Web Caching and Replication

Web Caching and Replication

Michael Rabinovich
Oliver Spatscheck

↟↟ Addison-Wesley

Boston • San Francisco • New York • Toronto • Montreal
London • Munich • Paris • Madrid
Capetown • Sydney • Tokyo • Singapore • Mexico City

Many of the designations used by manufacturers and sellers to distinguish their products are claimed as trademarks. Where those designations appear in this book, and Addison-Wesley was aware of a trademark claim, the designations have been printed with initial capital letters or in all capitals.

The authors and publisher have taken care in the preparation of this book, but make no expressed or implied warranty of any kind and assume no responsibility for errors or omissions. No liability is assumed for incidental or consequential damages in connection with or arising out of the use of the information or programs contained herein.

The publisher offers discounts on this book when ordered in quantity for special sales. For more information, please contact:

Pearson Education Corporate Sales Division
201 W. 103rd Street
Indianapolis, IN 46290
(800) 428-5331
corpsales@pearsoned.com
Visit AW on the Web: *www.aw.com/cseng/*

Library of Congress Cataloging-in-Publication Data
Rabinovich, Michael
    Web caching and replication / Michael Rabinovich and Oliver Spatscheck
        p.   cm.
    Includes bibliographical references and index.
    ISBN 0-201-61570-3 (alk. paper)
        1. Cache memory. 2. Electronic data processing—Backup processing alternatives.
    3. World Wide Web.   I. Spatscheck, Oliver. II. Title.

    TK7895.M4 R32   2002
    004.5′3--dc21
                                                             2001053733
                                                                  CIP

For information on obtaining permission for use of material from this work, please submit a written request to:

Pearson Education, Inc.
Rights and Contracts Department
75 Arlington Street, Suite 300
Boston, MA 02116
Fax: (617) 848-7047

ISBN 0-201-61570-3

Text printed on recycled paper.

1 2 3 4 5 6 7 8 9 10 –CRS–0504030201
First printing, December 2001

To my wife Irina and daughter Becky,
who were both very much part of this effort!

– Michael Rabinovich

To my wife Inge K. Pudell-Spatscheck
and my parents Bruni and Helmut Spatscheck
for their support.

– Oliver Spatscheck

Contents

Preface

In the past few years, the Web has transformed the Internet from a research tool of the few to an essential part of the everyday life of many. As its proliferation in all aspects of human activities continues, it becomes more important for users to get acceptable performance when using the Web. At the same time the demand for Web capacity and the Internet in general increases, not only due to the growing number of users who spend more and more time online, but also because of the emergence of new resource-hungry applications such as video and audio on-demand and distributed games. In addition to human users, computer applications increasingly rely on the Web; their demand for performance is even greater. While a human may not notice or care about a delay of a few hundred milliseconds, the same delay may be intolerable for a computer application, especially if it is incurred repeatedly during the execution of a task.

Web caching and replication address the issues of capacity and performance, and they have become essential components of the Web infrastructure. Broadly speaking, both Web caching and replication refer to satisfying requests by servers other than origin servers where the requested resources reside. Caching and replication can increase Web performance and effective capacity by shifting the work away from overloaded origin servers and, by satisfying client requests from nearby servers, even if origin servers are far away. Moreover, these auxiliary servers are increasingly viewed not only as a means to increase Web performance and effective capacity, but also as platforms to implement a variety of extra functionalities that add value to the services offered by origin servers. These promises of Web caching and replication have given rise to new industries, including equipment vendors that supply cache servers and compatible network gear, as well as service vendors that offer caching and replication services to consumers and providers of Web resources. Web caching and replication have also become areas of active research.

This book describes existing Web caching and replication technologies and concepts. It discusses implications of and trade-offs between alternative approaches, allowing a reader to understand the reasoning behind various solutions and to develop an intuition about what may or may not work and why. The book attempts to provide a unified view of approaches by commercial products and concepts from academic research. By considering both deployed solutions and far-reaching proposals, the book is intended to help readers identify current and emerging issues in this area, as well as future trends.

Web Caching and Replication concentrates on the fundamental ideas behind different technologies as opposed to particular products that implement them. Products come and go, and change in the process, especially in such an immature field as the Web. By focusing on underlying concepts, we believe this book will remain relevant as the market evolves. At the same time, there are a number of references to companies and products that implement various approaches that we consider. We fully expect these references to become obsolete rather quickly, as companies merge, disappear, or change their market focus. Our reason for providing them is to indicate the stage in the evolution of a given approach or idea; thus, we believe the references will be useful even if they are no longer entirely valid.[1]

Caching and replication are ubiquitous in computers and computer networks, and it is not always easy to draw a line between caching and replication in general and Web caching and replication in particular. We chose to provide comprehensive coverage of Web caching and replication as defined earlier; that is, satisfying Web requests from servers other than origin Web servers where requested resources originally resided. This definition emphasizes distributed aspects of Web caching and replication rather than the internal architectures of individual components—browsers, Web proxies, routers, switches, and origin servers—comprising the Web and the Internet.

Intended Audience

This book should be of interest to IT professionals, engineers at companies providing Internet services or equipment, and to researchers and graduate students in such fields as computer and information systems and networking. Our goal is to equip IT professionals with enough knowledge about the technology to understand market offerings in this area (and to keep vendor representatives honest!). For engineers developing new technologies in this area, this book might suggest concepts that can improve their products and point out areas in which more research is needed. Finally, for researchers and graduate students, the book aims to provide a thorough understanding of major issues, current practices, and the main ideas in the field of Web caching and replication, to the point of them being able to start their own work in the area. This book could also be used as a text for courses in Internet-based information systems.

Organization of the Book

Organizing the book presented an interesting challenge. On one hand, caching and replication are two broad directions for improving Web performance that have completely different business models. Caching represents client-side solutions, and replication represents server-side solutions; they are usually thought of as separate and orthogonal approaches. Service providers that offer caching services often have only a peripheral interest in replication and vice versa. This suggested organizing

---

[1] These references should not be interpreted as our endorsement of the products or companies mentioned; they just indicate that a particular idea has been implemented commercially.

the book into distinct parts that address these two broad directions separately. On the other hand, both directions often use similar technologies and mechanisms. For instance, the same equipment can be used as cache servers in Web caching and as surrogate Web servers in replication; the same balancing switches are used to distribute load among servers, and so on. Thus, this book could have been organized around the technologies that both directions use. We chose the former way in order to reflect the different focus of the two directions.

The book contains an introduction and four parts.

- The *Introduction* describes the concepts of Web caching and replication and defines very basic terms.

- Part I, *The Background,* presents the prerequisite information, introduces more detailed terminology, and provides a broad characterization of Web behavior.

- Part II, *Web Caching,* discusses caching.

- Part III, *Web Replication,* is devoted to replication. Because of the already-mentioned commonality of technologies used by both caching and replication, the corresponding parts in the book could not be made completely independent. We provide cross-references to enable readers to identify corresponding sections in the other parts that they might want to review.

- Part IV, *Further Directions,* outlines new directions in the area of caching and replication. It discusses how new services can be implemented on servers used for caching and replication, and it outlines an emerging technology that allows caching and replication platforms operated by different enterprises to cooperate in improving overall Web performance.

Our intent was to write a self-contained book. Although general familiarity with the Web, the client-server model, and distributed computing would be helpful, reading Part I will provide sufficient information for understanding the remainder of the book. Extensive use of examples and illustrations helps clarify the presentation. In most cases, the examples use fictitious URL addresses and companies; however, when we felt that a real name was useful, we used AT&T—a logical choice given that we both work there.

Acknowledgments

We would like to fulfill the pleasant duty of thanking the many people without whom this book would not be possible. We wish to thank our collaborators in various projects, including Amit Aggarwal, Gourav Banga, Ramon Caceres, Jeff Chase, Fred Douglis, Anja Feldmann, Syam Gadde, Gideon Glass, Antonio Haro, Rajmohan Rajaraman, and Sandeep Sibal. The book borrows from the papers that we wrote together. We are grateful to Jeff Chase, Mark Crovella, and Mike Dahlin for discussions that influenced certain parts of the book.

A small army of reviewers, including Martin Arlitt, Jeff Chase, kc claffy, Brian Davison, Fred Douglis, Sally Floyd, Steve McCanne, Jeff Mogul, Jay Newman, Gary Tomlinson, and Amin Vahdat, provided numerous comments which significantly influenced the final form of the book.

We thank our Addison-Wesley editor, Karen Gettman, who approached one of us with the idea to write a book on Web caching and then made sure we would start it and finish it. Mary Hart, Stephane Thomas, and Emily Frey expertly managed the entire process. Rebecca Greenberg scrupulously read the final book draft for presentation flaws and provided many valuable suggestions.

We are indebted to Professor Daniel Duchamp of Stevens Institute of Technology for writing Chapter 12, Prefetching, at our request, filling an important gap in the book. We should note that, with Dan's permission, we edited his chapter so that it would blend in with the rest of the book. Thus, the fault for any mistakes lies squarely with us.

Finally, we would like to thank AT&T for creating and maintaining a superb research laboratory. One could not wish for a better place to do research.

Introduction

The Web is fundamentally a very simple idea. It consists of *Web servers* that accept requests from *Web clients* for pieces of information called *Web objects*. The interaction between Web clients and servers occurs by means of standard protocols, typically *HyperText Transfer Protocol* (*HTTP*). Web objects can form relationships that allow clients to download related objects together, by embedding one object into another, or allow users to move easily from one object to another, by defining links, also known as *hyperlinks*, between objects. These relationships among objects are specified by using *Hypertext Markup Language* (*HTML*). Chapters 4 and 5 describe aspects of HTTP and HTML relevant to this book.

Any computer or device on the Internet can access Web objects and thus become a Web client; all it needs to do is speak HTTP to the appropriate Web server. A Web client that obtains Web content for consumption by a human user or an application on the same computer is called a *Web browser*. Web browsers therefore represent final destinations of Web objects. Examples of Web browsers include personal computers, Web-enabled phones, handheld computers, and so on. Other Web clients obtain Web objects for use by other computers; we will see examples of nonbrowser Web clients shortly.

Every Web object has a globally unique name called a *Uniform Resource Locator* (*URL*) that Web clients can use to retrieve it. An object URL encodes the name of the server where the object resides and the name of the object within that server. For instance, the URL *http://www.research.att.com/info/* specifies object "info/" residing on server www.research.att.com. Web objects are created and owned by people and companies who are collectively called *content providers*. Web objects belonging to the same content provider form a *Web site*. Objects from the same Web site usually share a common prefix in the server name of their URLs, for example, "research.att" in www.research.att.com, library.research.att.com, and help.research.att.com. In fact, the common prefix often includes the entire server name. Still, it is important to realize that there is no inherent relationship between Web servers and Web sites, although in practice a Web site often resides on a single server, and the two terms are often used interchangeably. We distinguish between Web servers and Web sites in this book.

Figure I.1 shows a simple but fully functional architecture of the Web. When the user enters an object URL or otherwise instructs the browser to download the object (for example, by clicking on a hyperlink that points to the object URL), the browser sends the request with the object name to the Web server specified in the URL. The server responds with the requested object. Once the object arrives, the browser displays it to the user and waits for further instructions.

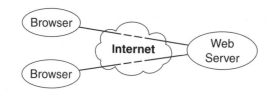

Figure I.1 Web browsers accessing a Web server

If network bandwidth and Web server capacity were unbounded, this simple architecture would be almost sufficient. We say "almost" because users might still experience noticeable delays when accessing a server halfway across the globe due to electromagnetic propagation delays. Unfortunately, bandwidth and server capacity are not unbounded. The Web continues to grow rapidly and this growth puts great stress on the Internet and popular Web servers.

Providing acceptable performance and reliability in face of this growth is often referred to as the Web scalability problem. To address this problem, companies operating network facilities (*Internet Service Providers*, or *ISPs*) are increasing their capacities. Server capacities are also growing at a rapid pace. But the demand for bandwidth and servers is also increasing. Indeed, as the bandwidth of user connections to the Internet increases, Web pages take less time to arrive and users are able to move from page to page more quickly; in addition, less frustrating performance of the Web is likely to increase usage further. Moreover, broadband connection to the user enables a wide use of new bandwidth-demanding applications, such as pay-per-view video. All this leads us to believe that the brute-force approach of adding ever increasing network and server capacities alone would not solve the Web scalability problem.

In addition to the brute-force approach, *caching* and *replication* are the primary means to scale up the Web. Caching refers to the simple idea that if you use some information and think you might use it again in the near future, you store a copy of this information in some easily accessible place. When you go to a library and take home a copy of an article, you perform caching. Replication, on the other hand, improves access to information by multiplying the source of the information. In our library analogy, replication would correspond to creating library branches and storing copies of popular books at every branch. Although both caching and replication create extra copies of information, the difference is that caching is done by and is under control of the consumer of information; replication, on the other hand, is the responsibility of the information provider, who retains full control over all the copies.

Just as caching and replication allow libraries to serve more readers more efficiently, these techniques can substantially improve Web scalability too. As Van Jacobson, one of the leading Internet experts, put it, "With 25 years of Internet experience, we've learned exactly *one* way to deal with exponential growth: caching" [Jacobson 1995]. And, we might add, replication, because it is so closely related to caching that the distinction is sometimes not drawn.

I.1 The Basics of Web Caching

While Web browsers routinely cache recently accessed pages on a local disk and in main memory, special cache servers called *Web caching proxies* are often used to provide a shared cache to a number of browsers. In the interest of brevity, we will use the term "proxy" instead of "Web caching proxy" in this book unless it could lead to confusion. As we will see in Chapter 17, however, a proxy can do many other things besides or even instead of caching.

Figure I.2 shows a number of Web browsers in an enterprise network sharing an enterprise proxy. A browser first attempts to satisfy requests from its local cache, then sends unresolved requests to the enterprise proxy. This proxy tries to satisfy the requests from its cache and forwards to the Web servers only those requests that could not be satisfied locally. A request that can be satisfied from a cache is called a *cache hit*; if it cannot be satisfied, it is called a *cache miss*.

Because browsers receive responses from the proxy, the proxy acts in some ways as a Web server to the browsers. At the same time, the proxy acts as a Web client to the Web server when it issues Web requests on its browsers' behalf. This role as a substitute server and client gave rise to the name *proxy*.

Just like other Web client requests, a request from a proxy can be satisfied from another proxy cache, and so on. For example, Figure I.3 shows browsers in an enterprise network that use an enterprise proxy, which in turn uses a proxy operated by the ISP that provides Internet connectivity to this enterprise. In this case, a browser sends requests that missed in its local cache to the enterprise proxy, which sends its misses to the ISP proxy, which finally forwards unresolved requests to their intended Web servers. The Web server where a Web object ultimately resides is called the *origin server* for that object. Web objects are placed on their origin servers by content providers; thus, origin servers act as authoritative sources of Web content.

Proxy caching promises important benefits to all parties on the Web—users, ISPs, and origin Web servers—as well as the Internet at large. For the user, a nearby cache

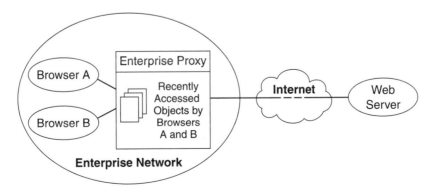

Figure I.2 Browsers using a Web proxy

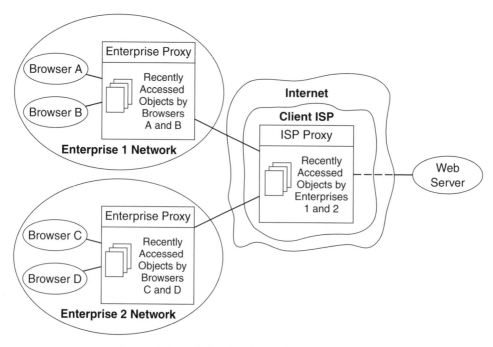

Figure 1.3 A chain of Web proxies from a browser

can often satisfy requests faster than a faraway origin server. For the user's ISP, the cache can reduce the amount of external bandwidth exchanged with other ISPs, since requests satisfied by an ISP cache terminate within the ISP network. Depending on the relationship of the ISP to its peer ISPs, such bandwidth reduction can directly translate into cost savings. For the origin servers, a cache reduces the load the servers have to handle, since the servers do not have to process requests satisfied by the cache. Finally, for the Internet at large, a cache offers the potential to improve scalability by reducing overall load on the network, because a cache that satisfies a request from a nearby client leaves the rest of the Internet free to carry traffic for others. Part II of this book discusses proxies in great detail, including what benefits to expect from them (Chapter 7), how to deploy them in various environments (Chapter 8), how best to leverage multiple proxies throughout the Internet (Chapter 9), and how to ensure that content cached by proxies is up to date (Chapter 10).

Caching alone, however useful, cannot solve the scalability problem of the Internet. There are a variety of reasons for this, some of which are nontechnical. Content providers are wary of caching because once their content is cached, they have limited control over it. Their primary concerns are copyrighted and other protected material. To prevent unrestricted access to such content, content providers typically prohibit caching it. Another concern is content freshness. Content providers have to rely on the consistency algorithms of caches they do not control to keep their content fresh. In some cases, content providers may even be held liable for delivering outdated information. This also compels them to disallow caching. Caching also complicates the collection of accurate statistics about content usage, which can be vital information for selling advertisements. Finally, some content is difficult or even impossible to cache because it is dynamically generated or personalized for a given user. Part II of this book describes various techniques for caching that address some of these problems (Chapter 13). However, there will always be plenty of requests that seep through all the caches to reach the origin servers. Handling these requests efficiently requires replication of popular servers, or Web replication for short.

I.2 The Basics of Web Replication

Unlike Web caching, which is performed by clients, Web replication is a server-side approach to scaling up the Web. An early and still widely used method for Web replication is *explicit mirroring*. In this method, multiple Web sites, called *mirror sites* or simply *mirrors*, are created with the same content, each site having its own set of URLs. Users choose one of the mirrors to receive their requests. If you have seen a page inviting you to click on one link if you are in the United States or on another link if in Asia, you have encountered explicit mirroring.

Many popular Web sites now have multiple mirrors. Figure I.4 shows an example of an explicitly mirrored site. Several problems make explicit mirroring inadequate.

- The existence of multiple mirrors is not transparent to the user. The user must explicitly choose a mirror for connection.

- This approach relies on proper user behavior to achieve load sharing. In other words, the content provider can request that certain groups of users connect to certain mirrors but cannot force them to do so. In an extreme case, users could conspire to connect to the same site, thus making it useless to have multiple mirrors. However, such undesirable user behavior also occurs without any malicious intent on the user side. Indeed, mirrors are generally not created when the service is first set up, but are added over time as the demand for the service approaches the capacity of the current set of servers. By the time the new mirrors appear, users may have already built links to the older sites into their applications. For example, they may have bookmarked the URLs pointing to those sites or embedded them into their own Web pages. Users may miss the announcement about the newly created mirrors or be unwilling to change their existing applications to point to the new sites.

- The decision to create a mirror is irrevocable: once created, the mirror cannot be brought down without invalidating its URLs. These URLs may be stored in an unknown number of user bookmark files and embedded in third-party applications; therefore, removing the mirror could cause an unknown level of disruption of access to the site. One could of course make the former mirror redirect clients to the currently valid sites, but that does not change the fact that the mirror site must always exist, even if in a skeleton form.

Mirrors of www.gnu.org

 [English I Korean]

Here is a list, by country, of the mirrors of www.gnu.org, the Primary GNU Project's World Wide Web server sponsored by the Free Software Foundation (FSF). Here is a list of our FTP mirrors.

If you would like to be a mirror site, please read this advice, and then ask *webmasters@gnu.org* to add you to this list once you have your mirror site set up.

The primary Web site for the GNU Project is fairly busy. Please use one of these mirrors of our primary Web site that is close to you.

Here are the countries that have Web mirror sites:

Australia I Austria I Belgium I Brazil I China I Colombia I France I Germany I Greece I Hungary I Hong Kong I India I Indonesia I Italy I Ireland I Japan I Korea I Mexico I Norway I Peru I Poland I Portugal I Russia I Spain I Sweden I Taiwan I Turkey I United Kingdom I United States I Yugoslavia

Figure I.4 A Web site with explicit mirrors
Source: Used with permission of gnu.org and Netscape.

The next step in the evolution of Web replication has been *transparent static mirroring*, where replication is hidden from the user. Each object on a transparently mirrored Web site has a single URL. Users cannot choose a server replica; in fact, they do not even know whether the site has been replicated. Instead, user requests are automatically directed to one of the mirrors (Chapter 14 describes mechanisms for doing this). As in explicit mirroring, each mirror has a full copy of the Web site, and the set of mirrors is determined and set up by humans (system administrators). Once deployed, the mirror set remains fixed until the system administrators reconsider their decision.

Transparent static mirroring can often be an adequate solution for a company running its own Web site, especially if its Web operation represents a relatively small portion of the overall business. Such a company can afford to deploy enough resources to handle the highest imaginable load. Although wasteful, such provisioning for the worst-case scenario would likely be feasible, since it would still represent a small portion of the total company costs. Given the limited scale of this environment, monitoring the load and periodically reconsidering resource deployment would also be manageable.

On the other hand, a *hosting service provider*—a company that provides facilities to host Web sites for third-party content providers—might host thousands of Web sites and millions of Web objects deployed on numerous Web servers around the globe. On this scale, the extent of the waste for worst-case provisioning would be multiplied by the number of hosted Web sites. Moreover, since running Web sites is the core business of the hosting service provider, the waste cannot be offset by other lines of business. At the same time, the number of possibilities for resource allocation, such as choosing how many mirrors of various Web sites to have and on which servers to deploy them, explodes. As the scale of hosting systems grows, administering them becomes increasingly difficult, labor intensive, and error prone.

In response to this challenge, the technology of *transparent dynamic replication* has emerged, where the replicas of various content are automatically created, deleted, or relocated based on observed demand. By automating resource allocation, one can afford to modify resource allocation much more often, according to the changing demand. Frequent resource reallocation also enables a quick adjustment to abrupt demand surges for a given site. Automating resource allocation also allows resource management at a finer granularity. For example, one could create mirrors of only the most popular pages of a given Web site instead of the entire site. A server that replicates a portion of a Web site is sometimes called a *partial mirror*.

As an illustration, consider a company that hosts two Web sites: one that provides news clips about the stock market and another that publishes sports news. If we assume that there is a factor of two diurnal variations of the average-to-peak demand for each site and that satisfying the average demand takes one Web server with a 40-megabit-per-second (Mbps) Internet connection, then provisioning for the worst-case scenario would require that either site be allocated four Web server replicas, each with a 40Mbps Internet connection (two servers for the peak demand, multiplied by two to be ready for unforeseen demand spikes, according to a common rule of thumb). The total resources for the two sites would amount to eight servers with 320Mbps total Internet connectivity. However, it is likely that the peak demand occurs in the daytime for stock market news and at night for sports events. Thus, dynamic replication might allow the hosting company to allocate only five servers for both sites with 200MBps total link capacity: one server with a 40MBps link to each site for routine demand,

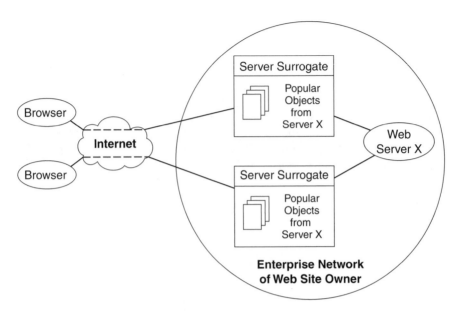

Figure I.5 Web server surrogates

one for both sites for peak demand, and two for unforeseen spikes. In this case, each site would be replicated as needed and, because the periods of peak demand do not coincide, both sites would share the same server for peak demand. Both sites would also share the same spare servers for unforeseen demand spikes, because it is highly unlikely that both sites would experience these spikes at the same time. By selectively replicating only the most popular content on either site, the hosting company may realize further savings in storage capacity.

Figure I.5 depicts a currently prevalent type of transparent dynamic replication using *surrogates*, also known as *reverse proxies*. In this scenario a Web site distributes incoming requests among surrogates as if they were static transparent mirrors functioning as full server replicas. A surrogate, however, processes a request as does a regular proxy, which is sometimes called a *forward proxy*, to clearly distinguish it: the surrogate satisfies the request from its cache if possible; otherwise, it fetches the requested object from the origin server, forwards it to the client, and perhaps caches it for future use. As a result, a surrogate acts as a partial replica with a state that dynamically changes with the demand.

The same surrogate can be shared by multiple Web sites, as is shown in Figure I.6. A shared surrogate caches objects from all participating sites; on a cache miss, the surrogate obtains the object from the appropriate site. A whole industry of *content delivery networks* (CDNs) has sprung up around the basic concept of shared surrogates. CDNs operate shared surrogates and sell their surrogate services to content providers. Shared surrogates introduce economies of scale and make it feasible for even a

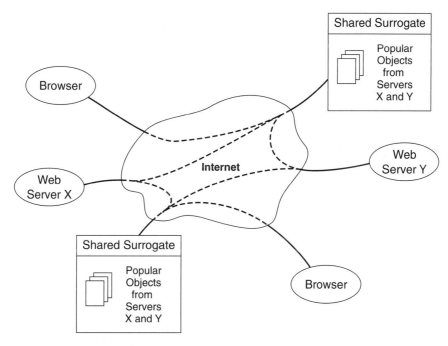

Figure 1.6 Shared surrogates (a CDN)

modest-sized Web site to benefit from a large number of well-connected surrogates deployed at highly prized locations in the Internet.

In the remainder of this book, we use the term *server replica* to refer collectively to mirrors, partial mirrors, and surrogates. A server replica does not have to be identical to the origin server, because the former may not have all the objects of the latter and also because a server replica may be shared by several origin servers. We also distinguish between server replicas, which refer to computers, and *content replicas*, which refer to pieces of content stored on those computers.

Web replication can help performance in several ways: first, it can improve the scalability of a Web site by distributing the load across multiple servers; second, it can improve the proximity of clients to the Web site by servicing requests from a mirror or surrogate that is close to the requesters; and third, communicating with nearby mirrors or surrogates localizes traffic on the Internet, improving its overall scalability.

These benefits are analogous to those of Web caching, which also reduces load on origin servers, improves proximity, and reduces network traffic. However, by leaving content providers in full control, Web replication addresses many limitations of Web caching mentioned previously in this chapter. Content providers are free to enforce the same access restrictions at server replicas as at the origin server. They can implement arbitrary nonstandard protocols between the origin server and its replicas to keep replicated content consistent.[2] They can collect accurate usage statistics by aggregating the statistics from individual replicas. They can also replicate applications that personalize Web pages or generate Web objects dynamically.

Like Web caching, Web replication has its own limitations. Not every content provider can afford replicating its Web site. For example, most academic sites are unlikely to deploy mirrors across the Internet or purchase CDN services. And while they probably will not make any of the "100 most popular sites" lists, they are of vital importance to certain classes of users, such as fellow academics. Also, as much as CDNs try to penetrate into every corner of the Internet, they would be hard-pressed to deploy surrogates as close to all Internet users as ISPs can deploy forward proxies. We believe that replication is unlikely to obviate the need for caching, just as caching alone is unlikely to solve the Web scalability problem.

Web replication issues are discussed in Part III, including the diversion of client requests to replicas (Chapter 14), CDN architectures and issues (Chapter 15), and choosing a server replica for a given request (Chapter 16). Because we discuss only transparent replication in this book, the word "transparent" is usually omitted.

I.3 Beyond Performance

Historically, Web proxies were used for security reasons. Corporate networks have special computers called firewalls that block direct communication of corporate computers with outside networks. Any application in a corporate network, including a Web browser, had to communicate with outside networks through special security gateways to get through the firewall, and a Web proxy served as such a gateway. Thus, early proxies played a functional role as a component of a security service rather than a performance enhancer. Two later developments had big implications for how enterprises used proxies. First, caching was added to these gateways, turning them into Web proxies as we know them today. Second, firewalls that can operate transparently to other corporate computers replaced many such explicit gateways. Because of these developments, the main motivation for using proxies in enterprise networks switched from providing essential functionality to improving performance.

Increasingly, however, proxies and surrogates are again being viewed as platforms to implement new functionalities. Examples of services that can be conveniently implemented on proxies or surrogates include content filtering (that is, restricting user access to certain kinds of content); content adaptation, where content is modified depending on the capabilities of the browser that requested the content; advertisement insertion; billing and accounting; and so on. Although the primary goal of Web

---

[2] Nonstandard protocols that do not require an inter-enterprise convention are called *proprietary*, as opposed to *open* protocols that have been standardized by an organization such as Internet Engineering Task Force (IETF).

caching and replication remains Web scalability, this book also covers, in Chapter 17, how these technologies can be used to implement new services.

I.4 Summary

Ultimately, both Web caching and replication involve creating extra copies of content. One can differentiate between the two approaches depending on who implements the approach and whom it is meant to serve.

Caching is implemented by clients and their ISPs. It is the responsibility of either the client or its ISP to deliver requests to the cache. At the same time, Web sites are oblivious to caches: to Web sites, caches are just other clients who request content. A cache, such as a forward proxy, serves Web clients, attempting to improve access for *a certain group of* clients to *any* Web site. Web sites have no control over forward proxies beyond what is stipulated in the standard protocols such as HTTP (see Chapter 5), and even then, Web sites cannot enforce compliance.

Replication, on the other hand, is performed by maintainers of a Web site, its ISP, or a CDN acting on its behalf. It is their responsibility to deliver requests to a replica. Web clients and clients' ISPs are oblivious to a replica's existence. Even with explicit mirroring, where human users are aware of multiple mirrors, the browsers and other clients remain oblivious to replication: for them, each mirror represents a distinct Web server. A replica, such as a mirror or surrogate, serves content providers, improving access from *any* client to *a certain group of* Web sites. Content providers have full control over replicas of their Web sites and can use proprietary protocols to communicate between Web servers and server replicas.

In short, Web caching is a client-side and replication is server-side approach to Web scalability. Web caching has a better chance of serving a client request from a nearby location in the case of a cache hit. Replication is applicable to a greater variety of content and allows content providers to retain more control over their content.

Caching and replication are pervasive in computers and computer networks; almost all Internet infrastructure components, including browsers, proxies, Web servers, routers, and switches, contain several levels of internal caches. Replication is also used by individual components, such as fail-over pairs of switches or servers. This book does not focus on the architecture of the individual components; instead, it concentrates on the *distributed* aspect of Web caching and replication, with the primary goal of describing techniques that can be used to improve Web scalability.

Although the basic concepts of Web caching and replication are simple, their implementation involves interactions with a variety of network elements and protocols. Thus, understanding of deeper issues around caching and replication requires some knowledge of how networks operate. Part I introduces the networking concepts required to understand the rest of the book.

Part I
Background

Part I of this book contains a brief introduction to the protocols and concepts that concern the Web, focusing on aspects that are relevant to caching and replication. It provides the background necessary to understand the remainder of the book. Chapter 1 introduces basic networking terms and concepts. Chapter 2 provides background about the Internet Protocol and routing. Chapter 3 introduces TCP, the protocol that transports most Web traffic. In Chapter 4 we describe more standards and protocols used by the Web, including URL, DNS, HTTP, and HTML. Chapter 5 provides an overview of the components involved in caching and replication on the Internet. Part I ends with Chapter 6, which discusses the basic characteristics of the Web. This information is important in Parts II and III because it allows one to understand the rationale behind the performance tradeoffs.

The novice to the subject should read all of Part I. More knowledgeable readers may want to skip some of the material in Chapters 1 through 4. To help decide which chapters to read, we recommend a brief look at each chapter's summary, which highlights the important concepts introduced; if the reader feels comfortable with all the concepts, that chapter may be skipped. We recommend that everyone at least skim through Chapters 5 and 6, as they introduce some less established terminology and include material that may be less commonly known.

Chapter 1
Network Layers and Protocols

Computer networks and network protocols are extremely complex. Network designers realized early that, to deal with this complexity, they needed to define some abstractions. Therefore, the concept of *layering* was introduced to provide increasingly complex functionality through standardized interfaces. With layering, network functionality is implemented as a stack of layers, where each layer uses a standard interface provided by the layer directly below in the stack and exposes a standard interface to the layer directly above. Layering hides the complexity of each layer from the next layer up the stack.

1.1 The ISO/OSI Reference Model

The International Standards Organization (ISO) was one of the first organizations to define such a set of layers in the Open System Interconnection (OSI) Reference Model [Day and Zimmermann 1983]. It defines the stack of layers shown in Figure 1.1 as a set of standards for the interfaces a layer should provide to the next layer up the stack and the services a layer should offer. Despite the fact that the ISO/OSI model has been overshadowed by the Internet protocols, its terminology is still in use. We therefore introduce the ISO/OSI protocol stack, which includes the following seven layers.

The physical layer: The physical layer, also referred to as Layer 1 or L1, deals with the physical medium such as a copper or fiber-optic cable. It defines the low-level encoding and protocols required to transmit information over this physical medium. It also deals with the electronic and physical properties of the medium. The physical layer never interprets the data being transmitted, treating it as an unstructured *bit stream*.

The data link layer: The data link layer, also known as Layer 2 or L2, introduces *Medium Access Control* (MAC) addresses, which are used to address hosts within

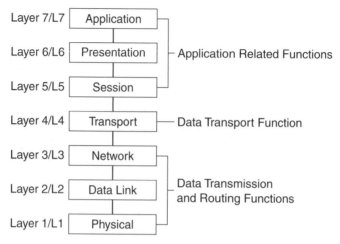

Figure 1.1 The ISO/OSI Reference Model

the same physical network. In addition, this layer is responsible for generating chunks of data called *frames*. The data link layer marks the beginning and end of frames so that the receiver can identify the frames within the bit stream provided by the physical layer. The data link layer also performs frame retransmissions in case of a transmission error.

The network layer: The main purpose of the network layer (Layer 3 or L3) is to provide a global address for each host in the Internet and to route chunks of data called *data packets* or *datagrams* to those hosts. As a packet is routed along a path of physically connected hosts, it is encapsulated into frames by the data link layer on each host and is transported over the physical network to the next host.

The transport layer: The transport layer is also known as Layer 4 or L4 and it introduces *port numbers*, an addressing scheme that allows data to be addressed and delivered to individual applications on a host. It breaks continuous data from a higher layer into chunks called *segments*. It also provides the notion of a *connection* between a pair of applications and offers such services as reliable in-order delivery of data packets within a connection.

The session layer: The session layer (Layer 5 or L5) and all layers above it are usually implemented within an application,[1] whereas all lower layers are commonly implemented within the operating system or within the network hardware. Therefore, the separation of the remaining three layers is only rarely enforced. In theory, the session layer is responsible for services that span multiple transport layer connections. An e-commerce transaction on a Web

---

[1] Notable exceptions here are network file systems that in most environments implement their session and presentation layers within the operating system.

site potentially spans multiple transport layer connections with the client and would be considered a session.

The presentation layer: The presentation layer (Layer 6 or L6) is responsible for the encoding of user data in globally understood formats, such as the HTML format, which is used to encode Web pages so that an arbitrary Web browser can display them.

The application layer: The application layer (Layer 7 or L7), as the highest layer in the architecture, deals with the actual processing and generation of the data. Web browsers, Web servers, or Web caches are considered part of the application layer.

1.2 Network Components at Different Layers

The ISO/OSI model defines L2 as having responsibility for addressing hosts within a physical network and allowing hosts on the same physical network to send data to each other. There are two general flavors of physical network: broadcast medium and switched network. In a broadcast medium network, all hosts on the physical network see every frame, regardless of the frame address. However, only the host whose MAC address matches that of the frame will accept it; all other hosts will ignore this frame. In addition, one can efficiently broadcast a packet to all hosts on the network by giving it a special MAC address that all hosts recognize. In contrast, a switched network uses interconnected switches to deliver frames to intended hosts only. Each switch uses a simple forwarding table that tells it on which link to forward a frame with a given MAC address. These switches use only L2 information and are appropriately called *L2 switches*.

While L2 delivers information between hosts on the same physical network, L3 is responsible for providing globally unique addresses to every host and routing packets within this global namespace. We define a *host* in the context of L3 as any equipment that is connected to the network and has at least one such L3 address. Packets are routed between an arbitrary pair of hosts via a chain of special hosts called *routers*, in which all neighboring routers are connected by a physical network. A router uses a forwarding table that maps global host addresses to the next-hop router (or the end host if this is the last router in the routing path) where packets with a given L3 address should be sent next. The advantage of defining global addressing at L3 is that routing has minimal complexity and is independent of the underlying networking hardware. This simplicity allows the development of extremely fast routers necessary to keep up with the increases in hardware networking speeds.

A disadvantage of limiting routing to L3 is that the only information available to make routing decisions is the global host address. Thus, all higher-level information that might have an impact on routing has to be folded into this global address. Unfortunately, the global addresses on the Internet can not easily be used to convey higher-layer information (see Chapter 4). This has led to the development of *L4* and *L7 switches*.

L4 switches, as well as routers with L4 capabilities, use L4 information to make routing decisions. Instead of looking only at the global address conveyed in L3 as routers normally do, they also consider such L4 information as destination port numbers and a connection to which the packet belongs (the L4 information in a packet is detailed in Chapter 3). L7 switches go a step further by routing packets using application-level data carried by these packets. This makes L7 switches application specific and only useful for a predetermined small set of applications. L7 switches are mainly found in the Web environment, where they route packets from Web clients based on the documents requested and other application-specific information. As we show in Chapters 8 and 14, L4 and L7 routing plays an important role in the Web environment.

1.3 Overview of Internet Protocols

This section provides an overview of the commercially successful rival of the ISO/OSI model: the Internet that was standardized in the 1980s. The availability of the Internet protocols at this early stage resulted in their adoption and the rise of the Internet. Figure 1.2 depicts a selection of Internet protocols commonly found on Internet hosts. The figure also highlights the fact that the Internet does not readily map to the OSI seven layers. Some of the layers separated in the OSI model are combined in the Internet. The following layers are usually distinguished in the Internet:

The physical layer: The Internet physical layer typically combines the physical and data link layers in the ISO/OSI model and is implemented in the networking hardware and the device driver that a host uses to communicate with its direct neighbors. The most common representatives in this realm are the *Ethernet* and

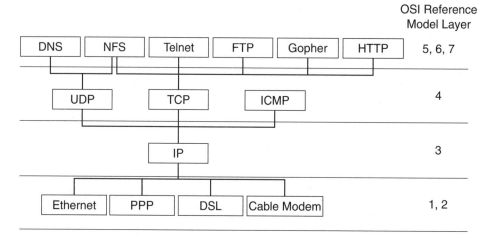

Figure 1.2 Common protocols in the Internet

the *Point to Point Protocol* (*PPP*), which are used to connect hosts within *local area networks* (*LANs*) and single hosts from remote locations, respectively. Later, *digital subscriber lines* (*DSL*) and cable modems were introduced as additional protocols at the Internet physical layer providing much higher bandwidth to individuals for connecting remote hosts. From the perspective of the higher layers, it is irrelevant which of these technologies are used. They differ only in their latency, bandwidth, and ability to broadcast information to all hosts on the physical network.

The network layer: The protocol in the Internet at this layer is the *Internet Protocol* (*IP*) [Postel 1981a], which provides the global addressing and routing capabilities of the Internet. This protocol is the only one that every Internet host must implement, and it is discussed in more detail in Chapter 3.

The transport layer: At this layer the Internet provides the *Transmission Control Protocol* (*TCP*) [Postel 1981c] and the *User Datagram Protocol* (*UDP*) [Postel 1980]. Those two protocols fulfill two extreme requirements of higher levels. UDP adds an additional address, the port number, to the functionality provided by IP. The port number addresses an individual application on a host rather than the host itself.

The other extreme, TCP, provides most of the services an application could require. In addition to port numbers equivalent to those used by UDP, it provides reliable in-order delivery and congestion control to prevent overloading the network. Since TCP is the protocol used by the Web, we discuss TCP in more detail in Chapter 3.

The last protocol shown in Figure 1.2 at the transport layer (Layer 4) is the *Internet Control Message Protocol* (*ICMP*) [Postel 1981b]. This protocol is shown at the transport layer because it uses the network layer to exchange messages. However, ICMP does not provide any transport-layer functionality to higher-level protocols. It is used to exchange control messages about host reachability, status, congestion, datagram flow, local route change requests, and other network layer problems.

The application layer: This Internet layer corresponds to layers 5 through 7 in the ISO/OSI model. The Internet does not distinguish between layers 5 through 7. It combines the entire functionality provided in those layers into the application layer. The application-layer protocols shown in Figure 1.2 highlight some important applications found on the Internet. The *Domain Name System* (*DNS*) resolves symbolic host names like www.att.com to the integer numbers used within the IP protocol to address hosts. DNS is discussed in detail in Chapter 4. The *Network File System* (*NFS*) is commonly found on LANs to allow remote file system access. It is interesting because it is one of the protocols that can operate on top of UDP and TCP, depending on which transport-layer protocol is more appropriate for its specific use. The remaining protocols shown provide remote access to hosts. *Telnet* was designed to remotely log into computers and was one of the first services offered on the Internet. Another early protocol is the *File Transfer Protocol (FTP)*. FTP was designed to allow the sending of files to, retrieval of files from, and deletion of files on remote hosts. It was one of the predecessors of the current Web in that it was one of the first applications allowing the remote retrieval of documents using the Internet. *Gopher* was the next step toward the Web. It combined the transfer of remote documents with hyperlinks.

The Web uses the HyperText Transfer Protocol. HTTP is discussed in more detail in Chapter 5. HTTP not only enables remote access to textual documents as does Gopher, but it also enables access to graphical and dynamic content.

1.4 Summary

The concept of layering is used in networking to help understand its complexity. The ISO/OSI seven-layer model was one of the first and most widely known layering models and its terminology is still used on the Internet. The family of Internet protocols can be categorized into four layers. The physical layer corresponds to layers 1 and 2 in the ISO/OSI model. The Internet network layer (IP) and the transport layer (ICMP, TCP, UDP) correspond, respectively, to layers 3 and 4 in the ISO/OSI model. Protocols and devices operating at these layers are often referred to as L3 and L4 protocols and devices. The fourth layer in the Internet, referred to as the application layer, corresponds to layers 5 through 7 in the ISO/OSI model. Protocols and devices belonging in this layer are often denoted as L5, L7, or L5+ protocols and devices. We use the L7 notation, as it seems more popular than the others.

The IP (L3), TCP (L4), HTTP (L5–L7) and DNS (L5–L7) protocols play an especially important part in this book and are discussed in more detail in the next three chapters.

Chapter 2
The Internet Protocol and Routing

The design of the network layer, including the Internet Protocol (IP) and routing, has a major influence on many issues in Web caching and replication. These issues range from how Web proxies are deployed (Chapter 8), to how Web requests are redirected to server replicas selected to process these requests (Chapter 14), to how server replicas are selected (Chapter 16). This chapter describes the most important aspects of IP in the context of Web caching and replication.

The fundamental goal of IP is to deliver *datagrams*—the L3 data packets containing a header and data portion—between hosts on the Internet. This means that IP is supposed to hide the physical (L1) and data link (L2) layers of different networks from higher layers and make the Internet appear as a single, homogeneous network. This chapter describes the main parts necessary to achieve those goals in the IP version 4 (IPv4) protocol [Postel 1981a]. As we will see, IPv4 has many drawbacks, some of which have been addressed in IP version 6 [Deering and Hinden 1998]. Because a wide deployment of IP version 6 is progressing very slowly and knowledge of its features is not required to understand the remainder of this book, a detailed discussion of IP version 6 is not included here.

2.1 Addressing

To build a global network, it is necessary to identify every host on the network. The Internet achieves this by assigning each host at least one 32-bit-long unique Internet address (*IP address*). Typically, IP addresses are written in decimal dotted notation where each decimal number represents 8 bits in the address. For example, the IP address of www.att.com, which is 11000000 00010100 00000011 00110110, is written as 192.20.3.54.

If IP addresses were assigned randomly, routing between hosts would be extremely difficult. As we mentioned in Chapter 1, the functionality of a router is to forward datagrams received by the router toward the datagram's destination. We discuss IP routing in more detail in Section 2.3. However, in the context of addressing, routing difficulties arise because each router would have to know exactly which neighboring router is the next hop on the way to each of the more than four billion possible IP addresses. In other words, the table on each router that maps an IP address to the next-hop router would need one entry for every existing IP address. This table is commonly called the *state* of the router or the *routing table*, and the size of this state is a crucial factor in router cost and performance. The IP designers reduced the router state substantially by making the IP address space hierarchical. That is, they split the IP address into the network ID and the host ID. Routers maintain entries for individual hosts that belong to their own physical networks. For all outside networks, routers keep only entries that correspond to network IDs rather than individual hosts. Thus, a router routes packets to any host on an outside network in the same way, and leaves the routing to an individual host up to the internal routers within the host's network.

To allow different networks to have different numbers of hosts, the IP addresses are divided into several *classes*. Each class allocates a different number of bits for the *network ID* and *host ID* fields, as shown in Table 2.1 . The more bits are allocated to the host ID field the more different host IDs can be encoded and, therefore, the more hosts the network can have. At the same time, more bits for the host field leaves fewer bits for the network ID, meaning a smaller possible number of networks. For example, a Class A address allocates 7 bits for network IDs and 24 bits for host IDs; consequently, the IP addressing scheme allows for only 127 Class A networks (the maximum number that 7 bits can encode), and each Class A network can have up to 16,777,214 hosts (the maximum number that can be encoded by 24 bits minus two reserved addresses). Similarly, there can be up to 16,384 Class B networks, each containing up to 65,534 hosts, and up to 2,097,152 Class C networks with 254 hosts each. Given the scarcity of Class A network IDs, these networks are usually assigned to large network providers and the military. Class B networks are found in big corporations and universities, and Class C networks are assigned to smaller businesses. This assignment of IP addresses to organizations within North America is administered by the American Registry for Internet Numbers (ARIN), which is also responsible for South America, the Caribbean, and sub-Saharan Africa.

There also exist two additional classes not shown in the table that have a special structure. Class D addresses are used for multicast (discussed in Section 2.4), and

Table 2.1 Three Classes of Internet Addresses

Class	Size of Network ID	Size of Host ID	Number of Networks	Number of Hosts
A	7 bit	24 bit	127	16,777,214
B	14 bit	16 bit	16,384	65,534
C	21 bit	8 bit	2,097,152	254

Class E addresses are reserved for future use. The initial few bits in the IP address identify the address class so that routers can interpret the rest of the address correctly.

In 1981 when the IP protocol was standardized, using a 32-bit address seemed a good compromise between the resources required to store, parse, and transmit an address and the number of hosts that are connected to the Internet. It seemed that the more than four billion addresses contained in 32 bits would be more than enough for future Internet growth. The problem with this assumption is that there are not really four billion addresses available. The only addresses available for individual hosts are Class A–C addresses. In addition, it is not possible to use the entire space of an individual network ID, since networks rarely deploy the maximum allowed number of hosts. As an extreme example, a network with only 256 hosts would require a Class B network ID because it does not fit into the smaller Class C network. The IP address utilization of this network would only be $256/65534 = 0.39\%$.

To avoid such poor use of address space, this network could be given two Class C network IDs instead of a single Class B network ID. However, this arrangement detracts from the optimal situation in which an outside router has to know only one route per network, because now there would be two routes to the network in question, one for each Class C network ID. A better solution to the problem is *Classless Interdomain Routing (CIDR)* [Fuller et al. 1993]. CIDR allows the network ID part of an IP address to have an arbitrary length. This allows the combination of Class A–C networks with adjacent IDs to merge into a single entry in routing tables while maintaining a high IP address utilization within a network. Conversely, CIDR also allows a single Class A–C network to split into several smaller networks. In our previous example, the network with 256 hosts could be given a block of, say, 512 adjacent Class B IP addresses instead of the entire Class B network ID. The remaining portions of the address space with this Class B network ID would still be available for other networks and organizations.

Despite CIDR, the number of available IP addresses is still rather limited. This shortage is currently being handled by a set of protocols like *network address translation (NAT)* [Egevang and Francis 1994] and the *Dynamic Host Configuration Protocol (DHCP)* [Droms 1993]. Both protocols help to use the IP address space even more efficiently by allowing sharing of a single IP address between multiple hosts. However, the ultimate solution will be the deployment of IP version 6, which offers an address space increased to 128 bits.

2.2 IP Datagram Header

The Internet Protocol was designed to be as simple as possible. The reason for this approach is to allow many hosts and existing networks to participate in the Internet with minimal effort. The consequence, however, is that the IP protocol guarantees neither in-order delivery of multiple datagrams nor the delivery of datagrams at all. The only guarantee it provides is that all parties involved will make their best effort to deliver the datagram.

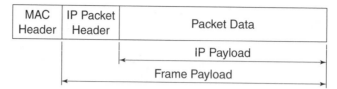

Figure 2.1 An IP datagram encapsulated into a frame

What IP does support is datagram fragmentation, which is necessary to transfer IP datagrams over different physical networks with different maximum datagram sizes. For example, consider a router connected to two physical networks with maximum datagram sizes of 1500Bytes and 512Bytes. If the router receives a 1200Byte datagram on the first network, it must fragment this datagram into three smaller datagrams before forwarding it to the second network. While fragmentation occurs at the routers connecting different networks, reassembly of the original datagram from the fragments is always performed at the final receiver.

Figure 2.1 shows the layout of an IPv4 datagram transmitted by the physical layer. The MAC header added by the physical layer is followed by the IP header, which is followed by the payload of the IP datagram. The next list introduces the most important fields found in the IP header and explains their functionality as required within the context of this book. A more detailed description of IP can be found in [Postel 1981a].

- The *protocol* field indicates to the receiving host which higher-level protocol it should use to process the data section of the datagram. For example, the TCP protocol is represented by the number 6.

- The *IP source address* identifies the sender of the datagram.

- The *IP destination address* identifies the receiver of the datagram.

- The *TTL* (*time to live*) field puts a lifetime on the datagram. The primary reason for this field is that most routing protocols allow transient or permanent loops in the routes. Therefore, if a packet is not restricted in its lifetime, it could in theory circulate indefinitely in the network. To avoid this problem, a sending host always puts a counter into the TTL field of each IP datagram, which is then decremented by each router on the datagram path. If the TTL reaches zero, the datagram is discarded and an ICMP error message is sent to the source of the datagram.

  This behavior is exploited by the *traceroute* program. Traceroute discovers intermediate routers on a path between two hosts by sending a sequence of datagrams with increasing TTL counts (starting at one) to the other host. Since datagrams with low TTL will likely not reach the destination, the program can gather the IP addresses of intermediate routers by inspecting the source IP addresses of the ICMP error messages.

- The *identifier*, *fragment offset*, and *flags* fields are used to fragment and defragment datagrams.

- The *total length* field contains the total length of the datagram in bytes. Because the total length field has a size of 16 bits, the maximum datagram size is theoretically 65,535Bytes. However, as few physical networks allow such large datagrams, a datagram of maximum length will almost always be fragmented. Fragmentation slows down processing within the network, and therefore higher-level protocols try to avoid it. The higher-level protocols try to determine the maximum datagram size that can be used between two hosts. In many cases it will be the Ethernet maximum transfer unit (MTU), which is 1492Bytes.

2.3 Routing

So far we have discussed how IP solves the global addressing problem and how individual IP datagrams are composed. Now we discuss how the Internet routes datagrams from their source host to their final destination. This process determines the path packets take through the network, and, as we show in Chapter 8, this has a large impact on Web proxy deployment.

The Internet is a packet-based store-and-forward network, which means that the source host sends a datagram not directly to its final destination but to a router on the same physical network. The router forwards the datagram to another router with which it shares another physical network, and so on until the datagram reaches the final destination. This process is called *routing*. The problem routers must solve is how to determine the next router to send a datagram to so that it reaches its final destination rapidly. This problem is addressed by a *routing protocol*.

As described in Section 2.1 the hierarchical nature of IP addresses uses some high-order bits as the network ID and the remaining bits as host IDs within the network. This two-level addressing reduces the amount of state a router must maintain. The Internet also uses a hierarchical approach to reduce the complexity of route computations. Internet routing tries to hide entire groups of individual networks from the remainder of the Internet. This goal has led to a two-level routing scheme. In this scheme the Internet is divided into regions under single administrative control, each of which is called an *autonomous system* (*AS*) and which contains groups of network IDs. Routing within an AS is completely hidden from the rest of the Internet. Routes between ASs are computed in terms of AS hops (that is, lists of intermediary ASs from the source AS to the destination AS). In other words, while a router maintains a routing entry for every outside network ID, all outside networks that belong to the same AS share the same route, expressed as the list of intermediary ASs. To route to arbitrary ASs on the Internet, a router need only know the next hop router to every AS, rather than the individual destinations. Figure 2.2 shows an imaginary Internet fragment that we use throughout this section to illustrate

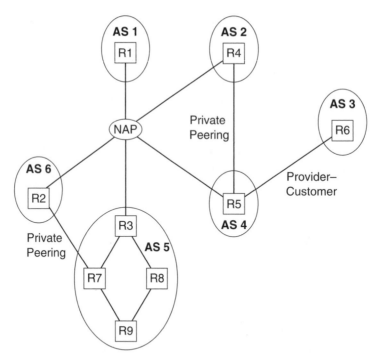

Figure 2.2 An imaginary Internet fragment with six ASs and nine routers

routing concepts. At this point, we note only that this fragment shows six ASs and nine routers.

2.3.1 Routing within ASs

The routing within an AS is under complete control of the owner of the AS. Small ASs might have only one router and be responsible for just one network, as is shown for AS 1 in Figure 2.2. All hosts within such an AS will send all datagrams destined for hosts outside their physical network to this router. The router then delivers the datagrams addressed to hosts within the AS and forwards the datagrams addressed to outside ASs to the appropriate next-hop routers. The router also receives and delivers all traffic from outside ASs to all hosts within the AS.

Larger networks might have many internal routers connected to multiple networks and use multiple network IDs. In addition, they might have multiple externally visible routers (called *border routers*) connecting them to other ASs. AS 5 in Figure 2.2 is an example of such an AS. AS 5 contains four routers, of which two (R3 and R7) are connected to other ASs. All traffic from an internal host to an internal host will be routed between the internal routers and all traffic going to or coming from other ASs will be handled by the border routers.

How the internal routers determine the next hop within an AS depends on the protocol chosen by the owner of the AS. The *Open Shortest Path First* (*OSPF*) protocol

[Moy 1998] is commonly used for this purpose. OSPF is based on an algorithm that allows every router to build a complete map of the AS and to determine the best route from each host to every other host. The meaning of the term "best" depends on the cost metric used in the OSPF configuration. Possible meanings include the highest-bandwidth route, the lowest-delay route, or the route with the lowest packet loss. Because the best routes may change over time, OSPF routers recalculate them periodically.

OSPF has two side effects that impact Web caching. The first side effect is that subsequent datagrams between two hosts may take different routes. This might happen either because the best route changes, or because there are two routes with identical cost. In the latter case, OSPF explicitly allows routers to distribute traffic between the two routes, sending one datagram along one route and the next along the other. The second side effect is that the best route between host A and host B may be different in each direction. This phenomenon is called an *asymmetric route;* it implies that a network element may see only one-half of the communication between a pair of hosts.

2.3.2 Routing between ASs

Autonomous Systems can be differentiated into three categories:

Transit AS: An AS that has connections to more than one other AS and is willing to carry datagrams that neither originated nor terminate on hosts within the AS. In other words, such an AS serves as a transit for traffic between outside ASs.

Multihomed AS: An AS that is connected to more than one other AS and that does not accept datagrams not destined for itself.

Stub AS: An AS that is connected to only one other AS.

Figure 2.2 shows all three AS types. AS 4 is a transit AS since it carries traffic between AS 3 and all other ASs. AS 2, AS 5, and AS 6 are multihomed ASs. AS 3 is a stub AS. AS 1 might be a multihomed or a stub AS, depending on the number of other ASs with which it is configured to exchange traffic.

The figure also illustrates three ways in which ASs can connect. The first way is via a *network access point (NAP)*. A NAP is a physical network that connects routers from many different ASs; it serves as a public exchange point where different ASs hand over Internet traffic to each other. AS 1, AS 2, AS 4, AS 5, and AS 6 connect via a NAP. The second way to connect ASs is through *private peering links*, which are private physical networks connecting only the routers from the two ASs. AS 2 and AS 4, as well as AS 5 and AS 6, have such a private peering connection. Private peering links are governed by peering agreements, which usually limit traffic over the peering link to nontransit traffic only and may require one AS to pay a fee to the peering partner (called *settled peering*). In Figure 2.2, AS 2 is not a transit AS because it cannot route transit traffic via its private peering link. The third way ASs can connect is through a *provider-customer* relationship. In our example, AS 3 is a customer of an Internet Service Provider (ISP) that owns AS 4. Technically, there is little difference between a

provider-customer link and a peering link, as both involve a physical network between routers belonging to the two ASs in question. The only important difference
is in the business relationship between the two. The provider-customer relationship
assumes that the provider delivers transit traffic to the customer, while peer ASs, as
mentioned earlier, usually only exchange traffic that originates from or is destined to
one of the peers.

The major routing protocol used between ASs is the *Border Gateway Protocol (BGP)*
[Stewart 1999]. In BGP, each router *advertises* reachability information to neighbor
routers for all networks within its AS and, in the case of a transit AS, for outside
networks reachable via its AS. The reachability information contains a list of reachable
networks and the performance cost to reach those networks from the router. The
performance cost is expressed as the number of ASs on the path from the router to the
destination. For example, router R6 would advertise to router R5 that R6 can reach all
networks in AS 3 with cost 0. Router R5 would then advertise to routers R1, R2, R3,
and R4 that it can reach those networks with cost 1, and so on. With this information,
each router can compute the best route to each destination network.

BGP allows an AS to set *routing policies* that determine which reachability information is advertised to which routers and, ultimately, which routes are used for inter-AS
traffic. In Figure 2.2, R5 would not advertise a route to AS 2 at the NAP because R5
connects to AS 2 by a private peering link with the peering agreement that disallows
transit traffic. However, R5 would advertise a transit route to AS 3, because AS 3 is a
customer of AS 4.

In the context of Web caching, important aspects of BGP are that subsequent datagrams from one AS to another may travel via different routes or that traffic between
two ASs can flow asymmetrically. One common cause of asymmetrical routes between
ASs is caused by so-called *hot potato routing*. Hot potato routing refers to an intra-AS
routing approach that attempts to get traffic off the internal networks as quickly as
possible to minimize internal bandwidth consumption. Figure 2.3 illustrates this scenario. In the figure, AS 1 and AS 2 peer with each other in two locations. One location

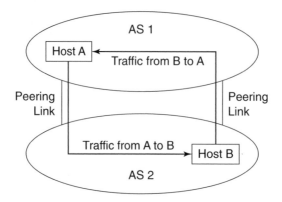

Figure 2.3 Hot potato routing

is close to host A in AS 1 and the other peering location is close to host B in AS 2. According to the hot potato routing approach, traffic from host A to host B uses the closest peering link to A, while traffic from B to A takes the route via the peering link next to B. As a result, the routes of traffic in each direction are asymmetrical.

2.4 Multicast

IP *multicast* is a mechanism that allows efficient delivery of a datagram to multiple hosts on the Internet. Multicast is useful in situations when many hosts, called a *multicast group*, are interested in the same content. For example, the Internet video broadcast of the Victoria's Secret fashion show draws hundreds of thousands of users every year. The datagrams sent to the hosts of all those users are, for the most part, identical. The idea behind IP multicast is to optimize the transmission of IP datagrams in such a way that an identical datagram traverses the link between two routers only once. Therefore, multicast is directly relevant to our subject in that it allows the efficient distribution of content to many browsers, proxies, or server replicas at the same time (see for example Chapters 10 and 15).

Figure 2.4 illustrates multicast's potential for performance improvement. The figure shows a host connected to the Internet via a dial-up link that needs to send a datagram to two receivers. With unicast, the host would generate two IP datagrams and send them both via the dial-up link to the receiving hosts. If the host used multicast instead, it would send one IP multicast packet into the network. Ideally, this multicast packet would only be duplicated at the latest possible point in the network, which is the point at which the routes to the two receiving hosts diverge. Thus, the common portion of the

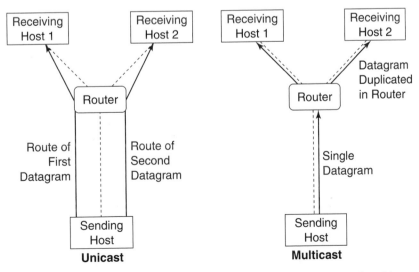

Figure 2.4 Delivery of an IP datagram to two hosts via unicast and multicast

routes would carry no duplicate packets. In particular, only one IP datagram would have to traverse the slow dial-up link in this example.

Although the advantages of IP multicast are clear, the disadvantages are difficult to overcome. The problems are rooted in how multicast groups are addressed and how they are routed.

Multicast groups are addressed using Class D IP addresses. Once an IP address is allocated to a multicast group, a host can send a packet to all hosts in the group simply by using the group's multicast IP address as the packet destination address. To receive multicast packets, a host must join the multicast group, which the host can usually do by notifying its next-hop router that it would be interested in a particular multicast address. That router then cooperates with other Internet routers to ensure the delivery to this host of packets with this destination address.

The problem with this addressing approach is that it scales poorly. Using Class D addresses to address all multicast groups in the Internet requires every router on a path from any host on the Internet to any member of a multicast group to know about this multicast group. For many routers in large networks this means they have to know about virtually all active multicast groups on the Internet. This requires an amount of routing state that is substantially greater than regular routing state, because the latter uses only the network portion of IP addresses, which is the same for many hosts. Moreover, as we will see shortly, some multicast protocols route multicast packets in a way that depends on the sender of the packet, requiring a router to maintain an entry in its routing table for each multicast group and for each sending host. Thus, the amount of state a router must maintain becomes proportional to the number of multicast groups *times* the number of potential senders to these groups, which obviously does not scale. Today's routers are barely capable of keeping up with ever-increasing line speeds. This additional burden does not seem appropriate.

Now, let us turn to the problem of routing multicast packets. Consider a graph containing all sources of multicast packets, all *sinks* or receivers (that is, members of the multicast group), and all routers on the paths from the sources to the sink. The problem is to deliver a packet from a given source to all the sinks with as few duplicate packets as possible. (A duplicate is the same packet sent over the same link more than once.) Currently, there are two basic approaches to this problem. The first approach builds a family of spanning trees over the router graph, one tree for each source. Each tree, called a *multicast distribution tree*, has its corresponding source host as the root and all group members as leaves. Multicast packets from a source are routed along its distribution tree. Figure 2.5 depicts two such distribution trees for two source hosts illustrating that this routing mechanism has to compute a different tree for every sender in a multicast group. Multicast routing protocols following this approach are called *dense-mode protocols*. This type of protocol makes routing dependent on the source of the packet, because a router sends a multicast packet to all its descendants in the distribution tree, which is specific to the source. As we already mentioned, this can result in a dramatic increase in routing state.

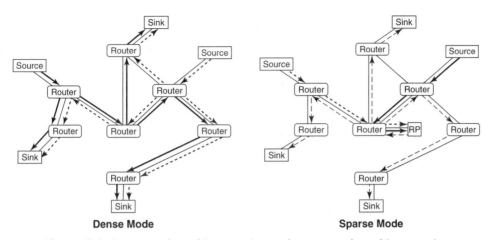

Dense Mode   **Sparse Mode**

Figure 2.5 Dense-mode multicast routing and sparse-mode multicast routing

The second approach includes *sparse-mode protocols*. Sparse-mode protocols build a single multicast distribution tree, rooted at a special host called the *rendezvous point*, denoted RP, as shown in Figure 2.5. All senders of packets to this multicast group send their datagrams to the rendezvous point, which distributes them using the multicast tree. The advantage of these protocols is that the routers only have to manage one tree per multicast group and not one tree per multicast group and sender. Consequently they have to keep only one forwarding entry per multicast group. The disadvantages are that all senders and receivers have to discover the rendezvous point and that the rendezvous point is a single point susceptible to congestion and failure.

Neither approach has solved the scalability problems of IP multicast in a global Internet. Recent proposals have tried to address these problems by dividing multicast routing into inter- and intradomain routing, similar to the division of unicast routing within an AS and between ASs. However, it is still an open question whether native multicast will be deployed on the entire Internet. Early attempts such as MBone (Multicast Backbone) [Eriksson 1994] have gained only limited acceptance.

Another less technical issue that delays the deployment of native multicast is the question of who pays for the bandwidth consumed by multicast distribution. A single IP datagram sent to a multicast address could generate millions of IP datagrams within the network. Therefore, network service providers will only be willing to enable multicast on their networks if they can charge somebody for the traffic generated.

Chapter 15 discusses the idea of providing multicast service at the application layer rather than the network layer. The advantage of this approach is that multicast can be specialized for a particular application and that no cooperation from network providers is required. On the other hand, detailed knowledge about the network is useful to build the optimal distribution tree. This knowledge is often absent at the application layer, and therefore systems with application layer multicast do not use the network optimally.

2.5 Summary

The Internet Protocol version 4 is at the core of today's Web. This protocol connects a large number of highly diverse networks into a single network called the Internet and delivers datagrams between individual hosts on this network. To achieve this goal, IP specifies a global address space to address hosts on the Internet, called the IP addresses.

IP uses hierarchical approaches to make its task manageable. To reduce the amount of state routers must maintain, IP divides IP addresses into two parts, which identify a network (network ID bits) and a host on that network (host ID bits). To reduce the complexity of route calculations, IP groups networks into autonomous systems and separates routing into two classes: routing within an AS and routing between ASs. Routing within an AS is the sole responsibility of the AS and is typically done using the OSPF protocol. Routing between ASs most likely uses the BGP protocol and is performed via NAPs or private peering points that connect neighboring ASs.

In addition to the basic functionality of IP, there are many extensions. IP multicast is the one most relevant in the context of caching and replication. Multicast can be used to distribute the same content efficiently to many receivers. Its main drawback is limited scalability because of the overhead it introduces in the network. This overhead and the fact that it is difficult to bill for multicast traffic accurately have so far prevented the large-scale deployment of IP multicast.

Chapter 3
Transmission Control Protocol

The *Transmission Control Protocol* (*TCP*) is the transport protocol used by the Web to deliver requests from clients to servers and Web objects from servers to clients. TCP properties have a profound effect on the performance of the Web in general and on many design choices in Web caching and replication in particular. This chapter introduces TCP at a level sufficient for understanding the rest of the book. There are a number of sources for more detailed information on TCP, including books by Comer [1991] and Peterson and Davie [1996].

The IP protocol described in the previous chapter provides the minimal functionality necessary to connect multiple networks: it allows one host to send a datagram to another, without any guarantee that the datagram will arrive or that a sequence of datagrams will arrive in the same order as they were sent. However, applications often require these and other guarantees to work properly. The TCP protocol was built on top of IP to provide this extra functionality that applications commonly need, so that each application would not have to implement it anew. In particular, TCP tries to provide the following properties to an application:

Reliable delivery: The IP protocol only provides "best-effort" delivery. IP datagrams can be lost because of congestion on routers or the underlying physical networks. Lost datagrams usually have to be resent by the application. TCP retransmits lost data, removing this burden from the application.

Exactly-once delivery: A related problem is that IP may deliver a datagram more than once. Such datagram duplication may occur in the underlying layers or be introduced by TCP itself when it retransmits a seemingly lost packet that in fact arrives eventually at the destination. In either case, TCP at the receiving host recognizes duplicate data and guarantees that data is only delivered once to the application.

In-order delivery: Another shortcoming of IP is data reordering. IP does not guarantee to deliver datagrams in the order in which they were sent. For example, reordering may occur when subsequent datagrams take different routes to the destination. TCP fixes this problem by storing the out-of-order datagrams in its internal buffers at the recipient host and delivering the datagrams to the application only after all preceding datagrams have been delivered. As a result, TCP guarantees in-order data delivery.

Stream-based transfer: From an application perspective, data sent via TCP represents simply a stream of bytes. Any division of data into datagrams, including any headers added by lower-level network layers, is invisible to the application. The concept of a stream is convenient for applications, which do not have to identify and strip the headers from the application data, and for the TCP protocol, which can fragment the data any way it likes to optimize network performance.

Full duplex transfer: Since the design goal of TCP was to support a wide range of applications, TCP allows data transfer between two applications in both directions at the same time. This TCP functionality is called *full duplex transfer*.

Flow and congestion control: One of the biggest benefits of TCP is that it regulates the rate with which the sending host transmits the data. The sender must limit its transmission rate to the rate at which the receiver can absorb the data (flow control) and to the rate at which the network can transfer the data (congestion control). By providing this functionality, TCP relieves applications from having to implement their own mechanisms for limiting their transmission rates.

Connection orientation: IP does not maintain any state after processing an individual datagram on the sending or receiving host. In contrast, providing the above properties necessitates maintaining state on both hosts. To limit the lifetime of this state, TCP introduces the notion of a *connection*. An application must open a connection to communicate with another application over TCP, and TCP provides its properties only for the data sent over the same connection. Once the connection is closed by an application or the other end stops responding for a period of time called *connection timeout*, TCP can free up the connection state.

Providing these properties in the transport layer greatly simplifies the development of applications that require them. On the other hand, TCP forces applications with simpler needs to use an overly complex protocol.

The remainder of this chapter discusses mechanisms used by TCP to implement some of the properties mentioned above.

3.1   Segment Header

To facilitate a stream-based transfer of data over a packet-based network, TCP has to break the data stream into *segments*, which the network layer will then encapsulate

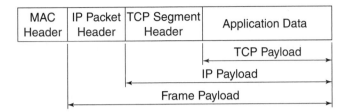

Figure 3.1 A TCP segment encapsulated into a datagram and a frame

into IP datagrams. Figure 3.1 shows the resulting segment structure. Each segment contains a TCP header in front of the application data, which allows the reassembly of segments into a data stream and supports connection management, reliable delivery, and flow control. The IP layer adds its own header to the segment; for the IP layer, the TCP header is just part of a regular datagram payload. And finally, the physical layer encapsulates the datagram into a frame by adding the MAC header. For performance reasons, TCP tries to choose a segment size that does not require additional fragmentation at the IP level [Postel 1983].

The following fields of the TCP segment are relevant to this book:

SOURCE PORT and DESTINATION PORT numbers: As described in more detail in Chapter 1, port numbers extend the host-to-host addressing provided by the IP protocol to application-to-application addressing. A port number identifies an application on a particular host. Well-known port numbers identify well-known applications willing to communicate with other applications. For example, port 80 is a default port number that identifies a Web server on a particular host. In the case of TCP, the receiving host uses the source and destination port numbers to determine the TCP connection to which an individual segment belongs.

The SEQUENCE and ACKNOWLEDGMENT numbers: The SEQUENCE number indicates the offset of this segment in the byte stream. More precisely, it is the sequence number of the first segment byte in the byte stream. The ACKNOWLEDGMENT number confirms that the sender of the segment received all bytes up to this number from the other host. Therefore, the SEQUENCE number in a segment sent from host A to host B refers to a position in the byte stream from A to B, while the ACKNOWLEDGMENT number in the same segment is related to the byte stream from B to A. Both of those numbers might grow beyond the maximum stipulated by the field size. Should this happen, the numbers will wrap around (that is, start from zero again). TCP ensures that this does not impact the correctness of the protocol; however, the details on how this is achieved are not important for the purpose of this book.

The CODE BITS field: This field contains a set of flags that deals with connection management and urgency of the content of the segment. The following list includes the most important bits for our purposes. Their use will be further clarified in the subsequent sections of this chapter.

SYN (synchronization bit) is used to establish a new connection.

FIN is used to close a connection gracefully.

RST is used to terminate a connection instantly.

ACK indicates that the segment's ACKNOWLEDGMENT number contains valid information (not all segments have to fill in this field).

Segments are often called by the name of the bit in the CODE BITS field that is set to 1; for example, a SYN segment, an ACK segment, and so on.

The WINDOW field: This field is used for flow control (see Section 3.4).

There are several other fields in the segment header, but because understanding all these fields is not necessary for the remainder of this book, we do not describe them here.

3.2 Opening a Connection

The connection-oriented nature of TCP stipulates the need to establish and terminate connections. Figure 3.2 shows message exchange for connection establishment. The initiator (host A) sends a TCP segment with a SYN bit set to the recipient (host B). Host A also picks an initial sequence number for the data stream from A to B. If host B accepts the connection, it responds with a segment that acknowledges the SYN segment sent by A, has the SYN bit set, and contains an initial sequence number that B picks for the data stream from B to A. After host A acknowledges this segment, the connection is considered to be established, and the applications on both hosts are notified of the presence of the TCP connection. This message exchange, called the *three-way handshake*, is necessary because TCP uses the unreliable IP protocol to transfer its segments. Combined with appropriate timeouts and retransmission, the

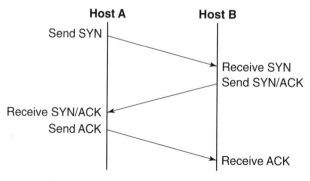

Figure 3.2 TCP connection establishment

three-way handshake guarantees that both hosts agree that a connection has been established. If host B were unwilling to accept the connection, it would have replied to the initial SYN segment with a segment with the RST bit set, notifying the initiator that the connection will not be accepted.

Before the initiator starts the handshake it must choose the destination and source port numbers. The destination port is usually fixed, since it identifies a well-known service (such as port number 80 for a Web server). The source port is usually chosen out of a pool of available port numbers on the initiator. The initiator should not reuse the port number to connect to the same listener until it knows that no segments from the previous TCP connection are still delayed in the network. This prevents old segments from being processed in the context of a new connection. The maximum possible delay of a segment in a network may be quite high, in the order of hundreds of milliseconds. This can lead to a problem, especially for Web proxy caches that must open many connections to a particular server in a short period of time. It is possible for such a cache to consume its port number space (which allows for 65,535 ports) before the maximum possible network delay is reached. In this case, most TCP implementations opt to reuse port numbers earlier to avoid the denial of service. They implicitly run the risk that a TCP connection may be corrupted by a delayed segment from a previous connection.

The initial handshake is one of the major reasons why TCP performance is suboptimal for transfers of small Web objects. Nearly all TCP implementations send the first data after the handshake is completed, adding an additional *round trip time* (*RTT*) to the application-layer data transfer. Figure 3.3 shows the maximum theoretical throughput TCP can achieve for 1KByte transfers over a typical backbone link with the raw throughput of 2.48Gbit per second (Gbps) and various RTTs, assuming that the data is transferred after the initial handshake. For example, the average AT&T backbone RTT delay between New York and Los Angeles is 85 milliseconds (ms). For this RTT, the

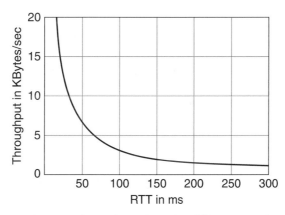

Figure 3.3   Theoretical TCP throughput for different RTTs for a 1KByte document over a 2.48Gbps link with zero loss

maximum throughput is less than 4KByte per second. This is particularly worrisome because bandwidth is increasing rapidly but average RTTs are improving only slightly and are bound by the speed of light. Therefore, as long as current TCP implementations are used, increases in backbone performance will not have any major impact on small data transfers. This performance limitation had a direct effect on the design of HTTP (see Chapter 5). Chapter 7 discusses some implications of this phenomenon on Web caching and Sections 15.2 and 16.2.3 on replication.

The seemingly good news is that the TCP standard does not require that data be transferred only after the completion of the initial handshake. Instead, data could be transmitted with the SYN segment (first round of the connection establishment). However, in current TCP implementations, even if the initiator sends data in the first segment, the recipient would most likely drop the data anyway. This would trigger a retransmission of the data after the handshake has completed. There is a good reason for this behavior. It is essential for a busy server to allocate as few resources as possible to a new connection early on in order to complicate denial-of-service attacks and to reduce the overall resource usage. When it receives the initial SYN, the server does not know yet if the sender's IP address in the datagram is correct or even exists. Therefore, the server should not commit buffer space for the data at this point.

3.3 Closing a Connection

After all data has been transferred, the TCP connection has to be closed. Figure 3.4 shows the segment exchange for the so-called graceful termination of a TCP connection. Each party is closing its part of the TCP connection independently. This means that in Figure 3.4 the FIN segment sent by host A indicates that host A is finished sending data but not that host B is done. In fact host B can still send data to host A even after host B has acknowledged the FIN segment sent by host A. Therefore, the TCP connection is considered closed and all state can be removed only after both

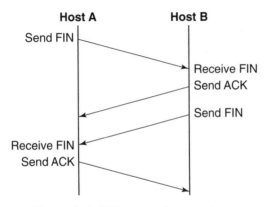

Figure 3.4 TCP connection tear-down

hosts have agreed to close the connection. In case either host has to terminate a TCP connection instantly while risking the loss of data, it can send an RST segment to the other host. This will trigger an instant termination of the connection.

3.4 Flow Control

The sending host must limit its transmission rate to the rate at which the receiver can absorb the data. Otherwise, the receiver would drop packets, which the sender would then have to retransmit, wasting bandwidth and the sender's own resources. Limiting the transmission rate to avoid overwhelming the receiver is called *flow control* in TCP.

TCP implements flow control by making the sender wait for an acknowledgment after transmitting a certain amount of data. To decide how much data to send between acknowledgments, TCP uses the *sliding window protocol*. This section covers the basics of the sliding window protocol, while the next section examines congestion control, another aspect of TCP that regulates the sending rate.

Figure 3.5 illustrates the sliding window aspects of TCP data transfer. The figure focuses on the data transfer from host A to host B and assumes for simplicity that only acknowledgments come in the other direction. (Recall that in reality TCP is bidirectional and allows a concurrent data transfer from B to A. In the presence of this transfer, acknowledgments in Figure 3.5 would be piggybacked on data segments from B to A.)

With every acknowledgment segment, B's TCP advertises a window size in bytes using the WINDOW header field. This window size indicates how many more bytes B is able to accept into its buffers. Consequently, A is allowed to transfer this many bytes beyond the last acknowledged byte (indicated by the ACKNOWLEDGMENT number in B's segment). As more bytes are acknowledged, A can transfer more new

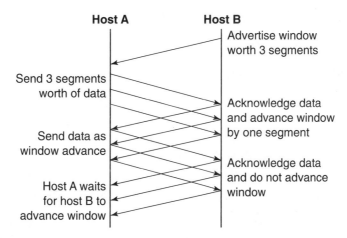

Figure 3.5 An example of the TCP sliding window protocol execution

bytes, always making sure that the number of unacknowledged bytes remains within the advertised window. One can intuitively visualize this process by imagining that A slides the advertised window forward in the data stream and transmits all data that show through. Note that B can dynamically readjust A's sending rate by changing the window size during transmission. In Figure 3.5, beginning with its fourth acknowledgment, B starts reducing the window size by exactly the number of newly acknowledged bytes. That forces A to stop transmitting any additional bytes, since the maximum byte sequence number that A is allowed to transmit remains the same.

The size of the WINDOW field in the segment header is 16 bits. This limits the advertised window to 65,535Bytes, allowing at most this number of bytes in transit at each instant for a single TCP connection. The effective size of the advertised window is, in addition, artificially reduced to 32,767 because of an incorrect implementation of sequence number calculation by some operating systems.

As network speeds increase, the maximum size of the TCP window becomes a performance bottleneck unless the entire transfer fits into the advertised window. Although most Web transfers currently fit into the advertised window, this bottleneck affects transfers of large Web objects such as video files or software packages. Going back to our example of a New York–Los Angeles connection with an average RTT of 85ms, the 32,767Byte window limits the throughput of a single TCP connection to at most 376KBytes per second, regardless of the physical capacity of the link, even if the handshake overhead is not taken into account. This limitation has been recognized, and TCP has been enhanced to increase the maximum window size [Jacobson et al. 1992]. In practice, however, this enhancement is rarely used.

3.5 Congestion Control

In addition to dealing with the capacity of the recipient, TCP also must adapt the transfer rate because of congestion on the network. If TCP did not adapt to congestion, an overloaded network would result in dropped packets, which would cause retransmissions that would further increase the congestion, for a snowball effect. To address this problem, TCP reduces its transfer rate if it detects congestion, by increasing its transfer rate until packets are lost and then drastically reducing the transfer rate. Subsequently, TCP increases the transfer rate again in order to probe continually for the network's bottleneck bandwidth between the two end hosts of the connection.

TCP implements this functionality by maintaining a *congestion window* on each end of the connection that specifies the number of unacknowledged segments one host may send to the other. The congestion window, like the advertised window introduced earlier, limits the amount of data outstanding in the network. In contrast to the advertised window, it is never explicitly transmitted over the network and is only kept in the sender's local TCP state.

After the initial handshake, each side of the TCP connection sets its congestion window to allow two unacknowledged segments and then increases the window as acknowledgments are received. Initially, the sender increases its congestion window size by one segment each time an acknowledgment arrives. Thus, at the beginning of the transmission, the sender sends two segments. Assuming no packet loss, the sender will receive the acknowledgments for these segments after the RTT. As a result, the congestion window increases to four segments, allowing the sender to double its transmission rate during the next RTT interval. The rate will double again after the data in the next congestion window has been transmitted and acknowledged, and so on, resulting in an exponential increase of transfer rate. This phase is called *TCP slow start*.

Later during the connection, TCP probes the network more carefully and increases the congestion window by one segment only after the sender receives acknowledgments for the number of segments equal to the current size of the congestion window. For example, if the current congestion window is five segments, the sender waits for five previously sent segments to be acknowledged before setting the window to six segments. After that, the sender will not increment the window again until it receives acknowledgments for another six segments. In this phase, the transfer rate increases only linearly with time.

Once the sender detects a packet loss, it reduces its congestion window by half. Several packet losses in quick succession may trigger the repeat of the slow start from scratch.

The fact that a TCP connection must increase its transfer rate over time indicates that the throughput of one large TCP transfer is usually higher than the throughput of many short ones, with the exception of extremely short connections that fit into the initial congestion window of two segments, or about 3KBytes.

Note that the amount of unacknowledged data a sender can transmit, and hence the effective throughput of a TCP connection, is limited by both the advertised window and the congestion window. As we have seen in the previous sections, the former affects large TCP transfers, while the latter affects mostly short transfers. In combination, the flow and congestion controls limit throughput of all TCP transfers over 3KBytes. But such short transfers are affected most by the TCP handshake overhead (Section 3.2), since this overhead cannot be amortized over the life of a connection. Thus, no transfer size escapes TCP overheads. Overall, the overheads are less severe in large transfers than in short ones. This provides a motivation for *persistent HTTP connections* (described in Chapter 5), which increase the size of TCP transfers by transferring multiple Web objects over the same TCP connection.

We refer the interested reader to the book by Peterson and Davie [1996] for further details on the congestion control algorithms. However, it is important to get a rough understanding of the impact of packet loss and round trip time on the overall performance of TCP to fully appreciate caching and replication. To this end, we applied the TCP performance model introduced by Padhye et al. [1998] to derive the throughput curves for a steady state TCP connection with different loss rates and RTTs. The resulting plot is shown in Figure 3.6. To isolate the effect of packet loss and RTT, we derived the throughput curves assuming that TCP is not limited by the advertised window or the underlying network bandwidth. This plot shows the extent to which the throughput depends on loss rate and RTT. Using the previous example

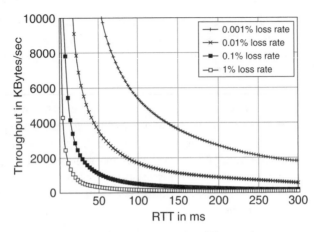

Figure 3.6 Theoretical TCP throughput for different drop rates and RTTs

of a connection on the AT&T backbone between New York and Los Angeles with an RTT of 85ms, the connection must keep the loss rate below 0.01 percent to sustain the 2.48Gbps throughput of the backbone link.

3.6 Retransmission

A major goal of TCP is to transmit data reliably. However, reliable transmission of data over an unreliable network layer like IP requires the retransmission of lost data. A general approach is that the sender would retransmit the TCP segments that have not been acknowledged by the receiver within a certain time after the initial transmission. This poses an interesting problem: how long should the sender wait before retransmitting such data? If data is retransmitted too soon, the data might actually not have been lost, and the retransmission might be redundant. If the data is retransmitted too late, the advertised window will not advance as discussed in Section 3.4, causing the sending host to limit its transmission rate unnecessarily.

TCP tries to solve this problem by adapting the timeout used to trigger retransmissions depending on the previously observed RTT and RTT variance between the two hosts. Typically, TCP sets the initial timeout to a predefined value and, as it learns the RTT, adjusts the timeout to the RTT plus four times the RTT variance.

3.7 Summary

TCP is the most-used transport layer protocol on the Internet: it carries nearly all of today's Web traffic. TCP provides most services that an application could expect including reliable delivery, exactly-once delivery, ordered delivery, connection-oriented service, stream-based service, full duplex delivery, and flow and congestion control. In addition, TCP introduces port numbers that address individual applications on a host.

On the other hand, TCP introduces overheads that may limit transfer throughput below the physical network capacity, especially in modern high-speed networks. In particular, the TCP handshake adds an initial delay before the actual data transfer begins; TCP slow start limits throughput in the initial phase of the transfer and in the high-loss conditions; the advertised window size imposes the upper bound on the throughput of any TCP connection regardless of the physical network capacity. While these overheads are being addressed by current research and TCP extensions, the proposed solutions are still not widely used. Therefore, the performance limitations of native TCP for Web traffic in high-speed environments present a real limitation in practice.

Transport protocols such as TCP provide the foundation for the implementation of application-level protocols that are used to build a variety of network services, including the Web. The next chapter considers the most important application-level protocols that implement the Web.

Chapter 4
Application Protocols for the Web

The Web is an application that runs on the Internet and is implemented using a set of application-layer protocols and standards. Some application-layer protocols, such as DNS, NFS, Telnet, FTP, Gopher and HTTP, were briefly introduced in Chapter 1. This chapter expands this introduction for the protocols used by the Web focusing on application-layer standards and protocols important in the context of Web caching and replication. It starts by describing the Web's naming convention (URLs), which extends IP addresses and port numbers to allow the naming of arbitrary objects on the global network. Next we outline the DNS protocol that allows hosts to have human-readable host names like www.att.com. We then provide a basic introduction to HTTP, which is used to retrieve those globally named objects, and concludes with some highlights of HTML, which allows individual objects to interconnect into a "web of objects." A more detailed study of the concepts and protocols introduced in this chapter can be found in the book by Krishnamurthy and Rexford [2001].

4.1 Uniform Resource Locators

URLs, or Uniform Resource Locators, allow the naming of arbitrary objects within a global network. Most URLs are specified in Web objects and either are automatically downloaded by browsers or are only indirectly—as hyperlinks—visible to an end user. If URLs are advertised directly to users, they are usually incomplete and rely on a Web browser to expand them to their correct form. For example, AT&T's advertisements direct customers to "att.com," which a browser expands to "http://att.com"—the correct URL for the entry page into AT&T's Web site.

Figure 4.1 shows the general syntax of a URL as introduced in RFC 1738 and later updated in RFC 1808 and RFC 2368 [Berners-Lee et al. 1994; Fielding 1995; Hoffman et al. 1998]. The URL contains information about the name of the object and how it

```
<protocol>://<username>:<password>@<host>:<port>/<url-path>
```
Figure 4.1 The general URL syntax

```
http://<host>:<port>/<path>?<searchpart>
```
Figure 4.2 Web-specific URL syntax

should be retrieved. It starts with the `protocol` field. The `protocol` field determines the protocol that should be used to access the object. Common possibilities are `file`, `news`, `mailto`, `http`, and `ftp`. The `file` protocol is used to retrieve local files, `mailto` to send email, `http` to download Web objects, and the `ftp` protocol is used to retrieve objects from an FTP server. The `protocol` field is followed by the optional `username` and `password` fields. These fields enable the authentication of a user, allowing a simple form of access control for the object. A serious limitation of this authentication scheme is that the username and password are passed insecurely over the Internet. For this reason, this scheme is rarely used in practice, and the `username` and `password` fields are commonly omitted, together with the associated delimiters, the colon (`:`) and the at sign (`@`). The next URL field is the `host` field. It contains either the IP address or the *fully qualified domain name* of the host where the document resides. Fully qualified domain names are described in Section 4.2.1. The `host` field is followed by a `port` field that identifies the port number used by the server to accept client connections for this object. In many cases `port` is omitted, since all common protocols have well-known default port numbers. The last field of the URL, `url-path`, identifies the object within the host. The `url-path` field can be as simple as a filename or may be a complex protocol- or host-specific encoding of arguments used by the server to dynamically generate the object. For example, the URL *http://www.spatscheck.com/oliver* points to a Web object belonging to one of this book's authors.

Figure 4.2 shows the structure of URLs that identify objects within the Web. The protocol used by the Web is HTTP, and it is specified in the `protocol` field of the general URL syntax. The `host` and `port` fields are identical to the `host` and `port` fields defined in the general URL syntax. For HTTP, the `port` field is generally omitted and defaults to TCP port number 80. The general `url-path` field is more specifically defined here as `path` and `searchpart`, which are separated by a question mark (`?`). The path usually contains either a single filename or the pathname of the directory that has the object and the filename of the object. For example, the path `/public/index.html` identifies the file index.html in the server directory `/public/` as the desired object. The searchpart is only present for *dynamic objects*. Unlike *static objects* that are stored in files and do not change unless explicitly modified, dynamic objects are generated by programs that the server executes at the time of access. Programs that generate dynamic objects are also known as *CGI scripts* because they must conform to the *Common Gateway Interface* [Gundavaram 1996]. In the case of dynamic objects, the path identifies the program that will generate the object and the searchpart contains arguments that are passed to this program. Both the path and the searchpart can be omitted, in which case the server returns a default object specified in its configuration file. The presence of the searchpart is signified by the question mark delimiter.

The presence of the question mark delimiter is generally a good indication that the content is dynamically generated. Another heuristic that can be used to deduce a dynamic object is the presence of the term "cgi-bin" or the ending "cgi" in the `path` part of the object, because these substrings usually identify CGI scripts. However, there are no firm requirements in the URL specification that force a URL to indicate whether the corresponding object is dynamic or static. Identifying dynamic content is important in the context of caching and replication, because proxies and surrogates usually do not cache dynamic content, although HTTP 1.1 does not preclude doing so. We introduce HTTP features that affect caching in Chapter 5 and discuss the problem of uncacheable content in Chapter 13.

4.2   The Domain Name System

So far we have seen how an individual host is identified by its IP address. This numerical address is perfectly suited for processing by routers or computers, but it is rather user unfriendly. Therefore, it is desirable that, in addition to the IP address, hosts should have symbolic names. For example, AT&T's Web server is known to most users as www.att.com and not as 192.20.3.54. The mapping between the symbolic name and the numerical IP address used to address IP packets is performed by the Domain Name System (DNS).

4.2.1   Name Hierarchy

To decentralize both the management of host names and their translation into IP addresses, DNS organizes host names into hierarchical *domains*. Each domain is given a name, which is unique within the higher-level domain to which this domain belongs. A list of domain names from the bottom to the top level in the hierarchy, where each name belongs to the next domain in the list, uniquely identifies a host and is called a *fully qualified domain name* (or a *domain name* for short).

For example, www.att.com is the domain name of the main Web server of AT&T. It consists of three levels of the hierarchy. At the highest level, "com" represents the domain of commercial names; "att" identifies the domain of names that belong to AT&T; and finally, "www" identifies a particular host (in this case a Web server) within AT&T. Notice that, unlike filenames and directories, fully qualified domain names list domains from left to right in the ascending hierarchical order—that is, starting with the most specific domain and ending with the top-level domain.

Figure 4.3 shows the basic hierarchy in the DNS. The so-called top-level domains are, not surprisingly, U.S.-centric. They are *.com*, the commercial domain; *.net*, the network provider domain; *.org*, the nonprofit organization domain; *.gov*, the U.S. government domain; *.mil*, the U.S. military domain; and *.edu*, the educational organization domain. In addition, there are country-specific top-level domains such as *.de* for Germany and *.uk* for the United Kingdom.

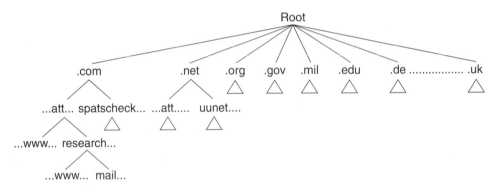

Figure 4.3 The Internet name hierarchy

Below the appropriate top-level domains, organizations or individuals can register their own domain names. For example, AT&T registered the "att" subdomain within both the .com and .net domains for different parts of its business. Another example is provided by one of the authors of this book, who registered subdomain "spatscheck" in the .com domain for his personal use. Because each name in the top-level domains can be reserved by only one organization much controversy has arisen over who should own domains with catchy words in the .com domain space, especially if the names contain a trademark.

All levels below the second-level domain are under the complete control of the organization or individual that registered the second-level domain. For example, it is AT&T's choice to further deepen the hierarchy with names like www.research.att.com, or to name individual hosts at this level of the hierarchy using names like www.att.com.

4.2.2 The DNS Protocol

The job of the DNS is to map host domain names into IP addresses (this is also called *resolving a domain name*). Hosts obtain these mappings by interacting with the DNS using the *DNS protocol*. The DNS protocol involves two major parties: a client host that wants to resolve a domain name to an IP address and a set of name servers, also called *DNS servers,* that provide the resolution.

The DNS protocol typically runs over UDP [Postel 1980]. A DNS server receives a *request* to resolve a domain name from a client or another DNS server and returns one or more *response* records. These records may have a wide variety of record types. The most common ones are:

- *A:* The A record is used to return a name to IP address mapping.

- *NS:* The NS record refers the requester to another DNS server that knows how to resolve subdomains within the domain.

- *CNAME:* The CNAME record maps one domain name to another domain name.

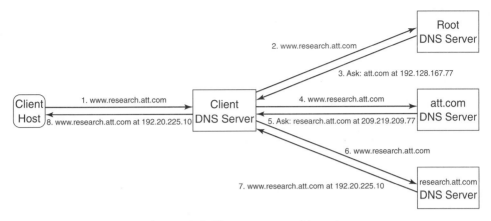

Figure 4.4 The name server hierarchy

Every host that wants to obtain services from the global DNS must know the IP address of at least one DNS server, called the *client DNS server* for this host. Hosts are either statically configured to record the IP address of their client DNS server(s), or they obtain that IP address using an autoconfiguration protocol such as DHCP [Droms 1993] when they connect to the network. For residential clients, client DNS servers reside in their ISPs and are shared by all customers; organizations often maintain their own DNS servers for the hosts contained within that organization.

Figure 4.4 shows a typical scenario for name resolution. In this example, a client needs to resolve the domain name www.research.att.com. The client sends the request to resolve this name to its client DNS server. The client DNS server then contacts one of the *root name servers* to resolve the name provided by the client. The root DNS servers are a well-known set of name servers with the knowledge of all domains registered directly under top-level domains. A root DNS server knows about att.com but not about www.research.att.com.[1] Therefore, it will not be able to resolve www.research.att.com. However, it will be able to point the client name server to the name servers responsible for att.com by returning the appropriate NS record. Each domain that is directly below a top-level domain, such as att.com, must have at least two such servers registered with root name servers to allow for fault tolerance.

Once the client's name server receives the NS record, it contacts one of the servers responsible for att.com. This name server may be able either to provide the IP address for www.research.att.com or, as shown in Figure 4.4, to redirect the client's name server again to a name server responsible for research.att.com. This last name server finally returns an A record to the client name server with the IP address corresponding to www.research.att.com. The client name server then forwards this response to the client.

---

[1] To reduce the load on root servers, separate name servers for top-level domains were recently introduced into the DNS architecture. This does not change the principles behind the DNS system; however, it introduces another layer of indirection.

Figure 4.4 shows two different types of DNS resolution, *iterative* and *recursive* resolution. With iterative resolution a DNS server returns the final answer (that is, the IP address corresponding to the requested domain name) only if the answer is locally available. Otherwise, the DNS server redirects the requester to other DNS servers that might know the answer by responding with NS or CNAME records. In this case the requester iterates through multiple DNS servers until it obtains the final answer. The client DNS server in our example uses iterative DNS resolution to resolve www.research.att.com. It contacts iteratively a root name server, an att.com name server, and a name server for research.att.com.

On the other hand, the client uses recursive resolution when obtaining the answer from its local DNS server. The local DNS server itself does all the work and returns the final answer to the client.

Because recursive resolution puts a substantial load on the name server, recursive resolution must be requested by the requester and accepted by the DNS server receiving the request. In practice, DNS requests always include the request for recursive resolution. However, the root DNS servers refuse to perform recursive resolutions and redirect requesters to lower-level DNS servers instead. The roots do not perform recursive resolutions both to avoid extra load and also for security reasons. Lower-level DNS servers often do honor recursive requests.

The complexity of our simple example in Figure 4.4 also makes it obvious that the latency of such a name resolution and the load it places on the root name servers, which are involved in every such resolution, are extremely high. To reduce latency and the load on the root DNS server, all name servers involved, as well as clients, cache DNS responses. To ensure that responses are reasonably up-to-date, each record contains an explicit time to live in seconds. This TTL is not related to the IP TTL introduced in Chapter 2. The DNS TTL limits the lifetime of a DNS record while the IP TTL limits the lifetime of an IP datagram. Unfortunately, Web browsers commonly do not honor the TTL field of DNS responses and cache these responses longer than their TTLs allow. Chapter 14 and Chapter 15 discuss the implications of DNS response caching for Web replication.

4.3   The HyperText Transfer Protocol

Because the Web has become the driving force of the Internet, the HyperText Transfer Protocol (HTTP) now carries a large majority (currently around 70 percent) of Internet traffic. HTTP is a simple request-response protocol using URLs to name objects it retrieves. HTTP 0.9 was the first widely used version, which was replaced by HTTP 1.0 [Berners-Lee et al. 1996] and then HTTP 1.1 [Fielding et al. 1999].

An HTTP message consists of an HTTP header and an entity body, the two being delineated by the carriage return (CR) and line feed (LF) characters. There are two types of HTTP messages: an HTTP request issued by a client and an HTTP response generated by a server. For both types of HTTP messages, all header fields are encoded in clear text (ASCII) so HTTP messages are easily readable by humans.

4.3.1 The HTTP Request

The HTTP request has grown from a simple message in HTTP 0.9, containing just the URL of a requested object, to a message with many header fields that can span multiple kilobytes. The layout of an HTTP 1.1 request is shown in Figure 4.5. It contains a request line, followed by multiple general, request, and entity header fields (or *headers* for short), possibly followed by an entity body, which contains data that the client wants to upload to the server.

The request line describes the action requested from the server, and headers describe various qualifiers of the request, such as content encodings the client understands and client authentication information. General headers are those that can be used by both the HTTP requests and responses, request headers are specific to request messages, and entity headers describe the data contained in the request. When it causes no confusion, we do not distinguish between the general, request, and entity headers of a request, referring to them all simply as *request headers*.

Request headers describe client capabilities, authorization credentials, and other information that helps in fullfilling the request. A header comprises a keyword that identifies the header and a value containing the information. In particular, request headers often provide information that controls the use of caches in fulfilling the request. These headers are described in detail in Chapter 5.

The request line contains the method, the path part of the URL, and the version of the protocol. The standard methods are GET, HEAD, OPTIONS, POST, PUT, DELETE, and TRACE.

GET is the most common method; it is used to retrieve from the server the object specified by the path portion of the URL. For example, the request line "GET/index.html HTTP/1.1" can be used to retrieve the object index.html from a

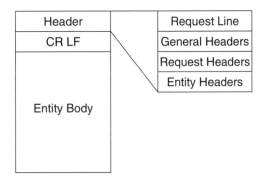

Figure 4.5 The HTTP 1.1 request format

Web server using HTTP 1.1. The HEAD method is similar to GET except that only the headers of the response are returned. Clients use the HEAD method to retrieve meta-information about the returned object. This information allows a client, for example, to check that the content type of the object is suitable for the client without retrieving the document.

The POST and PUT methods are used to upload information to the server. In both cases, the entity body will contain the data in question. POST is commonly used to transfer to the server information from Web forms that users fill out. PUT places a new object on a Web server. The DELETE method allows a client to remove an object from a server. To protect their content, Web servers usually restrict the use of the PUT and DELETE methods. The OPTIONS request retrieves details on the server capabilities and features applicable to either the particular object listed in the request or the server in general. Chapter 5 describes the TRACE method, which returns the request back to the sender. The TRACE method can be used to discover proxies between a client and a server.

The GET, HEAD, OPTIONS, and TRACE methods are *safe* according to the HTTP specification. This means requests with these methods do not cause a side effect on servers. In particular, these methods are *idempotent*—that is, they can be submitted multiple times with no harm, and they will return the same responses each time. In addition, the DELETE method is considered idempotent (but obviously not safe) because it has the same side effect at the server whether it is executed multiple times or just once.

4.3.2 The HTTP Response

Like the HTTP request, the HTTP response evolved from simply carrying an object in HTTP 0.9 to a complex message with an elaborate set of headers. Figure 4.6 shows the layout of the response. It starts with the status line, followed by general headers, response headers, entity headers, carriage return and line feed characters, and an entity body. As we do with the request headers, we often refer to all headers in the

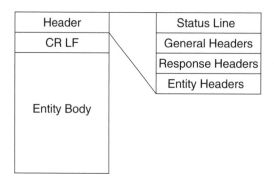

Figure 4.6 The HTTP 1.1 response format

Table 4.1 The Five Status Code
Categories in HTTP 1.1

Status Code	Response Category
1xx	informational
2xx	successful
3xx	redirection
4xx	client error
5xx	server error

response message as *response headers*. Response headers have the same format as their request counterparts, comprising a keyword and value. The discussion of header fields is in Chapter 5.

The status line of a response contains the status of the response, including the protocol version used, a numeric status code (also referred to as *response code*), and a textual explanation of the status code. Currently, HTTP 1.1 defines about forty status codes in five categories (see Table 4.1).

The most common response code is the OK response code (code 200) in the successful category. For example, the status line "HTTP/1.1 200 OK" indicates that the Web server will return the object using the HTTP 1.1 protocol. Less common in this category is the "partial content" code, which indicates that only parts of an object have been returned. Separate response codes indicate success of a PUT or POST request.

Response codes in the client error category describe errors in the request submitted by the client. These errors include such conditions as malformed URLs, unauthorized accesses, wrong method used, or unacceptable encoding requested. The server error response codes are used to describe various server errors such as temporary server unavailability and unimplemented functionality on a server.

The redirection category, which plays a central role in Web caching and replication, is described in Chapter 5.

4.4 The HTTP Message Exchange

The basic HTTP interaction includes a client request and a server response. The simplicity of the protocol results from its being *stateless*: it does not require either the client or the server to record any information beyond the boundaries of this simple interaction.

An HTTP exchange can generally be carried over any Layer 4 protocol. However, for all practical purposes, TCP is used in the Internet environment. Figure 4.7a shows the message exchanges between the client and the server in the simplest HTTP interaction, which is also the only possible case for HTTP 0.9. In this example, the client

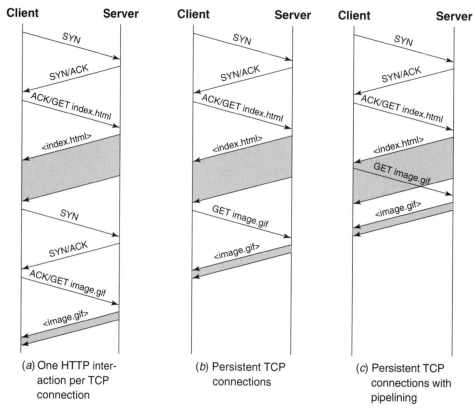

Figure 4.7 The TCP-level message exchange in an HTTP interaction

downloads the page index.html from the server and then image.gif that is embedded into this page.

The client first establishes a TCP connection to the server specified in the URL. Once the connection is established, the client requests index.html using the HTTP "GET /index.html" request. The server then delivers the object and closes the TCP connection after the document has been sent. (Closing the connection is not shown in the figure.) Obtaining the embedded image.gif occurs in the same way.

In this simplest mode, the protocol pays the overhead of TCP connection establishment for every object downloaded. Modern Web documents often contain dozens of objects, and this overhead causes a significant increase of user latency. It also increases network load for carrying TCP control messages and server load for initiating and closing connections. Trying to reduce the latency penalty, HTTP 0.9 browsers open multiple parallel connections to servers, but that increases server load by increasing the number of connections they must handle. An extension to HTTP 1.0 allows the client to request the server not to close the connection after the object transfer, so that subsequent object downloads can reuse the same connection. A TCP connection used for multiple object downloads is referred to as a *persistent connection*.

Figure 4.7b shows message exchange over a persistent connection. Only the first download incurs the connection establishment overhead; the rest of the objects can be fetched without it. The current version of HTTP—HTTP 1.1—makes persistent connections a default. In HTTP 1.1, either the client or the server can indicate to the other party that it would like to close the connection after the current download is complete. However, without such notification, it is assumed that the connection will persist beyond the current interaction.

In Figure 4.7b, the client sends the next request only after obtaining the response to the previous one. This creates pauses in transmission after the server sends an object and before it receives the next request. HTTP 1.1 introduces a *pipelining* mechanism that avoids these pauses. Pipelining allows the client to issue several HTTP requests without obtaining the responses. When the server obtains pipelined requests, it sends all responses one after another, in the same order as the requests arrived. As Figure 4.7c illustrates, pipelining often avoids transmission pauses and results in lower document download time.

Pipelining has a performance pitfall that concerns the requirement that the responses be sent in the order of the requests in the pipeline. Thus, a large or computationally intensive response that takes a long time to download will delay all subsequent responses in the pipeline. Such a delay is called *head of line blocking;* we will encounter other examples of it later in this book (see Chapter 8). To reduce the possibility of head of line blocking, HTTP 1.1 allows clients to open two parallel connections to a server. In practice, clients sometimes open many more, but this is a violation of HTTP 1.1 specifications.

4.5 Hyperlinks and Embedded Objects

HTTP can be used to retrieve arbitrary objects including images, JavaScript files, or HTML pages [Berners-Lee and Connolly 1995]. While the encoding and other details of those objects are outside the scope of this book, it is important in the context of caching and replication to understand the basic functionality of hyperlinks and embedded objects in HTML documents. An HTML document is the basic framework of a Web page. In general, it contains the text, formatting instructions, hyperlinks, and embedded objects displayed in a Web browser as part of the document.

Figure 4.8 shows a simple HTML object. It contains some text, two embedded objects, and a hyperlink. If the HTML object is retrieved by a Web browser, the browser automatically retrieves the embedded objects (`picture1.gif` and `picture2.gif`) and displays them as embedded pictures in the Web document, as shown in Figure 4.9. The hyperlink to AT&T's main Web page is highlighted in the rendered document, and if the user clicks on the link, the object specified in the hyperlink is retrieved and displayed in the browser.

This example illustrates three kinds of structural content for which, to avoid confusion, we need some terminology. A piece of Web content addressable by a URL

```
<html>
  <head>
    <title>Test Page</title>
  </head>
  <body>
    This is a test page.
    It includes embedded images
      <img src="picture1.gif"> and <img src="picture2.gif">
    and the following hyperlink:
    <a href="http://www.att.com/index.html">Hyperlink to the AT&T Web site</a>
  </body>
</html>
```

Figure 4.8 A simple HTML object

This is a test page. It includes embedded images   and   as well as the following hyperlink: Hyperlink to the AT&T Web site

Figure 4.9 A screenshot of the simple HTML object in Figure 4.8

we call a Web *object*. In Figure 4.8, both the HTML page and the embedded images are Web objects. An HTML object that includes embedded objects we call a *container object* or a *container page*. The HTML page in Figure 4.8 is a container object since it includes embedded objects. A semantically distinct piece of Web content viewable by the user we call a *document*. In our example, the Web page together with the pictures displayed in the browser is a document. Downloading a document entails several Web interactions to download its container page and all its embedded objects.

We should note that our terminology does not reflect any established practice. One can encounter the terms *document, object, page,* and *resource* applied interchangeably to the three kinds of content we distinguished previously. In fact, the term *resource* was originally proposed by HTTP creators to denote what we call an *object* (it appears in the term URL—Uniform Resource Locator). However, the term *object* appears to be more popular now. We will use the term *resource* to denote a Web application that produces a response, as opposed to the response itself.

Figure 4.8 also illustrates another aspect of referencing objects in HTML documents: the objects can be referenced using either absolute or relative URLs. The embedded images picture1.gif and picture2.gif are referenced by relative URLs, which contain only a portion of the path information. The browser reconstructs the actual URL of this object by prepending the default protocol part ("http") as well as the domain name and the path of the container object in which it is included. For example, if the URL of the page in Figure 4.8 is http://www.firm-x.com/test.html, then the full URL of the embedded object picture1.gif will be http://www.firm-x.com/picture1.gif. In contrast, the hyperlink to AT&T's Web site is an absolute reference, specifying the entire URL within the container object.

4.6 Summary

The Web is an application that runs on the Internet. It provides access to Web objects, which Web clients retrieve using objects' global names, called URLs. The two most important application-level protocols used by the Web are DNS and HTTP. DNS is used to provide hosts with human-readable names; it is used by many other Internet applications besides the Web. HTTP is specifically a Web protocol that Web clients use to talk to Web servers. In fact, Web servers are also known as HTTP servers. HTTP is a request-response protocol that runs on top of TCP. Two important performance optimizations are persistent connections, which allow multiple Web interactions to reuse the same TCP connection, and pipelining, which lets a client send a request without waiting for the full response to the previous request.

While the Web now provides access to many different types of objects, the objects that started the Web and remain at its core are HTML objects, which are textual objects written in the HTML language. HTML includes instructions for text formatting and, most importantly, for linking different objects into a hypertext structure. HTML defines two kinds of links: hyperlinks, which the user can click on to move from one document to another, and embedded links, which reference Web objects that the browser retrieves and inserts automatically into the encompassing document. Because there is no established terminology in this regard, we call an HTML object that includes embedded objects a container object and distinguish it from a Web document, by which we refer to a semantically distinct piece of Web content such as a container object together with all its embedded objects. Web servers may serve HTML objects from static files or generate the objects dynamically at the time of the request.

Combined with the background provided in the previous chapters, the information presented in this chapter allows the reader to understand the retrieval of Web objects in sufficient detail. For example, the retrieval of the AT&T Research main Web page usually starts by the user clicking on a hyperlink pointing to http://www.research.att.com/ or typing this URL into the URL window of the Web browser. The user browser then starts the retrieval process by resolving the DNS name www.research.att.com to its associated IP address 192.20.225.10. This resolution might involve the client name server, the root name servers, and various other name servers. The client name servers will request an A record for the domain name and might be redirected to other name servers using NS records.

After the browser has resolved the domain name to an IP address, the browser establishes a TCP connection to port 80 on the Web server identified by this IP address.

Port 80 is the well-known HTTP port on which a Web server accepts requests. After the TCP connection is established, the browser will request the object "/" using the HTTP GET method. The Web server will then reply with an HTTP response header followed by the content of the object.

At this point, the browser parses the HTML instructions of the container object and tries to retrieve all embedded objects using the same steps outlined above. After all embedded objects have been retrieved, the browser waits idle until the user clicks on yet another hyperlink or provides another URL in the URL window of the Web browser.

Chapter 5
HTTP Support for Caching and Replication

The previous chapters discussed Internet basics, including a basic introduction to HTTP. This chapter highlights the most important HTTP features relevant to caching and replication. While many of these features can be used for a wide variety of purposes, we will concentrate on their uses for caching and replication support.

5.1 Conditional Requests

An HTTP feature central for caching and replication is support for *conditional requests*. These requests specify certain conditions in their headers. A server executes a conditional request and responds with the message body only if the condition is true. Otherwise, the server simply responds with a special status code, either "304 Not Modified" or "412 Precondition Failed," which indicate that the condition does not hold. The headers that specify the conditions are called *conditional headers*.

Clients formulate conditional requests using metainformation about the objects. Servers provide this information together with the objects in `last-modified` and `ETag` headers of their responses. The `last-modified` header contains the date and time of the last modification of the object. `ETag`, which stands for *entity tag*, is a unique identifier for a particular instance of an object. For example, the MD5 hash function[1] [Gonnet and Baeza-Yates 1991] can be used to generate a unique digital identifier, or *fingerprint*, of an object, which can serve as its entity tag. Entity tags provide a more general and reliable way to identify object versions, because last-modified dates have a granularity of a second, making it impossible to identify changes that occur in less than a second from a previous object access.

---

[1] MD5 is an algorithm that maps an arbitrary object—that is, a set of bytes—into a 16Byte value; the algorithm is designed to map, with extremely high probability, different objects into different values.

Table 5.1 Conditional Headers Common in Caching

Header Keyword	Value	Meaning
`if-modified-since`	last-modified date	execute request if requested object updated since last-modified date
`if-none-match`	`ETag`	execute request if `ETag` of requested object is different

5.1.1 Conditional Headers Used for Caching

Table 5.1 lists the most important conditional headers used in the context of caching. The `if-modified-since` header contains the last-modified date of the cached object. When a server receives a request with this header (typically a GET request), the server only returns the object if the last-modified date of the object at the server is different from the date contained in the `if-modified-since` request header. Otherwise, the server returns a "304 Not Modified" status code.

The `if-none-match` header contains the entity tag of the cached object. In response to a request with this header, the server returns the object only if the object's entity tag on the server does not match the tag from the `if-none-match` header of the request. Otherwise, the server returns a "304 Not Modified" status code.

Clients use these headers to check whether their cached copies of objects are still valid and, if not, to download the current objects in one server access. Although the `if-none-match` header using entity tags provides a more direct way to compare objects, the `if-modified-since` header is far more common because it was introduced in earlier versions of HTTP; requests with this header are often referred to as *IMS requests*.

5.1.2 Conditional Headers Used for Replication

Conditional requests can also be used in replication if servers employ HTTP to propagate new object versions to each other. Recall that HTTP provides several methods for updating information on a server: POST, PUT, and DELETE. A server can use POST to send object updates to another server with an object replica, PUT to send the new version of the object in its entirety, and DELETE to delete object replicas when the object itself has been removed.

In any of these methods of update propagation, it is important to detect conflicting object versions. For example, two replicas of an object may be independently updated on two servers. If one server attempts to PUT its object copy on the other, doing so blindly may result in losing the updates performed on the other server. Instead of overwriting one conflicting copy with another, the system should call attention to the exception and let system administrators reconcile the replicas. Similarly, if an object

Table 5.2 Conditional Headers Useful in Replication

Header Keyword	Value	Meaning
if-unmodified-since	date	execute request if the object's last-modified date matches the supplied date
if-match	ETag	execute request if the object's ETag matches the supplied ETag

has been deleted on one server and independently updated on another, an attempt by the first server to DELETE the object on the second server should not succeed.

Two conditional headers can be used in conjunction with update requests to make sure that the update is performed on an intended version of the object; they are shown in Table 5.2.

The if-unmodified-since header is the inverse of the if-modified-since condition. When receiving a request with this header, a server executes the request only if the object's last modified date is the same as the date supplied in the if-unmodified-since request header. The if-match header specifies the inverse of the if-none-match condition. A server executes the request with this header only if the entity tag supplied in the if-match request header matches the current ETag of the object at the server. If the condition described in either header does not hold, the server does not execute the request and returns a "412 Precondition Failed" status code.

5.2   Age and Expiration of Cached Objects

HTTP also provides support for caches to decide when to check the validity of the cached objects. This support is based on a *time to live* (*TTL*) concept, which is similar to the concept with the same name that we already encountered in DNS caching (Section 4.2). The time to live of an object is the time during which the object is considered valid in a cache. An HTTP object that has been cached longer than its time to live is said to *expire*. When an HTTP request for an expired object arrives, the cache must validate the object by sending a conditional request to the server before serving the object from the cache. A related concept that plays an important role in HTTP 1.1 is the *age* of a cached object, which is the time since the object left or was last validated by the origin server. Table 5.3 lists response headers used to limit the time before a cache must validate cached objects.

An HTTP server can supply an explicit time to live value for the object by using the expires and max-age headers. The expires header provides the date (with the granularity of a second) up to which the cached object may be considered valid. Rather

Table 5.3 Headers Used to Limit Caching Time

Header Keyword	Value	Meaning
`expires`	date	date until which the object is valid
`max-age`	seconds	maximum age the object may reach before validation
`age`	seconds	estimated time since the object was served or last validated by the origin server

than being a header, `max-age` is actually a directive in a complex `cache-control` header described in detail in Section 5.5. This directive provides the maximum age of a cached object before it requires validation. The `expires` header provides the absolute value of the TTL while the `max-age` directive specifies TTL relative to the time the object left or was last validated by the origin server. Historically, `expires` is the older header, coming from HTTP 1.0; if both headers are present, the `max-age` directive takes precedence.

When a relative TTL is used to control object expiration, a cache must be able to determine the age of an object. This may be difficult when the cache receives the object via multiple proxies as in Figure I.3 in the Introduction. To enable age determination, a proxy that obtained the object directly from the origin server inserts an `age` header in any of its responses that involve the cached object. This header is then updated by all intermediate proxies, based on the value of the age header when they obtained the object and the time the object stayed in their cache. Thus, any cache in the chain can estimate the object age.

Unfortunately, servers often fail to supply an explicit TTL for objects they serve. Without an explicit TTL, caches resort to heuristics to decide when to validate their objects. We describe these heuristics in Section 10.1.2.

5.3 Request Redirection

Other HTTP features important for caching and replication are its mechanisms for redirecting a request from one server to another. A server may redirect a request to a proxy cache or a mirror server, or it may notify the client of the set of proxies and mirrors that can service the request. HTTP servers implement request redirection by returning a response with special redirection status codes. The main redirection status codes are shown in Table 5.4.

A server can use a response with the "300 Multiple Choices" status code to provide a client with a list of locations that can satisfy the request. The locations and their characteristics are specified in the entity portion of the response.

Table 5.4 Status Codes for Request Redirection

Status Code	*How Redirection Information Supplied*
300 Multiple Choices	entity body
301 Moved Permanently	`location` header
302 Found	`location` header
303 See Other	`location` header
305 Use Proxy	`location` header
307 Temporary Redirect	`location` header

The "301 Moved Permanently" status code indicates that the requested object has permanently moved to another location. The response provides the new URL in a `location` header. The client should use the new URL in the future. The "307 Temporary Redirect" status code also provides the client with a different URL for the request; however, this status code indicates that the object has moved only temporarily, so the client should use the original URL in the future.

The "303 See Other" status code indicates that the response to the request should be retrieved using a URL provided in the `location` header and the GET method. For example, a Web application normally accessed using a POST method can use this status code to redirect the client to a static object.

The "305 Use Proxy" response redirects a client to a proxy for the retrieval of the object. The `location` response header provides the identity of the proxy.

HTTP also provides a "302 Found" status code for historic reasons, which most browsers incorrectly treat in the same way as the "303 See Other" status code, despite the fact that the former is by definition identical to the "307 Temporary Redirect" status code.

5.4 Range Requests

When an object download has been interrupted, the client may already have received a large portion of the object. The client could then use a `range` request header to download only the missing parts. The `range` header specifies the byte range of the entity being requested. In principle, the request may contain several `range` headers that specify multiple disjoint portions of the entity. Requests with range headers are called *range requests*. The server executes the request with range headers normally, but it may return just the specified portions of the object, in which case it uses "206 Partial Content" status code instead of "200 OK."

In addition, if the interrupted download included the `ETag` header, the client also has the entity tag of the entire object (since the headers are typically transmitted before the message body). Having the entity tag allows the client to ensure that the missing parts being requested in the range request and the portion the client already has both belong to the same instance of the object. To this end, the client can include an `if-range` conditional header in its range request. When replying to such a request, the server returns the requested parts of the object only if the entity tag supplied in the `if-range` request header matches the current `ETag` of the object. Otherwise, the entire object is provided in the response.

5.5 The `cache-control` Header

The `cache-control` header can contain multiple directives that control the use of all the caches (if any) that are situated between the client that originally issued the request and the origin server. Thus, the value of the `cache-control` header is a list of directives, and each directive consists of the keyword identifying the directive and, optionally, the directive value. For example, the following is a valid `cache-control` header containing three directives.

```
cache-control:max-age=120,no-transform,proxy-revalidation
```

The `cache-control` header may be present in both requests and responses and is thus considered a general header. However, most directives in this header are specific to or interpreted differently in requests and responses. The next two subsections discuss the use of the `cache-control` header in HTTP requests and responses. Section 5.5.3 illustrates some of the directives with an example of a hypothetical Web site.

5.5.1 `cache-control` Header Directives in Requests

In HTTP 1.0, the `pragma:no-cache` header in a request forced a reload from the origin server. However, it was quickly realized that the functionality provided by this header was not sufficient, which led to the introduction of the `cache-control` header in HTTP 1.1. The `cache-control` header of an HTTP request may contain the directives listed in Table 5.5.

The `no-cache` directive in a request forces any intermediate proxies to obtain a new copy from the origin server. This directive has the same semantics as the `pragma:no-cache` header found in HTTP 1.0.

The `no-store` directive is even stronger and prevents the inadvertent storage of information in a cache. In a request, this directive prohibits either the request or the response from being stored in any cache. The intent of this directive is to prevent the inadvertent release or retention of sensitive information (for example, on backup tapes). This directive is especially useful to prevent browser caches, which frequently cache private information on a local disk, from retaining sensitive information.

The `max-age` and `min-fresh` directives allow a client to impose more stringent consistency requirements on a proxy that is processing a client's request. The `max-age` directive indicates that a client is willing to accept a cached response only if its age

Table 5.5 `cache-control` Directives That Can Be Used in an HTTP Request

Directive Keyword	Value	Meaning
no-cache	none	Cached objects cannot be used to satisfy the request.
no-store	none	The response to this request cannot be stored in a cache.
max-age	seconds	Only younger cached objects can be used to satisfy the request.
min-fresh	seconds	Only cached objects that will not expire for a specified time can be used.
max-stale	seconds	Cached objects that expired up to the specified time ago can be used.
no-transform	none	Only the precise response as provided by the origin server can be used.
only-if-cached	none	A proxy should not forward the request on a cache miss.

does not exceed the specified value in seconds (see Section 5.2); older objects cannot be used to satisfy this request even if those objects have not expired. The `min-fresh` directive specifies that the client is willing to accept a response from a cache only if the response will not expire for at least the time specified as the argument.

In contrast, the `max-stale` directive relaxes the consistency policy normally used by a proxy. This directive signals the willingness of the client to accept an expired response, provided it expired no longer than the given number of seconds ago.

The `no-transform` directive prevents an intermediate proxy from changing the representation of the object. For example, some proxies serving wireless devices degrade the quality of pictures to reduce their size. This directive prevents that type of degradation.

Finally, the client uses the `only-if-cached` directive to indicate that the request may be executed only if the first proxy that receives the request has the requested object in its cache. This directive is useful, for example, if bandwidth is limited between the proxy and the rest of the Internet; by using this directive, clients do not download noncritical information unless the information is already cached in the proxy.

5.5.2   `cache-control` **Header Directives in Responses**

A variety of `cache-control` directives can be used in a response. These directives are shown in Table 5.6. Two of them, `no-store` and `no-transform`, are identical to the same directives in a request. The rest of the directives are either specific to responses or have different meanings from the similar directives used in requests.

The `no-cache` directive prevents the caching of the response. The `private` directive allows caching but indicates that the response is intended for only the client that

Table 5.6 `cache-control` Directives That Can Be Used in an HTTP Response

Directive Keyword	Value	Meaning
`no-cache`	none	The response cannot be cached.
`no-store`	none	The response cannot be stored in any client (proxy or browser).
`private`	none	The response can be reused only for the client that originally requested it.
`public`	none	The response may be cached and shared among different clients.
`must-revalidate`	none	A cache must always validate the cached object before using it.
`proxy-revalidation`	none	Same as `must-revalidate` but applies to proxy caches only.
`max-age`	seconds	A cache must validate this object before serving it to any client once the object age reaches the specified value.
`s-maxage`	none	Same as `max-age` but applies only to proxies.
`no-transform`	none	Only the precise response as provided by the origin server can be used.

requested it. This directive therefore prohibits serving the cached copy to any other client. The `public` directive indicates that the response may be cached by any cache and shared among different clients.

The `must-revalidate` directive allows a server to specify that a cache must always validate the cached object before using it; validation is done using conditional requests to the origin server (see Section 5.1). This directive guarantees that users will see the current version of the object. The guarantee comes at the expense of having to access the origin server on every request. The `proxy-revalidation` directive is similar, except that single-client caches, like those found in Web browsers, do not have to perform the revalidation.

If the `max-age` directive is present in a response, the object is cacheable and is considered expired once its age exceeds the number of seconds specified by the `max-age` directive. The `s-maxage` directive is identical to the `max-age` directive, except that it applies only if the response is stored in a shared cache, such as a proxy. It overrides the `max-age` directive in this case.

5.5.3 Example of the `cache-control` Header

To illustrate some of the uses of the `cache-control` header, consider a hypothetical Web site, bigmoney.com. This site has two Web objects it wants to serve. The first object is a static welcome page, welcome.html; the second object, mysecrets.html, is dynamically generated for each individual user.[2] Two users, Bill and Bob, connect to bigmoney.com through a shared proxy cache. The `cache-control` headers can control the browser caches in Bill's and Bob's Web browsers and the shared cache on the proxy.

Consider the caching decisions made by all parties involved. During the setup of bigmoney.com, the Web designer must decide which objects can be cached, where, and for how long. The object welcome.html is the same page for all users and can therefore be cached by both the shared proxy and the private browser. Since shared caching is allowed by default in HTTP 1.1, no response headers need be specified for this page. If the Web designer wants to be extremely careful and avoid the possibility of another HTTP header overwriting this default and preventing welcome.html from being cached, the designer may explicitly specify the object as `public` using the `cache-control` header.

On the other hand, the dynamically generated mysecrets.html page is intended for a single user only. Therefore, the Web designer might have included the `private` directive in the `cache-control` header for the object. However, this directive still allows both the browser and the proxy to cache the object. Moreover, the page might inadvertently be stored on disk or backed up while in a cache. Assuming that the page contains sensitive information that should be kept secret, the Web designer adds the `no-store` directive that prevents the object from being cached or stored inadvertently by either component.[3]

After deciding which objects can be cached, the Web designer must determine how long they can remain cached. The only cacheable object in our example is the entry page, welcome.html. Assume that this page contains promotional discounts that change every hour. The Web designer specifies that the `max-age` directive be set to the remaining time of the promotion. In addition, suppose bigmoney.com decides that they may add extra promotions for new users on their first visit to the Web site. Since these promotions may come at random intervals, the Web designer decides that shared caches should always validate welcome.html before serving it from the cache. This validation is forced by specifying the `proxy-revalidation` directive in a response.

At this point the Web site of bigmoney.com is ready, and we turn to the users making the requests. Users typically rely on their browsers to set the right `cache-control` directives. However, for the purpose of this example, let us assume the user personally sets these directives.

Assume that Bill connects to the Internet via a high-bandwidth cable modem. Consequently, he specifies the `no-transform` directive on requests, to make sure he sees the page in its full quality. He also does not care about the bandwidth consumed on the Internet and wants to receive fairly fresh content. He therefore chooses

---

[2] We discuss how users are identified in Section 5.6.
[3] In the real world a page so critical would probably also be encrypted.

Table 5.7 `cache-control` Headers in the Hypothetical bigmoney.com Web Site

HTTP Message	cache-control Header
Bill's requests	`cache-control:no-transform,max-age=60`
Bob's requests	`cache-control:max-stale=86400`
bigmoney.com's responses containing welcome.html	`cache-control:public,max-age=`*t*`,` `proxy-revalidation`
bigmoney.com's responses containing mysecrets.html	`cache-control:no-store`

Note: t = time in seconds remaining until the next scheduled promotion.

to accept only content that is at most one minute old by setting the `max-age` header to one minute. As a result, a cache will use its cached copy of the welcome.html page for Bill's request only if the page was retrieved from the origin server less than one minute previously. This behavior is enforced whether or not the cache considers its cached copy of the page valid.

Bob, on the other hand, uses his wireless PalmPilot to access the Internet. He cannot afford to waste bandwidth. Therefore, he does not specify the `no-transform` directive, in the hope that the shared proxy cache will reduce the object sizes sensibly, if possible. He also specifies a `max-stale` directive of one day, thereby reducing the bandwidth required to update stale objects, while increasing the risk of viewing stale content.

Table 5.7 summarizes the `cache-control` headers in requests by the two users and responses from bigmoney.com. This small example should provide a taste of the complexity of the HTTP directives and their interactions.

5.6 Storing State for a Stateless Server: Cookies

HTTP allows Web clients and servers to introduce new headers that are not specified in the standard, as long as these headers follow the general "keyword:value" structure. HTTP stipulates that clients and servers that do not understand the new headers should ignore them. This provision for new headers has become a great facilitator of innovation, allowing the graceful introduction of new functionalities to HTTP. The *cookie* mechanism [Kristol and Montulli 1997], which is not part of standard HTTP, is a prime example of such innovation. It provides an elegant mechanism to store state between Web interactions while retaining the stateless nature of HTTP servers. For example, a cookie can record the state of a shopping cart on an e-commerce site or a user profile that stores user preferences such as choice of language.

If the server needs to preserve some state for a future interaction, it may return this state in a `set-cookie` response header to the client. The client never looks at this state (called a cookie) but simply stores it locally. The next time the client sends a request to this server, it will include a `cookie` request header containing this state. The server will therefore have the desired state without having to maintain it.

The attributes specified in the `set-cookie` header include (among other fields) a cookie name, a cookie value (the state being preserved), a timeout value, a path, and a domain. The cookie name and value will be returned on subsequent HTTP requests in a `cookie` request header if the requested URL matches the path and domain given in the `set-cookie` header. The timeout is used to limit the time during which a client must store the cookie.

The ability to set a cookie selectively for URLs matching a given pattern provides much flexibility to the Web site. For example, the bigmoney.com site from Section 5.5.3 can include a header `set-cookie:name=profile,domain=www.bigmoney.com,` `path=mysecrets.html,cookie=day-trader` with a response to Bill. Then, any future request from Bill's browser for mysecrets.html will include a header `cookie:` `name=profile,value=day-trader`, which the Web server can use to customize the mysecrets.html page. Bill's requests to welcome.html, however, will not include a cookie, because one is not needed for this generic page. Furthermore, requests for any objects embedded into mysecrets.html will not include a cookie, either. As we show in Chapter 13, setting cookies judicially is important for getting the most benefit from Web caching.

The path and domain attributes of a cookie also allow different applications on the same server to store different cookies on a client. For example, if site firm-x.com contains auction and stock-quote applications that use domains auction.firm-x.com and quote.firm-x.com, respectively, both applications can maintain independent cookies by specifying their respective domains in their `set-cookie` response headers.

Besides allowing a stateless server to store state on clients, another typical use of cookies is to record the identity of the user. In this case the server does maintain state about the user, and it employs a cookie to avoid asking the user repeatedly for identification. Using the IP address of the user's browser to identify the user is not sufficient: the user may use different browsers at home and at work, and dial-up browsers can be assigned different IP addresses every time they connect to the Internet (by the mechanism called *dynamic IP*). In the first case, the Web site would identify the user by storing the same cookie on all browsers, asking the user for identification only when a new browser is being used for the first time. In the second case, the browser sends the same cookie that identifies the user regardless of the browser's current IP address.

Because servers use cookies to personalize content for a particular user, the obvious problem with cookies in the context of caching is that responses with the `set-cookie` header cannot be stored in a shared cache and requests with the `cookie` header cannot be satisfied from a shared cache. However, HTTP 1.1 allows caching of responses containing `set-cookie` including the `set-cookie` header itself [Kristol and Montulli 1997]. Thus, strictly speaking, a Web site must use explicit `cache-control` headers to prevent caching of these responses. In practice, many sites do not, and proxies often do not cache these responses as a precaution. Chapter 13 discusses the interaction of cookies with caching in greater detail.

5.7 Support for Server Sharing

HTTP's request line contains only the path portion of the requested URL. An HTTP 0.9 server could not know to which domain the URL belonged. The assumption of the designers of HTTP 0.9 was that a server always shares the domain name with all its URLs and therefore sending the domain name part of the URL was redundant.

However, the emergence of Web hosting companies has invalidated this assumption. These companies deploy shared servers that host Web sites with different domain names, a practice known as *virtual hosting*. Different Web sites often have URLs with common path portions, such as www.firm-x.com/home.html and www.firm-y.com/home.html. In the absence of the domain name information, hosting companies used to assign multiple IP addresses to a shared server, one per hosted Web site. Then the server could determine to which site the requested URL belonged by the destination IP address of the request. Obviously, this is wasteful of the scarce IP address space. Consequently, HTTP 1.1 defines a mandatory host request header that contains the host name and part of the URL. This information, combined with the path specified in the request line, allows a server to determine the entire URL, even if multiple domain names are mapped to the same IP address. The host header is also used in some deployments of forward proxies (see Section 8.3.7) and surrogates when they are shared among multiple Web sites (Section 15.3).

5.8 Expanded Object Identifiers

Because objects are identified by their URLs, caches also normally use URLs to identify cached objects. However, servers sometimes serve different content for a given URL based on the value of certain request headers. We have already encountered one example of this behavior in Section 5.6, where servers customize content based on the cookie request header. More generally, servers can use other request headers to customize content or choose between different object representations. In effect, these headers become part of the object identifier. To avoid serving wrong object representations, proxies must also use these expanded identifiers for objects they cache.

The origin server can list request headers that must be used to identify the cached object in the vary response header. These request headers are called the *selecting* headers. A cached object with a vary field can be used for a request only if all selecting headers in the request match the corresponding stored headers from the original request that placed the object into the cache.

5.9 Learning the Proxy Chain

A client may want to know the chain of proxies its requests take on their way to origin servers. As we show in Chapter 8, a proxy in some cases affects (or even disrupts) the service clients receive from certain Web sites; it is therefore important that a client

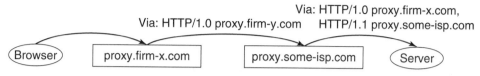

Figure 5.1 An example of the use of `via` headers

be aware of the existence of the proxy so that the client can use appropriate request headers to go directly to the origin servers in such situations.

HTTP 1.1 provides a `via` header and a TRACE request method, which together allow the client to know if a proxy exists. The `via` header keeps track of proxies and protocol versions involved in transferring the request from the client to the server. Every proxy that processes the request must append an entry to the request's `via` header, including the proxy name and the protocol used to receive the request. For instance, Figure 5.1 shows a browser whose request traverses a chain of two proxies on its way to the origin server. If the browser uses HTTP 1.0 to communicate to the first proxy and the two proxies use HTTP 1.1 to communicate between themselves, the figure shows the `via` request header at different points on the request route. The first proxy inserts the `via` header that specifies the proxy name and HTTP 1.0, since that is the protocol by which the proxy received the request. The second proxy adds an entry to the header that contains its name and the protocol used to receive the request (HTTP 1.1).

The TRACE request method stipulates that the final recipient of this request sends it back to the client in the entity body of the response. Responses to TRACE requests are never cached, and so the final recipient is typically the origin server to which the request is sent. Since every proxy on the way to the server inserts a `via` header, the request accumulates the entire list of proxies between the client and the server. It is this final state of the request that the server reflects back to the client, allowing the client to learn the proxy chain.

The client can limit the number of proxies the TRACE request traverses by including a `max-forwards` header in the request. This header contains an integer that the client initially sets to the maximum allowed number of proxies. Each proxy decrements this integer before sending it further. However, the proxy that receives a request with `max-forwards` 0 will not forward the request; instead, it will respond to the request itself as if it were the request's final destination. Thus, the client learns only the initial portion of the proxy chain to the origin server if this chain exceeds the original value of the `max-forwards` header.

The `via` header has several other uses. It includes the versions of HTTP used by intermediary proxies. The set of protocol versions involved in the transfer becomes important if the server intends to use functionality specific to HTTP 1.1. In this case, the server has to verify that all intermediate proxies use HTTP 1.1, which can be inferred from the `via` header of the request. The `via` header also allows the detection of request routing loops, thus preventing a situation where a request travels endlessly along an enclosed loop of proxies.

5.10 Cacheability of Web Content

A response is called *cacheable* or *uncacheable* depending on whether or not it can be stored in a cache and used to satisfy future requests. Similarly, we call a request cacheable if it can be satisfied by a cached response, and uncacheable otherwise. In particular, a request to an uncacheable object is always uncacheable.

With a few exceptions, HTTP 1.1 provides a simple rule to decide whether a request or response is cacheable or not: the protocol allows any response to be cached and any request to be satisfied from a cached response, unless doing so is expressly prohibited by HTTP headers. In practice, however, requests and responses do not always include these headers, and proxies and other caches use heuristics, in addition to HTTP headers, to identify content that should not be cached.

The following are the main rules and heuristics that proxies use to decide the cacheability of requests and responses.

- Most proxies consider requests uncacheable if requested URLs contain the string "cgi-bin," a question mark (?), or the suffix ".cgi." This heuristic is based on the fact that URLs of this form usually identify dynamically generated objects. Dynamic objects are often specific to the particular request, or requests for these objects have side effects beyond generating a response, such as purchasing physical goods. In these cases, it is essential that the request reaches the origin server. In other cases, however—for example, queries to a dictionary or a map-drawing application—it might be perfectly safe to cache dynamic responses, and this heuristic can be overly restrictive. In addition, not all dynamic objects can be identified by this heuristic, as we discuss in Section 13.3.3.

- Requests with a `cookie` header and responses with a `set-cookie` header are typically considered uncacheable by proxies. This is, again, just a heuristic. Its rationale is that cookies are often used to personalize a Web object to a particular client or even a particular request. Thus, the object sent in response to one request may not be reused for another request.

- Proxies usually do not cache requests using methods other than GET or HEAD. In fact, HTTP 1.1 provides elaborate rules that specify when requests using other methods can be cacheable, but such situations are so infrequent that implementing these rules is not worthwhile.

- Proxies usually consider requests with certain headers, such as the `authorization` header, and responses with certain response codes, such as "307 Temporary Redirect," to be uncacheable. Again, HTTP 1.1

specifies certain conditions under which these requests and responses could still be cached, but in general one can assume they are uncacheable.

Uncacheable content greatly reduces the benefits from Web caching. Section 6.3 provides some indication of how widespread uncacheable content is, and Chapter 13 discusses various ways to expand the scope of caching so that it includes content traditionally considered uncacheable.

5.11 Summary

This chapter introduces the most important HTTP features used in the context of caching and replication. One such feature is conditional requests, which retrieve objects only if a certain condition is true. An HTTP request is made conditional by including in the request special request headers, such as `if-modified-since`.

Another group of headers is used to specify which objects can be cached, how long they can be cached, whether they can be shared among different clients, and so on. In particular, the `expires` and `age` response headers are used by caches to expire cached Web objects. The complex `cache-control` header can be used by either requests or responses to control cache behavior in a variety of ways. Perhaps the most important directive of the `cache-control` header is `no-cache`. It allows a request to prohibit the use of any cached responses, and it allows a response to prevent any caches from caching the response.

An important aspect of HTTP in the context of caching and replication is the ability to redirect Web clients from one server to another. The redirecting server accomplishes this by using one of the special response codes in its response to the client.

HTTP 1.1 also allows the client to request a portion of the object by issuing a range request. Range requests are specified using `range` and `if-range` request headers.

An important extension to HTTP is the cookie mechanism. It allows a Web site to store state on a client between interactions and to identify users when they revisit the Web site from the same browser. We also discuss in this chapter the use of the `host` header to facilitate virtual hosting and mechanisms for the discovery of a proxy chain between the client and server.

Chapter 6
Web Behavior Rules of Thumb

Any serious exploration of techniques for Web caching and replication must begin with some understanding of the properties and usage of objects being cached. How big are the objects? How often are they reused? How frequently do they change? All these issues have a profound effect on policies and on the design of caches and mirrors.

Unfortunately, it is very difficult to characterize the Web. First, studying the Web is like chasing a moving target. Results often become obsolete by the time they are published. This makes Web behavior (or, in more "scientific" terms, *characterization*) a great area for writing papers, but frustrating in terms of lasting results. Second, because of the huge size of the Web, it is hard to obtain meaningful samples. These difficulties have led to many contradictory reports on Web characteristics. Here are some examples:[1]

- "We observed that both remotely [that is, requested by remote clients— *authors*] popular and globally popular documents were updated very infrequently" [Bestavros 1996].

- "Considering all data types, more frequently accessed resources are clearly younger than less frequently accessed ones" [Douglis et al. 1997a].

- "There is no strong evidence that popular documents change less often. In the design of any Web cache consistency scheme or any Web access model, it is perhaps best to assume that there is no correlation between document popularity and its rate of change" [Breslau et al. 1999].

---

[1] These quotations also illustrate the unsettled terminology mentioned in Section 4.5. They refer to what we call Web "objects" as "documents" and "resources."

These claims cover all possible answers to the question of the relationship between object popularity and modification rate! Some of these differences may be due to the differences in studied environments: as explained by Douglis et al., Bestavros's study is based on accesses to a single university Web server, while the study by Douglis et al. examines access logs of a proxy server that processed all requests from a group of clients. However, both Douglis et al. and Breslau et al. use proxy access logs and still arrive at different conclusions. In any case, these differences demonstrate the difficulty of staging a representative experiment and obtaining globally meaningful conclusions.

This chapter summarizes the little knowledge concerning Web behavior that is accepted as significant and more or less stable—which we refer to as "rules of thumb" of Web behavior. We pay special attention to aspects that are most pertinent to caching and replication. A more detailed survey of Web characterizations can be found in Pitkow [1999].

6.1   Evaluation Methods

Before we start our discussion of Web properties, it will be helpful to outline the main methods that are used to discover these properties and evaluate new technologies. Performance evaluation methods fall into three main categories: live measurements, trace-based methods, and benchmarking. The next subsections briefly consider these categories.

6.1.1   Live Measurements

Live measurements refer to observations of real Web behavior as it occurs. Live measurements are especially useful to evaluate the actual performance of the Web, either end-to-end (that is, the performance as seen by Web users) or from the perspective of individual components, such as proxies and Web servers. On the other hand, live measurements are often difficult to implement. For instance, observing end-to-end performance as seen by real users would require instrumenting their browsers. Live measurements are also inappropriate for stress testing because one would never want to overload components in real use. Finally, live measurements are usually not repeatable, since it is impossible to fully replicate the conditions under which the initial measurement was taken.

6.1.2   Trace-Based Methods

Web traces record information such as the time of requests, URLs requested, the size of responses, and response status codes. Access logs collected by Web servers and proxies represent a common type of trace (although IP packet traces of Web traffic have also been used). Access logs can be collected at a browser, proxy, or server. Browser and proxy logs are client-centric: they reflect access from one or a limited group of clients to an unlimited number of Web sites at large. Server logs are site-centric, representing accesses only to the Web site(s) hosted on the given server; access can come from any client on the Internet. While proxies and servers collect logs by default, a browser must be specially instrumented to do so. An easy method to instrument the browser without any code modifications is to run a local proxy on the browser machine, configure the browser to use the local proxy for all its requests, and set the browser main memory and disk cache sizes to zero. The local proxy will receive and log all browser requests and will also serve as a local cache on the browser machine.

Various Web properties, such as the distribution of response sizes or interrequest time intervals, can be inferred by tabulating trace data in various ways, a process often referred to as *trace analysis*. Other experiments using traces involve simulating the behavior of various Web architectures under a given trace of accesses. These experiments are called *trace-driven simulations*. *Trace-driven execution* involves studying real equipment when it processes requests from a log rather than from live client requests.

Conclusions drawn from a trace always raise the question of how representative the trace is of general behavior. Any given trace may exhibit some patterns that are particular to itself only [Paxson and Floyd 1997]. A trace of proxy cache accesses from a research lab or university may exhibit quite different properties from a similar trace from residential users. Traces obtained during the Olympic Games may be different from traces during the time students take finals or during stock market turbulence. Still, an experiment with a real trace provides conclusions that are at least valid for a particular slice of real Web usage.

6.1.3 Benchmarking

Benchmarking and *microbenchmarking* are experiments that test real equipment using a synthetic (that is, artificially generated) workload. Benchmarks are synthetic workloads designed to mimic real-life workloads, while microbenchmarks are artificial workloads designed to test a specific aspect of equipment behavior.

The ultimate goal of generating a synthetic workload is to mimic actual Web behavior as closely as possible. A typical method of generating a synthetic workload is to analyze real traces of Web accesses, extract workload characteristics, and replicate these characteristics in the synthetic workload. Although we are not aware of a better alternative, this approach has several problems.

First, as we mentioned in the previous subsection, a trace may have properties that are particular to one trace only. Separating typical patterns from all patterns exhibited in a trace can be difficult. It is often a subjective matter whether a characteristic can be considered typical enough to be reflected in the synthetic workload. Usually, one would like a pattern to be independently observed by multiple studies on independent data sets.

Second, generating a synthetic workload may require very detailed assumptions about Web behavior, much more detailed than the rules of thumb discussed in this chapter. Instead of the mean and median object sizes, one needs the actual size distribution. In addition to popularity distribution, one also may need correlation of Web references. It is difficult to decide when to stop considering more and more subtle aspects of Web behavior. But the more detailed assumptions one makes, the more risk of reflecting nontypical patterns. Even if all reflected patterns were typical at the time of the study, excessively detailed assumptions may quickly fall behind the fast-changing behavior of the Web [Paxson and Floyd 1997].

Another problem with attempting to generate a representative request stream is the subjective interpretation of what "representative" means. For instance, PolyMix-3, one of the workloads generated by the Web Polygraph workload generator [Rousskov et al., 2000] would not be representative at all if used for evaluation of object prefetching, because this workload does not model the correlation between accesses to different objects.

This suggests using microbenchmarking or actual traces whenever possible. A microbenchmark does not attempt to faithfully emulate Web behavior. Instead, it emphasizes certain aspects that are particularly important for the given experiment. For example, to study how a system tolerates sudden increases of user demand, one could use a benchmark that produces frequent exaggerated bursts of accesses.

Unfortunately, there is still often the need to evaluate complete systems under stress conditions, for instance, to find out how a Web server behaves when the demand is higher than provided by available traces. In these situations, using a synthetic workload becomes unavoidable. We refer the reader to Abdulla [1998], Barford and Crovella [1998], Almeida et al. [1996], Standard Performance Evaluation Corporation [SpecWeb 1999], Mindcraft [Webstone 2001], Almeida and Cao [1998], and Rousskov et al. [2000], for more information on benchmarking, including pointers for downloading benchmarking software.

The reader should be aware that sometimes benchmarks are proposed by vendors of certain components. These vendor benchmarks must be viewed with caution, as they could be designed to favor a particular product.

6.2 Object Size

The first Web property of concern is typical object size. Objects can have drastically different sizes. Icon images, banner advertisements, and small textual objects are typically very small, about 1KByte. Examples of large objects include video and audio files, which can easily reach multiple megabytes. Knowing prevalent object sizes is useful in many design decisions, for example, in deciding on proper storage capacity of a cache or the bandwidth of a network connection. We also use these numbers for "back-of-the-envelope" calculations in this book (see Chapters 9 and 11).

There is a difference between sizes of objects that exist on the Web and sizes of object transfers from servers to clients. The former reflect sizes of distinct objects, regardless of the number of times any particular object is downloaded. The latter count every transfer, even if the same object is downloaded many times. Studies that consider object sizes are often vague on which of these two characteristics they measure. Arlitt et al. [1999] and Barford et al. [1999] are the most explicit in this regard by reporting both characteristics. Fortunately, both studies indicate that both characteristics are fairly close: Arlitt et al. observed a mean distinct object size of just over 21KBytes and a mean download size of around 14.5KBytes. Barford et al. reported values of 7.6KBytes and 7.2KBytes for the mean size of distinct objects and downloads, respectively. The difference between the median sizes of distinct objects and object downloads is even smaller—4.3KBytes versus 3.4KBytes in Arlitt et al. and 2.8KBytes compared to 2.4KBytes in Barford et al. These differences are within the range of values of the same metric reported by other studies.

Overall, the following values appear to be safe assumptions, both for the sizes of distinct objects and the sizes of downloads [Arlitt and Williamson 1996; Bray 1996a; Abdulla 1998; Williams et al. 1996a; NLANR 2001; Arlitt et al. 1999].

- The average object size retrieved by clients is on the order of 10–15KBytes.

- The median object size is much smaller than the average, around 2–4KBytes.

These numbers show that a majority of accesses are to small objects. In fact, Abdulla [1998] reports that 75 percent of all retrieved objects are significantly smaller than the mean size. This tells us that small objects are accessed much more frequently. For one thing, there are just many more small objects on the Web. However, the fact that the mean and median size of downloads are somewhat smaller than those of distinct objects indicates that small documents are also disproportionately more popular than large ones, although this skew is not very pronounced. On the other hand, the fact that a few large objects are able to affect the average size so dramatically means that the few large objects are really large. In fact, objects of tens of megabytes in size can be encountered [Abdulla 1998].

A large number of very small objects could be explained by proliferation of small icons and advertisement images. Large objects typically contain PostScript and PDF files,[2] large images, or especially, video or audio files or software distribution packages. As we will see in the next section, very few such objects are visited. However, we can expect the number of large object requests to increase in the future, as more multimedia objects are published on the Web and bandwidth improvements make downloading these objects less painful.

The highly skewed concentration of accesses toward small objects creates an interesting phenomenon for caching policies. A cache can increase its hit rate by favoring small objects (for example, by not retaining large objects in the cache). However, the benefits of a cache hit are greater when the cached object is large. So, the overall cache benefits might be higher in a cache with a lower hit rate. We furnish other examples of unequal value of cache hits later in the book, in Chapters 9 and 10.

---

[2] Postscript and PDF are common formats for storing electronic books and articles.

6.3 Object Types and Cacheability

In the "good old days" (which were only a few years ago, come to think about it), there were only a few kinds of Web objects: static HTML pages and images and documents generated dynamically by CGI scripts. Today, a plethora of object types can be accessed via a standard Web browser.

At the present, an overwhelming majority of all downloads, in terms of both the number of accessed objects and bytes downloaded, involve HTML pages and images, with images outnumbering HTML pages. Together, they account for around 90 percent of all Web accesses and, typically, over 70 percent of downloaded bytes, although the reported byte fraction varies more widely, from 60 percent to over 80 percent [Douglis et al. 1997a; Williams et al. 1996a; Wolman et al. 1999a; and Arlitt et al. 1999].[3]

Multimedia objects account for very few accesses but a sizable fraction of downloaded bytes: 14 percent were observed by Wolman et al. [1999a], 24 percent by Arlitt, et al. [1999], and up to 6 percent by Douglis et al. [1997a] (assuming that most of the "others" content type reported in the last study is multimedia content).

Another interesting observation is that the number of accesses to dynamically generated objects is rather small, with reported values from under 1 percent [Williams et al. 1996a; Manley and Seltzer 1997] to 10 to 20 percent [Feldmann et al. 1999; Wolman et al. 1999a]. The small number of dynamic objects may contradict one's intuition on the often dynamic nature of Web content. However, recall from Section 4.5 that a Web document typically consists of a container page identified by the document URL and a number of objects embedded into the container page. In the case of dynamic documents, only the container page is usually dynamic, while all embedded objects are static (typically, images). According to Turau [1998], a document contains on average ten embedded images. Thus, the percentage of accesses to dynamic *documents*, among all document accesses, can be as much as ten times that of accesses to dynamic *objects* among all object accesses.

An issue of particular importance to caching is how often requests occur that cannot use a cache. As described in Section 5.10, a request can be uncacheable either because of certain features in the request itself, or because the request is for an uncacheable object. Table 6.1 summarizes the main features of a request or requested object that make a request uncacheable under HTTP rules or heuristics most commonly used by proxies.[4] The most important factor affecting cacheability is the presence of a cookie. Feldmann et al. [1999] found cookies to be present in 30 percent of requests from residential users and about 20 percent of requests from a community of computer scientists. These findings generally agree with Turau [1998], who also observed that

---

[3] One should realize that individual servers can deviate greatly from these numbers. However, we are interested in statistics reflecting typical Web usage by clients. This perspective is better captured by proxy traces, since they reflect client accesses to all servers. All studies cited here used proxy traces in their analyses.

[4] Note that an object may be uncacheable for more than one reason, so the individual reason percentages do not add up to the total percentage of uncacheable requests.

Table 6.1 Frequency of Occurrence of Features in Web
Interactions That Make Them Uncacheable.*[a]*

Uncacheability Feature	Frequency of Occurrence (%)
`cache-control/pragma` headers	9–15
`cookie/set-cookie` headers	19–30
`authentication` header	1–1.7
Method is not GET or HEAD	1.4–2
"cgi-bin" or "?" in URL	1–20
uncacheable response code	22.8
Total uncacheable requests	37–43

[a] See Williams et al. 1996a; Feldmann et al. 1999; Wolman et al. 1999a.

commercial Web sites use cookies about four times as often as educational sites, and American sites use them about three times as often as German sites. A wide use of cookies is sometimes an artifact of sloppy design of a Web site, with Web developers using cookies without realizing their effect on caching.

Overall, around 40 percent of all requests are uncacheable [Feldmann et al. 1999; Wolman et al. 1999a]. This clearly presents a big obstacle to caching. Better technology (as well as a higher level of cache-awareness on the part of Web developers) is needed to address this problem. We devote Chapter 13 to the problem of uncacheable objects and proposals that address it.

6.4   Object Popularity

The Web exhibits very uneven object popularity: most accesses are for a relatively small set of objects, while the vast majority of objects are hardly ever accessed. Arlitt and Williamson [1996] examined six different Web sites and found that 10 percent of objects accounted for 80 to 95 percent of all requests received by each site. More specifically, several studies [Glassman 1994; Almeida et al. 1996; Cunha et al. 1996; Barford et al. 1999] observed that object popularity conforms to *Zipf-like distribution* [Zipf 1949]. Applied to the Web, Zipf-like distribution states that the popularity (that is, the frequency of accesses) of the ith most popular object is proportional to $1/i^\alpha$, for some constant α between 0 and 1. In particular, for $\alpha = 1$, the most popular Web object is twice as popular as the second most popular object. This popularity distribution of objects is known as *Zipf's Law*.

Conformance of object popularity to Zipf-like distribution with α close to 1 has been reported by analyzing end-user URL requests [Cunha et al. 1996]; browser requests [Barford et al. 1999] which, unlike the end-user requests, are already filtered by the browser cache; request logs of a proxy cache [Glassman 1994]; and access logs of individual Web servers [Almeida et al. 1996]. Moreover, Breslau et al. [1999] showed that Zipf-like distribution of object popularity explains other Web characteristics that were observed independently. Thus, we can add Zipf-like popularity distribution to our rules of thumb for the Web. We should note, however, that more recent studies [Breslau et al. 1999; Arlitt et al. 1999] of several proxy traces reported α smaller than 1 (in the range from 0.64 to 0.83), suggesting a somewhat more even object popularity distribution at large proxies. These findings could possibly be explained by the fact that repeated accesses to popular pages are serviced from client caches so that high-level proxies do not see them.

The popularity of entire Web sites is as uneven as the popularity in individual objects. Traces of requests to several proxies showed that 25 percent of Web sites are responsible for 90 percent of all accesses and 90 percent of downloaded bytes [Abdulla 1998]. Williams et al. [1996a] found that site popularity distribution also conforms to the Zipf-like distribution.

Actual concentration of site and object popularity is probably even higher, since repeated accesses to the same resources from the same user are often satisfied from the user's browser cache and are not accounted for in the studies mentioned here. A high concentration of accesses, as explained in the next section, is generally good news for caching and replication.

6.5 Locality of Reference

Uneven popularity distribution is a manifestation of *locality of reference*. Locality of reference characterizes the ability to predict future accesses to objects from past accesses. There are two main types of locality: temporal and spatial. *Temporal locality* refers to repeated accesses to the same object within short time periods. High temporal locality implies that recently accessed objects are likely to be accessed again in the future. *Spatial locality* refers to access patterns where accesses to some objects frequently entail accesses to certain other objects. For example, an access to an HTML page can entail accesses to objects embedded or hyperlinked in this page. High spatial locality implies that references to some objects can be a predictor of future references to other objects.

Locality of reference is exploited to formulate caching policies, such as deciding which objects to keep or remove from the cache and which objects to *prefetch*, that is, load into the cache before they are accessed (see Chapters 11 and 12). Although not enough results on locality of reference have been published to add them to our rules of thumb, it is useful to understand the methodologies for characterizing (that is, defining a measure of) this important aspect of Web behavior. These methodologies are the focus of the remainder of this section.

6.5.1 Temporal Locality

An important tool in characterizing temporal locality is the notion of *stack distance* [Mattson et al. 1970]. Consider a stack of infinite depth, with elements corresponding

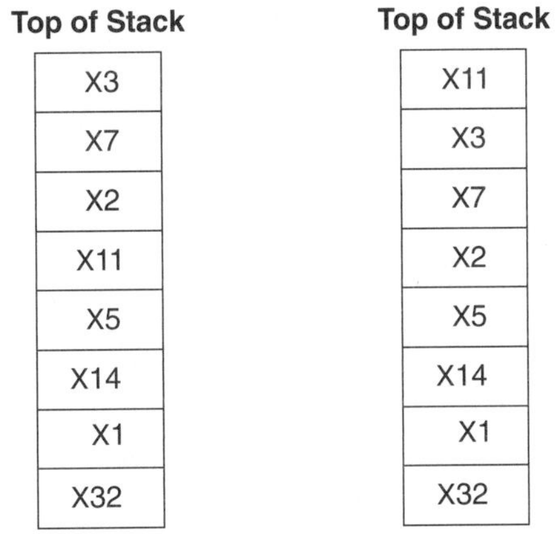

Top of Stack   **Top of Stack**

| X3 |
| X7 |
| X2 |
| X11 |
| X5 |
| X14 |
| X1 |
| X32 |

| X11 |
| X3 |
| X7 |
| X2 |
| X5 |
| X14 |
| X1 |
| X32 |

(*a*) Stack before access   (*b*) Stack after access
to X11.   to X11.

Figure 6.1 An example of stack transformation

to objects. When an object is requested, it is moved to the top of the stack, vacating its old position in the stack (if this is a repeated reference) and pushing other objects down the stack. The stack distance of an object reference is equal to the position of this object in the stack at the time of the access. As an example, Figure 6.1 gives a possible state of the stack before and after the request for object X11 occurs. The stack distance for this access is 4.

Repeating the above transformation for each access, the object reference stream can be translated to the stack distance stream. For example, starting with the stack in Figure 6.1a, a reference stream X11, X3, X3, X11, X14 translates into the stack distance stream 4, 2, 1, 2, 6. Furthermore, a distance stream can be translated back to the reference stream using symbolic object names. In our example, to convert the distance stream 4, 2, 1, 2, 6 to the corresponding reference stream, assume an initial stack state of $a_1, a_2, a_3, a_4, a_5, a_6, \ldots$. The first access has distance 4, hence it translates into reference to a_4 and results in stack $a_4, a_1, a_2, a_3, a_5, a_6, \ldots$. The next access translates into reference to a_1, bringing the stack to state $a_1, a_4, a_2, a_3, a_5, a_6, \ldots$. Continuing in this fashion, we obtain the reference stream a_4, a_1, a_1, a_4, a_6. This stream is the same, up to object names, as the original reference stream where object X11 corresponds to symbolic name a_4, object X3 to name a_1, and object X14 to name a_6.

The mean or median value of the stack distance can characterize the level of temporal locality [Barford and Crovella 1998; Arlitt and Williamson 1996; Almeida et al. 1996]. In a steady state, the stack distance measures the number of references to distinct objects between consecutive references to the same object. The lowest temporal locality occurs when all objects are accessed in turn, in a round-robin fashion. In this case, the stack distance of all accesses is equal to the number of unique objects in the access trace. Smaller values of the stack distance indicate that requests to the same object arrive closer to each other, and hence the temporal locality is higher. Thus, the ratio of the average stack distance to the total number of unique objects in the trace can serve as a measure of the trace temporal locality. Barford et al. [1998] calculate this ratio, which they call a *normalized stack distance*, using their university proxy trace. They find the mean and median values of the ratio to be 0.2340 and 0.00399, respectively, indicating a significant level of temporal locality in their trace. Considering a much larger trace of an ISP proxy, Arlitt et al. [1999] found a much lower value of the mean normalized stack distance, 0.04, indicating an even higher degree of temporal locality. However, their result may be biased by the presence of accesses to the ISP's Web site in their trace, which may have unique access characteristics.

Note that Zipf's popularity distribution of objects by itself captures temporal locality of Web accesses to a large extent: very popular objects tend to be accessed repeatedly in short succession, and these accesses have low stack distance. However, popularity and temporal locality are not identical properties, because accesses to equally popular objects can be clustered together or uniformly spread throughout the trace, resulting in more or less locality. An initial attempt to characterize the relationship between the two was made by Almeida et al. [1996], who compared the mean stack distances of their original trace and a trace constructed as a random permutation of all requests in the original trace. The random permutation obviously preserves the popularity of objects in the original trace; yet the mean stack distance of the random permutation was found to be somewhat higher, indicating that some temporal locality present in the original trace was lost. Jin and Bestavros [2000] proposed another method to characterize specifically the extra temporal locality that cannot be explained by object popularities. By analyzing accesses to only equally popular objects, they also found some temporal locality that cannot be explained by the popularity distribution.

6.5.2 Spatial Locality

It is hard to define a measure that would characterize spatial locality. One method, described by Almeida et al. [1996], observes that if references to objects can predict references to other objects, then the entire trace of references must exhibit a large number of repeated sequences of object references. For example, if an access to page A often entails access to page B, then the access sequence A,B will occur repeatedly. Conversely, such a trace will contain fewer *unique* sequences of references than a random permutation of the same trace. Thus, the ratio of the number of unique reference sequences in a trace to that in a random permutation of the same trace indicates the level of spatial locality: the lower this ratio, the higher the spatial locality of the trace. Of course, obtaining the total number of unique sequences in the trace is computationally very expensive, so one would normally limit the maximum length of sequences being considered. Considering the trace of accesses to their departmental Web server, Almeida et al. found that the original trace had a significantly smaller number of unique sequences than a random permutation of the trace. Thus, at least that particular Web site exhibited a measurable level of spatial locality.

6.6 Rate of Object Modifications

Another Web characteristic on which the utility of caching and replication depends is the update rate of Web objects. Update rates are important because they affect mechanisms for ensuring that a cache does not serve obsolete content to clients (see Chapter 10).

Douglis et al. [1997a] report some results based on accesses from several hundred research lab workers.[5] While it is unclear how representative this data is of general Web usage, the results should still give a rough idea of the tendencies.

The study finds that most accesses fetch objects whose age is well over one week, where the age is defined as the difference between the time of access and the last-modified timestamp. In fact, the most frequent object age observed was over one month.

To characterize the effect of object changes on caching, Douglis et al. studied the *change ratio*, the fraction of accesses that returned an object that has been modified since the previous access. Among all responses for which it was possible to determine whether or not their objects were modified, the change ratio was around 15 percent. In other words, 15 percent of repeated requests could not be satisfied by the cache from old cached copies of objects because the objects had changed. In fact, the change ratio that actually affects caches would be somewhat lower, because the number included dynamically generated pages that are not cacheable anyway. Caches with larger user populations should deliver even more hits between object modifications because of higher request rates relative to the rate of object changes.

Overall, these numbers indicate that the rate of object modifications is high enough to cause worry about cache and replica consistency but not high enough to negate the benefits from caching and replication.

6.7 Other Observations

Among the many other characteristics relevant to Web caching and replication is the burstiness of Web traffic, which affects many aspects of designing a scalable Web platform.

Gribble and Brewer [1997] measured the request rate generated by 8,000 dial-up clients. They observed that the request rate is quite bursty when measured in seconds but smoothes out at time scales of minutes and higher. On the other hand, Crovella and Bestavros [1995; 1996], by considering aggregate Web traffic (as measured in down-loaded bytes) from 37 client workstations, found traffic burstiness over a wide range

---

[5] The extended version of this paper [Douglis et al. 1997b] also analyzes a trace from more than 7,000 clients. However, these results are not useful for our purposes because that trace excluded requests for images, which play a crucial role in caching.

of time scales, even at 1,000-second intervals. Such traffic behavior can be described as *self-similar*, where self-similarity refers to the property of an object (in our case, traffic shape) to appear similar regardless of the scale at which it is viewed.

Another characteristic worth mentioning is the percent of aborted Web accesses. As we show in Chapter 7, aborted connections may affect performance gains one can obtain from a proxy. Feldmann et al. [1999] found that almost 11 percent of HTTP connections over modem lines were aborted. Presumably, higher-speed connections experience fewer aborts. However, the data from proxies installed at several foreign ISPs also showed about rates of 5.8 percent to 8.3 percent [Danzig 1998b].

Two other important characteristics that influence Web behavior are the number of embedded objects and number of hyperlinks in a typical page. The embedded objects are fetched immediately after the encompassing page, which results in a fast sequence of Web requests. Embedded hyperlinks often affect where the user will go next after visiting the current page. Unfortunately, as in so many other areas, existing studies do not converge. Turau [1998] reports that a page contains, on average, 10 embedded images and 25 hyperlinks. This number of embedded images is close to the one reported by Arlitt and Jin [1999] in their analysis of the Web site for Soccer World Cup '99.

An earlier study by Barford and Crovella [1998], using a trace of accesses by Boston University students collected in 1995, fitted the number of embedded images with Pareto distribution with $\alpha = 2.43$. This distribution produces a mean of 1.6 embedded images. Around the same time, Bray [1996b] analyzed some 1.5 million HTML pages and reported histograms of the embedded objects and links counts. The mean number of embedded images suggested by these histograms is closer to Barford and Crovella's results than to Turau's or Arlitt and Jin's. From the dates of these studies, we can speculate that the usage of embedded images grew with time.

A further relevant property is the distribution of ports utilized by Web servers, because it determines how useful so-called interception proxies are (see Chapter 8). As mentioned in Chapter 3, port 80 is the default port for Web servers. Intuitively, most Web servers use the default port since one does not often see URLs with explicitly specified port numbers. This intuition is confirmed by Woodruff et al. [1996] and Douglis et al. [1997a], who found over 93 percent and 99 percent, respectively, of accesses use port 80.

Finally, it is useful to realize the general scale of the Web. Lawrence and Giles [1999] estimated that the Web contained 800 million pages in 1999, totaling 15 terabytes of data. The Web has grown considerably since then: in October 2001, the Google search engine claimed to search over 1.6 billion pages. In 1997, HTTP traffic constituted 70 percent of total Internet traffic on the MCI backbone [Claffy et al. 1998].

6.8 Summary: Rules of Thumb for the Web

We conclude this chapter with a concise list of simple observations that we believe can serve as rules of thumb in reasoning about the Web.

- The mean object size is on the order of 10 to 15KBytes, and the median is 2 to 4KBytes. The distribution of object sizes is strongly skewed toward small objects. However, there is a nonnegligible number of large objects (on the order of megabytes).

- Most Web accesses are to graphic objects, followed in popularity by HTML pages. A very small fraction of accesses, in the order of 1 to 10 percent, are to dynamic objects. However, the fraction of access to dynamic *documents* (a container page with all embedded objects) is much higher than the fraction of accesses to dynamic objects.

- An HTML page contains, on average, on the order of 10 embedded images and multiple links to other pages.

- Around 40 percent of all accesses are for objects that are currently considered uncacheable by most caches.

- The popularity of Web objects as well as entire Web sites is very uneven: a small fraction of objects is responsible for a majority of accesses. The popularity distribution of Web objects can be approximated by a Zipf-like distribution.

- The access rate for static objects is typically much higher than the modification rate. While this rule may not hold for very unpopular objects considered in isolation, these objects usually matter less in design decisions.

- On a time scale below one minute, Web traffic is very bursty. Because of the burstiness, characteristics averaged over a period of a few tens of seconds or less are in general unreliable.

- A nonnegligible fraction of Web accesses, between 5 and 10 percent, are aborted.

- Virtually all Web servers use port 80.

Part II
Web Caching

Part II concentrates on issues surrounding forward caching, or more specifically, forward proxies. Recall from the Introduction that forward proxies operate on behalf of the consumer of Web content: a forward proxy attempts to improve Web access to a selected group of Web clients no matter which Web sites these clients access. To origin servers, forward proxies look a lot like any other Web clients that consume their content. In fact, before HTTP 1.1 introduced the `via` request header, origin servers could not even tell if a Web request came from a browser or a forward proxy.

The decoupling between forward proxies and origin servers and the resulting lack of control of the latter over the former is a fundamental issue with forward proxies that gives rise to many of the challenges they face. This part of the book describes approaches that address these and other challenges. It begins in Chapter 7 with a discussion of the benefits one can reasonably expect from forward proxies. Chapter 8 describes methods of deployment of forward proxies in ISPs and enterprise networks. Chapter 9 then concentrates on building sets of cooperating proxies that share their cached content with each other. Various mechanisms for maintaining cached content consistent with their origin servers are presented in Chapter 10. The next two chapters discuss two types of policy decisions that proxies face. Chapter 11 considers replacement policies, which determine which pieces of content a proxy should evict from its cache when a new object must be added to the cache that is already full. This chapter also explains why replacement policies, usually central to research in the caching area, are hardly ever mentioned in the otherwise fiercely competitive proxy product landscape. Chapter 12 discusses how a proxy can improve user experiences by performing certain work before clients request it. These techniques fall under the umbrella term of *prefetching* and include (but, as we will see, are not limited to) downloading Web content into a proxy in anticipation of client demand. Finally, Chapter 13 discusses uncacheable content.

As a final note, since Part II focuses on caching forward proxies, we usually refer to them simply as "proxies," omitting the words caching and forward unless this causes confusion.

Chapter 7
Proxy Caching: Realistic Expectations

The amount of literature and information on proxy caching is staggering. With all the hype around proxy caching, it would be useful to step back and consider how much benefit a proxy cache offers realistically. In this chapter, we analyze this issue in detail. We should emphasize that this chapter considers proxies as they exist today and concentrates only on performance. We talk about efforts for increasing the utility (and hence the benefits) of proxies, and caching in general, later in Chapters 13 and 17. Further, our discussion is based on studies performed in North America, which has very good network connection to most Web servers. A study in Europe or another region where requests have to traverse transcontinental links to reach much of the Web content would probably produce different results.

As discussed in the Introduction, a proxy can reduce network traffic and user latency, that is, the time it takes a browser to download a Web object. These benefits improve user experiences of accessing the Web. In addition, enterprises and ISPs also have direct business interests in proxy caching. For an enterprise, proxy caching promises to reduce the bandwidth consumption from the Internet. Consequently, the enterprise might be able to buy less bandwidth capacity from its ISP. A more controversial business benefit is that a proxy enables the enterprise to block Web access to content that is unrelated to company business, such as fiction or other entertainment sites. Doing so can improve productivity by reducing the amount of time workers spend on nonwork activities. At the same time, reducing latency for the allowed content also improves productivity by reducing the time workers waste waiting for the information they need.

An ISP can benefit from a proxy in several ways. If a client request can be satisfied from a proxy near the entry point to the ISP backbone traffic, the rest of the backbone does not have to handle the request, which saves bandwidth. Bandwidth is what ISPs sell to their customers. With the growth of the Internet, the number of customers is often limited by the amount of available bandwidth. Bandwidth savings, therefore, translate into more business for the ISP.

A proxy can also reduce the amount of external traffic that flows into the ISP by satisfying some requests for outside content locally. Depending on the relationship of the ISP with outside ISPs (see Section 2.3.2), this inflow traffic may directly affect the operating costs, in the case of a customer-provider relationship, or trigger contract renegotiation at renewal time, in the case of a peer relationship.[1] In either case, an ISP is interested in decreasing its incoming traffic.

A proxy can also improve the quality of service of the ISP. As discussed in Section 2.3, a request from ISP customers often traverses several other ISPs and NAPs before reaching the origin server. Thus the performance that the ISP delivers to its own customers depends on a variety of factors that the ISP does not control. These factors include peer ISPs' performance and load, NAP load, and origin server performance and load. By servicing more requests locally from its proxy, the ISP reduces its susceptibility to unpredictable performance of the outside Internet. Finally, a proxy provides a convenient platform to implement a variety of extra services that can help differentiate the ISP from its competitors, such as parental control over Web browsing.

We discuss extra services that can be implemented on a proxy in Chapter 17 and focus on performance benefits of a proxy in this chapter. As already mentioned, these benefits revolve around reducing latency and traffic. At the same time, the most frequently studied proxy cache performance metrics are *hit rate* and *byte hit rate*. Hit rate refers to the number of requests served from the cache divided by the total number of requests served, while byte hit rate is the number of bytes served from cached content divided by the total number of bytes served. We discuss cache performance metrics in more detail in Chapter 11; however, one of the points of this chapter is to emphasize that these metrics are not the ultimate goal in themselves. They are useful only insofar as they reflect improvement in the user-perceived and ISP-perceived performance, which is latency and bandwidth savings. In fact, we will see that hit and byte hit rates do *not* directly translate into latency and bandwidth savings.

7.1   Do Proxy Caches Deserve a Hearing?

Given large local caches in Web browsers, we can assume that most repeated accesses to the same page from the same user will be satisfied from the browser cache and thus be filtered from the requests seen by the proxy. This by itself does not imply that

---

[1] In the customer-provider relationship, the customer typically pays the provider based on the total volume of traffic exchanged between the two ISPs. Peers usually do not pay each other. To negotiate between these two types of relationships, the two ISPs usually decide based on their relative size (the bigger one becomes the provider, or equals become peers), where a common measure of size is the amount of traffic an ISP sends to the other ISP relative to the amount of traffic it receives back [Huston 1999].

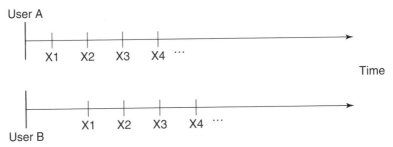

Figure 7.1 An example of request streams with shared hits. (The points
on the time axes denote requests for Web objects.)

the utility of proxies diminishes with the rapid growth of local storage on browser
machines. Consider the time diagram in Figure 7.1, which shows two streams of
requests generated by two users. The name of the objects requested are marked on
the time axes as X1, X2, and so on. Since neither user ever revisits any object in their
individual request stream, both will have a zero hit rate at their browser caches,
regardless of the cache size. However, if both users are connected to the same proxy,
all requests from user B will be satisfied from the proxy cache, because each requested
page will be in the cache after the previous request from user A. Thus, the hit rate at
the proxy cache will be a respectable 50 percent. Proxy cache hits that could not be
satisfied by even an infinite-sized browser cache are referred to as *shared hits*, because
they occur only if the same page is accessed by multiple users. The hits that are caused
by repeated accesses from the same client are called *locality hits* [Duska et al. 1997].

An important question is in order: Are there enough shared hits for proxy caches to
be worthwhile? Multiple studies have provided an affirmative answer. As an example,
Duska et al. [1997] analyzed access traces of seven different proxies and found that
sharing accounted for more than 85 percent of all hits in every trace. Whatever locality
hits might have been filtered by browser caches, the requests that did reach proxies
delivered the overall hit rate of between 20 percent and 45 percent. Proxies at the low
end of the range were those with fewer clients. As another example, some of the proxies
operated by the National Lab for Applied Network Research exhibited both hit rates
and Byte hit rates of more than 50 percent in October 2001 [NLANR 2001]. We will
revisit the topic of how many clients a cache should serve to be effective in more detail
in Section 9.1. However, in general, the most commonly accepted ballpark value for hit
rates at a proxy of a sufficient size (a few thousand clients) is in the order of 40 percent.

7.2 Latency Reduction

In this section, we provide upper- and lower-bound estimates for the reduction in
retrieval time (also known as latency savings or latency reduction) that one can

expect from data caching by a current proxy. We also describe an often-overlooked source of latency savings, which is TCP connection caching. The savings derived from connection caching may actually overshadow the savings from data caching. We should note again that this section considers current proxies. There is ongoing research into improving the benefits of proxies, which we describe later in Chapters 13 and 17.

7.2.1   An Optimistic Bound on Latency Reduction

Having established that the level of sharing justifies talking about proxy caching, let us see how much performance benefit one can hope to get from them. Our first concern is latency. We start with the best-case scenario for average latency reduction studied by Kroeger et al. [1997].

Not including proxy overhead, the latency of a missed request consists mainly of two (possibly overlapping) components: transferring the object from the origin server to the proxy, called the *external latency,* and transferring the object from the proxy to the client, called the *internal latency* (see Figure 7.2). The external and internal latencies may overlap because the proxy typically transfers portions of the response to the client as they arrive from the origin server, instead of buffering for the entire response. A conservative estimate based on the large (more than 17,000 clients) proxy trace shows that external latency accounts for 77 to 88 percent of the total latency.

A hit eliminates the external latency. As Figure 7.2 shows, eliminating external latency removes only its nonoverlapping portion from the total latency. Thus for the most optimistic estimate, one can assume that the object transfer in a nonproxy

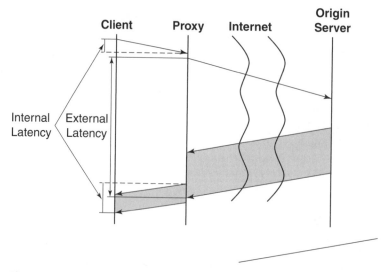

Figure 7.2 Latency components of fetching an object through a proxy

case occurs in two nonoverlapping phases: one from the origin server to the point in the network where the proxy would have been located, and the other from that point to the browser. In other words, the proxy hit would result in full 77 to 88 percent latency reduction compared to the nonproxy case. Furthermore, let us assume that a proxy miss does not increase the latency compared to the nonproxy scenario (another optimistic assumption that increases the benefit estimate). From the 45 percent proxy hit rate, one could have concluded that the best-case latency reduction could be in the order of $45\% \times 88\% = 40\%$. However, when Kroeger et al. [1997] simulated an infinite-sized proxy using the above assumptions, they found that the average latency reduction was only a little more than half that: 22 to 26 percent.

In fact, knowing that most accesses are for small objects (see Section 6.2), this finding should not be surprising. Since small objects are accessed more often, most of the hits are to small objects, which take less time to download. Therefore, the cache reduces small latencies more frequently. What this suggests is that *a proxy cache tends to reduce latency for objects whose latency was small to begin with*. On the other hand, user experiences would have improved most if the opposite were true, that is, if the longest delays were reduced. But if you think this is a discouraging finding for proxies, wait until you read the next subsection.

7.2.2 A Pessimistic View of Latency Reduction

The assumptions in the previous section were overly optimistic. They were optimistic on purpose, to show what latency reductions one can hope for in one's wildest dreams, and the wildest dreams turned out to be rather timid. So, what happens if we take a pessimistic approach? Here are a few things that the previous subsection did not consider.

- As we know from Chapter 3, before data starts flowing over a TCP connection, the connection must be established between the communicating parties. The connection establishment has to happen even on a hit, and on a miss it is likely to happen twice sequentially (first between the client and the proxy for the proxy to receive the request, and then between the proxy and the origin server). Thus, on a miss the proxy introduces extra delay, and on a hit the latency reduction is smaller.

- As has already been mentioned, the assumption of nonoverlapping external and internal latencies is a gross simplification. Moreover, when the proxy is inserted in the middle of the data flow from the origin server to the client, it may introduce additional overhead due to the interplay of congestion windows of the two TCP connections.

- When the client-to-proxy link is slow (for example, when a proxy is deployed by an ISP on its side of slow dial-up links to clients), the internal latency becomes the dominant factor, since the bottleneck shifts to the slow client-proxy link.

- The study by Kroeger et al. [1997] did not consider cookies, which have a large negative effect on data cacheability.

Note that this list does not include the delay due to internal proxy processing. A properly provisioned proxy may add at worst a few tens of milliseconds to latency when it needs to access disk storage, which is insignificant compared to the overall latency.[2] Furthermore, a well-designed proxy should be able to process most of the requests from its main memory with a latency overhead in single milliseconds.

Feldmann et al. [1999] accounted for the factors above, and found that data caching provides negligible latency reductions. For an environment with 28.8Kbps modem lines from clients to the proxy, the mean latency decreased by 3 percent; the environment with a 10Mbps Ethernet connection between clients and the proxy showed a 7 percent reduction. It appears that, for the modem environment, a dominant reason for this disappointing result is the modem bottleneck. For the Ethernet environment, the dominant factor is the additional overhead of the proxy in the middle of object transfers.

We should note that these are pessimistic numbers. First, they did not account for possible slowdowns in the external network (due to network congestion or origin server overload), which would make the ratio of external to internal latency more favorable to the configurations with the proxy. Second, some object transfers reused previously established TCP connections in the nonproxy case, while the simulated proxy required establishing new connections for each transfer. (TCP connections were reused for 18 percent of transfers in the modem environment and for 12 percent of transfers in the Ethernet environment.) Finally, there is active research aimed at increasing proxy benefits (for example, increasing the amount of data that can be cached—see Chapter 13).

Overall, one can expect latency savings from data caching at the proxy to be somewhere in between the optimistic and pessimistic estimates given here. These numbers provide a rather gloomy picture. Fortunately, the situation is not so bad, as we will see in the remainder of this chapter.

7.2.3 TCP Connection Caching

A significant portion of the total latency is contributed by the time needed to establish the TCP connection between the client and the origin server. Recall from Section 4.3.1 that HTTP 1.1 allows reuse of the same connection for multiple object transfers. Thus,

---

[2] Obviously an overloaded proxy may become the bottleneck in itself and a dominant factor in total user latency. Since we are interested in what performance benefits one may expect from a proxy, we assume that the proxy is powerful enough not to be overloaded.

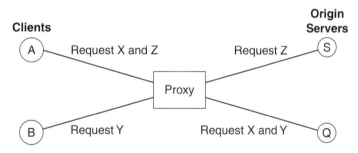

Figure 7.3 TCP connection reuse by a proxy

a proxy can maintain persistent TCP connections to its clients on one side and origin servers on the other, thereby eliminating the overhead of connection setup. One could argue that nothing prevents clients and servers from maintaining persistent connections without any help from the proxy in between. This is true, except the proxy can be much better at that, as the following examples show.

Consider two clients, A and B, requesting objects from origin servers S and Q. Let client A request a page from Q and then client B request a page from Q. Without a proxy, client B has to establish a connection first, since this is its first contact with server Q. If there were a proxy in between (Figure 7.3), it could have kept its connection to server Q alive after A's request and reused this connection for the request from B, by utilizing the persistent connection feature of HTTP (see Section 4.4).

In another scenario, client A might have requested a page from server Q and then one from server S. Without a proxy, it would have to establish a TCP connection for each request. A proxy, on the other hand, can at the very least reuse the connection between client A and itself (established after the first request) for the second request. Moreover, it might still have an open connection to S from servicing someone else's request in the past, in which case no connection setup will be required.

By aggregating requests from many clients in a single connection, a proxy can also significantly reduce the number of open connections that a server has to manage. Instead of managing connections with individual clients, the server need only deal with the proxy that acts on the clients' behalf. By analogy to reusing cached objects for multiple requests, reusing TCP connections by a proxy is called *connection caching* [Feldmann et al. 1999].

Caching connections at an intermediary has another potential advantage over direct persistent connections between clients and servers. Maintaining persistent connections requires the cooperation of the origin server. If each individual client requests a separate connection or two, popular servers may be inclined not to honor requests for persistent connections, to avoid being overwhelmed with the number of open connections. On the other hand, a proxy would open only a small number of connections to the origin server for all of its clients. Therefore, proxies can dramatically reduce the number of open connections that origin servers must deal with. As a result, origin servers may well favor proxies when choosing which connections to maintain, because they know this would benefit a large number of clients. Moreover, even if origin servers are unwilling to maintain persistent connections, proxies can at least maintain persistent connections with their clients, thereby still obtaining some latency reduction.

The proxy must be careful to only use *idle* cached connections to servers. For example, in Figure 7.3 the proxy should use its connection to server Q for request Y only if the transfer of response X has completed by the time request Y arrives. If no idle cached connections to the server are available, the proxy must open a new connection for request Y. Why not just pipeline request Y on the existing connection, regardless of the completion of request X? It is because pipelining in HTTP stipulates that responses be sent back by the server in the same order as the requests in the pipeline. Thus, response Y would have to wait until response X completes its transfer. If response X is slow to complete (which may be for a variety of reasons: a slow link to client A that backs up the transmission, the large size of X, a long-running script generating X, and so on), response Y would be needlessly delayed. Such delays are referred to as *head of line blocking* in networking literature.

In summary, a proxy can serve not only as a data cache, but also as a connection cache. In this capacity, it can maintain persistent TCP connections to clients and origin servers. When it reaches the maximum number of open connections and needs to open a new connection, it will choose a connection to close according to some policy. It may choose to close the oldest idle connection or the least frequently reused connection, and so forth. Connection management is therefore analogous to traditional cache management, where closing a connection corresponds to purging an object, hence the term *connection caching*.

7.2.4 Connection Caching versus Data Caching

The trace simulation by Feldmann et al. [1999] showed that connection caching provides generally much greater latency reduction than data caching. For the modem environment, the connection cache alone reduced mean and median latencies by 21 and 40 percent, respectively. Together with data caching, the total benefits were 24 and 48 percent. (Notice that the latency improvement due to data caching plus connection caching can be more than additive. This is because data caching shortens transfers of some objects and makes those connections available for reuse sooner.) Significantly, the study found that sizable benefits can be achieved by maintaining connections with clients only. This is important because clients are almost always willing to maintain persistent connections while origin servers may be incapable or too busy to do so.

For the Ethernet trace, the benefits of the connection cache alone were small, 2 percent mean and 20 percent median latency reduction compared to a nonproxy case.[3]

---

[3] Note that the nonproxy case included persistent connections between browsers and servers as indicated in the trace.

The reason is that, as with data caching, the benefits compensate only for the additional overhead introduced by the proxy. However, when combined with data caching, the total benefits become quite significant: 47 percent for mean and 40 percent for median latency. Another interesting point is that maintaining persistent connections only between the proxy and clients in the Ethernet environment did not have a significant impact on latency. This could be partially explained by the fact that clients are connected to the proxy via a fast LAN and by the fact that the study did not model processing overheads at the proxy for establishing TCP connections.

7.2.5 TCP Connection Splitting

The throughput of a page download affects the response time, especially for large objects. Because of TCP congestion control, the throughput on a link depends on the round trip time (RTT) of a packet between the link end points (see Section 3.5). By placing a proxy somewhere in the middle of the path between the end points, the RTT on both half-paths (between each end point and the proxy) could be reduced. In the case where the effective bandwidth is limited by the TCP congestion window rather than the physical bandwidth of the network, reducing RTT would increase the effective bandwidth on both half-paths, and hence increase the overall effective bandwidth [Cohen and Ramanathan 1997].

As an example, consider a Web server sending a large object to a Web browser over a link with infinite bandwidth and no packet loss. Under the TCP protocol, the server will increase its transmission rate (the TCP congestion window) until it reaches an upper limit. Given the infinite bandwidth and the absence of packet loss, once the TCP congestion window reaches the maximum, the sender will send a new data packet for every acknowledgment it receives. Figure 7.4a depicts the time diagram for this transfer, for a TCP congestion window size $n = 3$. Let RTT between the server and the browser be r and consider a packet p_1 sent by the server at time t_1. The server will receive the acknowledgment for p_1 at time $t_1 + r$. In general, if n is the window size, the transmitter then sends n data packets every RTT.

If a proxy is inserted somewhere on the path between the Web server and the browser, both the server-proxy and proxy-client RTTs will decrease. Figure 7.4b shows the time diagram under the assumption that the total server-browser RTT is split equally between server-proxy RTT and proxy-browser RTT. Since RTT between the server and the proxy is $r/2$, the proxy will receive packet p_1 at $t_1 + \frac{r}{4}$. At this time, the proxy will send the acknowledgment back to the server and send the packet to the browser. Thus, while the packet continues its way to the browser, the acknowledgment is traveling back to the server. In contrast, without the proxy, the acknowledgment to the server starts its journey only after the packet reaches the browser. This parallelism created by the proxy leads to increased effective throughput.

The server still sends n packets each RTT between itself and the receiver (the proxy), except this RTT is half of what it used to be. Similarly, the proxy sends n packets every RTT between itself and the browser, which is again half the old RTT. Thus, the

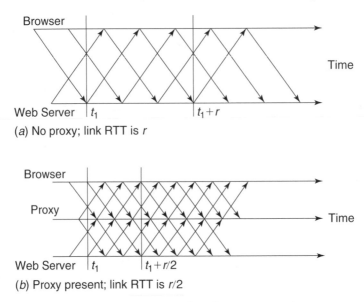

(a) No proxy; link RTT is *r*

(b) Proxy present; link RTT is *r*/2

Figure 7.4 The effect of a split TCP connection

throughput in this idealized example would increase by a factor of two. In fact, the TCP performance models mentioned in Section 3.5 show that the effective through-put strongly depends on RTT even if the congestion window does not reach the maximum.

Of course, the throughput will not double in reality, for a variety of reasons. RTT will not be equally divided between both connections. RTT will change sta-tistically on each connection, leading to variations in the effective throughput on each connection. A proxy itself will introduce extra delay. Still, measurements re-ported by Rodriguez et al. [1999] show that the throughput improvement can be significant. In an experiment where two proxies between the sender and the re-ceiver split total RTT evenly between the three path segments (sender-proxy, proxy-proxy, and proxy-receiver), the effective throughput almost doubled.[4] Lower RTT also speeds up the TCP slow start at the beginning of the transmission or when the sender times out while waiting for the acknowledgment for a packet [Bakre and Badrinath 1995].

We should note that only large objects will enjoy these gains in throughput, and only if the TCP congestion window rather than physical link bandwidth is the limit-ing factor in the transmission rate. As an extreme example, if the entire object fits in one or two packets, the throughput of its transfer will not go up. This is be-cause the congestion window at the Web server is usually two packets following the

---

[4] Note that the improvement is less than the ideal factor of three, due to the reasons mentioned.

connection establishment. Thus, the server will send the entire object immediately, regardless of the RTT value. Since connection splitting benefits mostly large objects, it nicely complements data caching, which favors small objects, as discussed in Section 7.2.1.

7.2.6 Environment-Specific TCP Optimizations

One could attempt to take the split connections idea one step further and gain more performance by tuning TCP differently on either side of the split point. TCP has been designed to work reasonably well in the general Internet, where network characteristics and the amount of competing traffic vary widely. There are many cases, however, where some links in the network exhibit a distinctive behavior. For example, wireless or cable modem links have high packet loss and error rates that are not caused by congestion. High packet loss may result in frequent triggering of TCP congestion control, but since the loss is not congestion related, TCP congestion control reduces the effective bandwidth unnecessarily [Bakre and Badrinath 1995; Cáceres and Iftode 1995; Cohen and Ramanathan 1997].

In some cases, the specifics of the link can be taken into account by the link-level protocol and therefore hidden from TCP. In particular, Balakrishnan et al. [1996] have shown that improvements in the link-level protocol can be just as effective in enhancing performance of transfers over links with high packet losses as split connections with modified TCP implementations.

In other cases, one can improve performance only by placing a proxy at one or both ends of distinctive links and modifying its TCP behavior [Bakre and Badrinath 1995; Cohen and Ramanathan 1997]. For instance, satellite links tend to have high RTTs, often in the order of seconds. Just the delay imposed by transmitting the signal over these links amounts to several hundred milliseconds due to the large distances involved. At the same time, these links sometimes have a high bandwidth capacity, up to multiple megabits per second.

High delay cannot be masked by the link-layer protocol. Therefore, it is up to the TCP implementation to put out enough packets on the link to fully utilize its capacity. Where satellite links are used to connect clients to an ISP point of presence (POP), a proxy at the POP could achieve this optimization by starting the transmission with a large congestion window.

However, unilateral changes in TCP are extremely dangerous, since they could destabilize the Internet at large. Therefore, they should be used only over links that are fully controlled by one organization. In particular, proxy connections to the public Internet should always use standard TCP implementations.[5]

---

[5] We are aware of proposals to tune TCP differently for Web traffic. However, given the complexity of the protocol dynamics and the consequences of wrong decisions, we believe any changes to TCP over the public Internet must be done by consensus through standards organizations such as the IETF.

7.3 Bandwidth Savings

Another major reason for using proxy caching is reduction in bandwidth consumption. Reducing bandwidth consumption not only has the obvious advantage of reducing the overall cost of a network, but it also reduces link- and origin-server utilization and therefore indirectly decreases latency. As a back-of-the-envelope calculation, HTTP constitutes over 60 percent of traffic on the AT&T Worldnet backbone. About 70 percent of traffic due to HTTP was reported on the MCI backbone [Claffy et al. 1998], and a study of cable modem clients found HTTP responsible for close to 90 percent of traffic [Arlitt et al. 1999]. Given the 30 to 40 percent byte hit rate reported for large proxies [Wolman et al. 1999b; Feldmann et al. 1999; NLANR; Danzig 1998b], proxy caching promises potential bandwidth savings on the order of 25 percent. As proxies try to cache other kinds of traffic (such as FTP, mentioned in Chapter 1) or extend caching to some currently uncacheable content (see Chapter 13), these savings may increase further.

As with latency, the situation with bandwidth savings is quite complicated. In this case the complicating factor is aborted object transfers. Transfers are aborted fairly frequently, mostly for two reasons. Users can explicitly abort a transfer by clicking on the Stop button of their browser windows. Or a user may follow a URL link on a partially displayed page, without waiting for the page to be completely transferred. When this happens, the transfer of the page and, more likely, its embedded images is interrupted. As mentioned in Chapter 6, overall abort rates of 5 to 10 percent have been reported [Feldmann et al. 1999; Danzig 1998b].

When the proxy learns about the abort, it can do one of two things. It can continue transferring the object from the origin server, so that it has the object in the cache for future use. Or, it can *forward* the abort, that is, abort its transfer from the origin server. The first option turns out to have a very negative effect on bandwidth consumption. Given that the byte hit rate is below 50 percent, the bytes retrieved despite the abort will most likely not be reused. Thus, the bandwidth for obtaining the object will be wasted. At the very least, the proxy should always forward aborts of transfers for objects that the proxy knows are uncacheable.

If the proxy forwards aborts, then the effect on bandwidth consumption depends on how much of the object the proxy had downloaded before aborting the transfer. The crucial factors here are the relative bandwidth of client-to-proxy and proxy-to-server links and whether or not the proxy employs flow control on the proxy-to-server connection.

To understand the effect of relative bandwidth of proxy links to the client and the Internet, consider a simple example. Assume a dial-up client with a 28.8Kbps line aborts the transfer of a 100KByte object after waiting for one second. Without the proxy, this transfer would consume on the order of 20Kbits of traffic. If there is a proxy within the client's ISP, the proxy's connection to the Internet might be faster, say 1.5Mbps. Thus, during that same second, the proxy might have downloaded the whole object, consuming 100KBytes of bandwidth (assuming there was no congestion at the time).

In general, if the client link is much slower than the link to the server, the proxy may download much of the content, if not the entire object, by the time it finds out about the client abort. Thus, a lot of bandwidth would be wasted even if the proxy forwarded aborts. Feldmann et al. [1999] show in a trace-driven simulation that the amount of bandwidth savings for 28.8Kbps modem clients with a 0.5Mbps, 1.5Mbps, and 45Mbps proxy-to-server link is in the order of 15 percent, −2 percent, and −8 percent, respectively.[6] Although the use of 28.8Kbps modems is declining, this study indicates the more general problem that the bandwidth mismatch between client-proxy and proxy-server connections can reduce bandwidth savings or even *increase* bandwidth consumption.

The negative effect of aborts could be reduced if the proxy reused the partially retrieved objects for future accesses. This can be done with HTTP 1.1, where the proxy can issue a range request (see Section 5.4) for just the missing portion of the object.

The proxy can also counter the disparity of bandwidth on the two links with flow control over the link to the Internet. On a miss, the proxy is in a mode where it receives an object on the proxy-server link and sends the object to the client on the proxy-client link. Typically, the data is streamed to the proxy cache (disk) and out to the client in parallel, to shortcut the disk write delay. Therefore, if the client link does not consume data quickly enough, the internal TCP buffers at the proxy will fill up, and it will stop consuming data from the origin server until more buffer space becomes available. In effect, the download from the origin server is throttled by the rate of transfer to the client. With standard TCP buffer sizes, the proxy cannot get more than 8 to 64KBytes ahead of a client in downloading information from the Internet. This implicit flow control largely negates the adverse effect of the bandwidth mismatch. For example, throttling the data inflow to a proxy to be no more than 64KBytes ahead of the outflow to the client turned an 8-percent increase in bandwidth consumption for the 45Mbps link into a 13 percent savings [Feldmann et al. 1999].

Interestingly, some proxy vendors try hard to defeat this implicit flow control. The rationale is that if the same object is downloaded by multiple clients at the same time, the rate of the download to all clients will be throttled by the rate of the download to the slowest client. However, one should be aware that the absence of flow control in an environment with a bandwidth mismatch may result in reduced or even negative bandwidth savings due to proxy deployment. If it proves common for slow and fast clients to simultaneously download the same content, perhaps one should consider a proxy implementation that would throttle the transfer rate from the Internet by the download rate of the *fastest* client among those currently downloading the content in question [Douglis 2000].

---

[6] This study did not include bandwidth savings from important new applications of proxies, such as channel concentration for live streaming media (see Section 7.4).

7.4 Proxies and Streaming Media

As the use of streaming media on the Web grows, proxy cache vendors are paying more attention to it. Inktomi's support for streaming media and InfoLibria's MediaMall are just two examples of this trend.

One can distinguish between *nonlive* streaming media—for example, video and audio on demand—and *live* streaming media—for example, live news transmission. Nonlive streaming media can in principle be cached like any other static data. However, streaming data objects are very large, in the order of tens or hundreds of megabytes. Caching just a few of these objects would occupy a large portion of the cache and deprive other object types of the cache space. By default, most current proxies do not cache such large objects for this reason; yet without the benefit of caching, latency of access to these data types remains high.

Instead of denying streaming data types cache benefits, a proxy can cache a small initial fragment of a nonlive data stream, enough for a few seconds of playing time [Rexford et al. 1999]. When the streaming object is accessed, the proxy can start transmitting it to the client immediately. Concurrently with that, the subsequent portions of the object can be downloaded from the origin server. This approach hides the access latency of streaming data without taking too much cache space.

Live streamed transmissions, known as *Webcasts*, can put an intense strain on the network. Popular Webcasts may cause surges of access, which by their nature occur all at the same time. An obvious solution is to use multicast to reduce bandwidth consumption. However, using multicast in a straightforward way has its own limitations. First, current routers treat multicast packets at lower priority than other data. As a result, the multicast packets may experience a huge drop rate—up to 40 percent in one study [Maxemchuk et al. 1997]. Second, a popular event with millions of recipients burdens routers with maintaining large multicast-related state. Third, such a large group of recipients will likely generate a very high rate of membership changes in the multicast group as users join and depart. Changing a multicast group entails modifying the multicast distribution tree, which can be a rather heavyweight operation that involves multiple routers. Finally, multicast is still far from being universally adopted.

In the absence of multicast, a proxy can significantly reduce bandwidth consumption and the load on the origin server. Without the proxy, individual recipients of a live stream connect independently to the origin server, as shown in Figure 7.5a. The server must deal with a large number of clients, and the network must carry a large number of streams with essentially the same content. When an ISP has a proxy, as in Figure 7.5b, the proxy concentrates requests for the event from all ISP clients into a single streaming connection to the server. This allows the ISP to drastically reduce the amount of bandwidth it consumes from an upstream ISP. The stream concentration also similarly decreases the load on the origin server and Internet traffic on the path from the server to the ISP.

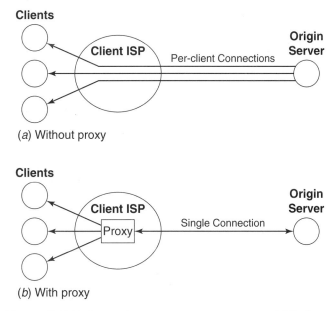

Figure 7.5 Delivery of a stream event to a group of ISP clients

7.5 Summary

This chapter examines the benefits one may expect from a forward proxy cache. We considered separately conventional HTTP traffic and the delivery of streaming media.

Overall, an HTTP proxy can deliver significant latency reductions. Data caching alone seems to promise only modest improvement in this respect, unless the connection to the Internet is extremely slow, congested, or has high delay. More benefits come from combining data caching with connection caching, optimizing TCP implementations for particular network characteristics of the client-proxy link, and reducing the round trip time of IP packets between the communicating parties.

In addition to latency reduction, caching also has the potential of reducing the bandwidth needs of HTTP traffic. However, care has to be taken to realize this potential benefit. For example, if the bandwidth of the client-proxy link is much lower than the bandwidth of the proxy-server link, the bandwidth utilization may actually increase. This phenomenon is due to client aborts and can be prevented if the proxy artificially reduces the throughput of the proxy-server link.

A proxy also promises important benefits for delivering streaming media. For video and audio on demand, it can reduce user latency and the bandwidth consumed by the ISP from the Internet. For live Webcasts, it can reduce ISP bandwidth consumption by satisfying all clients using a single feed from the origin server. Although we are not aware of studies quantifying these benefits, we believe bandwidth savings can be dramatic for popular Webcast.

Chapter 8
Proxy Deployment

Typical proxy users include individual departments such as academic units of a university, entire enterprises, and Internet Service Providers (ISPs). In this chapter, we discuss various alternatives for deploying forward proxy caching in enterprise and ISP networks. The general problem considered here is a mechanism to deliver a client request to the proxy instead of the origin server specified in the requested URL.

8.1 Overview of Internet Connectivity Architectures

Before discussing alternatives for proxy deployment, we need to understand at a high level how an enterprise obtains its Internet connectivity. Consider Figure 8.1, which depicts at a high level a typical ISP architecture. A large ISP has a backbone network consisting of backbone nodes. Each node has some *access routers* (*ARs*) that are the backbone entry points for enterprise customers of the ISP (such as other ISPs) and *backbone routers* (*BRs*) that provide connectivity between backbone nodes. Access routers are connected to their local backbone routers via LANs. Backbone routers in different nodes are connected via *wide area network* (*WAN*) lines, creating the *backbone topology*. In addition, some backbone nodes contain *gateway routers* (*GRs*) that link the backbone to the outside world. On the ISP side, GRs are connected to their local BRs via a LAN.

Residential dial-in customers connect to modem banks located in the ISP's *dial-in points of presence (dial-in POPs)*, otherwise known as *dial-in hubs*. These hubs are sometimes connected to backbone routers, bypassing access routers. Only the largest enterprise customers connect directly at access routers of a backbone node. Others connect at the ISP's *broadband points of presence (broadband POPs)*, which aggregate several enterprises into one connection to the backbone access router. These POPs are omitted in Figure 8.1 for simplicity.

Figure 8.2 shows typical ways in which enterprise networks connect to the Internet. An enterprise may buy its Internet connectivity from one ISP (Figures 8.2a and 8.2b) or multiple ISPs (Figure 8.2c). If using a single ISP, the enterprise network may be

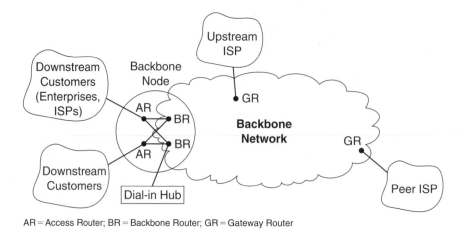

AR = Access Router; BR = Backbone Router; GR = Gateway Router

Figure 8.1 A high-level ISP architecture

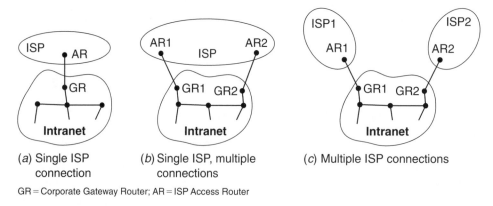

(*a*) Single ISP   (*b*) Single ISP, multiple   (*c*) Multiple ISP connections
connection   connections

GR = Corporate Gateway Router; AR = ISP Access Router

Figure 8.2 Typical examples of enterprise network connections to the Internet

connected to its ISP at a single access router or multiple access routers (Figures 8.2a and 8.2b). The main question for the purpose of our discussion is whether there is a single element in the enterprise network (a router, switch, or link) through which all Internet traffic flows. We refer to such an element as a *focal point*. Focal points may be undesirable from the fault-tolerance perspective, since a failure at a focal point breaks the Internet connectivity of the enterprise. At the same time, they create convenient points to deploy proxies, as we show later in this chapter.

Note that many enterprises with multiple ISP connections use only one connection for normal operation, with the rest serving as backups in case the main connection fails. These enterprise networks have a focal point despite multiple Internet connections. Other enterprise networks alternate between their Internet connections to balance traffic across all available links. Doing so eliminates a focal point for Internet traffic.

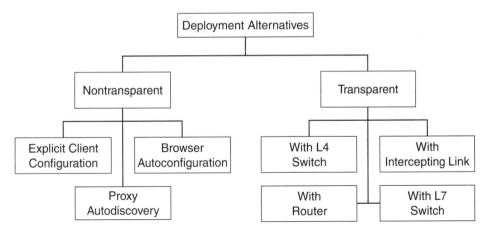

Figure 8.3 Deployment alternatives for a forward proxy

An ISP can deploy a proxy at a POP, at a backbone node to serve requests entering the backbone at this node (a *backbone entry point proxy*), or at a backbone node to serve any requests regardless of where they enter the backbone (a *backbone core proxy*). The main tradeoff here is between the amount of benefit from a cache hit versus the hit rate. A proxy at a POP is the closest the ISP can get to the customers. Therefore, a cache hit at a POP proxy can save the ISP the most bandwidth; such a hit can also reduce latency the most, compared to other ISP locations. On the other hand, a POP proxy only serves clients that connect at this POP; a limited client population can reduce the hit rate [Duska et al. 1997; Gribble and Brewer 1997]. Perhaps even more importantly, POP proxy deployment can get quite expensive, since a large ISP can have hundreds of POPs. A backbone entry point proxy can serve all clients from all POPs and enterprise networks that connect to the backbone at the corresponding backbone node, although this proxy is farther away from customers. A core backbone proxy can potentially serve all ISP clients but is the farthest away from them. Interproxy cooperation (see Chapter 9) can alleviate the tradeoff. We consider ISP proxy deployment in the form of a backbone entry point proxy. The same issues arise also in other locations, so our discussion applies to those locations as well.

The location of a proxy is less significant to enterprise networks because, with the exception of a few global corporations, enterprise networks do not have their own backbones.[1] Therefore, an enterprise or an enterprise department proxy can serve all clients in the enterprise or the department, regardless of the proxy location.

A fundamental issue in proxy deployment is how to deliver requests to the proxy. Figure 8.3 summarizes various methods for request delivery, which we consider in the

---

[1] Even global corporations often rely on ISPs for intracompany communication over a wide area, by means of so-called virtual private networks. For the purpose of our discussion, such a corporation can be assumed to have a collection of individual campus-size exterprise networks.

rest of this chapter. The main choice here is between nontrasparent and transparent proxy deployment.

8.2   Nontransparent Proxy Deployment

Nontransparent proxy deployment refers to a deployment in which client software is made aware in some way of the proxy's existence. Then clients send their Web requests to the proxy regardless of the origin servers specified in the URLs. In addition to document retrieval, these clients also delegate DNS resolutions to a proxy: a browser sends to its proxy the entire requested URL, including the host name part, and the proxy then, if needed, resolves the host name into an IP address and retrieves the object from that address. This is different from the actions of clients accessing the Web directly. Such a client itself obtains the origin server's IP address and sends the HTTP request containing just the path portion of the URL (see Section 4.1) to that address.

Proxies whose deployment is nontransparent to clients are often called *explicit proxies*. Let us now consider different ways of making clients aware of the explicit proxy.

8.2.1   Explicit Client Configuration

With explicit client configuration, clients (browsers or other proxies) are explicitly configured to send requests to a proxy instead of the origin servers.

There are several advantages to explicit client configuration. One advantage is its flexibility. Users can easily bypass the proxy if they choose to, by simply changing their browser configuration. Also, the proxy can be deployed at any convenient place in the network: since clients explicitly address their requests to the proxy, the requests will find their way to the proxy regardless of where it is located.

The main disadvantage of this deployment method is that clients must be explicitly configured. This causes administrative complications, especially for an ISP. In fact, the ISP often does not even know the clients at all, as, for example, when they belong to an enterprise customer or a downstream ISP. Switching the proxy off for maintenance or other reasons also becomes a problem. Still, explicit client configuration is a simple and valid alternative for proxy deployment in enterprise networks, and ISPs sometimes use it by preconfiguring browsers of their own residential customers.

8.2.2   Browser Autoconfiguration

Modern browsers implement proxy *autoconfiguration* capability [Netscape 1996]. Instead of being configured directly to use a certain proxy, a browser is configured to download a special URL every time it is started, called an *autoconfiguration file*, which identifies the proxy the browser should use. This level of indirection allows the administrator to maintain the proxy configuration information in a centralized manner. For instance, when a browser should be assigned to a different proxy, the administrator need only change the autoconfiguration file that is returned to the browser. The browser itself need not be reconfigured, though it must be restarted for the change to take effect.

In addition to simplifying administration, an autoconfiguration file can specify backup proxies and also different proxies for different Web sites and URL types. For example, the file can specify that the browser should use proxy P1 for all URLs matching the "*.gif" pattern, proxy P2 for those URLs matching the "*.html" pattern, and go directly to the Web site for all URLs that match the "*/cgi-bin/*" pattern, where the asterisk denotes an arbitrary string.

The autoconfiguration facility simplifies administration of explicit proxies but does not change the fact that every browser must be explicitly configured. The next step in automating browser configuration is a mechanism that allows the browser to *discover* automatically the autoconfiguration file URL.

8.2.3 Proxy Auto-Discovery

A mechanism for discovering an explicit proxy, called *Web Proxy Auto-Discovery (WPAD)* [Inktomi 1998], utilizes various protocols that hosts may use to discover resources on the network, such as printers, name servers, and so forth. For example, when using DNS, all browsers using this method essentially agree on a well-known relative domain name of the Web server that must provide the autoconfiguration file—such as wpad. At start-up, the browser queries its DNS server for this name (after expanding it into a fully qualified name as it normally would, like wpad.research.att.com). The DNS server returns the IP address of the Web server where the autoconfiguration file resides. The browser then constructs the autoconfiguration URL by adding a well-known path portion to the discovered IP address of the server, such as wpad.dat. If, for example, the IP address of the autoconfiguration server is 127.200.27.11, then the autoconfiguration URL would be http://127.200.27.11/wpad.dat. Once this URL is constructed, the browser can download the autoconfiguration file and start using the specified proxies.

With autodiscovery, the administrator need only maintain a Web server with the well-known domain name and an autoconfiguration file on that server with the well-known URL. The browsers could be used "out of the box," with no configuration, and still find proxies to use.

The proxy auto-discovery mechanism is in the proposal state. Moreover, it works only when the browser and the proxy are in the same administrative domain, such as an enterprise network. In other cases, *transparent deployment*, achieved with *interception proxies*, became a popular alternative.

8.3 Transparent Proxy Deployment

Transparent deployment of a proxy relies on some network element (a switch or a router) to intercept all traffic from Web clients to Web servers and divert it to a proxy server instead of its actual destination. For this reason, proxies deployed in

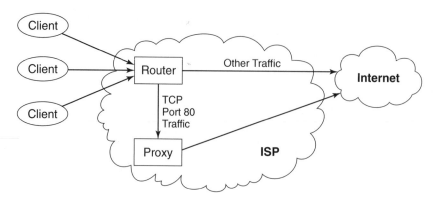

Figure 8.4 Transparent proxy deployment in an ISP

this manner are called interception proxies.[2] The network elements that intercept and divert packets to interception proxies are called *intercepting elements* or simply *intercepters.*

The network element identifies packets to be intercepted by examining IP headers of all incoming packets. Packets transported by TCP and adressed to port 80 are intercepted. Since HTTP communication occurs over TCP transport and an overwhelming majority of Web servers use the default port 80 [Woodruff et al. 1996; Douglis et al. 1997a], this method captures most of the HTTP request traffic flowing through the network element.

Figure 8.4 shows an example of interception proxy deployment in an ISP network. In this example, an ISP router serves as the intercepter and sends all TCP port 80 packets to a proxy instead of their intended destinations. Deployment in an enterprise network is similar: a gateway router connecting the enterprise network to its ISP can divert Web request traffic to an enterprise proxy.

When returning an object to the client, the interception proxy *impersonates* the originally intended destination of the request (that is, the origin server of the requested object), by putting into the IP headers of the response packets the IP address of the original destination rather than its own IP address. The client therefore never realizes that it communicates with a proxy and not the origin server. Such forced traffic interception and impersonation of the origin server is often referred to as *connection hijacking,* or *connection interception.* Connection interception has been expanded to include NNTP (the Network News Transfer Protocol, which carries newsgroups) and FTP traffic, in addition to HTTP communication.

Because clients are unaware of the interception proxy, they act as if they accessed the origin servers directly. In particular, unlike with explicit proxies, clients themselves

---

[2] Interception proxies are also referred to as *transparent proxies.* However, the HTTP 1.1 description uses the term *transparency* to mean semantic transparency (that is, referring to a proxy whose presence does not affect Web behavior semantically) rather than deployment transparency.

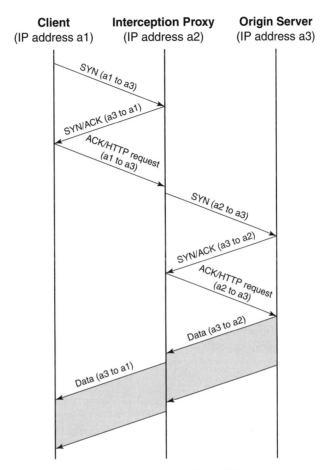

Figure 8.5 Packet flow in interception caching (Information in parentheses indicate source and destination IP addresses of the packets.)

resolve origin servers' domain names into their IP addresses and send HTTP requests containing only the path portion of URLs. However, when the interception proxy needs the domain names of origin servers (as described in Section 8.3.7), the proxy can extract this name from the host header of client requests.

Figure 8.5 illustrates packet flows for an HTTP interaction with an interception proxy.[3] The proxy impersonates the origin server and establishes the TCP connection with the client (packets SYN and SYN/ACK). The client then sends the packet containing the HTTP request. Assuming that the proxy does not have the requested object, it sends its own request to the origin server, using its own IP address. After the object starts to arrive, the proxy sends it back to the client.

---

[3] Although most TCP implementations send data only after fully completing the handshake, we assume for simplicity that the HTTP request is sent together with the final acknowledgment of the handshake. This assumption does not affect in any way the issues discussed here.

Transparent proxy deployment offers several major advantages to an ISP. First and foremost, the administrative obstacle of configuring clients is removed. Managing the proxy becomes a purely internal affair. The ISP can bring it down at will by simply switching off connection interception at the appropriate switches or routers (of course, the interception will stop only for new connections, and the proxy will be brought down only after it completes serving existing connections). The proxy DNS name and IP address are not exposed to clients and can be easily changed. Another advantage is that interception proxies behave better than explicit ones under failures and overload. The intercepting element constantly monitors the health of the proxy (see Section 8.3.2 for details on how monitoring is done). Once the intercepting element detects a failure, it simply stops diverting the traffic to the proxy; at this point, clients retain their Internet connectivity, perhaps at a diminished performance. Network elements, based on hardware and firmware, are generally more reliable pieces of equipment than software-based proxies. Thus, the ability to quickly shortcut a failed proxy improves the overall system behavior under failures.[4]

At the same time, transparent deployment has several pitfalls. Some of these are serious enough for this deployment method to remain controversial despite its wide use. The main controversy surrounding transparent proxy deployment and interception proxies stems precisely from the fact that clients are unaware of the proxy existence. Clients address their datagrams to origin servers and assume that the responses come from the origin servers. Thus, interception proxies violate the *end-to-end principle* of the Internet, which says that an application function "can completely and correctly be implemented only with the knowledge and help of the application standing at the end points of the communication system" [Saltzer et al. 1984]. HTTP 1.1 improves the situation slightly by requiring proxies to identify themselves to origin servers and allowing clients to find out whether any proxies stand between them and particular origin servers (see Section 5.9). While not changing the fact that hosts to which clients address packets may be different from the hosts with which clients end up communicating, these HTTP features at least allow one to diagnose a problem that may arise from this fact.

The most important limitation of interception proxies is a direct corollary of the violation of the end-to-end principle. We call this limitation a *multipath problem*.

8.3.1 Multipath Problem

The main limitation of interception proxies is that they can only work properly if *all* packets from a given client to a given destination flow through the same intercepting element. This limits the kinds of clients for whom interception proxies can be used and

---

[4] With explicit proxies, clients can also learn about failures of their proxies and stop using them. However, because clients and explicit proxies are more loosely coupled (and, in particular, not always connected by a fast LAN as the interception proxy and its intercepting router or switch are), detecting proxy failures and recoveries is slower and less reliable in this case.

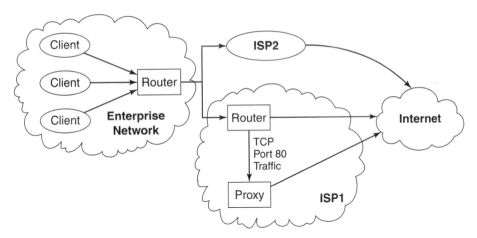

Figure 8.6 An incorrect use of the interception proxy

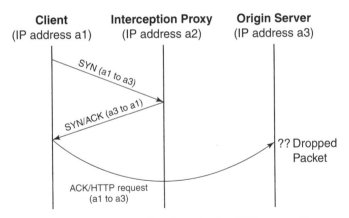

Figure 8.7 A packet flow for a broken TCP connection

the number of places in the network where the proxies can be deployed. Figure 8.6 illustrates a network setup that may cause a problem for an ISP proxy. It shows a client that buys its Internet connectivity from two different ISPs, as many enterprise customers do.

Consider the packet flow shown in Figure 8.7. The client starts an HTTP interaction by sending the SYN packet to the origin server. This packet is sent using ISP1 and is intercepted by the proxy, which responds with SYN/ACK, impersonating the origin server. The client now sends the HTTP request over the established connection. The request chooses ISP2 and is delivered directly to the origin server. Because the latter has not established a connection with this client, it discards this packet. The effect is a broken HTTP interaction; the client perceives it as lost connectivity to the Internet. Thus, interception caching may disrupt client connectivity even though the entire network functions properly. One may argue that the routing instability illustrated in this example occurs infrequently. However, most ISPs will find it unacceptable to introduce even a few percent additional connection failures.

At an ISP, interception proxy deployment is typically safe when it is used for customers who have this ISP as their only provider of Internet connectivity *and* utilize a single primary connection to this ISP. Having backup connections to this or other ISPs is also possible as long as these connections are used only when the primary connection fails (in other words, the primary and backup connections are never used concurrently). The intercepting element for these customers can be installed at any point along the primary connection, up to the point where the packet flow can first be divided among multiple paths.

A similar problem occurs with interception proxies in enterprise networks when they have multiple connections to the Internet, as shown in Figure 8.2b and 8.2c. It follows from this discussion that an enterprise network can safely deploy interception caching if it uses a single primary gateway to the Internet, or if it cleanly divides all Internet destinations among all its gateways, so that all packets to a given destination are always routed through the same gateway. These gateways could then be used as intercepting elements.

8.3.2 Interception Mechanisms

Let us take a closer look at the mechanisms behind transparent proxy deployment. The packets from the client carry the client IP address as the source IP address and the origin server IP address as the destination IP address. Once intercepted by the intercepting element, these packets must be delivered to the proxy. Delivering packets to an unintended destination can be accomplished at the data link layer (Layer 2 solution) or IP layer (Layer 3 solution).

Layer 2 solution: The intercepting element delivers packets to the proxy by sending them to the proxy's data-link-layer address (MAC address, see Section 1.1). No information in the IP packets themselves is changed. This simple scheme is very efficient but implies a restriction, in that the intercepting element and the proxy must be directly connected by the same data link network. This is because the packets still carry their original destination IP addresses, so if there is a router on their path from the intercepting element to the proxy, the router will faithfully send them back to their original destinations. Nortel's ACEDirector switch is an example of an intercepting element using the L2 diversion mechanism. This mechanism also requires a change to the proxy protocol stack: it must be changed so that packets would be accepted and passed up to the application regardless of their destination IP addresses. Most modern proxies already implement this functionality.

Layer 3 solution: The intercepting element wraps the packet into another IP datagram, the technique called *IP-in-IP encapsulation* [Hanks et al. 1994]. The

IP headers in the outer wrapper have the proxy IP address as the destination address. The packets are therefore delivered to the proxy using normal IP protocols. This option does not impose restrictions on the network connection between the intercepting element and the proxy. They may even be connected via a wide area network and have any number of routers in between. Also, no changes to the proxy protocol stack are required: all changes can concentrate at the application layer. Cisco routers follow this approach.

It may seem that the intercepting element could also deliver packets to the proxy by simply replacing the destination IP address of intercepted packets with that of the proxy. However, a major problem with this approach, which is called *network address translation (NAT)* is that the packets lose the information about their original destination. When the proxy needs to obtain the object from its origin server, how will it know where to send the request? It could use the HTTP host header of the client request, which contains the identity of the Web site, but that would require a DNS lookup by the proxy, since the site identity in the host header is usually represented by its domain name. This lookup would add extra latency to the misses because the client has already performed this DNS lookup before sending the request. As we show in Section 14.1.2, NAT as a mechanism for packet forwarding is more viable in the server surrogate setting, although IP-in-IP encapsulation remains a more general approach even there.

Several other basic questions must be answered when considering interception solutions.

1. How does an intercepting element detect and bypass a failed proxy?

2. How can an intercepting element distribute load among multiple proxies?

3. Can multiple intercepting elements divert packets to the same proxy?

4. Can an intercepting element be efficiently configured to selectively intercept packets based on some configured rules? For instance, can it be told not to intercept packets originating from or destined for specific IP addresses?

We have already touched upon the first question. Network elements, being implemented in hardware and firmware, are usually more reliable than proxy caches and can be deployed in *fail-over pairs*, that is, as a primary unit and a similar backup unit that takes over when the primary fails. The ability to quickly shortcut a failed proxy is one of the main advantages of interception proxies.

The second question arises because network elements typically have substantially higher performance than proxies. A typical backbone link with a throughput of 2.4Gbps can in principle tranfer up to 26,000 Web objects per second (assuming an average object size of 10KBytes). On the other hand, the best proxy in the benchmarking study by Rousskov et al. 2000] had a throughput of 2,400 objects per second.

Therefore, to balance the system, multiple proxies must be able to share the load sent to them by a single network element.

The third question addresses the multipath problem (Section 8.3.1). Normally, ISPs would not use interception proxies when packets from a client to an origin server can take multiple paths. However, if the intercepting elements on all these paths diverted packets to the same proxy, then that proxy would receive all packets from the client regardless of which path they took, and interception caching could still be used. In other words, the answer to this question affects how flexibly one can choose where in the network to intercept the packets.

Consider, for example, Figure 8.1 again. Assume that each AR alternates between the two local BRs when sending packets further in the network. If multiple intercepters could use the same proxy, the ISP could place the intercepting elements on the lines between ARs and BRs. Otherwise, intercepting on these lines would not be an option, since the proxy servicing each line would not be guaranteed to see all packets for any TCP connection, due to the multipath problem. As another example, if a corporate customer connects at both ARs in Figure 8.1, request interception normally would not be done at ARs for clients belonging to this customer because of the multipath problem. However, if both ARs divert intercepted packets to the same proxy, using ARs as intercepting elements becomes an option.

Another motivation for using the same proxy is more efficient cache sharing. Assume that ARs in Figure 8.1 act as intercepting elements. If each AR uses its own proxy, then a client connected to one AR cannot use an object cached at the other AR's proxy without proxy cooperation (see Chapter 9). If both ARs share a proxy, then clients connected to either AR can share the content cached by the proxy directly.

Note that there is no contradiction between the second and third questions. Multiple intercepters can distribute load among the same *set* of proxies in such a way that packets from the same client going to a given destination are always sent to the same proxy.

The fourth question is very important. As we discussed earlier, interception caching is only appropriate for customers who are not affected by the multipath problem. Further, we will see in Section 8.4.1 that interception caching is not appropriate for requests to some Web sites. One needs the flexibility to describe, by specifying filtering rules, which connections should or should not be intercepted. Most if not all intercepting elements provide this functionality but differ in the expressiveness of the rules and the performance overhead. In addition to the intercepter, the proxy could also identify the packets that should not have been diverted to it. The proxy could return these exception packets back to the Internet unchanged.[5] These packets would then be forwarded to their intended destination with their original source IP addresses (that is, the client IP addresses), and the destinations would respond directly to the clients.

---

[5] If IP-in-IP encapsulation is used to deliver the packets to the proxy, the proxy would obviously remove the wrapper.

The only danger in making the proxy handle exception packets is that the proxy's connection to the intercepter is often the only network connection of the proxy. Thus, all proxy communication, including the returned exception packets, flows through the switch or router that acts as the intercepter. Consequently, the intercepter might faithfully divert the exception packets right back to the proxy (after all, these are TCP port 80 packets from the original source IP)! Fortunately, most intercepters can be configured not to intercept packets that arrive on certain network connections. One only need take special care to configure the intercepter so that it never intercepts packets arriving on the connection from the proxy.

Four types of intercepting elements are used for transparent proxy deployment: Layer 4 switches, routers, Layer 7 switches, and intercepting links. Layer 4 switches, intercepting links, and, in most cases, routers use only the information in IP and TCP packet headers, whereas Layer 7 switches also consider the packets' application data. Let us now consider these types of intercepting elements in turn.

8.3.3 Layer 4 Switch as an Intercepter

An L4 switch is a network switch capable of reading and interpreting the IP and TCP headers of a datagram (hence the name, since it operates at the transport layer in the ISO protocol stack). There are a variety of applications for L4 switches, and different switches target different applications [Conover 1999]. Nortel, Foundry, Cisco, and Radware are examples of companies offering L4 switches for interception Web proxies. These switches look at the IP headers to determine packets sent by TCP, and then at TCP headers to detect packets destined to port 80. The switch then sends these packets to a proxy instead of their original destination.

Figure 8.8 illustrates using an L4 switch in a backbone node.[6] The L4 switch is placed between clients and the access router they connect to, so that all traffic between these clients and the access router flows through the switch. The switch then examines the packets arriving from the clients, intercepts those packets that carry Web traffic, and diverts them to an interception proxy or proxies.

L4 switches can distribute load among several proxies by a variety of methods. One method involves partitioning the IP address space among the proxies and diverting a packet to the proxy responsible for the packet's destination IP address. For example, in the case of three proxies, one possible partitioning would assign IP addresses from 0.0.0.0 to 85.255.255.255 to the first proxy, IP addresses from 86.0.0.0 to 170.255.255.255 to the second proxy, and IP addresses from 171.0.0.0 to 255.255.255.255 to the third proxy. A function that maps all possible values of a data item (in our case IP addresses)

---

[6] Note that this and other similar figures present a simplified view of the backbone node. In fact, clients do not connect to an access router directly, but rather they first terminate at some sort of an aggregation point, which then connects to the router via a LAN. It is on this LAN that the L4 switch is deployed.

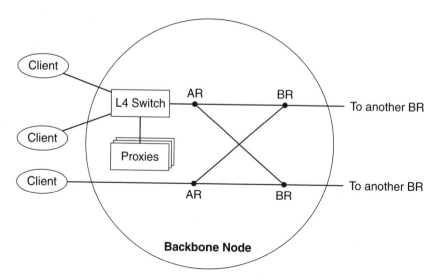

Figure 8.8 An interception proxy deployment with an L4 switch

to a set of numeric values (in our case the proxy number) is called a *hash function*, and applying a hash function is called *hashing*. In reality, switches use more complex hash functions than the one described here.

   This load distribution in effect implements hash-based intercache cooperation (see Section 9.3.3) at the switch level: all objects hosted at a given IP address will be cached at one proxy only (no duplicates), and all clients that request these objects will be directed to the proxy responsible for them. Switch-level cooperation is much more efficient than proxy-level because the same request does not have to be processed by multiple proxies. This cooperation breaks down, however, when a Web site is mirrored on multiple servers and the site's DNS server balances load by assigning IP addresses of different mirrors to different requests, because the switch is oblivious to mirroring and treats each replica with a different IP address as if it were a different site. In particular, a request for an object may result in fetching the object from the origin server even if a different replica of the same object (with the same URL) is cached at another proxy connected to the switch.

   In addition to distributing load based on the destination IP address, L4 switches can also be configured to distribute load among proxies by hashing the source IP address of packets instead. Other available mechanisms can select an arbitrary proxy for any given connection using a variety of algorithms. However, these mechanisms are more useful for distributing load among multiple replicas of an origin server on a LAN, which we discuss in Section 14.1. In the context of proxy load balancing, destination IP hashing has an important advantage over all these methods: it reduces duplication of cached objects and avoids situations where a request experiences a cache miss at one proxy while another has the requested object. We assume destination IP hashing for proxy load balancing in the rest of this chapter.

L4 switches can share the same set of proxies. For example, in Figure 8.8, one could deploy two switches on the links from one of the ARs to the two BRs. These two switches can share the same set of proxies, and the configuration will work even though neither switch sees all the packets for a given TCP connection. For proxy sharing to make sense, it is essential that all the switches use the same hash function in distributing requests among the shared proxies. Without this requirement, different switches could divert packets with the *same* source and destination IP addresses to *different* proxies. In particular, packets belonging to the same TCP connection could end up at different proxies, resulting in a broken connection.

L4 switches typically monitor the health of their proxies using standard HTTP. They place a small dummy Web page at each proxy and periodically fetch it. Failure to fetch this page from a proxy indicates a failure of the proxy. This elegant trick allows L4 switches to monitor proxy health without any special protocols, making these switches compatible with any proxy. The downside is that, since fetching pages uses TCP, failure to fetch the dummy page is detected through TCP retries and timeouts, and can take several seconds, with a corresponding service interruption. As we describe in Section 8.3.4, intercepting routers and links implement a quicker failure detection using special protocols designed for this purpose. Nothing prevents L4 switches from implementing such quicker failure detection as well; the only problem is compatibility with various proxy products which would have to implement the special protocol. This has become less of an issue as many proxy products now implement two competing intercepter-proxy protocols that include failure detection: Cisco's *Web Cache Communication Protocol* (WCCP) [WCCP n.d.] and *Network Element Control Protocol* (NECP) developed by an industrial consortium [NECP 2001]. We come back to these protocols in the next subsection.

8.3.4 Router as an Intercepter

Packets can also be intercepted by a router, which can look at the relevant IP and TCP headers of a packet just as well as an L4 switch does. One difference from switches is that routers (at least intercepting routers by Cisco) use IP-in-IP encapsulation to deliver packets to proxies while switches typically use the data link approach. Like L4 switches, several intercepting routers can share the same set of proxies and balance the load among multiple proxies based on hashing the destination IP addresses. We should note that unlike switches that are often configured to use other methods of load distribution, especially among origin server replicas, routers are hardly ever configured to use other methods. The reason is that routers are highly optimized for examining destination IP addresses in hardware, and having to consider other information can slow them down significantly.

Intercepting at a router is attractive because it does not require any additional network elements. Routers are also natural traffic aggregation points that are more likely to see all packets from a client. In the architecture of Figure 8.1, intercepting could be done at ARs. While customers often connect at more than one backbone node and

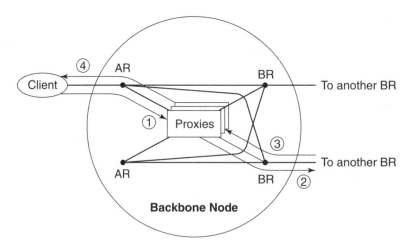

Figure 8.9 A router-based deployment of interception proxies

more than one AR, they typically can be configured to use a single primary AR, with other connections acting as backups. Thus, in the absence of failures, the same client sends all its packets via the same AR and no connection disruption—of the type shown in Figure 8.7—may occur. We discuss handling exceptions later in this subsection.

Figure 8.9 shows a backbone node using a router-based interception proxy deployment. Arrows indicate information flow on a cache miss. First, the AR intercepts request packets and diverts them to one of the proxies (the proxy is chosen by hashing the packet destination IP address). The proxy detects a miss and fetches the object from the origin server using its connection to BRs (steps 2 and 3). The proxy then sends back the object to the client via the AR (step 4). It is important that the proxy communicate with the Internet via BRs rather than use its link to the AR again. If the proxy sends these packets to the AR, then the AR will have to handle all packets related to missed requests *twice:* once when delivering them from the Internet to the proxy, and the second time when delivering them from the proxy to the client. If we assume 70 percent of all Internet traffic to be Web traffic (see Section 6.7) and a rather conservative miss ratio of 50 percent (see Chapter 7), this could easily cause a 35 percent load increase on the router. In practice, proxies are often connected only to ARs and use them for all communication, but unless there is a port shortage at BRs, such a configuration is suboptimal.

Another reason for connecting the proxy to a BR for communication with the Internet is efficient handling of exceptions in intercepting connections. There are always going to be cases (clients or Web sites) that should be excluded from interception. A Cisco router allows elaborate configuration rules to specify such exceptions. The trouble is, the rule processing occurs mostly in software, on a so-called slow processing path. The result is significantly lower router throughput and higher message delays. Moreover, all packets, whether or not they fall under the exception, must be tested against these rules, so the performance degradation applies to all Web traffic.

As previously mentioned, one could offload some of this rule processing to the proxy. In this case, the router would more or less blindly divert all Web traffic to the proxy, while the proxy would identify the exception packets and return them back to the Internet. This works especially well when the proxy is connected to the BRs for its communication with the Internet, as shown in Figure 8.9, since the returned packets bypass the intercepting router and do not increase its load.

Almost all models of Cisco routers are now able to intercept connections. Unlike L4 switches, they employ a special protocol, WCCP, for control communication between the router and the proxies. Cisco developed WCCP as a proprietary protocol but later opened it for use by others.

With WCCP, proxies use periodic "I am alive" messages to let the router know they are operational. While HTTP could also be used for failure detection (as we saw in Section 8.3.3), explicit messages allow a finer-grained failure detection. WCCP also gives proxies some control over how the intercepter distributes requests among them. Essentially, the proxies elect a master proxy that can communicate to the router the (re)assignment of IP address space partitions to proxies (see Section 8.3.3 for details on partitioning IP address space among proxies). The router then sends a packet to the proxy assigned to the packet's destination IP address. This type of feedback from proxies to the intercepting element cannot be accomplished over HTTP. Thus, an intercepting element that only uses HTTP for communication with the proxies can only perform "blind" request distribution, without any feedback from the proxy.

NECP, developed by an industrial consortium as an open (that is, nonproprietary) protocol, is an alternative to WCCP for intercepter-proxy communication. In some ways it is even more flexible than WCCP. It allows the proxy to choose between data link and IP layer methods for delivering packets to proxies. It also allows a proxy to dynamically install simple filtering rules at the intercepter, specifying that packets with certain source or destination IP addresses should not be intercepted.

8.3.5 Layer 7 Switch as an Intercepter

A Layer 7 (L7) switch operates at the application layer in the ISO stack. It intercepts requests for opening TCP connections to Web servers (that is, TCP SYN packets directed to port 80, the default port for Web servers) but, unlike an L4 switch, it does not forward these packets immediately to a proxy. Instead, the L7 switch itself performs TCP handshake with clients, impersonating their intended destinations. It then intercepts and interprets HTTP requests (or those of other application-level protocols) and only then forwards client packets to a proxy or the Internet. Because of its ability to interpret requests, L7 switches are otherwise known as *content-aware* switches. Arrowpoint Communications (now part of Cisco) was among the first vendors to bring these switches to the market. Several L4 switch vendors have added content awareness to their products as well.

Content awareness opens several possibilities. In the context of forward proxies, the main advantage is that the switch can be configured to send requests for different types of content to different proxies. For instance, requests for images and HTML files can be sent to one proxy, requests for video and audio files to another, and requests for live streaming data to yet another proxy. Thus, different proxies can be tuned to different content types. A proxy serving video files can be tuned differently, or even have an entirely different architecture from a proxy serving relatively small HTML pages. An L4 switch without content awareness is oblivious to what object is requested; it therefore cannot take content type into account when distributing requests among proxies.

Another advantage of L7 switches has to do with providing differentiated quality of service to different Web sites. Since this feature is mostly relevant to hosting service providers and other server-centric platforms, we defer further details of this feature until Section 14.3.3 in Part III of the book.

An alleged advantage of L7 switches is that they can avoid diverting packets when requests are for uncacheable content [Johnson 1999]. Since the proxy does not have to process these requests, its load is reduced; at the same time, the processing path for these requests (and, hence, their response time) becomes shorter. This might look like a great advantage of L7 switches except that it interacts in an unfortunate way with persistent connections.

Consider an uncacheable page with many embedded images. When an L7 switch receives a request for this page, it sends the request directly to the origin server, bypassing the proxy. But then the client may decide to reuse this TCP connection for embedded objects. Since the connection has been established between the client and the origin server and not between the client and the proxy, *all* requests over this connection must go to the origin server. Indeed, the proxy will discard any packets that belong to this connection since it has no information about this connection. In other words, once the switch chooses where to send a request, it must send all other requests over the same TCP connection to the same host, regardless of their cacheability. This may severely degrade the hit rate because it is common for a dynamically generated page to contain multiple embedded images on the same server, and these images account for much of the hit rate.

Arguably, a switch can fix this problem by maintaining its own persistent TCP connection with the client and merging responses from the origin server and proxies onto that connection. Figure 8.10 provides a simplified illustration of the approach. In this example, a client requests an uncacheable object X and then a cacheable object Y over the same connection. The switch maintains the connection to the client on behalf of the origin server; at the same time, the switch uses separate connections to the origin server, to get X, and to the proxy, to get Y. It then forwards X and Y to the client over the persistent connection between the client and the switch. In other words, the data that the switch receives over the persistent connection from the client it splits between the two connections, one to the origin server and one to the proxy; the switch then merges the data received over these two connections back into the single connection to the client.

No vendor, to our knowledge, has implemented this approach at the time of this writing. In fact, it remains to be seen if the approach is worthwhile. It triples the

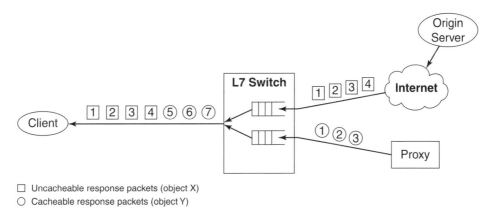

Uncacheable response packets (object X)
Cacheable response packets (object Y)

Figure 8.10 TCP connection merging by an L7 switch

number of connections the switch must handle when downloading a Web document that includes a dynamic container page and static embedded objects. Indeed, whereas the switch had to deal with one connection from the client to the proxy before, now the switch must handle one connection between the client and the switch itself, one between the switch and the origin server, and one between the switch and the proxy. Moreover, without this approach, once the switch establishes the TCP connection with the client and chooses the proxy for the HTTP request, the switch passes all packets between the proxy and the client without any buffering. Now the switch must maintain full TCP state for each of the three connections. In some cases, this approach forces the switch to buffer even more data than TCP would normally. In our example, if the client pipelines the request for Y after the request for X, then the responses from the switch must return in the same order. In the worst case, if object Y arrives before X, the switch must buffer the entire object Y to send it after sending X, as stipulated by the response ordering in the pipeline.

Thus, TCP connection merging will undoubtedly increase the performance cost of content awareness, and content awareness already comes at a hefty performance cost. Depending on the required amount of processing at the application layer, it can easily decrease throughput of the switch by 40 percent or more. Imposing additional penalty for TCP connection merging may not be worthwhile. Without connection merging, selective interception for HTTP 1.1 clients seems a bad idea.

8.3.6 Intercepting Link

One can also use a network link to intercept packets. Cobalt Networks, now part of Sun Microsystems, and InfoLibria offer such a device, which we call an *intercepting link*. The intercepting link is a box consisting of a tightly coupled pair of modules: a simple switch and a proxy (Figure 8.11). The switch contains only two exposed network interfaces and one internal interface to the proxy. Logically, a network link

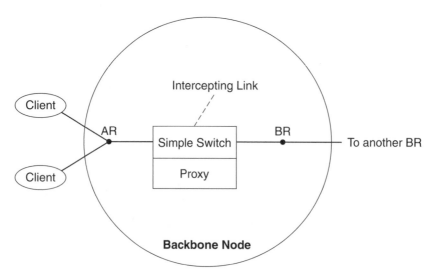

Figure 8.11 An interception proxy deployment with an intercepting link

is "cut" and the device interposed by connecting the two "loose" ends of the link to the two switch interfaces. The switch monitors all traffic on the link and diverts all Web request packets (the TCP port 80 packets) to its internal proxy. For example, Figure 8.11 shows the deployment of an intercepting link in a backbone node with only one pair of access and backbone routers. In this figure, the intercepting link is inserted into the link between the routers.

The main advantage of the intercepting link is its simplicity. The switch is a very simple device, easy to make reliable and efficient. This simplicity also makes the device easy to configure and administer (vendors claim these are truly plug-and-play devices). The intercepting link also avoids the overload of existing routers and switches for handling missed objects twice, once when they flow from the origin server into the proxy and once when they go from the proxy to the client (see Section 8.3.4). Finally, tight coupling of the switch and the proxy facilitates fast detection of proxy failures and efficient shortcutting of the failed cache [InfoLibria 2001].

The main limitation of this approach is that it may be difficult to find a link where an intercepting link could be interposed. A candidate link must see all traffic from a given session. Large ISPs, however, usually ensure that there are always redundant paths between any points in their networks. If traffic is distributed across redundant paths, then no single link can be guaranteed to see all packets. If redundant links are used only as backups, then finding a link appropriate for interception becomes easier. Figure 8.11 shows an appropriate link because the system has only one access router and one backbone router.

A backbone node more typical for a large ISP, shown in Figure 8.1, does not contain an appropriate link if each access router splits its traffic between the two backbone routers. In this case, intercepting links could only be used on the links between ARs and

BRs if ARs were configured to split traffic at the granularity of TCP sessions, so that all packets from a given session would go on the same link. While this mode of operation is available in modern routers, it places an extra load on routers and therefore is unlikely to find acceptance from network administrators. Another disadvantage is that the tight coupling of the switch and the proxy means that multiple switches cannot feed the same proxy cache and, conversely, the same intercepting link cannot feed multiple proxy caches.

Overall, it appears that the most likely market for intercepting links is small low-cost ISPs as well as enterprise networks. Their network administrators will find the ease of administration most appealing. There will also more likely be a convenient point in these networks to deploy an intercepting link.

8.3.7 Performance Pitfalls

We already discussed the main limitation of interception proxies: the violation of the end-to-end principle of the Internet and the multipath problem that stems from it. This limitation prevents some clients from using a proxy and requires careful placement of intercepting elements in the network. This subsection considers more subtle pitfalls of interception proxies that do not cause service disruption but that may degrade the performance of interception proxies when they are compared to their explicit counterparts.

Replicated Web Sites

When a client is configured to use an explicit proxy, it sends the proxy an entire URL including the host name portion, for example, http://www.firm-x.com/index.html. With interception proxies, the client assumes it speaks to the origin server; it therefore does not send the host name portion in the request line of the HTTP request. The request line would contain only the "/index.html" portion of the URL. How can the interception proxy distinguish in its cache similarly named objects from different sites, such as http://www.firm-x.com/index.html and http://www.firm-y.com/index.html? A simple way to extract the DNS name of the Web site from the HTTP host header of the request and use this name as the host ID. Studies have shown that over 98 percent of HTTP 1.0 requests and virtually all HTTP 1.1 requests contain this header [Feldmann 1999], so this mechanism largely solves the problem but can reduce bit rate for accesses to replicated Web sites.

Consider a Web site that performs DNS-level request distribution among replicated servers. We discuss this mechanism in detail in Chapters 14 and 15. In short, an object can be replicated on several hosts, and different requests can be directed to different hosts by the DNS system of the object's site. When the intercepting element divides load among multiple proxies, requests to different server replicas may well arrive at different proxies. This is because the intercepter chooses a proxy for a given request based on the destination IP address in the request (see Section 8.3.3), and different server replicas have different IP addresses. When one proxy has an object in its cache and a request for this object arrives at another proxy that does not have the object, this request will be a miss. Only cooperation between the proxies (described in Chapter 9) can avoid the reduction in hit rate. The degree of this hit-rate reduction in practice has not been adequately studied. Note that L7 intercepting switches can balance the load among proxies based on the requested URLs rather than destination IP address. They would not be prone to the hit-rate reduction described here, because all requests for a given object go to the same proxy.

Limited TCP Connection Reuse

Interception proxies have less potential than explicit proxies in reducing latency for users. As discussed in Section 7.2.3, a large portion of latency reduction comes from connection caching, that is, reuse of TCP connections for requests from multiple origins by multiple clients. An interception proxy can cache its TCP connections to origin servers just as an explicit proxy can. However, caching connections to clients becomes impossible when clients are not aware of the proxy [Danzig 1998a].

The situation is illustrated in Figure 8.12. Assume the client sends a request to Web site firm-x.com, and that the client requests a persistent connection. The proxy intercepts the request and agrees to maintain the persistent connection with the client. Recall that the proxy impersonates firm-x.com to the client, so the client thinks it has a TCP connection with firm-x.com. Assume that the client now wants to send a request to firm-y.com. From the client's perspective, it has not spoken to firm-y.com, so it needs to establish the TCP connection first. The proxy must accept this new connection on behalf of firm-y.com. The result is that the client has not reused the existing TCP connection to the proxy, even though it is available and idle, whereas if the client communicated with the proxy explicitly, it could send both requests over the same connection.

At this writing, the impact of this phenomenon on performance has not yet been investigated. Note that the interception proxy does not make matters worse compared to the no-proxy case: when a client uses a persistent connection to fetch multiple objects from the same server, the client also uses the persistent connection in the presence

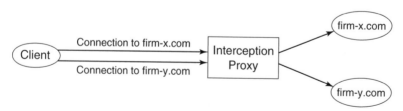

Figure 8.12 Duplication of TCP connections between a client
and an interception proxy

of the interception proxy. However, the interception proxy reduces *additional* opportunities of using persistent connections that can arise when an explicit proxy is used.

8.4 Security and Access Control Issues

Every time a new component is added to the Internet, it is vital to consider the impact this component has on the security and reliability of the Internet as a whole. In the case of proxies, this impact can be profound; it affects how Web servers implement access control—that is, limit the clients that can use their services—as well as a variety of security issues.

8.4.1 Proxies and Web Server Access Control

Many Web sites provide services only to specific clients, for example, those who agree to pay for the service. To enforce access restrictions, Web servers must implement client access control. Some Web servers implement access control at the IP layer. In this mechanism, a server maintains a list of IP addresses of authorized clients and accepts requests only from those clients. Unfortunately, a proxy may break IP-based access control. If a proxy intercepts requests and issues its own requests on a client's behalf, these requests carry the proxy IP address as their source IP address. The Web site will not recognize this IP address and will refuse to service these requests.

An actual example of this problem involved three companies, CyberCache, Gleim, and Digex. CyberCache is a company that signs up business customers to execute their monetary transactions with their clients (we refer to them as end-customers). Gleim was CyberCache's customer, and Digex was the ISP providing connectivity to Gleim. Once Digex deployed an interception proxy, CyberCache stopped honoring Gleim's requests, which were now conveyed to CyberCache by Digex's proxy. Gleim was unable to process orders from its end-customers and was considering suing Digex for losses it suffered from Digex's interception proxies.

Of course, an explicit proxy would cause the same problem; the difference is that the business customer would have to configure its client software to use the proxy. Presumably it would not do this or would reconfigure its software so as not to use the explicit proxy once the problem transpires. With an interception proxy, the client is not aware of the proxy and cannot unilaterally bypass the proxy even if it learns about its existence.

One could say that a proxy should impersonate the client when sending its request to the origin server; then situations such as CyberCache's would not arise. Unfortunately, asymmetric routing (see Section 2.3) invalidates this solution. Considering Figure 8.6 again, we note that asymmetric routing could cause the bottom route to be the primary route for packets from a client to a server while the top route would be the primary route for responses from the server. Then, if the interception proxy at the bottom ISP impersonated the client, the server packets would bypass the proxy and arrive at the client. The proxy would get no response, assume that the connection to the server is broken, and return an error to the client.

Thus far, the only current technical remedy to the IP-based authentication problem is for the proxy to identify this problem from the error messages of the origin servers. Once an origin server is suspected of performing IP-based access control, the proxy should stop caching this server and simply forward the client packets to the origin server unchanged. In a transparent deployment using the NECP protocol, the proxy can also inform the intercepter to stop intercepting packets destined for this server.

A nontechnical remedy is for the Web sites to avoid this method of access control. There are better methods for authenticating clients and restricting access to information that could be used instead. These methods include HTTP authentication, cookie headers, digital signatures, and encryption.

8.4.2 Proxies and Security

Proxy deployment leads to security concerns that can be classified in four major areas. The first is secure systems management. Proxies are generally high-performance, well-connected computers running complex software. This makes them prime candidates for hackers to break into and to use for various attacks. On the other hand, proxies do not score worse than other well-connected computers such as popular Web servers. Therefore, the problem of secure systems management is not really specific to proxies. Still, experience has shown that this important issue is frequently neglected, and a reminder in the context of this book seems advisable.

The second area of concern is the protection against denial-of-service attacks. In a denial-of-service attack, the attacker overloads either the proxy, the network connection to the proxy, or other necessary components like DNS servers, to prevent legitimate users from receiving service. There are multiple possible methods an attacker can use to achieve this goal. For example, the attacker could send IP fragments to the proxy, overloading the proxy and thereby preventing legitimate clients from receiving service. In contrast to a single Web site, such an attack on a proxy blocks not only a single site, but all sites for all clients using the proxy. This makes it extremely important that proxies provide a fail-over mechanism in case they become unavailable.

The third area of concern is the security of a client browsing the Web. The Secure Socket Layer (SSL) protocol is generally used to secure traffic between a client and a Web server. The use of SSL protects the privacy and integrity of the data transmitted. Since SSL aims at ensuring end-to-end privacy, it by definition precludes the use of proxies, which stand in between the intended communicating parties. The SSL issue is therefore a concern for proxy caching because SSL narrows the applicability of the latter: ubiquitous use of SSL would push proxies into oblivion.

The last area of concern is integrity of the content. Since caches do serve data for a Web server, it is important to ensure not only that the content is up to date (as described in Chapter 10), but also that the content cannot be substituted or altered by an attacker. In the context of proxies, there are two potential problems. The first is the retrieval of the content from the origin server. The attacker could pose as the origin server to the proxy by, for example, subverting the routing infrastructure. Requests to the origin server would then be fulfilled by the attacker, which could replace the content of the Web site arbitrarily. The second possible problem is that an attacker could target the proxy itself. An attacker breaking into the proxy can add, delete, and replace cached documents arbitrarily.

In terms of integrity, explicit proxies have one additional area of concern. An explicit proxy has to perform a DNS resolution to find the origin server. This DNS resolution could be intercepted by an attacker that could trick the explicit proxy into retrieving the content from the wrong server. Interception proxies do not face the DNS problem, since they already know the IP address of the origin server and do not have to resolve a DNS name to reach it.

8.5   Summary

A key issue in proxy deployment is delivering client requests to the proxy. The main alternatives include nontransparent deployment, where clients explicitly send requests to the proxy, and transparent deployment, which leaves clients unaware at the IP layer of the proxy's existence.

With nontransparent deployment, the client knows at the IP layer that it speaks to a proxy and not the origin server; therefore, the client must somehow be told to communicate with the proxy. This can be achieved through explicit client configuration, an autoconfiguration file using a configured URL, or autodiscovery of the configuration file. Proxies deployed in a nontransparant manner are called explicit proxies.

Transparent proxy deployment relies on a network element that intercepts requests from clients to origin servers and diverts these requests to the proxy. Proxies deployed using this method are called interception proxies. Request interception can occur at the transport layer (L4) or application layer (L7), and can be accomplished by a switch (L4 or L7 switch), a router, or a special device interposed in a network link (an intercepting link). L4 elements interpret only IP and TCP headers of packets and use destination IP addresses to choose a proxy for the request. Some routers, intercepting links, and L4 switches operate at this layer. L7 elements, represented by L7 switches, can interpret the contents of the request and use this content in choosing a proxy for the request or for implementing fine-grained quality of service policies. However, such content awareness comes at a cost and significantly reduces the throughput of the network element. L4 elements are simpler and leave more processing to the proxy itself but have less sophisticated policies. Recently, intercepting elements that historically operated at the L4 layer have been adding optional content-aware features, while L7 elements have allowed operation in the L4 mode. With this convergence, the choice between L4 and L7 interception is becoming a choice between operation modes rather than products, and the product choice is increasingly based on issues such as price and performance.

Explicit proxies require client configuration and rely on cooperation from the clients. Interception proxies have their own limitations, such as a need for careful placement in the network to avoid a possibility of connection disruptions, disruption of IP-based access control, and more limited reuse of TCP connections. These pitfalls stem from the fact that interception proxies violate the end-to-end principle of the Internet.

For an environment such as an enterprise network where both proxies and clients belong to the same administrative domain, deciding between explicit and interception deployment is a matter of the tradeoff between upholding the end-to-end Internet principle versus administrative convenience and proxy enforcement (forcing clients to go through a proxy may be motivated by the desire to monitor or control users' Web surfing). In environments where clients are outside the control of the network administrator deploying the proxy, interception proxies may be the only feasible alternative.

Chapter 9
Cooperative Proxy Caching

The main mission of a proxy server is to provide a shared cache to multiple clients. This shared cache allows a client to take advantage of a cached copy when the client retrieves an object for the first time if that object was previously requested by another client. Intuitively, the benefit from the shared cache increases with the size of the client population using it.

There are two potential problems in serving a very large client community. First, as the client population grows, so does the request rate that the proxy must process. We refer to the problem of handling the request rate as the *load scalability* problem. Second, a large client population is necessarily dispersed over a wide geographical area. Therefore, a proxy serving a large client population is far removed in the network from many of its clients. The advantage of obtaining objects from the proxy cache rather than from the origin server becomes questionable. We call the scalability limitations due to the geographical dispersion of clients the *geographical scalability* problem. Cooperative proxy caching has the potential to provide both load scalability, by sharing requests from many clients among individual caches, and geographical scalability, by servicing requests coming from nearby clients.

This chapter discusses different methods of *cooperative proxy caching*, which is defined as individual proxies sharing their cached objects with each other's clients. While all the cooperation models described here have been implemented and most of them are available for free download, not all of them have been widely deployed. Further, existing deployments sometimes combine several of the models we describe.

Before discussing the details of cooperative proxy caching, let us first introduce some terminology. Consider a client that sends a request for an object to a proxy cache that participates in a cooperative caching scheme (Chapter 8 examines various ways in which a request may arrive at this proxy). If the proxy has the object locally in its cache, the request is a *local hit*. If the request does not hit locally, it is a *local miss*. In the context of cooperative caching, the proxy can fetch the object from another proxy, in which case the request is called a *remote hit*. Finally, if the proxy fetches the object from the origin server, the request is called a *global miss*.

9.1 Shared Cache: How Big Is Big Enough?

Much research effort has gone into enabling cooperation between different proxies. The underlying belief has been that the more clients that can share the cache, the better. In addition, early proxies were capable of processing only around fifty requests per second, so a central proxy often became a performance bottleneck. Great strides have since been made in improving proxy performance. The best-performing proxy in an independent evaluation conducted in 2000 [Rousskov et al. 2000] sold for around $51,000 and processed 2,400 requests per second. The best-performing proxy per dollar in the same study could process 1,450 requests per second for less than $15,000. According to Wolmann et al. [1999a], 23,000 clients in their study generated a peak rate of 290 requests per second. Using the results from Rousskov et al. and allowing for spare capacity by a factor of two to ensure that the proxy is not overloaded, we calculate the cheaper proxy can sustain 725 requests per second. This request rate allows the cheaper proxy to serve over 60,000 clients in this specific setting. While browsing characteristics of residential or industrial users may differ, a single modern proxy can clearly serve entire companies, universities, or small cities.

Now let us consider the question of how large a client population should ideally share a proxy. To give a definitive answer to this question, one would need to analyze access logs from millions of clients. Unfortunately, it is very difficult to obtain such access logs. In the absence of this data, various researchers analyzed smaller client populations, on the order of tens of thousands of clients, and found that the hit rate grows logarithmically with population size [Duska et al. 1997; Gribble and Brewer 1997; Wolman et al. 1999b]. By extrapolating the logarithmic curve until it reaches the maximum possible hit ratio (equal to the fraction of cacheable requests), Wolman et al. [1999b] found that no additional benefit could be gained by sharing the proxy beyond 2.4 million clients. In fact, benefits become marginal for populations of more than 5,000 clients. This part of the analyses by Wolman et al. did not take into account that Web documents change over time. The analyses assumed that once a document is accessed by one client, all subsequent accesses to this document from any other client in the population are satisfied from the proxy, regardless of the time interval between the accesses. In fact, documents do change and then must be refetched from the origin server.

The study by Wolman et al. also built an analytical model to account for document changes, using modification rates that they observed in one of their traces. They found that the cooperative hit rate is extremely sensitive to the modification rate. By varying the modification rate between the median and mean values observed in the trace, they found that the client population required to achieve 90 percent of the maximum possible hit rate ranged from 250,000 to nearly 20 million. We refer to the population that achieves 90 percent of the maximum hit rate as the *beneficial population*. At the low end of the estimate the beneficial population can be served by a small number of modern proxies. Thus the issue of load scalability has largely become a question of which is less expensive, a cooperative system of smaller proxies or a larger centralized proxy. However, as proxies implement more computationally intensive value-added services, the limits of proxy capacities may again be tested.

With respect to geographical scalability, Wolman et al. observed that at the low end of the estimate the beneficial population of clients can be assembled in a medium-sized city. In fact, the study showed that some cooperation mechanisms led to a degradation of the overall response time when the user population grew far beyond the beneficial size. The degradation occurs because the marginal extra benefits from a larger population cannot compensate for the increased latency of obtaining objects from far-away proxies. These observations led Wolman et al. to conclude that cooperative caching is advantageous at the level of cities with a population of 250,000 to 500,000 clients, but not in a broader geographical area.

Still, there are several reasons why it is useful to consider cooperative caching mechanisms for larger regions than cities with a population of 250,000 to 500,000 clients. First, an ISP is likely to favor caching within its own network over cooperation with proxies in other networks. The main reason is that most ISPs try to reduce the amount of traffic they exchange with upstream ISPs from whom they purchase bandwidth. Further, most packet delays and losses occur at the exchange points between ISPs, so avoiding inter-ISP traffic improves user experiences as well. Most ISPs would likely be unable to assemble hundreds of thousands users in a single metropolitan area: even the largest ISP, America Online, only has on the order of 30 million users; other large ISPs have client populations in single millions, spread across North America and beyond. A likely scenario is that an ISP would deploy proxies at individual points of presence over a broad area and make them cooperate to reduce traffic over its Internet connections. In this scenario, geographical scalability remains important even for low-end estimates of the beneficial population size.

In addition, the beneficial population size produced by the Wolman et al. model is very sensitive to the modification rate and the total size of the Web. As already mentioned, changing the modification rate between the mean and the median values observed in the trace results in the range of the beneficial population spanning two orders of magnitude. Increasing the total number of documents on the Web by a factor of 10 increases the beneficial population by a factor of 100. Moreover, the model in Wolman et al. assumes a fixed set of Web objects and a steady popularity distribution among them. Accounting for new objects and popularity shifts would increase the beneficial population size even further. Intuitively, if a new document becomes popular, the cooperative proxy must fetch it only once for the entire population; however, if the population is split among n independent proxies, the document would have to be fetched n times, and the aggregate miss rate for this document would be n times higher.

Finally, while any given user might not benefit from cooperating with more than half a million other users, the populations of cooperating users may overlap to improve the proximity of these users to their proxies. Compare Figure 9.1a showing isolated cooperating populations with Figure 9.1b depicting overlapping populations. User X

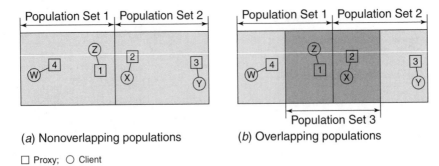

(*a*) Nonoverlapping populations   (*b*) Overlapping populations

☐ Proxy; ○ Client

Figure 9.1 Populations of proxy sharing users

in Figure 9.1a must cooperate with proxies in its cooperation area, while some proxies in an adjacent area may actually be closer. If instead cooperating populations overlap as in Figure 9.1b, proximity for user X to its proxies would improve. When cooperating populations overlap, proxies must participate in cooperation within all population sets to which they belong. For example, proxy 2 must cooperate with proxy 1, so that user X can obtain an object from proxy 2 via proxy 1; at the same time, proxy 2 must cooperate with proxy 3 to allow user Y to obtain objects from proxy 2 via proxy 3. The result is a wide area cooperation scheme. In fact, several large-scale cooperation schemes considered in this chapter exploit precisely this idea of cooperation among limited but overlapping populations.

9.2 Issues in Cooperative Proxy Caching

Cooperative proxy caching gives rise to two fundamental issues.

- How can a proxy find out which other proxies (if any) have a document it needs? We call this a *location management* problem of cooperative caching. Location management is discussed in Section 9.3.

- How can a proxy decide whether to fetch an object from a peer proxy or from the origin server? In a global network, the origin server may be closer or better connected than the proxy that has the requested object. We refer to this problem as a *proxy pruning* problem. We consider the pruning problem in Section 9.4.

Another issue that arises in cooperating proxies is how individual proxies cooperate to remove objects from the cache if no space is available to store additional objects. The rules governing this removal are called the *global cache replacement policy*. As we argue in Chapter 11, a replacement policy is not very important for a proxy considered as a whole system. We therefore assume that each proxy implements an independent replacement policy, and in this chapter we concentrate on location management and pruning.

Finally, we would like to reiterate the point that the ultimate performance goal of Web caching is to reduce user latency and network bandwidth consumption. In the context of cooperative caching, the bandwidth issue includes two aspects: bandwidth consumption external to a group of cooperating proxies and overall bandwidth consumption, including internal traffic between proxies. The relative importance of the two aspects depends on the environment. If cooperative caching is done within an ISP with the purpose of reducing traffic on its upstream connections, then external bandwidth consumption is the overriding concern. The same is true for a situation where cooperative caching is done within a region with a poor or expensive connection to the rest of the Internet. If cooperative caching is done to localize traffic and reduce general bandwidth consumption on the network, then interproxy traffic also becomes important. In particular, one must consider the traffic overhead of the cache cooperation mechanism itself in this case.

9.3 Location Management

Following are the main alternatives for location management.

- *Broadcast queries:* A proxy looking for an object issues a query to other proxies with which it cooperates.

- *Hierarchical caching:* The cooperating proxies are arranged into a hierarchy and a proxy sends all locally missed requests to its parent in the hierarchy.

- *URL hashing:* A hash function maps all possible URLs to individual proxies, so that each proxy becomes responsible for a well-known subset of all Web resources.

- *Directory-based cooperation:* An explicit directory service tracks the whereabouts of cached objects.

9.3.1 Broadcast Queries

The earliest cooperation model, and one that is still popular, is based on *broadcast queries*. The basic idea of a broadcast query is that when a proxy receives a client request for a cacheable object that is not in its local cache (a local miss), the proxy sends a probe for this object to all other proxies it cooperates with.

Broadcast queries were introduced by the Harvest hierarchical cache [Chankhunthod et al. 1996] The protocol used to exchange queries and responses, called ICP (Internet Cache Protocol) [Wessels and Claffy 1997] is supported by many proxy vendors. To improve scalability, ICP allows a hierarchical arrangement of proxies, and we concentrate on this *hierarchical query broadcast* model here.

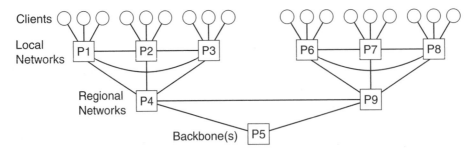

Figure 9.2 Broadcast query cooperation model

As Figure 9.2 illustrates, browser clients in this cooperation scheme are connected to *leaf* proxies; a leaf proxy is connected to several other leaf proxies, called *siblings* or *peers*, and to one or more *parent* proxies; parent proxies, again, connect to their siblings and parents. For example, in Figure 9.2 proxies P1, P2, and P3 are leaf proxies and siblings. Proxy P4 is the parent of P1, P2, and P3 and the sibling of P9; P5 is the parent of P4.

On a local miss, a leaf proxy broadcasts a query to all its siblings and parents. The query contains the requested URL, and the recipients respond with a hit or a miss, depending on whether or not they have the object in their cache. The requesting proxy fetches the object from the first proxy that responds with a hit. The rationale is that the proxy that was the first to respond to the probe might be closer in the network and/or less loaded than the rest of the proxies. Thus, it may also be the fastest proxy to service the object itself. Obviously, this is just a heuristic. If all probed proxies respond with a miss or if no hit responses have arrived within a timeout window, the requesting proxy sends the HTTP request for the object to the first parent that responded with a miss.

To choose between fetching an object from a proxy and fetching it from the origin server, the leaf proxy also sends an ICMP *echo* request to the origin server. In compliance with ICMP the server replies to this request with an ICMP echo response as soon as it receives the request. If this response returns before any hits from the proxies, the requesting proxy sends the HTTP request for the object to the origin server.

When the leaf proxy sends the HTTP request to a parent, the parent recursively executes the same protocol: it probes its parents, siblings, and the origin server and gets the object from the first server to respond with a hit.

This model has several advantages. First, little agreement is needed to join the hierarchy. All a joining proxy needs is permission from at least some parents and siblings to probe them. In the case of siblings, it is expected that the proxy joining a hierarchy at a certain level will agree to be probed by its siblings in return. Most importantly, it is easy to grow the hierarchy incrementally, because the effects of a proxy joining and departing the hierarchy are localized to the immediate neighbors in the hierarchy.

Another advantage is that the hierarchy can be arranged to reflect the network topology. In other words, proxies enter into leaf-sibling agreements if they are close in the network to each other (for example, they connect to the same regional network). A natural parent for such proxies is a regional proxy belonging to that regional network. Regional proxies can also peer and can use a national proxy as their parent. Only if the request misses at the national proxy does it travel outside the national backbone to the origin server. This method improves geographic scalability, especially when the Internet is arranged as a loose collection of internally well-connected clusters. European and Asian networks provide an example of such arrangements, where well-connected national backbones have rather limited-bandwidth external links. It is not a coincidence that proxy hierarchies became especially popular there.

A further advantage is that the simple heuristic used to choose a remote proxy also minimizes the time the requesting proxy must wait before fetching the object from another proxy. The object is fetched after the *fastest* hit response arrives.

There are also several important disadvantages to this model. The proxy hierarchy does not scale to large numbers of siblings and parents. Indeed, a proxy must wait for the *last* miss to arrive (or for a timeout) before concluding that none of the neighbors has the object and sending the request to the next level of the hierarchy. The likelihood of some response being delayed (or worse, not delivered at all because of a network or neighbor proxy failure) increases exponentially with the number of neighbors. This limits the number of neighbors a proxy can have before its miss latency (that is, the latency of a request that misses in lower levels of the hierarchy) increases unacceptably.

Another drawback is extra traffic and overhead on the proxy generated by ICP queries. According to National Laboratory for Applied Network Research statistics, each proxy has to deal with many more ICP queries than HTTP requests [NLANR 2001]. Running their benchmark through a four-sibling configuration of Squid proxies, Fan et al. [1998] observed around 20 to 24 percent CPU overhead and 8 to 13 percent data packet increase over noncooperating proxies, depending on the hit rates. Observe also that although network-level multicast could reduce the traffic overhead of ICP queries, each ICP response is inherently a unicast message.

Since these overheads limit the number of siblings, the other way to scale the hierarchy is to increase its depth. However, a deep hierarchy also hurts performance, albeit in a different way. Consider processing a global miss, that is, a request for an object not cached by any of the proxies. Assume that the origin server is always slower than a proxy's parent, meaning that a proxy always forwards a request that missed at its level to its parent. A global miss request will therefore be forwarded from one proxy to another on the path from the leaf proxy that initially received the request to the root of the hierarchy and then to the origin server. The server response will traverse the same path in return. Since every proxy on this path introduces a delay, such multilevel traversal increases latency for global misses. Tewari et al. [1999] studied the latency of downloads through a chain of Squid proxies and found that the length of the chain directly and significantly affects the latency.

In principle, deeper hierarchies may also exhibit lower hit rates. This is because "cousins" in the hierarchy are not probed. For example, assume proxy P1 in Figure 9.2 receives a request for an object cached only by proxy P6. Proxy P1 unsuccessfully probes its siblings (proxies P2 and P3) and parent (proxy P4) and then forwards the request to proxy P4. Proxy P4 probes its siblings and parent, again without success, and so on until the request reaches the root, proxy P5 in the backbone network. The object is then fetched from the origin server. Proxy P6 is never probed for this object and its cached copy is not utilized. In practice, ample disk space at high-level proxies would make this last limitation insignificant. For instance, the situation in our example can occur only if proxy P5 purged the object from its cache after serving it to proxy P6, which would not have happened if proxy P5 had had enough cache space. With disk prices falling steadily, it is likely that a proxy will cache most objects that it serves to its descendants, and so the situation in our example will occur infrequently.

Regardless of the hierarchy depth, another factor limiting the scalability of this model is that proxies at higher levels in the hierarchy must process essentially all the misses from the lower levels. Higher-level proxies can therefore become performance bottlenecks.

To summarize, various performance factors limit both the number of siblings and the depth of the tree hierarchy in the broadcast query cooperation model. We conclude that the overall scalability of this cooperation model in its pure form is limited.

9.3.2 Hierarchical Caching

The limited scalability of the broadcast query model gives rise to a variant of the model in which proxies in the hierarchy make no sibling queries. In this case, a proxy simply sends a locally missed request to its parent in the hierarchy, without any attempt at locating the object at another proxy. The hierarchy is similar to the one shown in Figure 9.2, except that siblings are not connected.

This scheme removes the problems associated with broadcast queries. It is also often more feasible administratively, as it allows different companies to have a common parent proxy without providing access to each other's proxies. Giving up on cooperation with siblings may reduce the overall hit rate, but as described earlier, sufficient cache space at parent proxies can effectively address this issue. The issues that remain in hierachical caching are an increased load on the parent proxies, which must now process every miss from a child, and the fact that each global miss has to traverse the entire hierachy.

ICP allows a mixture of the broadcast query and pure hierarchy models. This hybrid approach allows a proxy to selectively query *some* of its siblings. The set of siblings to be queried is defined in the proxy's configuration file. Besides administrative decisions on which siblings to allow queries from, the set of cooperating siblings must reflect their relative size. Krishnan and Sugla [1998] showed that when siblings serve drastically different client populations, it is beneficial for smaller siblings to query larger ones but not the other way around. A large proxy is unlikely to find an object at a small sibling, and querying it would only add overhead.

9.3.3 URL Hashing

A simple way to allow interproxy cooperation is to divide all possible URLs among participating proxies and make all proxies agree on the partitioning rules. For instance, in the case of two cooperating proxies, all URLs with a host name in the .com domain could be assigned to one proxy and all other URLs to the other. Then, each proxy becomes responsible for processing requests for the URLs that belong to its partition of the URL namespace. In other words, whenever a proxy receives a request for an object, it forwards the request to the proxy responsible for the object's URL according to the partitioning rules. This scheme, called the *URL hashing* model, is illustrated in Figure 9.3. All proxies are interconnected to indicate that each is contacted by all other proxies for its partition of the URL namespace.

Partitioning rules can be concisely expressed using a hash function that maps any URL to a proxy. An example of a simple (but, as we will see shortly, not very good) hash function is the following mapping. For an arbitrary URL u, let MD_u be its 16Byte integer hash value using the MD5 [Gonnet and Baeza-Yates 1991] hash function. Let n be the number of participating proxies and assume that all proxies are numbered in a well-known way. We can define the hash function as $u \rightarrow MD_u$ mod n. In other words, the proxy responsible for u is the one whose number is MD_u mod n. For example, consider twenty objects and assume for simplicity that their MD5 hash values are equal to $1, 2, \ldots, 20$. Table 9.1 shows a partitioning of these objects among five proxies. The object with a hash value equal to 1 will be assigned to proxy 1 because 1 mod 5 = 1, an object whose MD5 is 9 will be assigned to proxy 4 because 9 mod 5 = 4, and so forth.

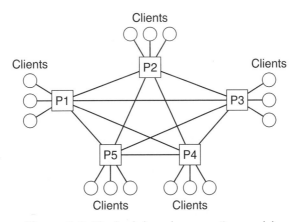

Figure 9.3 The hash-based cooperation model

Table 9.1 Object-to-Proxy Assignment Based on the Modulo Hash Function

Proxy 1	Proxy 2	Proxy 3	Proxy 4	Proxy 5
1,6,11,16	2,7,12,17	3,8,13,18	4,9,14,19	5,10,15,20

A protocol implementing URL hashing, called Cache Array Routing Protocol (CARP) [CARP n.d.] is supported by several proxy vendors, including Netscape, Microsoft, and, to a limited extent, Squid. It is easy to see that URL hashing is load scalable: to process an increased load one can always add more proxies and repartition the URL namespace. Another advantage of this cooperation model is extremely low-overhead location management. Indeed, no interproxy communication and no special information are required to locate a proxy where a requested object may be cached. Instead, each proxy autonomously computes the hash function for a requested URL and immediately knows where to forward the request. Finally, URL hashing uses cache space very efficiently, since in general it does not create duplicate cached copies of the same object.

On the other hand, CARP's geographical scalability is worse than that of the broadcast queries in Section 9.3.1, because the same proxy must process all requests for a given URL, regardless of where they come from. Further, by requiring a global agreement among all proxies on the hash function, CARP impedes incremental growth of the system. Another caveat is that the efficiency of the protocol depends on how evenly the hash function partitions the load among participants. For example, consider a simple partitioning of the URLs among 27 proxies, where all URLs starting with "a" (discarding the common prefix "http://") go to one proxy, those starting with "b" go to another, and so on, and all URLs that start with nonletter characters go to the twenty-seventh proxy. Such partitioning would result in an uneven load distribution, since a disproportionate number of URLs start with "www." Finally, a global miss generally incurs the overhead of being handled by two proxies, the one that receives the request and the one that is responsible for the requested URL. This increases the miss penalty of the scheme, although not to the extent of broadcast queries over a deep hierarchy.

Hash Disruption

An important question regarding URL hashing is what happens when a proxy is removed or added to the system. Obviously, the hash function must be redefined; otherwise, all requests for URLs assigned to removed proxies will fail, and the added proxies will never see any requests. With hash functions, even a small redefinition may lead to drastic changes in assignments of URLs to proxies. For example, consider again Table 9.1, which gives the assignment of 20 objects to 5 proxies using the modulo hash function. If proxy 5 fails, the assignments must be recalculated using mod 4 hash function. These assignments are shown in Table 9.2. Only objects 1, 2, 3, and 4

Table 9.2 Object-to-Proxy Assignment Based on the Modulo Hash Function When Proxy 5 Fails

Proxy 1	Proxy 2	Proxy 3	Proxy 4
1,5,9,13,17	2,6,10,14,18	3,7,11,15,19	4,8,12,16,20

remain assigned to the same proxies after the failure. In general, with the modulo hash function, if a proxy is added or removed, the fraction of objects that are reassigned to a new proxy (called the *disruption coefficient*) is $(m - 1)/m$, where m is the initial number of proxies [Thaler and Ravishankar 1998]. In other words, for a large number of proxies, virtually all objects get reassigned.

So why is object reassignment bad? It is bad because it makes all previously cached objects unusable. Indeed, proxies accumulate their content based on the current object assignment. In other words, a proxy can acquire only objects whose URLs hash to it. After the reassignment, requests for these objects go to a different proxy, according to the new assignment. Thus, the copy of the object cached by the old proxy is useless. When the disruption is high, the impact of the reassignments is as if all proxies purged their caches of all objects. High disruption therefore results in a great drop in hit rates and performance degradation until caches *warm up* (that is, fill with objects) again, according to the new object assignment.

Two factors further exacerbate this problem. First, because proxies tend to have large disk spaces, they warm up slowly (sometimes over a period of days); thus, hash disruption may degrade performance for a significant length of time. Second, the probability of a single proxy failure increases exponentially with the number of proxy servers. Given the catastrophic, if temporary, effect of a single failure on hit rate, this phenomenon may limit the scale of the system.

Fortunately, research into hashing addresses these and other issues related to URL hashing [Karger et al. 1997; Thaler and Ravishankar 1998]. We now turn to these solutions, one flavor of which has been implemented in Microsoft's ISA proxy.

Consistent Hashing

To avoid the problems of reassigning objects to proxies, the mapping of URLs to proxies needs to satisfy several requirements.

- When a new proxy is added, some objects must be reassigned from old proxies to the new one, so that the new proxy will be used. However, it is undesirable for objects to be reassigned from one old proxy to another, since such reassignment would increase hash disruption.

- When an existing proxy is removed or has failed, all objects assigned to it must be reassigned to the remaining proxies. Again, no objects should be reassigned from one remaining proxy to another.

- When a significant load imbalance between proxies is detected, it is desirable to reassign some objects from overloaded to underloaded proxies. However, the rest of the objects should remain assigned to their old proxies to minimize hash disruption.

Karger et al. [1997] called a hash scheme satisfying these requirements *consistent hashing*. The consistent hashing approach by Karger et al. works as follows. Consider

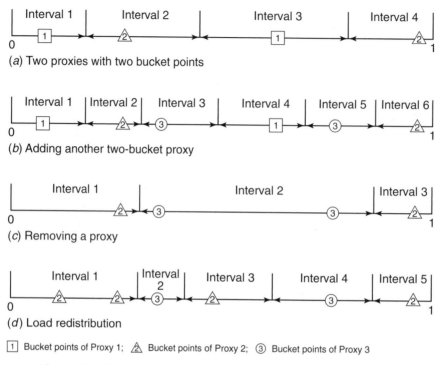

(*a*) Two proxies with two bucket points

(*b*) Adding another two-bucket proxy

(*c*) Removing a proxy

(*d*) Load redistribution

1 Bucket points of Proxy 1;   2 Bucket points of Proxy 2;   3 Bucket points of Proxy 3

Figure 9.4 Examples of consistent hashing bucket point assignments

the interval $[0, 1]$. Assume that C points on this interval are chosen at random for each proxy. We refer to these points as *bucket points*. For instance, Figure 9.4a shows bucket points for a system with two proxies where each proxy is assigned two bucket points. All proxies agree on this bucket point assignment. In other words, every proxy knows about all proxies participating in the cooperative and which points are assigned to each proxy. All proxies also agree on a hash function h that maps a URL to a random point on $[0, 1]$.[1] When a proxy receives a request for a URL, it decides which proxy is responsible for this URL by applying the following simple procedure.

1. The proxy hashes the URL to a point on the $[0, 1]$ interval using hash function h.

2. The proxy finds the closest bucket point and resolves ties consistently, for example, by always choosing the smaller among equidistant bucket points.

---

[1] These agreements are achieved by running a special protocol between proxies at system start-up and every time the bucket point assignment or hash function h changes. We do not consider the details of such a protocol here.

We refer to the interval of points closest to a particular bucket point as the *bucket interval.*

3. The proxy to which the chosen bucket point belongs becomes responsible for the URL.

Since the bucket point assignment and hash function h are well known to all proxies, a URL is assigned to its proxy unambiguously. For example, in Figure 9.4a, proxy 1 is responsible for URLs that hash into bucket intervals 1 and 3, and proxy 2 is responsible for bucket intervals 2 and 4.

When a new proxy joins the system, C new random bucket points are assigned to it, while the old proxies retain their old bucket assignments. Figure 9.4b shows possible bucket points after a third proxy joins the system. As one can see, the new proxy is assigned some of the URLs (those that hash to intervals 3 and 5 in Figure 9.4b) but no URLs are reassigned among old proxies. Thus, the first requirement on our wish list is satisfied.

To remove a proxy, one removes its bucket points from the interval (Figure 9.4c). In this way, the URLs of the removed proxy (proxy 1) are reassigned to the remaining proxies without affecting the rest of the URLs. Thus, the second desirable property is satisfied.

Satisfying the third requirement is a bit tricky, because it is not practical to construct a hash function that takes into account differences in the popularity and size of various URLs. However, one can easily adjust the load distribution among proxies if it is uneven. Increasing the load on a particular proxy entails assigning it some extra bucket points. Figure 9.4d shows that by adding extra bucket points, we add URLs that map interval 3 to proxy 2 without disrupting the assignment of other URLs.

9.3.4 Directory-Based Cooperation

Instead of probing other proxies or partitioning URL namespace, the location of cached objects in the system can be tracked explicitly by a *directory service*. In its purest form, the directory-based cooperation model has been implemented in the CRISP proxy cache [Gadde et al. 1997b; Gadde et al. 1998; Gadde 1999].

Figure 9.5 illustrates directory-based cooperative caching. Logically, the system consists of proxies and a directory service. Assume for the moment that the directory service is represented by a separate server (we explore various ways to implement the directory service in Section 9.3.5). Whenever the contents of an individual proxy change (that is, an object is added or removed), the proxy sends an appropriate notification to the directory server. The directory therefore possesses information about the location of objects cached anywhere in the system. On a local miss, a proxy queries the directory service for the requested object. The directory responds either with the identity of a proxy caching the object or with a global miss notification. Upon receiving the response the proxy fetches the object either from the proxy listed or from the

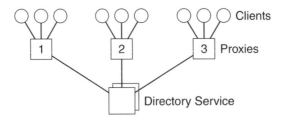

Figure 9.5 Directory-based cooperative caching

origin server. Since neither queries to nor responses from the directory service carry actual Web content, they are generally small in size. Consequently, communication between proxies and the directory service is carried over UDP, which does not provide connection-oriented, reliable delivery and therefore has less overhead than TCP.

It might appear that the directory could become the bottleneck limiting load scalability of the system. However, the directory service load can be easily distributed by partitioning the URL namespace among multiple directory servers. The mechanism for partitioning is exactly the same as in the URL-hashing cooperation model (with consistent hashing): namely, all proxies agree on a partitioning scheme among several directory servers, and, for a given URL, every proxy consistently communicates with the directory server responsible for that URL. An important difference with CARP is that since the directory does much less work per request than a proxy, there are many fewer directory servers than proxies. Also, the communication between a proxy and the directory service involves only an exchange of two UDP messages, as opposed to TCP sessions between proxies in CARP.

Another potential concern is that the directory may become a single point of failure in the system, hurting its overall fault tolerance. However, the Internet provides a ready fallback: when something goes wrong, one can always get the object from the origin server, at the cost of some additional delay.

Finally, proxies can use the same fallback to deal with an outdated directory, that is, containing some inaccurate location information. Such inconsistency may arise because of a delay between a change in cache content and notification of the directory about this change or when the directory server fails and a second directory server takes over without having current location information.

The directory-based cooperation model requires very limited agreement among proxies, resulting in a loosely coupled architecture. Individual proxies can be added to and removed from the system without the knowledge of other proxies. All a new proxy needs to know is the directory server and, in the case of multiple directory servers, the URL hashing function. The directory learns about the new proxy when the new proxy sends its first notification or query. To be removed gracefully, the proxy needs to notify the directory, which will invalidate entries that map objects to this proxy. When a proxy departs without warning (that is, fails), the directory finds out about the failure from the first live proxy that attempts to contact the failed one.

In summary, the directory-based cooperation model exhibits high load scalability and loose coupling. Its main limitation is the need for directory queries by locally missed requests. Since these queries occur synchronously with the requests that cause them (that is, the processing of the requests stalls until these queries are answered), the network delays between proxies and the directory must be low, say, 20ms at most. This limits the geographical scalability of the system.

9.3.5 Directory Structures

After our discussion of how one might use a directory service in building a cooperative proxy caching model, let us now focus on how such a directory service might be implemented. This section describes in particular fully replicated directories, partially replicated directories, coarse-grained directories, and summary caches.

Fully Replicated Directories

An obvious way to avoid synchronous directory queries is to replicate the directory on all proxy servers. Each proxy is then able to find remotely cached objects by consulting its own local copy of the directory. Figure 9.6 illustrates such a fully replicated architecture. This approach has been used in the Relais cache [Makpangou et al. 1999].

A replicated directory raises several issues. One issue is space overhead. The aggregate directory space grows linearly as the number of proxies increases. If we assume the directory for an individual proxy takes 1 percent of its cache space, the aggregate directory for a 100-proxy system will require doubling the space on every proxy. Worse, the directory should preferably be in main memory for fast access, and main memory is still a relatively limited resource.

Another issue is the overhead for keeping directory replicas consistent. This overhead includes extra traffic for sending directory updates between proxies and extra CPU time for processing these updates. Encouraging news is that studies indicate that consistency among directory replicas can be maintained well enough if proxies delay propagation of directory updates [Fan et al. 1998; Tewari et al. 1999]. Instead of

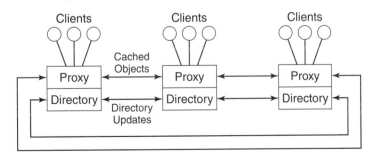

Figure 9.6 A fully replicated directory

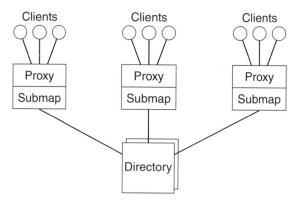

Figure 9.7 Separate directory with a replicated submap

notifying each other immediately about addition and removal events in their local proxies, they can batch multiple events and send a periodic update containing all batched events in a single message.

Partially Replicated Directories

To deal with the space overhead issue, one can try to limit directory replicas to only the most important entries. Figure 9.7 illustrates this approach, called replicated partial directory (RPD) [Gadde et al. 1997a]. The RPD approach retains a separate directory service that maintains full location information. A portion of the full directory is also replicated on every proxy. In addition to being the authoritative source of location information, the directory service in RPD determines the portion of the directory (called the *submap*) to be replicated and keeps the submap replicas consistent. For instance, the directory service may include in the submap directory entries for only those objects that are shared among multiple clients.

When a proxy receives a locally missed request, it first looks in its submap replica. If the submap contains an entry for the requested object, the proxy chooses a remote proxy among those listed as having the object and fetches the object from it. Otherwise, the proxy synchronously queries the directory service. Gadde et al. [1997a] found that replicated submaps achieve 40-percent space overhead reduction compared to replicated directories at the expense of having to generate synchronous queries in 6 percent of all requests.

Summary Caches

One could also reduce the space overhead by storing the directory in a compressed form. The key requirement here is that directory maintenance and lookups need no uncompressing and recompressing of the directory. Otherwise, CPU overhead would make this scheme impractical. An elegant solution proposed by Fan et al. [1998] employs *Bloom filters* [Bloom 1970] to represent directories in a very compact if imprecise way. An alternative implementation of the same idea is described by Rousskov and Wessels [1998]. These cache representations are called *summaries* by Fan et al. and *digests* by Rousskov and Wessels. The Bloom filter is a bit vector that represents a set of objects, URLs in our case. Bloom filters are constructed using a set of hash functions; the construction algorithm is described in the paper by Fan et al. [1998] and in Bloom's original paper [1970]. We note only the properties of Bloom filters that are important for our discussion.

Given the Bloom filter of a set X of URLs, one can efficiently but imprecisely determine whether a given URL belongs to the set. To do that, one computes the Bloom filter for a set that includes just the URL in question and compares this filter with the Bloom filter of set X. If all unity bits in the former filter correspond to unity bits in the latter filter, one assumes that the URL belongs to set X.

Bloom filters are imprecise because there is a remote chance that the test will erroneously indicate that a URL belongs to a set while in fact it does not. Such wrong answers are called *false positives*. At the same time, Bloom filters never produce falsely negative answers, that is, if the test indicates that a URL does not belong to the set, this answer is always correct. To keep the probability of false positives low, the number of bits in the Bloom filter must be at least around ten times the expected number of URLs in sets that the filter is supposed to represent. In addition, to allow efficient recalculation of the filter when an object is removed from the set, each bit in the filter is actually replaced by a four-bit counter. The result is that the size of the filter is on the order of 40bits times the maximum number of objects in the set, or 5Bytes per object.

In the summary cache approach, the global directory is represented by a set of Bloom filters, one per proxy. Each Bloom filter represents a set of URLs cached at the corresponding proxy. Every proxy stores a replica of this set of filters. On a local miss, a proxy constructs the Bloom filter for the requested URL and steps through the set of Bloom filters until it finds one for which the containment test returns a positive. The proxy then attempts to obtain the object from the proxy corresponding to that filter. If that proxy does not have the object (which would happen in the case of a false positive), the first proxy can either check the remaining Bloom filters or download the object from the origin server. To keep the Bloom filter replicas reasonably consistent, each proxy sends periodic updates of its filter to other proxies.

Spending only around 5Bytes per object, Bloom filters are obviously much more compact than traditional directories that explicitly list URLs. A main disadvantage of this approach is that it requires a very high level of agreement among proxies. They all must agree on the length of Bloom filters and the set of hash functions used in their construction. Consider, for example, the situation of a new proxy that wants to join the system and has a cache size significantly larger than that of the existing proxies. The larger cache size means that the number of objects the proxy can potentially store increases. To maintain accuracy of directory representations, all proxies must agree to increase the length of the Bloom filters. This limits the autonomy of individual proxies and the ability of the system to grow incrementally.

Coarse-Grained Directories

Another way to reduce space overhead for the replicated directory is to store coarser granularity entries there, the approach taken by the CacheMesh project [Wang 1997]. In CacheMesh, location tracking is done at the granularity of entire Web sites. Each proxy picks Web sites whose objects it wants to cache, based on the history of requests from its own clients (not from partner proxies). As it picks and drops Web sites to proxy, it announces these decisions to all other proxies. All proxies monitor each other's announcements and maintain a replicated directory that maps Web sites to proxies that cache them. On a local miss, proxy X checks its copy of the directory to see if the requested object's Web site is cached by any proxy. If so, X forwards the request to one of those remote proxies, Y.[2] The remote proxy Y serves the object to X, fetching it from the origin server if needed. Proxy X then sends the object back to its customer and may also store the object locally in a nonshared portion of its cache.

By maintaining only one entry per an entire Web site (as opposed to an entry per every object), the size of the directory is greatly reduced. On the other hand, requests are forwarded to remote proxies regardless of whether or not the requested objects are cached. Thus, some global misses incur the overhead of being processed by two proxies. Further, a proxy cannot share with other proxies any locally cached objects of sites for which it is not responsible. Hence, the degree of cache sharing is lower in CacheMesh.

9.4   Caching on a Global Scale: Proxy Pruning

None of the approaches considered so far is suitable for the scale of the global Internet. Centralized directories have limited geographical scalability because of synchronous directory probes. Replicated directories have limited scalability due to high storage overhead, which grows proportionally with the number of proxies times the individual cache size. In broadcast hierarchies, scalability is limited because either the fan-out or the depth of the hierarchy must increase with scale. Increasing the fan-out causes an exponential increase in the likelihood of query timeouts; increasing the depth increases the latency on a miss and reduces the hit rate. URL hashing does not take network proximity into account; increasing geographical scale causes objects to be fetched from increasingly remote proxies. Summary caches technically do scale; however, their scalability is limited by the high level of agreement among proxies (which on the global scale necessarily belong to numerous independent administrative domains). The high agreement level also inhibits incremental growth of the system. CacheMesh has probably the most scalable location management mechanism; however its scalability comes at the expense of limited cache sharing and a performance penalty for global misses.

In the global Internet, origin servers may often be closer, better connected, or more powerful than remote proxies. Therefore, the pruning problem—deciding

---

[2] In fact, CacheMesh ensures that only one proxy can cache a given Web site, but this feature is not central to our discussion.

between remote proxies and origin servers for processing a local miss—is of crucial importance for cooperative caching. In the absence of more systematic solutions,
network operators today resort to ad hoc measures in addressing this problem. For
instance, German backbone proxies could be configured to fetch .com objects from any
European proxy but never to go to any remote proxy for a .de object. The rationale
is that .de objects are most likely hosted in Germany, and such hosts are closer or
better connected than remote proxies; .com objects are typically hosted in the United
States, and such hosts are farther away than any European proxy. Such "manual"
pruning by statically configuring proxies is certainly better than nothing. However,
it is too static and coarse-grained, as it does not account for differences in connectivity and processing capacity of individual sites, nor can it react to changing network
conditions and server load. Furthermore, the global economy reduces the correlation of the higher-level domain names with network locations. An increasing number
of .com sites are hosted outside the United States, and, conversely, many sites with
non-American top-level domains reside there.

At first glance, pruning seems fairly straightforward. An individual proxy can
maintain some metrics regarding the distance between itself and Web sites and remote
proxies it has accessed. Examples of metrics include hop counts in network paths,
latency of previous downloads (perhaps normalized by the object size), or another
metric such as those considered in Chapter 16. On a local miss, once the proxy finds
out which remote proxies have the requested object, it can choose between the remote
proxies as well as between remote proxies and the origin server based on the distance
to these proxies and the origin. When the metrics for some proxies or the origin server
involved are not available, heuristics can come to the rescue.

Even this seemingly simple approach involves a lot of technical details, which we
describe further in Chapter 16. What metric should be used? How should the distance
values be collected: using active measurements (for example, using the traceroute
utility, ICMP echo requests to measure delays, and so on) or passive measurements
(such as measuring performance of HTTP downloads that occur anyway)? How often
should measurements be taken and *aged* (that is, how should old measurements be
phased out)? Which heuristics should be used when distances to some proxies or
origin servers are not available?

Answering these questions would require delving into low-level details in networking. Instead, we concentrate in this section on how proxy pruning can improve
scalability (and especially geographical scalability) of location management. By addressing the pruning problem, this section considers some approaches for building
truly global caching platforms that become an integral part of the global Internet
fabric.

9.4.1 System Model

So far we have assumed that proxies are willing to accept requests from all other cooperating proxies. This assumption is justified when all cooperating proxies belong to
the same enterprise such as an ISP. In the global Internet this is not the case. Different

ISPs, companies, and individuals might own proxies. They all have diverse performance, legal, and security constraints that have to be accepted by the users of their
proxies. To reflect these constraints we introduce the *agreement model*. The agreement
model assumes that each proxy negotiates cooperation agreements with other proxies
to share each other's objects and accepts requests only from its clients or other proxies
with which it has agreements.

Proxies that have a cooperation agreement with each other are referred to as *neighbors*. The agreement can be symmetric, in which case both sides agree to serve requests
from each other, or asymmetric, where requests can flow between the neighbors only
in one direction. On a local miss, a proxy may send the request either to the origin
server or to one of its neighbors. The proxy cannot send the request to a nonneighbor
remote proxy even if it knows that the remote proxy has the object. The proxy must
send the request to one of its neighbors, who can forward it to its neighbors, and so
on until the request reaches the target proxy.

While one would expect that agreements link proxies that are close to each other
in the network, there is no direct correspondence between proxy neighbors and their
underlying network topology. As an example, Figure 9.8 depicts an imaginary portion
of the Internet. Figure 9.9 shows a possible proxy topology graph, with proxies and
links corresponding to proxy agreements, for the portion of the Internet shown in
Figure 9.8. Note that P1 and P3 are not connected in the proxy topology graph despite
being close in the network, because there is no agreement between the two. Also,
P3 and P4 are connected even though their networks do not peer directly on the IP
layer.

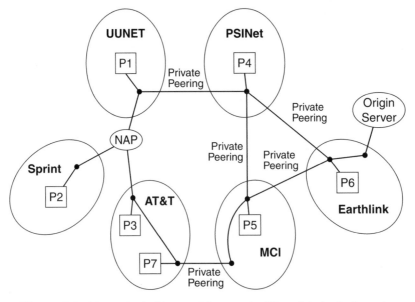

Figure 9.8 A hypothetical Internet fragment with a global set of proxies

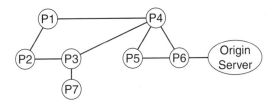

Figure 9.9 The proxy topology graph corresponding to the
Internet topology of Figure 9.8

9.4.2 Cache Routing

In the *cache routing* approach, a proxy sends a locally missed request to the neighbor proxy *in the direction of the origin server*. In this way both location and pruning problems can be circumvented. The location problem is eliminated because proxies do not track the location of objects cached at remote proxies. Requests are routed from proxy to proxy whether or not the proxies contain the requested objects. The pruning problem does not arise because cache routing effectively prunes all proxies that are off the path from the initial proxy to the origin server.

For example, consider again the network in Figure 9.8. When proxy P2 receives a request for an object residing on the origin server shown, the proxy forwards the request to proxy P1, since the latter is closer in the network to the origin server. Then P1 sends the request on to P4, which forwards it to P6, which finally sends it to the origin server.

Cache routing replaces the location management problem with the problem of maintaining cache routing tables. In our example, proxy P2 must know that the neighbor en route to the origin server for the requested object is proxy P1. In other words, each proxy must maintain the table that maps host portions of URLs to the next-hop proxy in the direction of that host. These tables are semantically very similar to routing tables used by network routers, and are called *cache routing tables*. One important difference between cache routing tables and regular routing tables is that the former do not have to be complete. If the routing table on a router misses the entry for a host, the router will be unable to handle packets addressed to that host. If a cache routing table misses an entry, the proxy can always simply obtain the object from its origin server.

Maintaining Cache Routing Tables

One way to maintain cache routing tables is by using network topology information from the routing tables of network routers [Grimm et al. 1998]. Assume for simplicity that each ISP in Figure 9.8 consists of a single autonomous system. In this approach, the system administrator of each proxy first manually assigns each bordering autonomous system to the neighbor proxy that is closest to that AS.

For instance, in Figure 9.8, AT&T connects to Sprint, UUNET, and MCI. According to the proxy topology in Figure 9.9, the AT&T proxy P3 has neighbors P2, P4, and

P7. P3's administrator would then assign the Sprint AS to neighbor proxy P2 and the MCI AS to neighbor proxy P7. No proxy will be assigned to UUNET, since neither of its neighbor proxies is closer in the network to UUNET than P3 itself. Turning to proxy P7, it has only proxy P3 as a neighbor. P7's administrator would assign Sprint and UUNET autonomous systems to P3; it will not assign any proxy to MCI. These assignments are based on the system administrator's knowledge of network topology and the location of neighbor proxies in the network. Given a relatively small number of bordering autonomous systems and neighbor proxies, this task is not impractical.

For each destination, a proxy determines the bordering autonomous system through which packets to that destination will be routed. This information can be extracted from the routing databases kept at the proxy's own ISP. (The proposal in Grimm et al. [1998] to use the traceroute utility for this purpose seems expensive, even with the described optimizations.)

Once the bordering autonomous system is determined, the proxy lists the corresponding neighbor as the next-hop proxy for the destination in its cache routing table. The cache routing table has a special entry for the bordering ASs that are not assigned to any next-hop proxy (like UUNET in the case of proxy P3 or MCI for proxy P7 in Figure 9.9). If the path to the origin server of a requested object goes through such an AS, the proxy will fetch the object directly from the origin server.

It is worth noting that this mechanism for building cache routing tables does not make use of a neighbor proxy if it belongs to a nonbordering autonomous system. For instance, in Figure 9.9 P3 never routes a request to neighbor P4, because P4's PSINet does not border AT&T. Another limitation is that a proxy builds its routing table based on routes from itself to various origin servers. Due to asymmetric routing, these routes are often very different from the routes that objects take from their origin servers to the proxy. Given that objects are typically much larger than requests, the latter routes are more important for bandwidth consumption and transfer times.

Another way to build cache routing tables is to mimic a *distance vector* protocol once used by network routers [Michel et al. 1998]. Without getting into the issue of various routing protocols, one simple scheme is as follows. Each origin server records in its configuration files the identity of a few nearby proxies (its neighbor proxies). This information is filled in by the origin server's system administrator based on knowledge of the network. Each origin server X notifies its neighboring proxies that they can access it in one hop. Each proxy records this information in its cache routing table and sends the notification to its neighbor proxies that it can reach X in one hop. A neighbor proxy records in its table that it can each X in two hops (unless the entry for X already indicates that it can be reached more quickly via a different path). In this way, each proxy knows how many hops away a given origin server is and what the next proxy in the direction of the origin is. Notice that, under the agreement model, this mechanism counts hops in the proxy topology graph. These hops do not directly correspond to network topology.

Instead of hops in the proxy topology graph, cache routing can use a variety of other distance metrics. For instance, another metric used by Michel et al. [1998] is the average time to obtain a page as the metric. In this approach, when proxy A advertises to proxy B that it can download a page from server X in time t_a, proxy B advertises that it can do so in time $t_B = t_A + t_{AB}$, where t_{AB} is the time it takes proxy B to obtain a page from A. The time-based metric better reflects user experience, while the hops metric changes less frequently and hence produces more stable cache routes.

Pros and Cons of Cache Routing

The amount of location information in cache routing is similar to that in the CacheMesh approach: one entry per Web site. Moreover, cache routing avoids bad decisions in choosing between a remote proxy and the origin server, in terms of the network proximity.

Cache routing does not always make optimal decisions. On a global miss, the network path through the proxy chain can be longer than going directly to the origin server. Considering the hops metric again, proxy P2 in Figure 9.9 will always forward missed requests for the origin server shown through proxies P1, P4, and P6. However, there might be a shorter route between proxy P2 and the origin server that will not be taken if it has no intermediate proxies. On a remote hit, cache routing guarantees that a proxy will fetch objects from a remote proxy only when it is closer than the origin server, assuming the distance between nonneighbors is always greater than the distance between neighbors. Since this is not always the case, routing decisions may be suboptimal even for hits.

Still, cache routing is intuitively appealing for reducing Internet bandwidth consumption. Also, cache routing performs location management at the granularity of Web sites rather than individual objects and thus has low location management overhead.

On the other hand, by always pruning all proxies that are off the path from the proxy receiving the initial request to the origin server, cache routing limits proxy sharing. In Figure 9.9, proxy P3 is closer to proxy P2 than the origin server. However, P3 will not fetch objects from P2 because P2 is off the shortest path toward the origin server. Also, cache routing forwards a missed request through a chain of several proxies on its way to the origin server. This increases the latency of a missed request unless all neighbor proxies maintain persistent connections. With persistent connections, the impact of proxy routing on latency is unclear. (As we saw in Section 7.2.5, splitting connections along the path may increase the effective end-to-end bandwidth, which would have a positive effect on latency.)

9.4.3 Vicinity Caching

Unlike cache routing, the *vicinity caching* approach [Rabinovich et al. 1998] performs proxy pruning explicitly, based on observed costs of object fetches from various proxies and origin servers.

In this approach, proxy A defines a *vicinity* of other proxies relative to a given Web site. Informally, proxy B is in the vicinity of proxy A relative to the origin server if it is preferable for A to fetch objects from proxy B. Note that a proxy defines different vicinities for different Web sites. A very distant, poorly connected, or slow site will have a large vicinity, since many proxies would be preferable to it. A fast and well-connected site may have a small or empty vicinity, since fetching an object from this site is faster than from almost any remote proxy. As in the example of the German backbone, a vicinity for most .com sites might include all European proxies while the vicinity of many .de sites would be empty.

The key idea is that each proxy tracks object location only in the vicinities that correspond to their origin server. Deciding between a remote proxy and the origin server becomes trivial: if proxy A's directory indicates that the object is cached on a remote proxy or proxies, the proxy looking for the object fetches it from one of the remote proxies, since any of them are preferable to the origin server by the definition of the vicinity; otherwise, the proxy looking for the object fetches it from the origin server. Limiting the locally stored directory to vicinities also reduces the directory size that each proxy must maintain.

Note that the directories kept by different proxies differ even if all updates have propagated to all proxies: they contain substantially different information, since different proxies have different vicinities for the same Web sites. For example, a German proxy may have an empty vicinity for a well-connected German site. Therefore, its directory will never contain any objects from this site. On the other hand, an American proxy will likely have many other American proxies in the vicinity for the same German site. Consequently, it will have directory entries for the site's objects.

Consider proxy A. As it communicates with its neighbor proxies and origin servers, it maintains a table of distances between itself and these proxies and origin servers. As in cache routing, the distance can be derived from a variety of metrics, including both performance and monetary costs. To be specific, we assume that it reflects the latency of arrival of the first portion of the response from the other party [Vingralek et al. 1999b]. Entries in the cache directory of proxy A contain the distance of the cached object from A as well as the neighbor proxy through which the object can be obtained. The entries have the form *object-key, neighbor-proxy, distance*, where *neighbor-proxy* is the neighbor proxy B through which A may obtain the object and *distance* is the distance between A and the proxy that caches the object. Note that the latter may be different from *neighbor-proxy*. Thus, this directory entry only indicates that A should send its request for the object to its *neighbor-proxy*, which might in turn have to fetch it from elsewhere to satisfy the request. The distance, however, indicates the actual total distance between A and the remote proxy that caches the object.

Neighbor proxies periodically exchange updates to their directories that have accumulated since the previous exchange. When processing a new batch of updates, a proxy applies pruning by accepting a new entry only if the distance to the cached object is smaller than the distance to the object's origin server and if the directory does not already point to a closer copy of the same object.

To be more specific, let proxy A receive a directory update from neighbor B, where the distance between B and A is d_{AB}. Then, if an entry in this update indicates distance d_A to the cached copy, the total distance from proxy A to the cached object is

$d_A = d_B + d_{AB}$. This is because d_B reflects the distance to the cached object from proxy B, and proxy A would have to fetch the object through B. Thus, A will accept the entry only if the distance to the object origin server *and* the distance to other cached copies of this object that A already knows about (if any) exceed d_A.[3] If A does not know the distance to the origin server (which can happen when A has never obtained any object from this site before, or if this is an obscure site not worth tracking), A can apply various heuristics to decide whether to accept the entry. For example, if A is in Germany, it may decide to accept the entry for a .de object if d_A is below 0.5 seconds and accept the entry for a .com object if d_A is below 5 seconds.

Vicinity caching does not have the proxy sharing limitation of cache routing; its usage of remote proxies is independent of whether or not they are on the path to the origin servers. It also does not forward requests to remote proxies unless it has a good indication that the object is cached there. Thus, vicinity caching has a low latency penalty on a global miss.

On the other hand, because vicinity caching performs location management at the granularity of individual objects, its location management overhead can be much higher than that of cache routing. Vicinity caching limits the location management overhead by propagating directory updates in batches periodically, and by pruning the updates once they reach proxies outside their vicinities. In fact, the location management overhead can always be controlled by pruning more directory updates. In other words, a proxy can arbitrarily reduce the amount of location information it propagates to its neighbors, to keep the location management overhead at acceptable levels (at the expense of reduced cache sharing).

9.5 An Overview of Existing Platforms

We have considered a large number of proxy cooperation models. Not all of them have been widely deployed. This section describes platforms for cooperative caching that are deployed on the Internet at the time of this writing.

9.5.1 Cache Hierarchies

Many geographical regions have built extensive caching hierarchies. They were initially constructed around the broadcast queries cooperation model and the ICP protocol that implements them. They have since evolved to include a mix of broadcast queries, cache digests,[4] and URL namespace partitioning (which is equivalent to URL

---

[3] We assume that a proxy maintains only the location of the closest cached copy of any object. For fault-tolerance or load balancing, it may actually make sense to maintain location information on more than one remote copy.

[4] Recall that cache digests is an alternative name for the summary cache scheme described in Section 9.3.5. We use the term *digests* in this section since it reflects the parlance of Squid, a dominant cache in caching hierarchies.

Table 9.3 Organizations That Maintain Caching Hierarchies

Region or Country	Organization	Web Site
U.S.A.	NLANR	http://ircache.nlanr.net/Cache/
Europe	TERENA	http://www.terena.nl/task-forces/tf-cache/
U.K.	National JANET Web caching service	http://www.cache.ja.net/
Germany	DFN University of Hanover	http://www.cache.dfn.de/
Italy	GARR working group for caching	http://www.cache.garr.net/
Far East	APAN cache working group	http://apan.net/groups/cache/index.html

hashing where the hash function is defined manually in the configuration files of individual proxies). Together, cache hierarchies comprise thousands of proxies. They are especially popular in the regions connected to the rest of the Internet via low-bandwidth, high-delay, or high-cost network connections. Table 9.3 lists organizations that maintain these platforms in several regions.

While any proxy product that supports some of the protocols used by a hierarchy can be utilized, an overwhelming majority of the caching proxies use Squid, because it supports a variety of cooperation protocols and is free. For lack of a better term, we refer to these hierarchies as Squid hierarchies.

A typical Squid hierarchy has two levels. Leaf proxies represent organizational proxies. Second-level (or root) proxies are connected to a backbone. Unlike the hierarchy in Figure 9.2, a typical Squid hierarchy is not a tree. A leaf may form sibling relations with some other leaves and child-parent relations with multiple roots. For example, in Figure 9.10, proxies 3 and 4 are siblings but have different parents, while proxies 5 and 7 have multiple parents. In the NLANR hierarchy, a leaf proxy is allowed to have up to two parents.

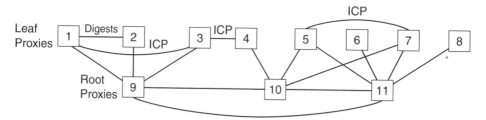

Figure 9.10 An example of a Squid hierarchy of cooperative proxies

From the perspective of an individual proxy, the difference between its leaf and parent peers is that the proxy never sends locally missed requests to a leaf peer unless it has a good reason to believe that the peer has the object. In contrast, the proxy routinely sends missed requests to its parents regardless of the parents' cache contents.

Leaf peers use either broadcast queries or cache digests to keep track of each other's cache contents. Agreeing on the protocol for location management is part of the establishment of a peering relation between the two proxies.

Any peering relationship can be qualified with the portion of the URL namespace for which this relationship is valid. In Figure 9.10 for instance, proxy 5 may be configured to use proxy 11 as a parent for URLs that match the "*.com/*" pattern, which would mean that this relationship is valid for URLs that contain the string ".com/," such as URLs on commercial Web sites.

This mechanism can be used to partition the URL namespace among a group of proxies. Consider, for example, the three cooperating root proxies 9, 10, and 11 in Figure 9.10. If 9 and 10 qualify their relation to 11 with the URL pattern "*.com/*," 10 and 11 qualify their relations to 9 with the pattern "*.edu/*," and 9 and 11 qualify their relations to 10 with "*.gov/*," then 9 will be asked to share only its cached objects that come from commercial sites, 10 will be asked for only objects from government sites, and 11 will be responsible for educational sites. The proxies will not cooperate for any other URL requests; these requests will be fetched from their origin servers on a local miss.

In theory, root proxies could use this facility to manually implement a CARP-like protocol for cooperation between each other. For that, each root proxy must specify all other root proxies as its parents, and all root proxies must be configured to identically partition the URL namespace among themselves. Then, missed requests from each root proxy will go to the root proxies designated for requested URLs, just as with CARP. However, in practice, root proxies are usually configured as siblings to each other and use broadcast queries for cooperation. They use URL namespace partitioning to concentrate objects from given Web sites at only a few root proxies to reduce the number of queries they must send. For instance, the NLANR hierarchy designates different root proxies to be responsible for different top-level domain names of Web sites (such as .com, .edu and .gov). Then the relation to a given root proxy from any other proxy (be it a leaf or another root) must be qualified accordingly.

Finally, root proxies periodically measure message delays between each other as well as between themselves and various Web sites. ICMP messages are currently used for this purpose with the hope that they will approximate the delays of data messages.[5] A root proxy uses these measurements to choose the other root proxy (or perhaps the origin server) to forward a locally missed request to. In this way, the Squid hierarchy implements some elements of cache routing and vicinity caching.

---

[5] ICMP messages may experience different delays and packet loss because they receive special treatment from routers.

9.5.2 Caching as a Service of a Network Access Point

Recall that the broadcast queries cooperation mechanism incorporates a cache hierarchy. As shown in Figure 9.2, the hierarchy structure is supposed to mimic the network topology. In other words, a proxy's parent should be located near the area in the network where the proxy would send missed requests anyway. In a sense, a cache hierarchy is trying to achieve the same thing as cache routing, except that cache routes here are defined statically and are "frozen" once the proxy starts up.

Existing Squid hierarchies blur the relation between request routes and packet routes. In these hierarchies, requests may be sent to different parents based on the domain names of sites being accessed. The goal is to maximize the global hit rate with the fewest ICP queries. This may make sense in situations where the parents are better connected to each other than to most Web sites on the Internet. Alternatively, one can emphasize the cache routing component of hierarchical caching (perhaps at the expense of the sibling queries component) by making root caching a service of major network access points. This approach is being pursued commercially by Mirror Image Internet and by NLANR (as a parallel project to the NLANR cache hierarchy).

A network access point is a local area network to which routers from various ISPs can connect and BGP-peer (see Chapter 2) with each other. It is a logical place to locate root proxies because it is where a lot of Internet traffic converges. To connect at a network access point, the proxy must act as its own little ISP, that is, have its own router that connects to the access point, as shown in Figure 9.11. However, an essential requirement is that this router BGP-peers with all ISPs that use the proxy. Otherwise, this deployment could cause harm that far outweighs any benefits.

To see this, compare the case when a proxy obtains its connectivity from a large ISP (proxy C2 in Figure 9.11) to the case when the proxy is connected directly to a NAP (cache C1). C2's large ISP likely peers with most other ISPs present at the NAP. So when a request is sent to C2 from or via one of these ISPs, say ISP3, it will be sent by

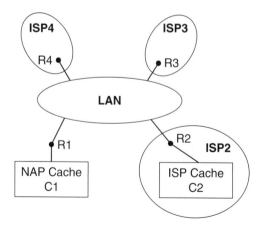

Figure 9.11 A network access point

the router of the sending ISP, R3, to the router of C2's ISP, R2. The response could be sent back via R2 and R3, or take a different path through another exchange or private peering point. Thus both the request and response traverse the exchange point at most once. On the other hand, if ISP3 sends a request to C1 without peering with C1's router R1, the request will have to first go to a router with which R1 does peer (say R4). R4 will then send the request to R1. The response will also have to traverse R4 on its way to ISP3. Thus, the exchange point LAN must handle the request and response traffic twice. Given that exchange points are already frequent bottlenecks and sources of packet loss, such load overhead is clearly undesirable. Therefore, NLANR requires that any proxy C that wants to use NLANR's NAP proxy must arrange for C's ISP to BGP-peer with the NLANR router that connects the NLANR proxy to the NAP. Thus two peering relationships must now be established, one between the proxies and one between their routers.

In summary, NAP caching works as follows. Individual ISPs can subscribe to the NAP caching service by BGP-peering with the proxy router at the NAP and having their proxies send their missed requests to the NAP proxy. The NAP proxy can download objects from their origins or from any of the ISP proxies that use its service.[6] Whether or not the ISP proxies also cooperate with each other is irrelevant to the NAP caching service.

9.5.3 Satellite Broadcast Cache Service

An interesting approach to cache cooperation is enabled by satellite networks. Recall that there are really two main advantages to cooperative caching. First, the effective cache size increases to the aggregate size of all proxies. Second, clients' first access to content can obtain cache benefits, if that content had previously been accessed by clients of another proxy.

Assume for a moment that each proxy has a cache storage so large that the first advantage becomes unimportant. In principle, the second benefit could then be achieved without any need for remote hits if content loaded into any one proxy was *pushed* immediately to all other proxies. Obviously, such content pushing would waste a great amount of bandwidth under normal circumstances. The main twist of satellite networks is that they *beam* the content to proxies, making the bandwidth consumption for content pushing independent of the number of recipient proxies. This approach has been implemeted commercially by a company called Cidera.

Figure 9.12 illustrates the system architecture. Individual proxies report to a central relay server (called the *master cache*) content they fetched from origin servers. The

---

[6] Mirror Image Internet requires that ISP proxies first send an ICP query to the NAP proxy to find out if it does have the object. The ISP proxies fetch objects that miss at the NAP proxy directly from their origin servers. Separately, the NAP proxy collects the request statistics and obtains objects that it deems valuable to have in its cache.

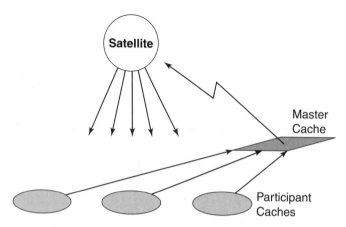

Figure 9.12 The satellite broadcast architecture

master cache obtains this content from the Internet and uploads it to the satellites, which then beam the content down to participating proxies.

The idea is appealing. Compared to other approaches we have considered, its advantage is that all hits become local, and there are no location management or pruning problems. Of course, we are painting a highly idealized picture so far. First, we assume individual proxies are large enough to hold most of the data obtained by all other proxies. In reality, only the largest ISPs could practically deploy such proxies, and then only in the core of their networks. But proxies save most bandwidth when they are deployed around the edges of networks, when requests are satisfied with minimal network traversal. Since each network entry point sees only relatively few requests, this seems to suggest that a higher number of smaller proxies would be a better investment than a centralized superproxy. Second, the bandwidth of the satellite downlink, while independent of the number of participating proxies, is limited.

These realities compel the master cache to be less aggressive in pushing content. Instead of pushing all content downloaded by any individual proxy, it tries to identify the "hottest" content to download. To this end, participating proxies send the master cache not just miss statistics (that is, what content they obtained from origin servers) but also hit statistics (what content was requested and how often). The master cache uses this information to limit content pushing to the most popular pages. This compromise introduces potential penalties. First, less popular pages will not be shared among proxies; second, sharing of hot pages is delayed until enough statistical data is collected to identify them as hot. The reduced proxy sharing may reduce the hit rate compared to more direct proxy-sharing approaches that we have considered.

Given these limitations, we see two compelling applications for the satellite broadcast approach. One is a service where content providers partner with the satellite cache provider to preload participating proxies with their content and to keep it fresh. In this model, a site (for example, cnn.com) ships its pages to the master cache whenever they change, to be pushed to the individual proxies even before they are referenced.

Thus content to be beamed is predetermined by partnering agreements and does not rely on statistics collection. This application might be of particular interest to CDNs discussed in Chapter 15. The other compelling case is when terrestrial links connecting individual proxies to the Internet have lower bandwidth than the satellite link and cannot be upgraded easily. Satellite broadcast then provides a way to alleviate this bandwidth limitation.

9.6 Summary

Table 9.4 summarizes qualitative comparisons between the various cooperation models we have considered. We are not aware of studies that quantify the involved trade-offs: various approaches have been compared to broadcast queries but not to each other. None of the methods marked with the asterisks address the pruning problem as proposed (and, to the best of our knowledge, implemented) by their authors, so the actual geographical scalability of all methods is low. High geographical scalability indicates that the method allows the cache to implement effective pruning.

Broadcast queries do not scale to many siblings because of degraded performance of missed requests. This method also generates traffic and CPU overhead for sending and processing queries. The scheme can reduce the degree of cache sharing unless the cache size of a parent proxy is sufficient to keep most of the objects cached at all its descendants. On the other hand, the scheme provides high autonomy to individual proxies. It can also scale geographically when the cache hierarchy follows the network hierarchy. Pure hierarchical caching eliminates query overhead at the

Table 9.4 A Comparison Summary of Cooperation Models

Cooperation Model[a]	Load Scalability	Geographical Scalability	Agreement Level	Location Overhead	Miss Penalty	Cache Sharing
Broadcast queries	low	high	low	highest	highest	medium
Cache hierarchy	low	high	lowest	lowest	highest	medium
URL hashing	high	lowest	high	lowest	high	medium
Pure directory	high	medium (*)	lowest	medium	low	high
Replicated directory	medium	high (*)	medium	high	lowest	high
Summary cache	high	high (*)	high	low-medium	lowest	high
Coarse-grained directory	high	low	medium	low-medium	high	medium
Cache routing	high	high	low	low-medium	(?)	medium
Vicinity cache	high	high	low	medium-high (?)	lowest	high

[a] Question marks indicate especially wild guesses. The asterisks in some boxes of the third column indicate that the degree of geographical scalability shown in the box reflects the potential scalability of the corresponding method if, in addition, the proxies address the pruning problem.

expense of further reducing cache sharing in the case of insufficient cache size of the parents.

URL hashing is best suited for a high-capacity Internet proxy implementation, or as an individual proxy in the global caching infrastructure. At the same time, URL hashing is oblivious to the network proximity factor: a locally missed request always goes to the proxy responsible for its URL, even if an object is cached at a nearby proxy.

A pure directory approach scales better geographically than URL hashing but is still limited by the need to query the directory responsible for the requested object. Replicated directories remove remote directory queries from the critical path of request processing. In addition, summary cache drastically reduces the space overhead for storing the fully replicated global directory. However, it requires a high level of agreement between participating proxies, thus inhibiting incremental growth of the system. Coarse-grained directories share many properties with URL hashing, except they allow dynamic assignment of Web sites to proxies. This may alleviate to some extent the geographical scalability limitations of URL hashing at the expense of some overhead for location management.

The two methods that incorporate proxy pruning and are directly targeted toward global deployment are cache routing and vicinity caching. Cache routing has low location management overhead. However, it does not fully utilize proxy sharing and, depending on whether or not neighbor proxies maintain persistent connections, can have high latency overhead on a miss. By using explicit cache directories, vicinity caching can provide better proxy sharing and lower miss penalty than cache routing. On the other hand, because it performs location management at the granularity of individual objects, its location management overhead can be significantly higher than that of cache routing.

Existing cooperative caching platforms include the Squid hierarchies, NLANR's and Mirror Image's NAP caching, and Cidera's satellite cache service. However, prototype implementations of most of the methods considered in this chapter are also available.

Chapter 10
Cache Consistency

As we have seen, caching creates numerous copies of Web objects scattered throughout the Internet. If an object is updated at the origin server, copies of that object cached elsewhere become *stale*. Without special mechanisms to enforce the freshness of cached data, a proxy may continue using a stale cached copy of the object. The problem of ensuring that proxies and browsers use only fresh cached content is called the *cache consistency problem*. While the cache consistency problem arises in numerous computer environments, it is especially difficult in the Web context, due to its scale and to loose coupling between origin servers on one side and proxies and browsers on the other. This chapter concentrates on approaches to the cache consistency problem on the Web.

Because much of our discussion applies to both browser and proxy caches and focuses on their interaction with origin servers where both browsers and proxies act as clients, we use the word *client* for both, except on occasions when it is useful to distinguish between the two.

There are two fundamental approaches to cache consistency: *validation* and *invalidation*. Validation refers to an approach where clients verify the validity of their cached objects with the origin server. With invalidation, the origin server notifies clients which of their cached objects have been modified. The clients mark those objects as invalid and assume that any objects they cache are always valid unless marked otherwise.

There are a variety of tradeoffs between validation and invalidation. Validation usually provides a weak consistency because objects are typically validated only periodically, to reduce the overhead of validation. Invalidation usually is done immediately after the update and has a potential for providing strong consistency. Although clients can validate objects without waiting until they are requested (such validations are called asynchronous and are discussed in Section 10.1.4), object validation in practice is typically done at the time of a request for the object. Successful validations at the request time (that is, those that find the cached copy still current) increase the response time of cache hits. Invalidation is by definition asynchronous in regards to requests and does not directly affect the response time.

On the other hand, validation simplifies life for the origin server. The origin server does not have to maintain state for consistency support. All it has to do is respond to freshness inquiries regarding specific objects. In contrast, invalidation requires the origin server to maintain lists of clients that have obtained and hence possibly cached its objects. Generally, such a *client list* must be maintained for every object on the origin server. When the origin server modifies an object, it must send a potentially large burst of invalidation messages to all the clients in its client list. These messages can cause performance degradation after object updates.

Validation may create unnecessary network traffic and increase origin server load by generating validation messages for objects that have not changed. Invalidation may also create extra traffic when an object invalidation message is sent to a client that no longer has the object or when the client will not use the invalidated object again before it is replaced in the cache with other objects.

Purely from the perspective of message overhead, the tradeoff between the two approaches is influenced by the correlation between document popularity and its rate of change. If frequently changed documents tend to be unpopular then (synchronous) validation can potentially outperform invalidation. This is because unpopular but frequently changing documents may generate many unnecessary invalidation messages. However, if there is a positive correlation between the rate of change and popularity of documents, then the validation approach must send frequent validation messages to minimize stale delivery, which may result in many unnecessary validations. In this case validation may perform worse than invalidation.

Studies trying to quantify this tradeoff arrive at contradictory conclusions. Gwertzman and Selter [1996] as well as Bestavros [1996] found that popular documents typically change infrequently, while Douglis et al. [1997a] and Wolman et al. [1999a] found just the opposite.

Currently, the Web uses validation rather than invalidation, mainly because validation greatly reduces the level of cooperation required from the origin server and because of security reasons, as described in Section 10.2. HTTP provides direct support for cache validation. The only case where invalidation is currently used is to maintain consistency of server surrogates and mirrors. Since surrogates and mirrors are under the control of content providers, origin servers can use proprietary protocols and products to perform invalidation, and security issues are also simplified.

10.1 Cache Validation

A key question for cache validation is when to send validation messages. The tradeoff is between the degree of consistency and the message and latency overhead. The more frequent the validation messages are, the lower the probability of delivering stale content from the cache, but the higher the message and latency overhead for validating unchanged objects. The extreme options are to validate on every access, which provides strong consistency at the expense of a large number of unnecessary validation messages, or never to validate, which has zero message overhead but a high probability of stale delivery. The following subsections discuss a number of intermediate solutions.

A further issue that arises with the validation approach is *synchronous* versus *asynchronous* validation. Synchronous validation of an object is done at object request time. With asynchronous validation, the client periodically checks its cached objects, identifies those objects that require validation, and validates them proactively without waiting for a request. Synchronous validation adds extra latency, while asynchronous validation has the danger of validating an object that will never be used until it expires again or is purged from the cache. We will refer to the latter as *wasted validations*.

10.1.1   The Basic Validation Scenario

Chapter 5 described a number of HTTP features that support caching. These features can be used to implement a variety of validation scenarios, all revolving around the time to live (TTL) concept (see Section 5.2). The simplest validation scenario is illustrated in Figure 10.1 in the example of the interactions between a proxy and an origin server.

The origin server, when serving a cacheable object to the proxy, supplies an explicit time to live value for the object using the `expires` or `max-age` header fields, and the timestamp of the last update to the object in the `last-modified` header in the response. Responses carrying the object and its TTL are denoted as "200 OK" in the figure.

When the proxy caches the object, the cached copy can be used until it expires, that is, it has been away from its origin server longer than its TTL. After that, the proxy must

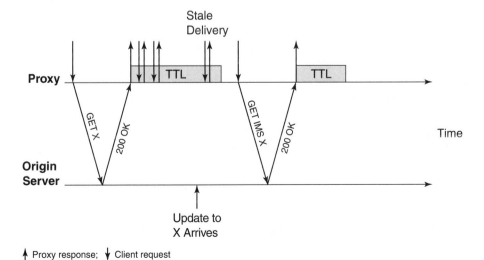

Figure 10.1 TTL-based cache validation and stale delivery

validate the cached object before using it again, by issuing a conditional request. The most common conditional request is a GET request with the `if-modified-since` (IMS) header containing the last-modified date of the cached object. Figure 10.1 shows one such request, denoted as "GET IMS".

In this validation scheme, one can distinguish two kinds of cache misses. One is when the proxy receives a request for an object that is not in its cache (*compulsory miss*). The other, called a *consistency miss* [Duska et al. 1997], is when the object is in the cache but is expired; furthermore, the subsequent validation has found that the object has changed and must be retransmitted.

There are also two kinds of hits. One kind of hit occurs when the proxy receives a request for an object that is found in the cache and has not expired. We refer to this as a *fast hit* [Dilley 1999]. Alternatively, the requested object is expired in the cache, but the subsequent validation finds it to be fresh. This outcome is called a *slow hit* [Dilley 1999].

Fast hits give the most value from the cache. Slow hits are still useful for reducing bandwidth consumption if not the latency of the response. One study found that the latency difference between slow hits and misses is several times smaller than the difference between fast and slow hits [Dilley 1999]. Finally, both compulsory and consistency misses result in additional latency due to extra processing at the proxy.

Another consequence of this validation scheme is that the proxy considers cached objects valid until they expire. Hence, it will not be aware of any changes to the object during its time to live; any such change may result in *stale delivery* as shown in Figure 10.1.

10.1.2 Implicit Time to Live

The validation scenario of the previous subsection relies on *explicit TTLs* supplied by origin servers. Explicit TTLs must be specified by Web developers as part of object creation. Unfortunately, the developers often neglect to do so, and a large majority of HTTP responses does not have any expiry information. In the absence of this information, a client must resort to heuristics to assign an *implicit TTL* to an object. The simplest heuristic, called *fixed TTL*, is to use a fixed default value—say, two hours—as an implicit relative TTL for any object without an explicit TTL.[1] Since different object types have different rates of change—images, for example, are changed much less frequently than textual objects [Douglis et al. 1997a]—it makes sense to have different default TTLs for different object types [Nottingham 1999]. Still, the fixed TTL heuristic results in too many unnecessary validation messages in some cases and too many stale deliveries in others.

Most current proxies use an *adaptive TTL* heuristic instead. This heuristic traces back to the Alex file system [Cate 1992], which was based on the assumption that the longer a file has been unchanged, the longer it tends to remain unchanged in the future. When an object is downloaded, its relative TTL is computed to be a fraction of

---

[1] Recall from Section 5.2 that time to live can be expressed in absolute form, as a future date when the object expires, or relative form, as the time since the object left the origin server.

the time interval from the object's last update to when the object was sent out by the origin server (indicated in the date response header) but not greater than a threshold:

$$\text{TTL} = \min\{(k \times (send\_time - last\_modified), threshold\}$$

where k is a constant (typically 0.1 or 0.2). The threshold is used as a sanity check, to make sure that even old objects are validated occasionally. Unlike the expires and cache-control:max-age headers, the last-modified header is supplied by the origin server automatically for all cacheable objects. In fact, most proxies do not cache objects without the last-modified header. Therefore, virtually all responses include the information necessary to compute the adaptive TTL.

A simulation based on AT&T's dial-up trace by Feldmann et al. [1999] showed that the adaptive TTL with $k = 0.2$ exhibited a very low stale delivery rate: 0.8 percent of cache hits, or 0.22 percent of all objects, were served stale. On the other hand, a majority of validation requests issued by the proxy (58.5 percent) resulted in a "Not Modified" response. These requests were in a sense unnecessary: the proxy would have delivered the correct content even if it did not do the validation. This data indicates that there is potentially room for improvement of the adaptive TTL validation scheme.

As with fixed TTL, one approach for improving adaptive TTL performance is to use different values of k for different object types. Other possibilities are described in Sections 10.1.4 and 10.2.1.

10.1.3 Fine-Tuning Validation

There will always be situations where either a client or an origin server will want to override the default validation behavior of HTTP. We already listed HTTP headers that can be used for this purpose in Chapter 5. This subsection describes additional, more complicated scenarios.

Consider a client accessing the Web via a proxy. The client may instruct the proxy to postpone validation of an object by including in the request the cache-control header with max-stale=<*seconds*> directive. This directive indicates to the proxy that the client is willing to accept a nonvalidated copy that exceeds its TTL by a given number of seconds. Postponing validation can be useful for a client with a slow Internet connection or a user who wants a fast, if perhaps inaccurate, response. In particular, by specifying a very large time value in the max-stale directive, the request will never cause validation.

In addition, the client can expedite validation of an object in two ways. It can specify the maximum object age (the time since the object was received from or validated by the origin server) it is willing to accept. To this end, the client can include a max-age=<*seconds*> directive in the cache-control header of the request. Older objects will be validated by the proxy regardless of their TTL. In particular, max-age=0 forces the proxy to perform immediate validation.

The client can also specify that it will only accept a cached copy of the object from the proxy if it will remain fresh (according to the proxy's TTL heuristic) for a given number of seconds. The proxy will validate objects that fail this condition. This requirement is specified in a `min-fresh=<`*seconds*`>` directive of the request `cache-control` header. Finally, the client can force the proxy to download the requested object from the origin server by using the `no-cache` directive in the `cache-control` header of the request.

An origin server may also prescribe to the proxy when to validate the content by providing an explicit TTL for the response. In particular, `max-age=0` forces the proxy to validate the object on every access. The server may also override relaxed validation specifications from the proxy's clients by including a `must-revalidate` directive in the `cache-control` response header. This directive forces the proxy to validate an expired object even when the client is willing to accept it without validation. Finally, the server may prohibit caching the object at all by specifying a `cache-control: no-cache` directive.

10.1.4 Asynchronous and Piggyback Cache Validation

Synchronous validation, as described so far, exhibits two problems. First, it generates additional message exchanges. Second, it introduces extra delay in request processing, since a client (a browser or a proxy) must wait for the answer to its validation request. In many or even a majority of cases, the object will not have changed at the origin server and the validation request will simply result in a "Not Modified" response. Such a validation is called a *positive validation* because the origin server confirms the validity of the cached object. In a sense, the latency overhead for positive validations is wasted, since the client could have used the cached copy of the object right away.

An alternative is asynchronous validation, which may be implemented in two ways.

- With a separate thread on the client: The thread periodically checks object ages in the client's cache and validates those objects that are expired.

- With time triggers: A trigger is set at the time an object is loaded into the cache or validated to go off when the object expires. When the trigger fires, it will validate the expired object that awoke the trigger.

Asynchronous validation eliminates the latency overhead. However, asynchronous validation retains or even increases the message and bandwidth overhead, due to wasted validations. Bandwidth overhead is especially high when a wasted validation entails downloading a new object version unnecessarily.

It therefore is desirable to have a validation scheme that would

- Avoid sending synchronous validation requests for objects that have not changed at their origins, to reduce the latency penalty, but at the same time,

- Reduce message overhead for validating objects that will not be requested, and

- Avoid wasting the bandwidth for downloading a changed object that will not be requested until it expires again.

Our first conclusion is that asynchronous validation should not be done by blindly issuing IMS requests for expired objects. Only objects that are valuable enough to prefetch into the cache should be validated using IMS requests. Other objects should be validated using conditional requests that do not return the content if validation fails. HTTP provides several mechanisms to accomplish this. The simplest way is to use the HEAD method for validation purposes. This method downloads only the headers of the object, including the current values of the `last-modified` and `date` headers. The client can use these headers to either invalidate or extend the TTL of the object.

Using HEAD requests reduces bandwidth overhead of asynchronous validation but not the number of validation-related messages. To reduce the number of messages as well, one could batch multiple validation requests to the same server into a single message. Further, a client could piggyback batches of validation requests and responses over normal HTTP traffic. This approach is called *Piggyback Cache Validation* (*PCV*) and was proposed by Krishnamurthy and Wills [1997].

To piggyback validations on normal HTTP traffic, the client has to generate a sufficiently active and constant stream of HTTP requests. Thus, piggybacking approaches are intended for proxies and not individual browsers. In PCV, when a proxy needs to send an HTTP request, the proxy checks if it holds any other objects from the same site, and whether any of those objects have expired or are about to expire. The proxy then piggybacks HEAD IMS requests for these objects with the original request. The proxy can use the pipelining feature of HTTP (see Chapter 5) to implement piggybacking. With pipelining, the proxy sends a TCP stream containing the main request followed by the IMS HEAD requests. The origin server sends back a stream of responses in the same order as they appeared in the request stream.

When there is enough traffic on which to piggyback validation, PCV avoids synchronous validation. Without enough traffic, a request may still find that the requested object has expired in the cache. In these cases, expired requests are validated synchronously. A trace study of two active proxies[2] indicated that these proxies would generate enough traffic for PCV to use piggyback validation in most cases [Krishnamurthy and Wills 1997]. Also, this study found the extra bandwidth consumption for wasted validations to be negligible.

10.2 Cache Invalidation

In principle, HTTP 1.1 allows an origin server to invalidate an object cached by a proxy by submitting to the proxy a PUT, POST, or DELETE request for the object. In doing so, the server acts as an HTTP client of the proxy. In practice, proxies behind firewalls

---

[2] The two proxies considered by Krishnamurthy and Wills [1997] had average request rates of around 40,000 and 2,800 requests per hour.

would most likely be unreachable for the HTTP requests from outside servers. Furthermore, there has been no accepted standard for a protocol that would allow invalidation of browser caches. However, cache invalidation can be implemented within enterprise networks, and open protocols for Web cache invalidation in the Internet at large are being actively discussed in the IETF.

Cache invalidation must address two interdependent issues: the client list problem and the *delayed updates* dilemma.

The client list problem is twofold. First, as we have already mentioned, just having to maintain client lists is undesirable since it makes the server stateful, that is, it requires the server to record prior interactions with all clients.[3] Second, it is unclear if the server can ever trim the lists, because expecting clients to notify servers when they drop objects from their caches is generally unreasonable.

The delayed update dilemma has to do with the guarantee of strong consistency, the main motivation for the invalidation approach in the first place. The question is, how should the server deal with an unreachable client that needs to be invalidated? That client will not receive the invalidation message and will continue using its cached content regardless of any updates. So, invalidation as we have described it so far can only provide strong consistency in the absence of Internet disconnections. In order to guarantee consistency, invalidation must be done before the update, and an object can be updated only after all clients on the client list confirm that they have invalidated the object. But this brings the next question: how long should the server delay the update waiting for some unreachable client (which may never get back online)?

The remainder of this section describes various approaches to these issues.

10.2.1 Leases

A general mechanism that addresses the client lists and delayed updates problems is *leases* [Gray and Cheriton 1989]. A lease is a promise by a server to a client that the client will be notified if the leased object is updated during the lease. With leases, the server must keep a client in the object client list only until the client lease expires. Further, an update can be delayed by an unreachable client by at most the duration of its lease.

Figure 10.2 illustrates interactions between a proxy and the origin server in the lease mechanism. For strong consistency, the server must invalidate a cached object during its lease, and the proxy must validate a cached object on its first access after lease expiration. This mechanism is thus a combination of invalidation (during lease period) and validation (after the lease expires). Validation in this context is often referred to as *lease renewal*, since the server typically extends the lease together with object validation.

---

[3] Formally speaking, most servers already record all client accesses in their logs. However, unlike the client lists, the logs are not essential for server operation and can even be turned off. Further, unlike client lists, logs do not require efficient read access and thus allow a simple implementation as a sequential file.

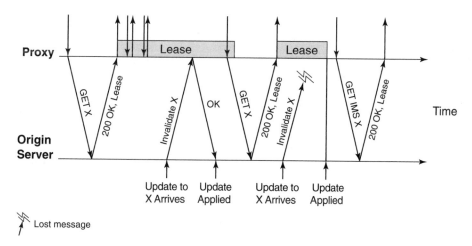

Figure 10.2 Cache invalidation with leases

A crucial question for the lease mechanism is choosing the duration of a lease. The overriding restriction on lease duration is imposed by an application-specific requirement on how long updates can be delayed. Within this restriction, longer leases increase the client lists and the number of invalidation messages. Shorter leases increase the number of lease renewal messages, which are often done at the time of the request and hence increase the response time as well as create extra traffic.

Given that cacheable objects are usually accessed more often than updated, the overall number of control messages can be expected to decrease with longer leases. Duvvuri et al. [2000] provide preliminary experimental evidence of this. Thus, there appears to be a direct tradeoff between the client list size on one hand and the number of control messages and the response time on the other. Based on this observation, Duvvuri et al. suggest adapting the lease duration dynamically to establish a desired balance. Figure 10.2 reflects this mechanism by showing unequal lease durations for the same object. In fact, one of their schemes lets the server choose a different lease duration for every object or lease renewal request. For example, it can use the same adaptive TTL heuristic used by proxies for cache validation. In this case, the lease duration for a given request D is calculated as

$$D = \min\{(k \times (current\_time - last\_modified)), threshold\}$$

The difference with adaptive TTL is that the server now prescribes when validation (or lease renewal in the invalidation parlance) must occur instead of the client applying a one-size-fits-all heuristic.

10.2.2 Subscriptions

Beside short leases, another way to reduce client lists is to let clients explicitly request, and servers grant, *subscriptions* to receiving invalidations [Dilley et al. 1999]. This approach exploits the observation that invalidations are useful only for those cached objects that are requested more than once without being invalidated between the requests. In fact, other objects do not benefit from caching at all. At the same time, it has been observed in many proxy traces that a large number of objects are requested only once. For example, Arlitt et al. [1999] found that such objects constitute 60 percent of all objects in their trace. So, to limit invalidations only to those objects that would benefit the most, the server may grant subscriptions only to clients that already have a valid cached copy of the object. In other words, the client can only request a subscription with an `if-modified-since` request, and the server will grant it only if the object is indeed not modified.

Subscriptions can be implemented at the application layer or IP layer using multicast. At the application layer, the origin server maintains the lists of subscribed clients and, when an object changes, invalidates clients from the corresponding client list by sending them unicast invalidation messages. In the multicast case, a multicast group is defined for each object and the server sends invalidation messages to the multicast IP addresses corresponding to the changed objects. Subscribing then reduces to joining a multicast group by a client [Li and Cheriton 1999], and client lists are stored in the multicast membership state maintained by routers. Multicast-based invalidation is more efficient than unicast invalidation from the network traffic and server load perspectives. The burden for maintaining client lists shifts in this case from servers to routers. The client may still need to negotiate with the server before being allowed to join the group. The server can enforce this by sending the multicast IP address only to those clients to whom it grants the subscription. In fact, having the multicast address for invalidation allows an efficient push of updated content from the server to the client caches.

Subscriptions can be naturally combined with leases [Dilley et al. 1999]. In this case, a subscription is granted only for the duration of a lease period. Put differently, in this approach not every object request results in obtaining a lease, and not every lease request or renewal is granted by the server. Without the lease, the client can choose to either validate on every access or use weak-consistency validations as described in Section 10.1.

Figure 10.3 shows an interaction between a proxy and an origin server using this combination, which we refer to as *leased subscriptions*. The first request from the proxy in Figure 10.3 does not result in a lease because it is the first request for this object from the proxy; the second request does not result in a lease because the object has changed on the server and so the cached object is not valid. The responses to the third and fourth requests from the proxy include leases because the proxy had the valid object when it made these requests.

Leased subscriptions are almost equivalent to the adaptive leases approach, with leases of zero duration corresponding to denied subscriptions. The only difference is that a zero-duration lease *prescribes* the client to validate on the very next access while a denied subscription leaves the client the flexibility to choose its validation policy.

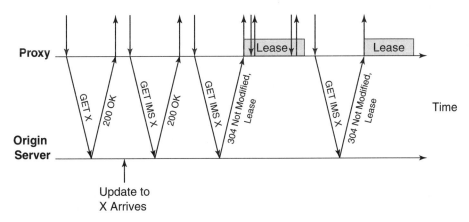

Figure 10.3 Cache invalidation with subscriptions and leases

10.2.3 Delayed versus Immediate Updates

One may argue that delaying updates until all clients are successfully invalidated or their lease expires is simply fooling oneself. The reason given is that if the need arises to update a page, then the page has changed semantically anyway, whether or not it is physically changed on the server; so the cached copy is obsolete regardless of any update delays [Yu et al. 1999]. The conclusion is that failed invalidations should not delay updates and that updates can be applied immediately. The role of leases then reduces to limiting the staleness of an object, instead of providing strong consistency. For example, if one of us wanted to add a new publication to his Web page, this publication exists whether or not the update is applied immediately. Delaying the update may keep cached copies of the Web page technically identical to the version at the origin server, but it would not make them any less obsolete semantically.

However, there are other examples where delayed updates do help enforce an expected behavior. Consider a teacher who wants to update the class homework posted on the school's Web site. A delayed update makes the teacher aware that students will still access the old homework. A successful update, on the other hand, creates an expectation that the students will see the new homework, which may not be the case with immediate updates. The teacher may tell students to check the new homework page, but when they do they may still unknowingly access the old cached copy.

So we have to conclude that choosing between delayed and immediate updates must be application-specific. Simply delaying updates in all cases just because it is desirable in some situations is extreme. Delayed updates have much higher cost, at least because every invalidation must be acknowledged. In contrast, immediate updates allow for unacknowledged best-effort invalidations since they tolerate disconnected clients anyway. Best-effort invalidations give the server some flexibility in managing client lists, such as simply dropping less active clients when the lists become too large.

Thus, the server should be able to choose between the two mechanisms based on some configuration rules. Enabling this choice requires a simple addition to the invalidation protocol. An invalidation message must carry a flag that tells the client whether or not the message must be acknowledged. When choosing delayed updates, the server sends out invalidation messages with this flag set. Then the clients will acknowledge the invalidations, allowing the server to decide when to proceed with the update. With immediate updates, the server uses invalidations with the flag unset and performs best-effort invalidations. Observe that immediate updates with best-effort invalidations provide no stronger guarantees than the current `expires` HTTP header. In fact, the `expires` header is equivalent to the lease without invalidations.

All this argues for much wider use of the `expires` header. Currently it is statically inserted into a page by the page's developer. In reality, it is hardly ever present in responses. Instead, server implementations could conceivably provide simple config-uration rules that would allow one to specify heuristics for generating and inserting the `expires` header automatically to all cacheable pages. An application may then forgo the complexities of invalidation and be content with bounded staleness, re-duce stale delivery by best-effort invalidations, or use delayed updates for strong consistency.

10.2.4   Volumes

So far we have assumed that cache consistency is maintained separately for in-dividual objects. Even with batched validations as in PCV (Section 10.1.4), each validation refers to an individual object. One could also combine several ob-jects into a *volume* and maintain consistency at the granularity of entire volumes [Krishnamurthy and Wills 1998; Yin et al. 1998; Yin et al. 1999; Li and Cheriton 1999]. Coarser granularity is especially attractive for invalidation because it may reduce its overhead in two ways. First, it reduces the amount of space for the client lists, since these lists are kept for every unit of content that is invalidated individually. Second, it reduces the number of messages between the client and the origin server, because a single lease renewal request obtains the lease for all objects in the volume. On the other hand, an update to a single object invalidates all objects in the volume. Thus, coarse granularity may lead to invalidating parts of content unnecessarily and to sending unneeded invalidation messages to clients that hold only unchanged parts of the volume.

Questions concerning the general granularity problem (what is the proper granu-larity and how to group objects into volumes) remain largely open. However, volumes turn out to be useful not necessarily instead of but in addition to maintaining consis-tency at the level of individual objects.

We have already noted that different access patterns and application requirements may suggest different lease durations. Specifically, application requirements on

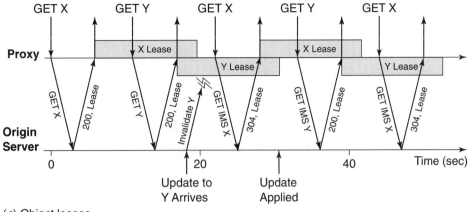

(a) Object leases

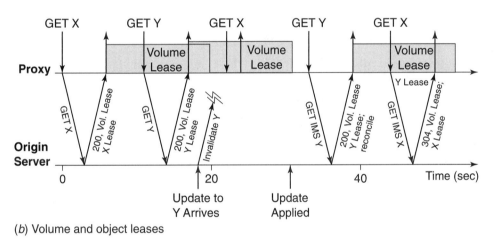

(b) Volume and object leases

Figure 10.4 Combination of short volume leases and long object leases

staleness bounds (for the immediate updates case) or update delay limits (for delayed
updates) may dictate a short lease duration. Short leases, however, may lead to a large
number of lease renewals relative to the request rate. As an example, consider a Web
site with delayed updates and assume that the application requires a limit of at most 13
seconds for an update delay. This limit dictates the same value for object lease duration
as shown in Figure 10.4a. When object changes are infrequent relative to this value,
such lease duration may cause many positive validations, that is, validation requests
that return a "304 Not Modified" response. In the particular scenario in Figure 10.4a,
every client request results in a positive validation, denoted as a 304 response.

A combination of volume and object leases can be used to address this problem
[Yin et al. 1998; Yu et al. 1999]. In this approach, a client must hold the leases on both
the object and its volume to use a cached object. Since clients cannot use an object
without the object lease, the server need not invalidate volumes. This eliminates the

unnecessary invalidation problem mentioned in the beginning of this subsection. Furthermore, because clients cannot use an object without the volume lease, short volume leases allow short update delays.

Figure 10.4b illustrates how this idea helps in the scenario of Figure 10.4a. In the figure, objects X and Y are combined into a volume, and the volume lease of 13 seconds satisfies the application limit on update delays regardless of the lease duration of individual objects. This allows the server to assign long object leases as justified by the object access and modification rates. (Figure 10.4b does not depict object leases; we assume they are longer than the time values shown in the Time axis.) Long object leases reduce the number of unnecessary positive validations. For example, the proxy is able to satisfy the second request to X locally in Figure 10.4b but performs a validation for the same request in Figure 10.4a. In more realistic scenarios, with volumes containing many objects, the combined volume and object leases can save a much higher number of validations.

10.2.5 Volume Lease Protocols

The following protocol implements the idea illustrated in Figure 10.4b [Yin et al. 1998].

- An origin server response carries the identity of a volume to which the object in the response belongs. Responses also assign separate volume and object leases.

- When updating an object, the origin server sends the object invalidation message to clients with valid object leases. It can proceed with the update once all invalidations are acknowledged or the volume lease expires. Clients that have not acknowledged the invalidation are added to an *unreachable list* for the volume.

- When using a cached object, a client checks for the valid leases for the object and its volume. If either of the two has expired, the client issues a request— if-modified-since—to renew the expired leases. If the client is not in the server's unreachable list, the server responds with lease renewals, including the object if it has changed. If the client is in the unreachable list, the server in addition sets a *reconciliation* flag that demands that the client renew the leases on all cached objects from this volume before using them. (Reconciliation is the reason for the GET IMS X request in Figure 10.4b.)

- The server removes a client from the unreachable list when it is removed from all per-object client lists (that is, when the client has no valid object leases from this volume) or when the client acknowledges receiving the reconciliation flag.

Since the origin server does not invalidate volumes, it does not need to maintain per-volume client lists. The server does perform normal object-level invalidation, maintaining per-object client lists. However, short volume leases allow trimming client lists quickly: the server can always remove a client from the client lists for all objects once its lease for the volume expires, by moving the client to the unreachable list for this volume. A client must renew the volume lease frequently, because the lease is short. The overhead for each such renewal, however, is amortized over all objects in the volume.

For better insight into this scheme, assume a particular case where all objects on a Web site form a single volume. Assume a volume lease of 10 seconds. When accessing a cached copy of an object, a proxy must contact the server unless it has renewed the lease within the past 10 seconds. In other words, the proxy experiences at least one slow hit per server per 10 seconds. However, the number of these slow hits is independent of the number of objects from this server that the proxy is accessing. Thus, for popular servers, slow hits will be amortized over many fast hits. Depending on whether the server uses delayed or immediate updates, the proxy will never serve stale content or will serve content that is at most 10 seconds obsolete.

Alternatively, a server may push volume lease renewals to all clients deemed active enough without client requests [Yu et al. 1999]. Still assuming a single volume for the entire site, volume lease renewals become simple periodic messages from the site to the clients that actively use the site. Because these messages are expected at equal intervals, they are called *heartbeat messages*. Clients need not acknowledge heartbeats. A client that misses an expected heartbeat from a server must renew leases on all objects from this server before obtaining the lease for this volume again. Once the server sends an object invalidation to a client, it stops sending heartbeats to this client until the client acknowledges the invalidation. To improve performance in the presence of packet loss, clients and servers can agree that a volume lease lasts a predefined number of heartbeat intervals. A client must miss the corresponding number of heartbeats before considering a volume lease to be lost, and servers delay updates by the corresponding number of heartbeat intervals. For example, if a Web site can delay updates by at most 30 seconds and a volume lease lasts three heartbeat intervals, the origin server must send heartbeats every 10 seconds, and clients lose volume leases after missing three heartbeats.

This scheme removes volume lease renewals from the critical path of request processing, further reducing the number of slow hits. It is achieved at the expense of sending volume lease renewals to clients even during periods of inactivity. The scheme also removes the need for the unreachable client lists because a client now always reconciles after missing a volume lease renewal.

A simulation study using a real access trace and a simulated update stream showed that this scheme[4] significantly reduced user response time for read-intensive objects compared to validation schemes [Yu et al. 1999]. We should note, however, that the study used an artificially low TTL threshold for validation schemes, which benefits the invalidation scheme.

---

[4] The scheme under study was actually a slight variation from the one here: it assumed immediate updates, multicast heartbeats, and object invalidations piggybacked on heartbeat messages.

10.2.6 Piggyback and Delayed Invalidation

Consider invalidation with immediate updates. As we discussed, this scheme does not provide strong consistency; it only bounds the staleness of the cached content. In other words, the scheme does not promise to invalidate content immediately. We could try to exploit this flexibility and gain some performance benefits by sometimes delaying invalidations deliberately.

Some potential benefits can be achieved by delaying individual invalidations so that several invalidations can be sent together in batches. This may reduce the number of invalidation messages in the system. The server might also send an unrelated message to the client on which the invalidation batch could be piggybacked.

In particular, volume lease renewals often provide an opportunity to piggyback object invalidations because volume leases are short and their renewals are sent often. Volume lease renewals sent as heartbeats are especially convenient since they are always there to piggyback invalidations. In fact, one could push this idea one step further and use it to avoid having to maintain per-object client lists altogether [Yu et al. 1999]. One can do this by including in the invalidation batch *all* objects that have changed since the previous volume lease renewal, regardless of whether or not the client has a particular object. Thus the server does not have to track which client has which objects—all changed objects in the volume are invalidated.

Furthermore, since the invalidation batch is no longer client-specific, the server can send the same message (the volume heartbeat plus the invalidation batch) to all clients. Thus, the message can be multicast to all clients that have the volume lease. To summarize, the consistency scheme, which is a slight generalization of the one proposed by Yu et al. [1999], matches the following outline, where n is the number of heartbeat intervals in the volume lease duration.

1. The server keeps a client list for every volume. It adds a client to a volume client list based on some policy, either when the client requests an object from the volume, or once the client explicitly subscribes to the volume invalidations. When the server decides to remove a client from the list, it stops sending the client heartbeats and then removes the client once its volume lease expires (after it was excluded from n heartbeats).

2. The server keeps an invalidation batch for a volume. When an object changes, it is added to the batch for its volume. Once added, the object is removed from the batch after having been transmitted in n consecutive heartbeats.

3. The server multicasts volume heartbeats to all clients in the volume client list. The heartbeat contains the current invalidation batch for the volume.

4. The client loses the lease on a volume after missing n consecutive volume heartbeats. Once it loses the lease, it must invalidate all objects from this volume before acquiring another volume lease. When receiving an

invalidation batch, the client invalidates all objects from the batch that it has in its cache.

A potential danger of this proposal is that many unneeded invalidations may be sent to clients that do not have the objects concerned. Further, each invalidation is sent n times. While the effect of the unneeded invalidations has not been analyzed by Yu et al. [1999], this study observed, using simulation experiments, that repeat invalidations did not result in any noticeable bandwidth increase.

Regular HTTP traffic provides another possibility for piggybacking invalidations [Krishnamurthy and Wills 1998]. In this approach, called *Piggyback Server Invalidation* (*PSI*), the origin server assigns version numbers to volumes. The server increments a volume version number any time an object in this volume is updated. Clients keep track of the volumes to which their cached objects belong. When a client sends an `if-modified-since` request for an expired object, it includes the version number of the object's volume. With its response, the server piggybacks the list of all objects from this volume that have been updated since the version was current. The client then invalidates those objects from the list that happen to be in its cache. Because clients include volume information in their requests, the server need not maintain any client lists.

Delaying invalidations until the next HTTP request means forgoing consistency guarantees. Thus PSI, like validation schemes, is generally best-effort. However, it can be used to reduce incidents of stale delivery, especially if used in combination with piggyback validation. Krishnamurthy and Wills [1998] found that this combined approach achieved stale delivery rate of only 0.1 percent in the traces studied.

10.2.7 Invalidation in Cache Routing

Invalidation is especially attractive in a cache routing proxy cooperation model. Consider the cache routing scheme of Michel et al. [1998], where the routing table at each proxy maps Web sites to the next-hop proxies and where cache routing table are maintained based on distance vectors (see Section 9.4.2). In this scheme, each proxy receives requests for a given Web site from only a small number of neighbors in the topology graph, those for whom it is the next hop toward this Web site. For example, in the topology of Figure 9.9, cache P6 can receive requests for the origin server only from P4 and P5, since requests from everyone else would arrive through those two caches anyway. If, for the sake of argument, most Web requests to origin servers arrived through cache routing, the origin servers would also receive requests mostly from their configured neighbor proxies.

Therefore the client lists for sending invalidations will be small both on origin servers and on intermediate proxies in the topology graph. Invalidations in this case will disseminate through the network of proxies in the reverse direction of the routing tables, with manageable fan-out at every hop. Invalidation schemes of this flavor for cooperating caches have been described by Yu et al. [1999] and Yin et al. [1998].

In general, proxies reduce the number of clients that an origin server sees and, therefore, facilitate invalidations.

10.3 Issues in Cooperative Cache Consistency

Cooperative proxy caching introduces some interesting consistency issues that are specific to this environment. Before discussing them further, we should stress that any such issues are important only insofar as there is a possibility of a stale delivery by individual proxies. Indeed, if each individual proxy always served fresh content, so would cooperating proxies. As we have seen earlier, cache consistency mechanisms of individual proxies achieve very low stale delivery rate. Thus, one may argue that the issues in this section are not very important. However, there is a difference between a *rare occurrence* of an undesirable event and a *guarantee* that the event would not occur. Our discussion includes solutions that provide such guarantees.

10.3.1 Validation with Cooperative Proxies

When proxies participate in cooperative caching, each proxy must be able to enforce its own policies. Such autonomy is especially important for policies regarding consistency maintenance, because these policies can be part of the quality of service agreements between a proxy and its clients. For example, a proxy may promise its clients that it would use adaptive TTL with $k = 0.1$ for cache validation. Then this proxy should be able to deliver this consistency level despite looser consistency policies used by other cooperating proxies.

Consider Figure 10.5 that shows two cooperating proxies, P and Q, using adaptive TTL with $k = 0.1$ and $k = 0.2$, respectively. Assume that on January 31, 2002, proxy P obtained an object X via proxy Q, so both proxies have this object. Applying their respective TTL heuristics, each proxy will assign a different expiration date to their copies of X based on the object's last modified date of January 1. Q will set the object to expire in $0.1 \times 30 = 3$ days and P in $0.2 \times 30 = 6$ days.

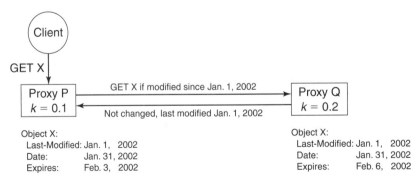

Figure 10.5 An example of cache validation in a cooperative proxy environment (the client request arrives on February 4)

Let a client of P request this object on February 4. Since the object has expired in P, P will validate the object by a GET IMS request. In a cooperative proxy environment, the request may arrive at Proxy *Q*, which will satisfy it from its cache because the object has not expired according to *Q*'s heuristic. Thus, P will receive a "Not Modified" response carrying the same `date` and `last-modified` headers. If P now returns the object to the client, P would do so because the object did not expire *according to another proxy's policy* [Dingle 1996].

A seemingly straightforward way to correct the problem by checking the freshness of the received response and revalidating it if expired would be grossly wrong. As mentioned in the HTTP 1.1 standard [Fielding et al. 1999], this can lead to an infinite cycle. In our example, P would compute TTL = 0.1 ∗ (Jan 31 − Jan 1) = 3 days and set the expiration date to Jan 31 + 3 = Feb 3.[5] Since the current date is February 4, P will again decide to validate the object and send the IMS request to Q, which will again respond with a "Not Modified" message, and so on.

An alternative is to validate such responses directly with the origin server. While correct, this alternative can reduce the value of cooperative caching. For instance, in our example, Q may cooperate with another nearby proxy, S, which has a fresh copy of the object. By forcing validation with the origin server, P forgoes the possibility of utilizing the fresh copy at proxy S.

A better way for P to enforce its validation policy is to include the `max-age=<`*TTL*`>` directive into the `cache-control` header of its IMS requests, where *TTL* is the object's TTL assigned by P. In our example, the IMS request from P to Q will contain `max-age=3 days`. That will force Q to validate its copy (because it is four days old), utilizing any upstream caches Q would normally use.

In other words, proxy P can enforce its own TTL heuristics in a cooperative HTTP 1.1 proxy environment by using the following simple rules:

- When P obtains an object from another proxy, it must check to see if this object needs validation according to P's own heuristics before serving the object to its clients.

- When P sends a validation request for an object to another proxy, it must include the `cache-control:max-age=<`*TTL*`>` directive in the request, where *TTL* is the TTL that P assigned to this object.

In fact, a proxy should follow the above rules regardless of whether it explicitly cooperates with other proxies. Indeed, with transparent proxies, one can never be sure if the responses arrive from the origin server or from a transparent proxy that intercepted the request and impersonated the origin server. Thus a proxy may be engaged in cooperative caching without knowing it.

---

[5] Note that P would use the date when the object was obtained from the origin server (January 31) in these calculations, not the current date (February 4).

10.3.2 Non-Monotonic Delivery Problem

A new issue that arises in cooperative caching is the consistency of object copies cached at different proxies. (Contrast this with the consistency problem we considered so far, which concerns cached content becoming stale relative to the content at the origin server.) When the consistency of a stand-alone proxy cache is violated, a user may receive a stale object version. However, the user has at least the guarantee that revisiting the same object again will result in the same or fresher copy of the object but never an *older* version than the one it has seen already. When cooperating proxies hold inconsistent object copies, this guarantee may no longer hold. In other words, repeated accesses to an object may return versions that are older than the version obtained previously by the same user. We refer to this phenomenon as *non-monotonic delivery* [Makpangou et al. 1999]. Let us consider some examples.

Consider two cooperating proxies P and Q and a sequence of events depicted in Figure 10.6. Suppose Q obtains object X, after which P receives a request for this object from client C1 with a `cache-control:no-cache` header. Consequently, P fetches X from the origin server. Assume that the server updates the object between the two downloads, so that the version obtained by P is newer than the version cached by Q. Assume that after that time, client C2 sends its request for X, which is satisfied from P's local cache.

At this time, assume that P purges X from its cache while Q still retains its copy. If C2 again requests X, P may satisfy the request from Q's cache, and thus send to C2 a version of X that is not only obsolete but is earlier than a version C2 had seen before.

As already mentioned, any instance of non-monotonic delivery implies also stale delivery, since the older version of the object in the non-monotonic delivery is

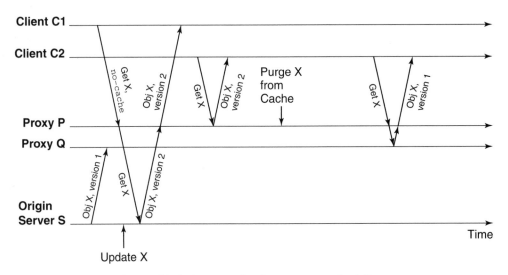

Figure 10.6 An example of non-monotonic delivery

necessarily stale. Thus, the rate of non-monotonic delivery is bounded by the rate of stale delivery, which can be made quite low using modern techniques described earlier in this chapter.

However, it is relatively simple to avoid non-monotonic delivery altogether. Consider a proxy that uses the adaptive TTL heuristic with threshold T for cache consistency, or a combination of this policy with other mechanisms, such as PCV or PSI. Threshold T serves as an upper bound on the relative TTL assigned to any object in P's cache (see Section 10.1.2). The following simple rules ensure monotonic delivery by P.

- P maintains a SERVED table where it keeps the last-modified date of any object it serves to any client (including other proxies with which it cooperates) until the elapsed time since the object's last-modified date exceeds the TTL threshold of P:

$$current\_time - last\_modified > T.$$

  The entry is stored whether or not the object is present in the cache.

- When P sends a request for an object that does not have an entry in the SERVED table, P includes the cache-control:max-age=<T> directive, where T is the TTL threshold of P.

- When P obtains an object, it accepts it only if this object does not have an entry in the SERVED table or if the last-modified date of this object in the SERVED table is no later than the last-modified date of the just-obtained object.

With these rules the same proxy will always send out monotonically increasing versions of an object. Indeed, if the proxy obtains an object and finds it in the SERVED table, it enforces the monotonicity directly by making sure that the new version is not older than the one served before. If the object is not in the SERVED table, it may be because the proxy has never served this object before or because it removed the entry for this object from the table. In the former case, monotonicity is satisfied trivially. For the latter case, recall that the proxy removes an entry only after the time since object's last-modified date at P exceeds T, the TTL threshold of P. A version of the object cached at a remote proxy can violate monotonicity only if that version left the origin server before the last-modified date above. Therefore, the age of the remote version would certainly exceed T. But the max-age=<T> directive in P's request prevents the delivery of such objects. Thus, even in this case monotonicity will be enforced.

Figure 10.7 illustrates how this approach prevents non-monotonic delivery in the situation shown in Figure 10.6. Assume that P purges object X from the SERVED table. By our rules, P can do so only if the time since the object's last-modified date, time_since_last_mod$_P$(X), exceeds T. Later, when P tries to obtain X from Q, the

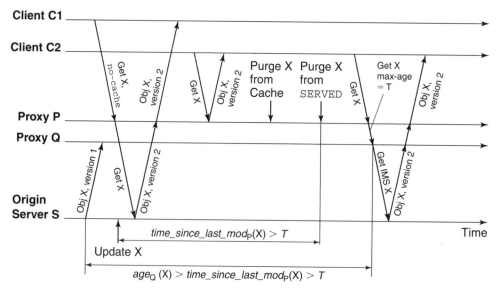

Figure 10.7 Prevention of non-monotonic delivery

age of the object at Q, age_Q (X), exceeds the TTL threshold of P. Therefore, the `max-age=<T>` directive in P's request forces Q to fetch the object from the origin server.

The above method guarantees that a proxy serves monotonic versions of any object. Thus, it prevents non-monotonic delivery *if* a client always connects to the same proxy for all its requests. If this assumption does not hold, a client that cares about monotonicity can enforce it by following the same approach described above for the proxies.

One may wonder if it is possible to enforce monotonicity without relying on the TTL threshold. The Relais project implements such a protocol [Makpangou et al. 1999]. Given that all existing proxies enforce a TTL threshold, we believe the complexities of such protocols are not justified.

10.4 Summary

The two fundamental approaches to cache consistency are validation and invalidation.

Cache validation provides weak (that is, nonguaranteed) consistency and a very simple tradeoff between the rate of stale delivery and validation overhead, which mostly manifests itself in turning fast hits into slow hits. Piggyback asynchronous validation can significantly reduce this overhead. It therefore makes maintaining near-strong consistency affordable. Still, any realistic validation scheme can fundamentally provide only weak consistency.

Cache invalidation can provide strong consistency if the origin server delays updates until all invalidations are acknowledged. Object leases can be used to limit the delay of updates. When immediate updates are required, leases guarantee bounded object staleness, limited by lease duration.

Invalidation overheads include the need to maintain client lists at origin servers and the need to send invalidation messages, which might be unnecessary if a cache no longer contains the object or if the invalidated object will not be used. Subscriptions can reduce these overheads by using invalidations only for the most important objects or the most active clients. Volume leases, especially in combination with object leases, are another mechanism to reduce these overheads. One can further minimize these overheads by piggybacking invalidations on volume lease renewals or on regular HTTP traffic. In fact, the latter relieves origin servers of the need to maintain any client lists or any other per-client state. On the other hand, piggybacking on HTTP traffic forgoes the strong consistency guarantees of other invalidation methods.

Validation places most of the burden of keeping caches consistent on the clients, while invalidation shifts the burden to the origin servers. Research on cache invalidation has produced preliminary evidence that strong consistency can be achieved with little impact on network traffic. However, the server overhead has not yet been conclusively quantified. In addition, it is unclear if clients would be willing to accept unsolicited invalidation messages from origin servers for security reasons. Consequently, validation has remained the prevalent method to maintain cache consistency. Invalidation is mostly used to maintain consistency of surrogates (see Section 15.7), where both surrogates and origin servers are under the control of the content provider.

Cooperative caching introduces two extra problems to cache consistency. The first problem has to do with cache validation. If one proxy sends its requests (in particular, `if-modified-since` requests) to another, then the second proxy may impose its own heuristics for object expiration on the first proxy. To avoid this, a proxy must always include the `max-age=<TTL>` directive in its validation requests to other proxies, where *TTL* is the relative TTL that the requesting proxy assigned to the object.

The second problem is non-monotonic delivery, where repeated requests for the same object from the same client return older object versions than earlier requests. Although non-monotonic delivery is a rare occurrence, we describe a relatively simple mechanism that avoids this problem altogether.

Chapter 11
Replacement Policy

Any proxy faces several policy decisions. One of them is to decide which objects, if any, to evict from the cache when no space is available to store additional objects. This chapter discusses various options for this policy decision.

The strategy used for eviction decisions is often referred to as a *replacement policy*. Traditionally, research in the area of caching has been almost synonymous with studying cache replacement policies (the decision on what to store was usually simple: store everything, assuming it is cacheable). Much work on proxy Web caching has also been devoted to clever replacement policies and their effects on hit rates. However, we argue that replacement policies are not the limiting factor in the progress of proxy caching. To put it differently, research in this area is not going to be a determining factor in proxy efficiency or Web performance in general. One indication supporting this opinion is that no cache vendor uses replacement policy as a distinguishing factor for the vendor's caching product. Before we justify this statement further in the last part of this chapter, let us first discuss the issues involved in determining a good replacement algorithm and describe some of the algorithms proposed.

11.1 Replacement Policy Metrics

The first question to answer while evaluating a replacement algorithm is, what is the metric? The second question is, what is the workload? Research papers on replacement algorithms typically propose an algorithm and show that it is superior to existing algorithms for a particular workload and metric. Unfortunately the consequence of this methodology is that no replacement algorithm is optimal for a wide range of workloads and metrics. Considering the uncertainty in determining the typical Web workload, it becomes quite difficult to find the optimal algorithm. In addition, there are multiple metrics of interest, which in many cases point to different algorithms. Some of the metrics described below were discussed in Chapter 7. Others are more specific to replacement policies.

Hit rate: The hit rate represents the percentage of requested objects that are served out of the cache. Since the hit rate is calculated by dividing the number of objects served from the cache by the total number of objects served, small objects are generally favored to remain in the cache by replacement algorithms that try to increase hit rates.

Byte hit rate: The byte hit rate represents the percentage of bytes of data served from the cache out of the total number of bytes served. The byte hit rate is different from the hit rate in that if the workload contains heavily used large objects, a hit rate metric might favor their early removal, while a replacement algorithm based on the byte hit rate would not remove them.

Saved bandwidth: The saved bandwidth metric tries to quantify the decrease in the number of bytes retrieved from the origin servers. It is an important metric for many ISPs to reduce their costs and is directly related to the byte hit rate. However, depending on the workload, it is usually not well represented by the hit rate.

Latency reduction: An important goal for the individual retrieving information from the Web is to minimize latency. Reducing latency generally decreases the saved bandwidth and in some cases might even increase the bandwidth requirements. Therefore it should not be surprising that replacement algorithms that optimize latency are different from those that optimize bandwidth savings.

Disk performance: Another important but less-studied metric is the impact of the replacement algorithms on disk performance. For example, for many high-speed networks, the latencies going to the origin server are similar to performing the multiple disk operations necessary to retrieve an object that has been spread over disjoint parts of the disk. This indicates, for example, that adjacent objects on a disk should be replaced together to avoid having to spread a newly arriving object over several disjoint disk areas.

CPU performance: Although it is increasingly rare that a simple proxy cache does not have enough CPU capacity, an overly complicated replacement policy could change this and make the CPU the bottleneck. It is also important to note that replacement policies which have to examine a large amount of data might overload the memory system and therefore reduce the CPU performance substantially.

11.2 Replacement Policy Algorithms

After describing some of the metrics of interest, let us now turn to the replacement algorithms. Broadly, they can be grouped into three categories as proposed by Aggarwal et al. [1999]. The first group of algorithms includes the classic replacement algorithms, of which the main representatives are Least Recently Used (LRU) and Least Frequently Used (LFU). As their names indicate, LRU replaces the object that was used least recently and LFU replaces the object that was used least frequently. Both algorithms can be implemented fairly easily and are used in many applications outside the Web. LFU and LRU often serve as the basis of comparison for newly proposed replacement algorithms.

The second class of algorithms can be broadly categorized as key-based. These algorithms use a primary key (that is, an attribute of an object) to decide which object to evict. Ties are broken using additional keys. An important primary key in the area of the Web is object size. For the workloads studied by Williams et al. [1996b], the best hit rate of the algorithms examined was achieved by two extremely simple key-based replacement algorithms, which replaced the largest objects first. These algorithms use either the object size or the $\log_2$ of the object size as the primary key. However, the same study indicated that these algorithms are the worst in terms of byte hit rate for most workloads. This should not be surprising, since removing large objects makes room for many small objects, increasing the hit rate. But at the same time, doing so also replaces popular large objects with many less popular small ones, decreasing the byte hit rate.

Another group of algorithms in this class includes LRU-based algorithms applied to a subset of the objects. For example, Abrams et al. [1995] introduced LRU-threshold, which applies the LRU algorithm to all objects with an object size below a certain preconfigured threshold. Abrams et al. [1995] also introduced LRU-minimum, which groups objects into large objects and small objects and uses LRU to replace objects within the group of large objects first. If there are no large objects, it replaces objects that are more than half the size of the largest object in the cache, using LRU to choose among them. The performance of these algorithms, while reasonably good in many cases, again heavily depends on the workload. In addition, their performance also depends on the thresholds chosen to classify objects into large and small.

The last group of algorithms in the category of key-based algorithms does not base its primary key on size at all. Lowest Latency First [Wooster and Abrams 1997], for example, first replaces the objects that can be retrieved fastest from their origin server. This algorithm, in contrast to the size-based algorithms, does not try to optimize the hit rate. It tries instead to decrease the latency perceived by the user of the cache.

The last class of replacement algorithms is the set of cost-based algorithms. A cost-based algorithm tries to optimize a given cost function derived from different factors such as time last used, usage frequency, cache transfer time, time of day, object's HTTP headers, and so on. One popular group of algorithms in this class is derived from the Greedy-Dual-Size algorithm [Cao and Irani 1997]. This algorithm associates a cost with each object and evicts the object with the lowest cost/size ratio. The Greedy-Dual*Web caching algorithm [Jin and Bestavros 2000] takes this approach one step further by accounting for the fact that objects that belong to the same document and were retrieved together will most likely be retrieved together again; so if any of the objects contained in the document generates a cache hit, all of them should be retained in the cache.

An important factor to consider while designing cost-based replacement algorithms is the cost of calculating the optimal solution according to the cost function used. In many cases this cost is high enough to prevent the use of the proposed algorithm in practice.

11.3   The Value of Replacement Policy

To return to our argument that the replacement policies are not the limiting factor of the progress in proxy caching, consider the proxy that showed the highest performance in a proxy performance evaluation conducted in January 2000 [Rousskov et al. 2000], capable of serving 2,400 requests per second. If the cache is provisioned properly, its average rate is at most a quarter of that, or 600 requests per second [Danzig 1998a]. At an average size of 10KBytes, this request rate translates into serving 48Mbps of data to clients. If we assume 40 percent of uncacheable data (see Section 6.3) that need not be stored and a 40 percent overall byte hit rate, the incoming data to be cached will arrive at the rate of 9.6Mbps, or roughly 1.2MBps. On the other hand, the cache used in the performance evaluation had a total disk capacity of 181GBytes. At 1.2MBps, it would require 41 hours to fill the cache. Once it is filled, the cache will hold 18.1 million 10KByte-sized objects.

While the opinions vary on how long it should take a cache to collect a working set for its clients,[1] a study of a large proxy [Arlitt et al. 1999] found the median stack distance to be 60,000, with a mean of 640,000 and a standard deviation of 1.5 million (see Section 6.5.1). Even the maximum stack distance was just over 16 million. This is 2.1 million fewer than the 18.1 million which could be held in the cache used in our example. Given the 18.1 million object cache capacity, these numbers indicate that even a basic LRU replacement policy would not cause a significant degradation of cache hit ratio.

11.4   Summary

Overall, a general consensus among vendors is that disk space is currently not the limiting factor in proxy performance. Therefore they never differentiate themselves based on replacement policies.

One can argue that cache replacement at a proxy will become more relevant once the proliferation of multimedia makes Web objects much larger. However, given the pace of change of the Web, today's studies of cache policies, based on today's Web behavior, will soon be irrelevant, because all studies depend heavily on the workload characteristics. For example, the LRU-threshold and LRU-minimum replacement policy, while increasing the hit rate of small objects, would discriminate against those large multimedia objects. Moreover, the computing environment is also changing, although not as quickly as the Web. Disk capacity grows at a rate of around 60 percent a year, while certain factors limiting disk throughput (like the number of disk operations per

---

[1] The opinions range from one week [Danzig 1998a] to a few minutes [Totty 1999].

second) lag far behind. Thus, by the time multimedia objects become prevalent, disk capacity will grow faster than the number of disk operations per second supported. In other words, the number of disks needed to provide the processing power will come with much larger storage capacity than in today's environments.

Replacement policies remain an important issue to determine the contents of the proxy's internal main memory cache. Unlike disk space, main memory is still a limited resource that must be managed wisely. The internal memory cache replacement algorithms, however, depend to a large extent on internal proxy components like the I/O bus, disk controller, disk and CPU caches. Like the internals of other components of the Web infrastructure, these issues are outside the scope of this book.

Chapter 12
Prefetching

Prefetching refers to performing work in anticipation of future needs. The idea of prefetching Web pages has surely occurred to many as they used their browsers. It often takes too long to load and display a requested object; by the same token, several seconds usually elapse between consecutive requests by the same user. It is natural to wonder if the time between two requests could be used to anticipate and prefetch the second Web object so that it could be displayed with little or no delay.

Despite such obvious motivation, prefetching remains largely a research topic, and the few commercial products use approaches that seem primitive compared to concepts discussed in the research literature. The main reason for this gap between concept and practice is that the most successful prefetching methods depend upon far-reaching techniques such as changing the HTTP standard, aggregating usage information from many sources, or both. In contrast, the existing commercial prefetchers are client-only packages that operate with limited knowledge.

This chapter explains both commercial and research approaches to prefetching. First we discuss metrics for evaluating the effectiveness of prefetching. Then we describe the bounds on how well prefetching can perform. Finally, we survey known prefetching techniques through a taxonomy.

12.1 Performance Metrics

The goal of prefetching is to display Web objects on the user's screen faster than if prefetching were not employed and the objects were *demand-fetched*, that is, downloaded after the user requested them. Therefore, the key metric that should be used in evaluating prefetching schemes is the latency seen by the user when requesting an object. Some methods prefetch objects into the browser's cache, whereas others alternatively or additionally prefetch to an intermediate point such as a shared proxy cache or a second cache on the client machine. Regardless, the value of a prefetching mechanism is measured by the user's experience. Typically, studies measure the time needed to deliver the object to the browser; an object that is already in the browser's cache requires zero time, while objects that have been prefetched to intermediate points require some time, which is ideally less than the time necessary to retrieve the object from the origin server. Latency is usually measured by its average or median value and, occasionally, variability.

Except for those discussed in Section 12.5.1, prefetching mechanisms are *user-transparent*, meaning that prefetching takes place without the user being involved or even aware of it. User-transparent prefetching is probably the only practical approach because of the highly dynamic and wide-ranging nature of many browsing sessions; usually, the user is unable to predict the URLs of objects to be visited, except possibly for the top-level object of a Web site. A transparent prefetcher is necessarily *speculative*, meaning that the prefetching system makes guesses about a user's future object references. For example, a prefetcher could infer future user behavior from past references to the same or similar objects made either by the same user or many users. Another source of information for the prefetcher is the content of the Web object that is currently viewed by the user. For example, hyperlinks in an HTML object are candidates for prefetching since a user might click on them.

Any speculative prefetcher will make some wrong guesses and, therefore, will make *more* requests than a nonprefetching system that is presented with the same stream of user requests. The extra requests contribute to the two costs of prefetching: the extra load placed on origin servers and the extra network bandwidth consumed. It is important to quantify the costs because they can lead to worse performance for the prefetching client, other clients, or both. Besides evaluating the costs through obvious measures such as total extra requests and total extra bytes, some studies attempt to be more precise, evaluating how prefetching affects the burstiness of requests and what portions of the network become bottlenecks because of the extra bandwidth demanded by prefetching [Crovella and Barford 1998].

Other prefetching performance metrics are more abstract: these are metrics for evaluating a prefetching algorithm in isolation from its surrounding system. The terms *precision* and *recall* are used to refer to these metrics. Precision is the percent of prefetched objects that are subsequently requested. It is a measure of the accuracy of the prefetching algorithm. Recall is the percent of client requests that were prefetched. It is a measure of the usefulness of prefetching: prefetching would not be worth much, even if highly precise, if few objects were prefetched (that is, if prefetching had low recall). We call these metrics abstract because they reflect only the algorithmic aspect of prefetching, that is, the quality of prediction. In practice, prefetching is not purely an algorithmic problem, because even if an algorithm correctly predicts a future access, prefetching of the predicted object would be successful only if the object can be retrieved before the user actually requests it.

12.2 Performance Bounds of Prefetching

There is substantial danger in prefetching. It is inherently difficult to predict the future actions of a user who does not provide any special information to the prefetcher, and incorrect guesses impose extra load on shared facilities. Therefore, it is valuable to know how much possible advantage prefetching can deliver and how accurate prefetching must be in order to succeed.

An important study by Kroeger et al. [1997] establishes bounds on the latency reduction achievable by prefetching into a shared proxy cache. These are not mathematical bounds, but rather the results of simulations applied to substantial traces (approximately 24.6 million requests) under idealized conditions. Their most notable result is that, even employing an unlimited cache, having a prefetch algorithm that knows the future, allowing up to 1Mbps of bandwidth for prefetching, and assuming that a major portion of end-to-end latency (77 to 88 percent) is incurred between server and proxy rather than proxy and client, prefetching into the shared intermediate proxy can reduce the total latency by no more than 60 percent. The primary reason for such limited latency reduction under such favorable conditions is the high number of uncacheable objects that are not cached or prefetched in the study.

Another bounds study, by Wang and Crowcroft [1996], focuses on mathematical analysis of prefetching. One of their results specifies how effective prefetch predictions must be (or alternatively, how lightly loaded the network must be) in order for prefetches not to sabotage the performance of demand fetches and thereby *increase* the overall latency seen by the prefetching user or by other users. Assuming that the network delivers objects one by one in the order of their arrival in the network and that both the time objects spend in the network and the time between arrivals of different objects in the network are exponentially distributed random variables,[1] the condition for avoiding latency degradation is $U < E/(1 + E)$, where U is network utilization excluding prefetch traffic and E is the ratio of prefetch recall to traffic increase caused by prefetching. For example, if U is 0.5, then E must be greater than 1 to satisfy the above condition. That means that for each 1 percent increase in traffic caused by prefetching, the prefetch recall must also increase by at least 1 percent. This gives some indication of the difficulty of prefetching. Granting that a utilization of 50 percent is high for a shared network, nevertheless most prefetching mechanisms do not come close to achieving $E = 1$, at least not for high-recall levels. (Typically, much less extra traffic is needed to raise recall one percent from, say, 10 to 11 percent than from, say, 56 to 57 percent.) For a more realistic utilization level of 25 percent, the prefetcher can generate up to 3 percent extra traffic for each 1 percent increase in

---

[1] In queuing theory parlance, we could say that the network connection is modeled as an M/M/1 queue.

recall before overall latency will worsen. Achieving a ratio of 3:1 or less is not trivial, especially at high-recall values.

12.3 Taxonomy

In this section we survey existing and proposed prefetching techniques. The survey is organized according to a five-dimension taxonomy:

1. What is prefetched? The term *prefetching* conventionally implies data, that is, a Web object and possibly its embedded images. However, other choices are possible and often less risky.

2. Is the prefetching transparent or nontransparent? A nontransparent prefetching mechanism may be based on user input at the client (being nontransparent to the user), rely on cooperation from the server (being nontransparent to the server), or both.

3. Is prefetched data pushed by the server or pulled by the client, and where are the prefetching decisions made? The answers to these questions are often determined by the answers to other questions in this list. For instance, server-transparent prefetching is necessarily done at the client. However, approaches that are nontransparent to the server often allow both pushing and pulling variants.

4. What type of information does the prefetching use? Some schemes operate with information gathered only from a single user. Others aggregate information from a group of users, and some use access patterns of Web clients at large.

5. What type of algorithm is used to predict the future? The most common choice is Markov modeling; however, some studies have made use of more intuitive methods, such as prefetching hyperlinks in recently accessed objects.

The intention of our taxonomy is to indicate the major ways in which Web prefetching schemes differ. Some prefetching methods that we survey are better developed than others, and these systems often serve as the best examples in more than one category. Therefore, some prefetching systems are mentioned more than once in the following sections.

12.4 Nondata Prefetching

The term *prefetching* was coined long before the existence of the Web. In other domains, such as computer architecture or file systems, prefetching conventionally denotes fetching data in advance of its need. However, the Web is a distributed system and is therefore more complicated. There are several steps that might be taken to speed up data delivery besides prefetching the data itself. These include reducing the connection setup time and preparing the origin server to respond more quickly to an upcoming request for a Web object.

Earlier, we discussed the idea of using a proxy to cache TCP connections (see Section 7.2.3). The motivation behind that idea was to reduce the overhead of establishing connections. The next logical step is to prefetch entries into the connection cache, that is, to preestablish connections to origin servers. This idea was investigated by Cohen and Kaplan [2000], who considered three types of nondata prefetching:

1. Opening a TCP connection to a server in advance of its use (called *preconnecting*)

2. Resolving a server's DNS name to an IP address in advance of opening a connection to the server (*preresolving*)

3. Sending an HTTP HEAD request (see Section 4.3.1) to the server in advance of the first real request (*prewarming*)

Preconnecting is motivated by the substantial overhead of TCP connection establishment and DNS resolution time. Preresolving is a subset of preconnecting: the only part of a GET request done in advance is to translate the server's name into an IP address. Prewarming is a superset of preconnecting: its purposes are to force the server to perform one-time access control checking in advance of demand requests, and to trigger any cache warming effects in equipment (such as routers, Web caches, and the server itself) along the path from client to server.

Cohen and Kaplan note that a small fraction of object requests are responsible for a disproportionate fraction of the user's latency. They further note that such requests are often "session starting"; that is, they are the first requests made to a server from that client in a long time. Their work aims not so much to reduce the average connection setup time, but to reduce the number of long setups. Their traces show that 7 percent of session-starting HTTP interactions exceed 4 seconds. Their techniques reduce the number of these interactions to 4.5 percent, 2 percent, and 1 percent, for preresolving alone, preconnecting (which subsumes preresolving), and all three, respectively.

Another type of nondata prefetching involves prevalidation of expired cached objects. Doing so removes validation from the critical path of processing demand requests. Several commercial proxies are capable of prevalidating their cached objects. Companies that offer forward proxy services, such as Cidera, also perform prevalidation.

Schechter et al. [1998] suggest that the server should use predictions to preexecute scripts that generate dynamic content. They note that many origin servers are configured with substantial excess cycles, typically double what is needed to cope with the expected average load. Since the latency of script execution is an enduring performance problem, preexecution of scripts might help to speed delivery of the type of objects that impose the highest latency on the user. An obvious complication of script preexecution is that the server must predict not just a script but also the arguments with which the script will be invoked. However, the Web sites explored by Schechter et al. were all found to be remarkably amenable to such predictions. Even considering arguments to be part of the URL and therefore including them into the prediction scope, they produced a prediction (right or wrong) over 80 percent of the time and a precision of over 40 percent on all sites. Put differently, these sites could eliminate computational latency for more than $80\% \times 40\% \approx 30\%$ of requests at the cost of computing at most 60 percent more responses than necessary.[2] Since most servers are provisioned to have significant spare CPU capacity anyway, using spare CPU cycles for preexecuting scripts could allow some sites to reduce user latency without acquiring additional equipment or network bandwidth.

12.5   Nontransparent Prefetching

As mentioned in Section 12.3, there are two aspects in transparent prefetching: user transparency and server transparency. User transparency refers to a lack of user input to the prefetching process. Server transparency refers to a lack of cooperation from the origin server side. A prefetching mechanism can either be fully transparent or rely on cooperation from the user and/or the servers.

12.5.1   User Nontransparency

Two prominent commercial products, PeakJet2000 and NetAccelerator, run on browser machines. Both are server-transparent but allow optional user input to guide prefetching (thus, they can be user nontransparent). Both products will prefetch all the hyperlinks in any object that is fetched on demand. With PeakJet2000, this behavior is optional. Both products allow the user to specify a set of interesting objects similar to a set of bookmarks; these objects are watched for changes and updated when they are observed to have changed. PeakJet maintains its own separate cache, whereas NetAccelerator loads objects into the browser's cache.

Another example of a prefetcher nontransparent to the user is the Coolist research prototype [Wang and Crowcroft 1996]. Coolist runs outside the browser and calls the browser to prefetch into its cache. Coolist allows the user to choose among three levels of prefetching aggressiveness: batch, startup, and pipelined. In each case, the set of objects to be prefetched is specified by the user (the "cool list"). Batch prefetching happens during quiet times, startup prefetching when the browser starts, and pipelined prefetching whenever the user commands.

---

[2] We should note that, while this study excluded static images, it did not exclude other static files. Thus the study left unclear how many of the successful predictions were actually for scripts. The study does mention that the explored sites were rich in dynamic content.

12.5.2 Server Nontransparency

Most prefetching proposals involve cooperation from the server side. Because such cooperation requires a protocol between servers and clients, the deployment of any of these schemes in real life is predicated on the acceptance of their protocols by a critical mass of clients and servers. A nontechnical factor that may limit the usefulness of these approaches is that they often require Web sites to disclose information that might be considered sensitive, such as lists of their most popular objects. For these reasons, these schemes still remain at the prototype stage.

There are several ways that a server can be involved with prefetching.

- It can passively gather access statistics and publish information about the relative popularity of individual objects or about patterns of usage; for example, after object X is referenced, it is likely that object Y will be referenced.

- It can accept usage reports from clients, aggregate and analyze them, and then send the results or make them available to clients.

- It can send prefetching hints to clients.

- It can actively push to clients objects that they are likely to request in the near future.

The first two cases limit server cooperation to providing the clients with information they can use in making prefetching decisions. The first case represents the most passive type of server involvement: it simply analyzes log records and makes the result of the analysis, such as lists of the most-accessed pages, available [Markatos and Chronaki 1998]. Clients can access this information and use it to prefetch some of these objects. The burden of making prefetching decisions rests with the clients.

Usage reports in the second cooperation type may contain richer information than what is available in server logs. In particular, these reports may include usage of other Web sites. This type of cooperation may require the server to accept extra messages, store extra information, and perform substantial extra computation.

In the last two cases, servers accept at least part of the burden of making prefetching decisions. With prefetching hints, servers only communicate their decisions to clients, but the final authority to prefetch rests with the latter. Sending hints requires extending HTTP or HTML to carry the hints. For example, the proposal by Padmanabhan and Mogul [1996] uses an HTTP extension for this purpose. An example of an HTML extension is provided by an early version of the Mozilla Web browser, which included code for processing a special ⟨PREFETCH⟩ tag that specified a URL to prefetch.

Server push is the most speculative type of cooperation, as the server not only makes prefetching decisions but also imposes them on the clients (although clients could decline to accept pushed content). There have been a few proposals for having the server push unsolicited content to clients, including one of the earliest prefetch algorithms proposed by Bestavros [1995], as well as a more recent study of push-prefetching over a dial-up connection [Fan et al. 1999].

12.6 Server Push versus Client Pull

Prefetched data can be pushed by servers onto clients or pulled by clients from servers. With server push, servers send prefetched data to clients without client requests for this data. Client pull is implemented by clients sending requests for prefetched data to servers before the data is actually demanded by the users. Clients use the same HTTP requests to pull prefetched data as they would use to obtain the data when it is actually demanded by users.

One method to implement server push is to return prefetched objects to the client in response to a single HTTP GET request issued by the client. This method reduces the number of requests to the server compared to the case without prefetching, because some future Web accesses of the client will be satisfied from prefetched data without requests to the server. In contrast, client pull increases the number of requests because of the additional requests for prefetched data that is never demanded.

A study by Fan et al. [1999] showed that push reduces the number of requests to the server by approximately 27 to 39 percent compared to the case without prefetching. Also, to preload the same set of objects into a client's browser cache, pushing uses slightly less bandwidth than pulling, due to the GET requests that pulling performs but pushing avoids. On the other hand, a service site that pushes either must be made aware somehow of the contents of the client's cache or risk pushing objects that the client already has cached. Therefore, a naive implementation of pushing carries the risk of greater bandwidth waste than pulling.

It is difficult to quantify the difference in load placed on the server by pushing versus pulling. Pushing might reduce the number of requests but does more work per request, loading each response with possibly several extra objects. However, there is a fixed cost for each request, which pushing amortizes over the included objects. This cost varies across Web sites, as does the cost of generating one object compared to several. Thus, from the server-load perspective, the trade-off between pushing and pulling is likely to be specific for a given Web site.

Another method a server can use to push content to the client is to include a Java applet with its response that downloads additional objects. This approach is limited to browser clients because proxies do not execute Java applets. The advantage of this approach is that it only utilizes existing protocols. The drawbacks are that the client does not participate in the decision-making process and that the client has to download the Java applet in addition to the Web objects involved. Also, some users disable Java on their browsers because of security concerns and, therefore, will not prefetch any content this way. This approach is offered by a company named Fireclick.

12.7   Information Used in Prefetching Algorithms

Most prefetching algorithms predict future Web accesses based on information about previous accesses. The type of information used by the prediction algorithm and the algorithm itself are closely related, so "algorithm" and "information" cannot be truly orthogonal axes of a taxonomy. Nevertheless, there is a range of information quality, and many algorithms can function (though perhaps not equally well) with several different types of information.

Three types of usage information have been used in prefetchers.

1. The usage patterns of a specific individual.

2. The patterns of a defined group, such as users sharing a proxy or individuals who choose to join a group based on their shared interests, which suggests that they might have similar access patterns.

3. The access patterns of Web clients at large. Many of the prediction algorithms [Bestavros 1995; Duchamp 1999; Padmanabhan and Mogul 1996] keep track of which objects tend to be requested in succession by the same client. Other algorithms use only coarse-grain statistics, such as which of a site's objects are most popular [Markatos and Chronaki 1998].

The first two kinds of information are client-centric; this means the information can be collected by the client or forward proxy, and prefetching can be done in a server-transparent manner. Further, the information in these cases reflects access patterns that span multiple servers. The third information type is typically collected on the server. This type of information can aggregate the access patterns of all users who access the server. However, the information is usually (but not always, as we will see in Section 12.7.3) server-specific: it only reflects accesses to the server that collects it.

12.7.1   User-Specific Information

Intuitively, one would expect prediction to be most accurate if it relied on past usage information of a specific user whose actions are being predicted. However, the problem with user-specific information is that the Web is large and gathering high-quality information from a single user is difficult. In addition, past access history of a user is no help at all when the user accesses objects the user has not seen before. This happens whenever the user goes to new Web sites or new parts of previously visited Web sites, or even if a known Web site reorganizes its URLs, which is a common occurrence. For example, Pitkow [1999] finds by examining multiple studies that roughly 50 percent of all objects are accessed only once by the same user. Even when the user revisits objects, the frequency of accessing them may be too low to draw any statistically significant conclusions.

Systems using user-specific information typically run on a browser machine and prefetch into either the browser cache or another cache on the same machine. These systems are server-transparent and for this reason can be autonomously deployed by any user. Note that the commercial systems PeakJet2000 and NetAccelerator mentioned earlier, while running on the browser machine, do not belong in this category because they do not use history information for predictions. (Recall that they prefetch hyperlinks in a visited object as well as user-specified objects.)

Cunha's work [Cunha and Jaccoud 1997; Cunha 1997] is an example of exploiting user-specific usage patterns. However, because of the above-mentioned difficulty with collecting meaningful information, prefetching is only done if a user's *aggregate* behavior is considered amenable to successful prediction. Considering aggregate behavior is useful because it forms a larger sample, which is more likely to be statistically significant. Two mathematical models—adapted from the areas of computer memory caches and linear predictive coding for speech processing—attempt to classify users' aggregate behavior as "surfing" or "conservative." In the surfing mode, the user seldom revisits old objects; therefore, prediction is considered unreliable and no prefetching is performed. On the other hand, the user displaying conservative behavior frequently re-references the same URLs. For these users, the system prefetches objects using the common prediction based on Markov modeling (see Section 12.8.2). A trace-driven simulation [Cunha 1997] showed that this strategy achieved around 25 percent latency reduction at very small bandwidth cost.

12.7.2 Group Information

Using group-specific information is typically facilitated by a proxy. In the simplest case, the proxy aggregates the access history of its clients and uses it to prefetch entries into its own cache in a server-transparent manner. However, proxy clients can also prefetch entries from the proxy into their caches. For this, the proxy and its clients can exchange information and hints, similar to the schemes used between clients and origin servers outlined in Section 12.5.2 As we already mentioned, the advantage of using only user-specific information is that it is not skewed by access patterns of other users, which may not be indicative of the given user, and that prefetching can be done autonomously by any client. On the other hand, aggregate information allows the collection of a much larger, statistically significant sample.

Examples of using group-specific information include approaches by Loon and Bharghavan [1997] and by Fan et al. [1999]. Loon and Bharghavan's proposal actually combines user-specific and group-specific prefetching. A browser machine performs autonomous user-specific prefetching; in addition, each browser sends usage reports to the proxy, which aggregates them and uses the aggregate group information to generate prefetch hints for browsers and to prefetch into the proxy's own cache from origin servers.

The study by Fan et al. focuses on push-prefetching from a proxy to browsers over dial-up modem lines. The proxy decides which objects to push based on the aggregate request history from browsers and usage reports by which browsers inform the proxy of all requests that were satisified from browsers' local caches. The motivation for this approach is, first, that the modem line is a bottleneck slow enough to negate caching benefits at the proxy and, second, it costs nothing—monetarily or in extra load on the Internet or origin servers—to push to a browser objects that are already cached at a proxy. Furthermore, extra bandwidth consumed on the link to the browser is considered to be free, so long as prefetch requests do not conflict with demand requests. The only cost in this approach is some increase of the proxy's load.

Both systems prefetch into browser machines only during idle times, to minimize the impact of prefetch traffic on the browser connection to the Internet. This restriction is important when the browser connection is the performance bottleneck, which is often the case for slow dial-up connections.

12.7.3 Multiuser Information

Multiuser information refers to information, collected from many unrelated users, about which objects tend to be referenced in sequence. Web servers usually collect this information and either use it themselves to make predictions or disseminate it back to the clients. A wide variety of algorithms, including all those presented in Section 12.8, build data structures that describe this information.

A simulation study by Jiang and Kleinrock [1998] compared prefetching quality using multiserver client-specific and multiuser server-specific information. They found that client-specific information yields the best precision, confirming the intuition that we discussed earlier. However, they also found that the combination of client-specific information with server-specific information yields higher prefetch recall than using either alone.

Multiuser information may differ in detail and content. One algorithm considered in the next section uses coarse-grain information on the aggregate popularity of different objects on a site. Other algorithms rely on finer-grained usage patterns that estimate probabilities of various object sequences.

The approach by Duchamp [1999] takes an interesting next step: there, servers aggregate usage reports containing not only accesses to their own objects but also outside objects that were followed from their objects. We describe more details of this algorithm later, in Section 12.8.5, focusing here on the information collection aspect. A usage report describes the fact that one or more hyperlinks contained within an object have been recently followed from that object.[3] The usage report also includes other

---

[3] Note that in general the server cannot infer this information from the HTTP `referrer` request header. Indeed, the `referrer` field specifies the object from which the current object has been accessed. In other words, it can help compute transition probabilities *to* the current object. On the other hand, the usage report in Duchamp [1999] describes which objects had been accessed from the current object in the past, allowing the server to compute transition probabilities *from* the current object. The latter is obviously more useful for prefetching, since the server may then pass hints to clients accessing this object about the objects they are likely to access next.

information useful for prefetching, such as the size of the followed documents and how much time elapsed between access to the referrer and access to the referee. The usage report is passed as an extension HTTP header in client requests to the server. The server accumulates the information from all usage reports that pertain to the same object and summarizes it in a usage profile of the object. Whenever the server delivers the object to a prefetch-enabled client, it piggybacks the object's usage profile as an HTTP response header. Decisions whether and how to prefetch rest with the client because the client best knows its own usage patterns, the state of its cache, and the effective bandwidth of its link to the Internet. Thus, unlike many other prefetching approaches, this more complicated information-passing method accounts for cross-server usage patterns. According to Duchamp, the cross-server usage is significant, comprising 29 percent of referenced hyperlinks.

12.8   Prediction Algorithms

Every prefetching system faces the problem of predicting a client's future accesses based on information about the past. Prediction algorithms differ in the level of past usage detail they consider and how far in the future they try to predict. Simpler, coarser-grain information may miss some prediction opportunities but is easier to collect and process. Some algorithms consider only coarse-grain history information such as aggregate object popularity. These algorithms do not use access patterns in their predictions. Using the terminology of Section 6.5, they do not exploit *spatial locality* of reference. Many other algorithms attempt to reach conclusions of the form, "if a client has accessed a sequence of objects $X_1, \ldots, X_m$, then it is likely to access a sequence of objects $Y_1, \ldots, Y_n$ soon after." Different algorithms use different values for m and n, and some determine these values dynamically. An important class of these algorithms use $m = 1$, thus basing their predictions on the client's last access only. Finally, some algorithms also exploit information about hyperlink relationships between objects available from HTML hyperlinks and HTTP headers, or so-called structure information.

Algorithms that exploit patterns of accesses (or spatial locality of reference) commonly use some variation of *Markov modeling*, a general technique for finding patterns within a sequence of events. We also describe representative examples of other types of prediction algorithms mentioned above.

12.8.1   Popularity-Based Predictions

The *Top 10* proposal by Markatos and Chronaki [1998] is an example of a system that uses purely popularity-based predictions. The basic idea of the Top 10 proposal is for servers to publish their most-accessed objects, called the "Top 10" (although there may be more than ten popular objects). Clients prefetch some fraction of the list.

A client has a *prefetching agent* that periodically creates the client's *prefetching profile*, which is the number of objects the client has fetched from various servers. The client uses the prefetching profile to decide how many objects to prefetch from which servers. The decision is based on a simple algorithm that uses two parameters: one indicates how many times a client must have contacted a server before the client will prefetch at all, and the other specifies the maximum number of objects it will prefetch from a server. The client prefetches from a server after the number of objects fetched from this server in the previous period reaches the threshold (the first parameter). Then the client prefetches the N most popular objects from this server, where N is the number of objects fetched in the previous period or the maximum number of documents specified in the second parameter, whichever is less.

Using a trace-driven simulation with traces from five Web sites, Markatos and Chronaki showed that the Top 10 approach achieves a precision of 3 to 23 percent, depending on the trace. Also, since objects on a given server typically have very uneven popularity distribution (see Section 6.4), the size of the Top 10 lists can be limited (Markatos and Chronaki suggest 100 to 500 objects but do not specify the total number of objects on the servers they studied). The two parameters used in the algorithm to limit prefetching keep extra traffic caused by unsuccessful prefetching at a low level (10 to 20 percent in their study). Another result is that Top 10 lists can be compiled and released rather infrequently, about every one or two weeks. What remains unclear is how to choose proper values for the two parameters in the algorithm.

12.8.2 Markov Modeling

Markov algorithms are used in many domains, including file system prefetching and speech recognition. When applied to the Web, a Markov algorithm regards the IDs of objects requested by a single client as a string, and attempts to discover patterns in the string. Detected recurrence of the initial part of a pattern triggers prefetching of the remainder of the pattern. In this subsection, we consider a simple case where predictions are based on the last-accessed object only. This case corresponds to first-order Markov models. We discuss longer patterns in Section 12.8.4.

The typical implementation of a Markov algorithm represents objects as graph nodes, as shown in Figure 12.1. A weighted, directed edge is drawn between two

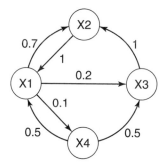

Figure 12.1 A Markov graph

nodes if the two objects they represent are ever accessed consecutively by the same client (or sometimes if the two objects have both been accessed in the indicated order by the same client within a certain period of time). The weight of the edge usually records the probability of the corresponding object transition: the more often the two objects are accessed in order, the greater the weight of the edge. To make a prefetch prediction, a search algorithm traverses the graph, looking for the most heavily weighted edges and paths. For example, the node for object X1 in Figure 12.1 has three edges leaving it, pointing to nodes for objects X2, X3, and X4. When object X1 is accessed, the prediction algorithm examines this portion of the graph and might choose to prefetch one, two, three, or none of X1's successors, depending on the edge weights, a cut-off probability value, and various system factors such as the amount of bandwidth available for prefetching.

To illustrate why the prediction algorithm should also examine longer paths in the Markov graph, consider the case when object X3 is accessed. In this case the prediction algorithm should prefetch both X2 and X1, since X2 follows X3 with probability one and X1 follows X2 with the same probability.

Compared to more intuitive approaches, the two advantages of the Markov approach are that it does not depend upon extra information such as object hyperlink relationships, which may not always be available, and that it can discover nonintuitive patterns.

There are a few significant disadvantages to Markov algorithms. One is that such algorithms often have a high cost, measured in storage and computation time. Predictive ability is improved by retaining as many nodes in the Markov graph as possible and examining as many paths as possible. To achieve high prefetch precision, large graphs must be maintained and searched. For example, the first-degree Markov graphs in the study by Zukerman et al. [1999] course graph size can be limited by discarding nodes representing infrequently accessed objects, but precision will be reduced. A second disadvantage is that Markov approaches are much more effective only after a "training" interval in order to build a graph that is big enough for statistical significance. For example, in the study by Zukerman et al., the first 80 percent of the trace data was used for building an initial graph, with results derived from only the last 20 percent.

Several Markov-based studies use training intervals that correspond to days of activity in their traces. Accordingly, the graph used by a Markov prediction algorithm is a precious data structure that should be checkpointed to safeguard against loss. The large size of the graph suggests a third disadvantage, which is the difficulty of answering the question of when data in the graph becomes too old and should be removed. On one hand, removing data about past accesses is desirable in order not to prefetch based on outdated patterns of use. On the other hand, it is important to retain a large record of past access patterns. The most common approach is to apply an *aging function* to the data in the graph so that, for example, 20 percent of the weight of an edge is determined by recent activity and 80 percent is determined by past activity. Such an aging function is somewhat arbitrary, and there has been little or no systematic comparison of different aging functions or parameter choices (such as the 20 and 80 percent coefficients and the dividing point between "recent" and "past").

Finally, Markov algorithms suffer a drawback of being too general. While it is advantageous not to depend on structure information, Markov algorithms spend considerable resources to rediscover information that is already evident in HTML or the HTTP `referrer` header and is more simply extracted therefrom. For example, the earliest Markov-based studies made no distinction between HTML and image URLs, with the result that most discovered patterns were links from an HTML object to its embedded images. Some studies now exclude image URLs on the basis that the prefetcher would deliver both the HTML object and all its embedded image objects.

Different algorithms use different notions of object transitions when building a Markov graph. An approach most closely following classic Markov modeling considers that a transition from object A to object B occurs if and only if the same client accesses B immediately after A [Nicholson et al. 1998; Zukerman et al. 1999]. Other algorithms consider that a transition from A to B occurs if and only if the same client accesses B within a certain time T after A [Bestavros 1995], or within a certain number of object accesses [Padmanabhan and Mogul 1996]. An important implication of these more general notions of object transitions is that transitions originating from the same node are not mutually exclusive. For example, if $T = 5$ seconds and the client accesses object B 2 seconds after A and object C 2 seconds after B, then the execution history will contain both transition A → B and transition A → C. Thus, the probability weights on the edges that originate from a node can sum up to more than 1. In Section 12.8.5 we will encounter more definitions of an object transition that depend on the object's contents.

12.8.3 Examples of Algorithms Using First-Order Markov Modeling

Among the earliest prefetch algorithms is that proposed by Bestavros [1995]. His algorithm uses the Markov graph with the time-based notion of an object transition; that is, transition A → B occurs when a client accesses B within time T after accessing A. When object D_i is requested, the server sends it plus any other object D_j that is reachable from D_i by a path in the Markov graph and whose access probability exceeds a probability threshold P. The access probability is computed as the product of probabilities that label all edges in the path. For example, in Figure 12.1 the probability of the path X1 → X4 → X3 is $0.1 \times 0.5 = 0.05$. Note that this product is a conservative estimate of future access probability of D_j, since the graph may have several paths from D_i to D_j. In Figure 12.1, there is a direct path from X1 to X3, in addition to the path considered earlier. If transitions starting from the same object were mutually exclusive, we could compute the total access probability of a successor node as a sum of all path probabilities that lead to the successor. In the models with nonexclusive transitions (such as Bestavros's), this may result in a gross overestimation of future access probabilities. Consequently, Bestavros only considers individual path probabilities, in effect using the path whose probability is the greatest. Continuing our example of Figure 12.1, if $P = 0.1$, the algorithm will explore the path X1 → X4 → X3 and the path X1 → X3 and will prefetch X3 because the latter has probability above the threshold. Bestavros's scheme never prefetches objects over a certain size, which is a common technique many algorithms use to limit the cost of a wrong prediction. The statistics for building the graph are gathered over 60 days and updated daily.

Bestavros analyzed the performance of his algorithm by simulating it on an access log gathered from Boston University's computer science department from January to March 1995, approximately 200,000 accesses. Table 12.1 shows the prediction recall and latency reductions that the algorithm achieves at various bandwidth costs. As more bandwidth is used (which corresponds to lower probability thresholds), the returns diminish. Another relevant result in this study is that updating statistics daily is better than weekly or every 60 days. For example, at 50 percent extra bandwidth, client latency is 67 percent, 63 percent, and 60 percent of the original when statistics are updated every 60, 7, and 1 days, respectively. Also, computing the Markov graph from 30 days of usage data is better than from 60 days. These results give a sense of how up-to-date the usage data must be for effective prefetching.

An algorithm using Markov graph with object transitions based on access counts is described by Padmanabhan and Mogul [1996]. In this approach, an object transition X → Y occurs, and the weight of the corresponding edge in the graph is updated, if the same client accesses Y within w accesses of the last access of X. The weight on the edge indicates the probability that a client accesses object Y within w accesses after X. Upon a request for object X, the algorithm considers immediate successors of X in the graph and selects those with transition probability above threshold P as candidates for prefetching. (Recall that as object transitions are not mutually exclusive, probabilities of transitions originating from an object do not sum up to 1.) An important difference between Padmanabhan and Mogul's and Bestavros's algorithms is that the former does not consider nonimmediate successors. Instead, Padmanabhan and Mogul's algorithm adjusts how far into the future it predicts by varying w, the maximum number of accesses between objects in an object transition,

Table 12.1 Performance of Bestavros's prefetching algorithm

Bandwidth Used	Requests at Server (Recall)	Client Latency
+5%	−30%	−23%
+10%	−35%	−27%
+50%	−45%	−40%
+100%	−52%	−46%

which they call a *lookahead window size*. Thus, Padmanabhan and Mogul's algorithm does not underestimate future access probabilities of objects.

Trace-driven simulations showed that Padmanabhan and Mogul's algorithm achieves up to approximately 40 percent latency reduction over a link with the bandwidth of 150Kbps, although at the cost of much increased network traffic (70 percent) [Padmanabhan and Mogul 1996]. In contrast, Bestavros achieved 40 percent latency reduction with only 50 percent extra traffic. However, a direct comparison of performance results obtained in different studies is virtually impossible because of the differences in study methodology and peripheral algorithm details. What is significant is that Padmanabhan and Mogul found only limited latency improvement when the lookahead window w is increased beyond 3 to 4 accesses. This result suggests that the prefetching algorithm needs to predict only the next few accesses.

12.8.4 Exploiting Longer Request Sequences

The algorithms of the preceding subsection predict future accesses of a client by considering the client's last request only. (These algorithms are called the *first-order algorithms.*) However, it may be beneficial to look at earlier accesses also. Consider, for example, a site where clients always access object C after accessing objects A and B, and object E after objects D and B. A fragment of the first-order Markov graph reflecting access patterns after object B is shown in Figure 12.2. It shows that both C and E follow B with equal probability; indeed, either object occurs 50 percent of the time after B is accessed. An algorithm using this graph could not discriminate between objects C and E when attempting to predict a client access after the visit to object B. As a result the algorithm would either give up on prediction (decreasing the prediction recall) or predict both successors (decreasing the precision). In contrast, an algorithm that bases its predictions on the past two accesses will confidently choose between these objects. We refer to algorithms that can take into account earlier requests as *high-order algorithms*. In the remainder of this subsection, a request sequence will denote a stream of requests from the same client, where the time between any neighboring requests does not exceed a certain time limit. (Sometimes such request streams are called client *sessions*.)

One way to account for longer request sequences is to use higher-order Markov models [Zukerman et al. 1999]. An *m*-order Markov model reflects probability of

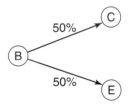

Figure 12.2 A Markov graph that cannot discriminate between object successors

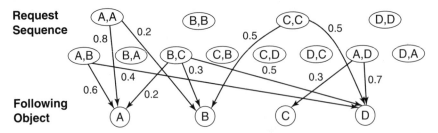

Figure 12.3 A second-order Markov graph

transitions of the form "given the last m requests from a client, the next request will be to object X." Graphically, these models can be expressed as bipartite graphs with one class of nodes corresponding to sequences of length m, the other class of nodes corresponding to objects, and edges from nodes in the first class to nodes in the second class labeled with the probabilities of corresponding transitions. For example, Figure 12.3 illustrates a second-order Markov graph for four objects, A, B, C, and D.

A problem with high-order Markov models is that long request sequences may not occur often enough to draw statistically significant predictions. In Figure 12.3, if A is a root object on a Web site that is always a starting point in any client session, then a second-order Markov model will never be able to predict a successor of A because it predicts based only on request sequences of length 2, and no such sequence is ever observed that would end with A. This suggests that to predict using sequences of length m, one must combine Markov models of orders $1, \dots, m$.

Fan et al. [1999] describe a *Partial Matching* high-order algorithm that is based on the Prediction-by-Partial-Matching data compressor [Bell et al. 1990; Curewitz et al. 1993]. The algorithm proposed by Fan et al. essentially implements the combined Markov model idea. Their algorithm is parameterized three ways: the number of past requests considered (m), the number of future requests predicted (l), and the probability threshold that an object must surpass to become a prefetch candidate (P). The algorithm maintains a data structure that lists all subsequences of up to $m + l$ URLs accessed by any user in the past and the number of times these subsequences were accessed. To conserve space, sequences with common prefixes are organized in a tree structure that stores the common prefixes once. Fan et al. call it a *history structure*.

For example, assume $m = 2$ and $l = 1$, and that users requested URL sequences (A, B) ten times, (A, C, D, C) five times, and (B, A, C) five times. Table 12.2 lists all subsequences of length up to $m + l = 3$ in this history and their occurrence count (note

Table 12.2 Subsequence Frequencies

A	B	C	D	A, B	A, C	C, D	D, C	A, C, D	C, D, C	B, A	B, A, C
20	15	15	5	10	10	5	5	5	5	5	5

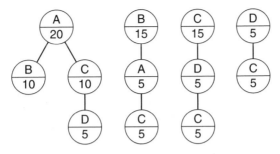

Figure 12.4 A history structure for the URL sequences in Table 12.2

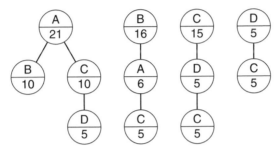

Figure 12.5 The history structure of Figure 12.4 after insertion of sequence (B, A)

that the subsequence (A, C, D, C) is omitted because it exceeds the length limit). The corresponding history structure is shown in Figure 12.4, where the number in a node indicates the count of the URL subsequence obtained by descending the corresponding tree from the root to the node in question.

To find prefetch candidates, the algorithm determines all subsequences in the history structure that match any suffix of the client's last m requests. URLs that follow these subsequences in the history structure within l tree levels with a probability that exceeds P are selected for prefetching. To limit the cost of a wrong prediction, objects larger than 50KBytes are not prefetched, and only up to eight most likely objects are prefetched at once. Continuing our example, assume that user request sequence (B, A) arrives. Figure 12.5 shows the history structure that reflects this new sequence. At this point, the prediction algorithm will try to match suffixes A and B, A of this sequence. The first suffix matches the subsequence that ends at the root of the left-most tree in Figure 12.5 and yields candidates B and C with the probabilities of 10/21. The second suffix matches the subsequence that ends at node A in the second tree from the left. The algorithm will add its sole successor C, which has probability 5/6, to the candidate list. Assuming threshold $P = 0.75$ the algorithm will prefetch only C. A lower threshold, say, $P = 0.25$ will cause all three candidates to be prefetched.

Fan et al. [1999] evaluated their algorithm in the specific environment where a proxy pushes predicted objects to the browsers over slow dial-up links. In particular, they assumed that prefetching is performed only during modem idle times and is interrupted once the user makes a demand request. Their study does not consider the purely algorithmic characteristics of their approach, such as recall and precision, a fact that complicates a comparison of their algorithm with other prediction algorithms. Under these conditions, a simulation study using dial-up traces showed a latency reduction of 17 to 23.4 percent, depending on parameter settings. Wasted bandwidth varied approximately from 1 to 15 percent.

Another high-order algorithm, proposed by Schechter et al. [1998], uses *path profiles*, a concept taken from compiler optimization. This algorithm differs from the partial matching algorithm in the way it tries to limit the amount of history information. The partial matching algorithm limits the state by storing subsequences of up to $m + l$ URLs; the path profiles algorithm does not limit the subsequence length but stores only subsequences that have occurred at least T times in the past, where T is a parameter of the algorithm.

An interesting implication of this difference is that the partial matching algorithm is able to construct its history structure on the fly, continuously updating it for every request received by the server, whereas the path profiles algorithm must periodically construct its history structure using server logs collected over the previous period. This can make the partial matching algorithm more responsive to changes in demand patterns, although it is unclear how important this difference is in practice. The path profiles algorithm cannot construct its data structure on the fly because when a new sequence appears, it will obviously have a count of 1 and not be stored in the history structure. When this sequence occurs again, it will again have a count of 1, since the previous occurrence has not been recorded, and again will not be stored. One can see that the new sequence will never be stored, regardless of how frequently it occurs. To bypass this problem, the path profiles algorithm uses server logs that contain all access sequences in the previous period to construct its history structure off-line.

As an example, consider a server log that contains eight occurrences of request sequence (A, B, C), two occurrences of (A, B, D), five occurrences of (A, C, D, A), two occurrences of (A, C, D), and three occurrences of (A, C, B). The subsequence frequency for this log is shown in Table 12.3, and Figure 12.6 gives the history structure for this log, assuming $T = 3$.[4]

Given a client access sequence S collected after the history structure was constructed, the path profiles algorithm finds the longest suffix of this sequence that occurs in the history structure. The algorithm then chooses the URL that most frequently follows that path in the history structure as the predicted URL. In our example, given a request sequence (B, A, C), the longest matched suffix will be A, C in the left-most tree, and D will be the predicted URL.

---

[4] We draw the history structure as a forest of trees to highlight the similarity with the partial match algorithms. Schechter et al. [1998] convert the forest to a single tree by connecting all trees to a fictitious root node.

Table 12.3 Subsequence Frequencies

A	B	C	D	A,B	A,C	B,C	B,D	C,D
25	13	18	9	10	10	8	2	7

D,A	C,B	A,B,C	A,B,D	A,C,D	C,D,A	A,C,B	A,C,D,A
5	3	8	2	7	5	3	5

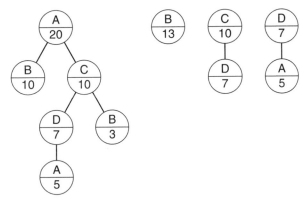

Figure 12.6 An example of the history structure used
by the path profile algorithm

By analyzing traces from several large Web sites, Schechter et al. found their algorithm to produce a prediction (right or wrong) in about 80 to 100 percent of the time, with prefetch precision of 40 to 50 percent. Similar to the partial matching algorithm, the path profiles algorithm could also predict multiple future URLs by descending further down the tree from the selected path (predicting A in addition to D in our example).

High-order algorithms maintain and process much larger state than their first-order counterparts. For instance, graphs in Figure 12.3 to Figure 12.6 would contain only four nodes, the same as the number of distinct URLs in the history, in a first-order Markov model. Overall, Fan et al. [1998] indicate that the size of the graph in practice is proportional to $(m+l) \times N$, where N is the number of requests in the history, m is the maximum length of past request sequences considered, and l is the maximum length of future request sequences predicted. Zukerman et al. [1990] in their comparative study found that going from first- to second-order Markov models increases the size of the graph by an order of magnitude, from around 17,000 nodes and 125,000 edges to around 123,000 nodes and 288,000 edges.

A natural question is how much high-order algorithms improve prediction. Unfortunately, existing studies give no satisfactory answer to this question. Fan et al. [1998] considered only cases where $m=1$ (equivalent to the first-order algorithms of

Section 12.8.3) and $m = 2$ (that is, considering up to the last two accesses). Although the latter case increases the number of times the algorithm is able to make a prediction (thereby increasing the number of prefetched objects), it does not appear to improve the prediction precision, as indicated by Figure 4 in Fan et al. [1999]. Schechter et al. [1998] did observe a considerable improvement in prediction precision over a first-order algorithm (which they call a *point prediction*). However, the first-order algorithm they studied prefetches the most likely successor of the last object regardless of the absolute probability value of this transition. Thus, the result may not be indicative of typical first-order algorithms, which use a probability threshold. Also, Schechter et al. [1998] did not compare graph sizes of their high-order algorithm and the first-order algorithm. A conclusive analysis of high-order versus first-order algorithms is therefore yet to be performed.

12.8.5 Structure Algorithms

While Markov algorithms consider purely past request patterns, *structure algorithms* make use of information in the objects themselves. Hyperlinks that connect different objects are a common type of such information. This information seems intuitively to be a good predictor of future accesses, because when the user accesses objects by clicking on links rather than typing their URLs, every future access follows a hyperlink in the object currently viewed.

A server using a Markov prediction algorithm can account for structure information by retaining only edges $A \rightarrow B$ in its Markov graph such that object A contains a hyperlink to object B [Zukerman et al. 1999]. Therefore, the algorithm will predict a future request only when the current object has a hyperlink to it. Like other server-centric schemes that collect request histories within a single Web site, a server using this method can predict future requests only to itself.

A more complicated algorithm that uses structure information was proposed by Duchamp [1999]. (We mentioned this algorithm in Section 12.7.3.) In this algorithm, clients and servers exchange information that can help clients prefetch objects from other servers. In particular, clients occasionally send *usage reports* to servers, which describe the fact that one or more hyperlinks contained in an object from this server were recently followed.

The server makes a best effort to accumulate the information from all usage reports that pertain to the same object, P. When the server delivers P to a prefetch-enabled client, it attaches a summary (called a *usage profile*) of the information that it has obtained from all clients' earlier usage reports for that object. The summary indicates how often hyperlinks contained in object P have been referenced, relative to the number of references to P in the same time period. A client can negotiate the time period it wants the server to use. Time in this case is measured by references to object P. For example, a client can request usage profiles that describe the frequency of hyperlink references relative to the last 10, 25, or 50 references of the originating object P. A client that receives a usage profile along with object P may choose whether or not to prefetch any hyperlinks, according to any algorithm it prefers.

In particular, Duchamp proposes the following algorithm. The client asks for two usage profiles over time periods spanning the last 10 and 50 references. The client continually measures the speed of its HTTP GET transfers, and maintains a running average effective bandwidth. Because of the inaccuracy of the bandwidth estimates, the client ensures that its outstanding prefetch requests can consume no more than 50 percent of the measured average bandwidth. Until this bandwidth limit is reached, the client prefetches hyperlinks described in the last-10 usage report, in descending order of hyperlink reference frequency, down to a limit of 25 percent. For example, assume that object P contains hyperlinks to objects A, B, and C, and P's profile says that among the last 10 times P was requested, this request was followed by a request to A five times, to B three times, and to C two times. Assuming the bandwidth limit allows it, the client will prefetch objects A and B but not C, since its probability of being referenced is below 25 percent. As prefetch requests complete, more are issued from the last-10 profile and then from the last-50 profile, again in descending order of popularity down to the 25 percent limit. A prefetch request is considered complete only when the HTML object and all its embedded images have been loaded. If a user initiates a request for an object that has not been prefetched, all prefetch requests are aborted until the user request is fulfilled.

On a trace of accesses from six clients over about five months, this approach produced prediction recall of 42 percent for HTML objects and 62 percent for all types of objects at the expense of a 24 percent increase in network traffic. That resulted in a latency reduction of 52 percent [Duchamp 1999]. Although it is dangerous to compare results across different studies, we have seen that structure-oblivious first-order Markov algorithms required 70 to 100 percent extra traffic to achieve these levels of latency reduction (see Section 12.8.3).

12.9 Summary

Prefetching can be an important tool in improving user experiences. Studies have indicated that it can potentially be more effective in reducing Web access latency than passive caching. A fundamental trade-off in prefetching is that it decreases latency at the expense of extra bandwidth consumption. Some techniques attempt to get around this trade-off by using only "free" bandwidth, for example, the bandwidth of the otherwise idle network connection. One should realize, however, that much of the network path between clients and servers is usually a resource shared among numerous computers on the Internet, so identifying truly idle connections can be done only in some specific computing environments. An important example of such an environment is prefetching between a browser connected to its ISP by a dial-up link and the proxy at the ISP side of the link. Other techniques reduce additional bandwidth costs by prefetching the means of data transfer (such as opening a TCP connection or performing a DNS lookup for a future request) instead of data itself.

Successful prefetching relies crucially on a prediction algorithm that anticipates the future requests of a client. The quality of the prediction can be judged using two system-independent metrics: recall and precision. However, it is difficult to compare algorithms proposed in different studies, since the studies often compare their proposals to the case with no prefetching rather than other prefetching schemes. On the other hand, comparing numbers from different studies is often impossible because they use different traces and specific system environments (such as performing prefetching only when the network link is otherwise idle), and they incorporate peripheral issues into their algorithms (such as off-line versus dynamic maintenance of the Markov graph, or a size limit on prefetched objects) that affect their results.

There are also nonalgorithmic factors that can affect the overall quality of the prefetching scheme. These factors include the transparency of prefetching to clients and servers, the space and computation overhead of the prediction algorithm, and whether prefetching avoids interference with servicing demand requests. Thus, when evaluating different prefetching schemes, one should also look at end-to-end performance metrics such as user-observed latency, network and server loads, and bandwidth costs.

Some of the most interesting prefetching schemes require cooperation between the client and the server. Unfortunately, this requirement greatly handicaps the deployment of these schemes. Until some scheme emerges as a clear winner and its underlying client-server cooperation is standardized, these schemes can only be used in situations where both the clients and the servers belong to the same administrative entity. In particular, these schemes can be used for prefetching between browsers and forward proxies, between surrogates and origin servers, or between clients and origin servers on an enterprise network.

Chapter 13
Caching the Uncacheable

The usefulness of proxy caching is limited by their low hit rates. Recall from Chapter 7 that realistic object hit rates are around 40 percent, and byte hit rates are even lower. The main reason hit rates are so low is that a large portion of Web requests—up to 43 percent in some studies [Feldmann et al. 1999]—are for uncacheable content. So proxies have just over half the requests to work with. If we factor out uncacheable content, hit rates would be much higher: assuming the above numbers, the hit rate would be around $40\%/(100 - 43)\% = 70\%$.

There are a variety of reasons why a content provider may wish to make some content uncacheable. These reasons include collecting accurate usage data, avoiding stale delivery, delivering dynamically generated content that changes on every access, and personalizing content for a given user. Section 6.3 mentions several types of uncacheable content and the frequency of their occurrence. With caches being useless for such a large portion of Web content, replication is currently the only tool for providing scalable access to uncacheable data. In Part III, we talk in detail about replication. But replication alone, as useful as it is, cannot fully replace the benefits of caching content close to the client.

There are always going to be legitimate reasons for making some content uncacheable. Unfortunately, Web developers often indiscriminately prohibit caching, a practice known as *cache busting*. In this chapter we discuss how a content provider can achieve its legitimate goals in a cache-friendly way. We also describe some new technology proposals that extend cache benefits to some uncacheable content.

13.1 A Note on Implementation

Various techniques considered in this chapter require various degrees of modification to browsers, Web servers, or proxies. Browsers can be extended in three basic ways.

1. *Co-locating a customized proxy with the browser*. In this approach, illustrated in Figure 13.1a, the computer that runs the browser application also runs a

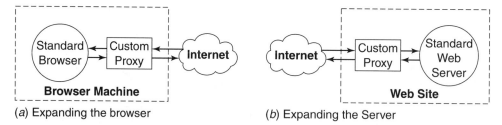

(*a*) Expanding the browser   (*b*) Expanding the Server

Figure 13.1 Customizing standard Web browsers (a) and servers (b) using custom proxies

```
<html>
<body>
<applet codebase="http://www.firm-x.com/custom-applet/"
   code="customizer.class">
<param name="content"
   value="raw content of page www.firm-x.com/foo.html to be processed">
any extra parameters needed to process raw content
</applet>
</body>
</html>
```

Figure 13.2 An example of wrapping a Web object into a Java applet
(The wrapped object's URL is http://www.firm-x.com/foo.html.)

custom proxy. The browser is configured to send its requests to the custom proxy. The custom proxy implements all new functionality; it receives a standard HTTP request from the browser and sends a standard HTTP response back. The browser itself is oblivious to any new functionality.

2. *Browser plug-ins.* A new content type is defined and a new plug-in is created to process this content type. The new functionality will apply to the new content type only.

3. *Java applets or JavaScript.* In the Java applets approach (the JavaScript approach is similar in spirit), pages that require extra functionality are wrapped into Java applet invocations as illustrated in Figure 13.2. When the browser downloads, say, http://www.firm-x.com/foo.html, it actually receives the response shown in Figure 13.2, which contains the invocation to an applet with the entire raw content as a parameter.[1] The applet then custom-processes the raw content and renders it. If the user clicks on a link contained in this page, the applet will catch the click event and hand over the requested URL to the browser, thereby completing its mission. The applet itself may be cached from a previous invocation. We call this approach *applet wrapping.*

---

[1] Alternatively, the parameter can include an internal URL of raw content, which is then downloaded by the applet.

The first two approaches require browser configuration and installation of the custom proxy or plug-in. A major advantage of the third approach is that it can be immediately used by most legacy browsers with no reconfiguration and no user intervention. On the other hand, some users disable Java and JavaScript on their browsers; these browsers will be unable to display pages that utilize this approach. Also, the last two approaches invoke custom processing only upon receiving a response. For modifications at the request-sending phase, only the first approach is applicable.

While all these approaches involve performance penalties, they often suffice as a way to introduce a new functionality. Once the new functionality gains wide acceptance, it can be added directly to the browser core.

Web servers provide APIs, such as servlets and CGI scripts, that allow a developer to extend their functionality without modifying the source code of servers themselves. In addition, servers are sometimes extended through a custom server-side proxy (Figure 13.1b), which acts like a surrogate server except that its role is to implement a desired new functionality. The last approach was used, for example, in a proof-of-concept implementation of IBM's Web Express product [Housel and Lindquist 1996], which we discuss in Section 13.5.2.

Commercial proxies are hard to extend. Hardware-based proxies that offer both hardware and software as a single piece of equipment (otherwise known as *appliance proxies*) can be modified only by their vendors. Software-based solutions where proxy software runs on a standard machine on top of a standard operating system, sometimes provide APIs that allow extensive customization. Inktomi's Traffic Server, for example, follows this approach. Open-source solutions, such as Squid, allow the greatest flexibility (and the greatest risk of introducing bugs into the core of the system). Chapter 17 discusses the issue of customizing proxies in detail.

Of course, one could always couple the appliance proxy, just like the browser or Web server, with a stripped-down custom proxy. However, the overhead of this approach would likely be prohibitive in situations where appliance proxies are deployed. An interesting proposal for injecting new functionality into a proxy using *cache applets* is described in Section 13.6.

13.2 Modified Content and Stale Delivery Avoidance

When an object is updated on the origin server, its cached copies become obsolete and must be refetched to avoid stale delivery. Since caching is largely outside the control of content providers, there is an inherent tension between caching and providers' desire to ensure their content freshness. Some Web developers simply make their entire content uncacheable to guarantee freshness. However, this approach is grossly misguided. It reduces user-perceived performance of the perpetrating Web sites and overloads the Internet for everyone else.

13.2.1 Cache-Friendly Approaches to Stale Delivery Avoidance

We have discussed throughout the book a multitude of mechanisms available to the Web developer to limit or avoid stale delivery. At the extreme, the developer can include the `must-revalidate` header with every response, forcing proxies and browsers to validate every object on every access. This approach is already a huge improvement over blind cache busting. However, a careful look at a Web site will always identify plenty of content that changes infrequently, or whose absolute freshness is not crucial. For this content, validation on every access is an overkill. Images in particular typically do not change, and when they do, they often receive new URLs, so no stale delivery is possible. In other cases, content can tolerate limited staleness. That can be achieved by assigning an appropriate TTL to an object through `expires` or `max-age` response headers. Even a short TTL of a few minutes can lead to significant cache utilization by busy proxies: the proxy at AOL or another large ISP can serve many requests from its cache during a short period of time.

Some content is modified at predictable points of time. For instance, a news Web site may be updated at the top of every hour. In these cases, the origin server can assign an absolute TTL to responses so that objects expire at the end of the hour on which they were downloaded. Then substantial caching becomes possible without sacrificing any freshness guarantees. Other content is modified at a predictable rate, such as stock quotes at a financial site that receives its data feed every 30 seconds. In these cases, the site cannot provide absolutely fresh content anyway, and allowing some staleness does not weaken consistency guarantees. In our example of the stock-quoting site, the origin server can assign a relative TTL of 15 seconds to its stock quotes (using the `max-age=15` response header), and still guarantee that the quotes will be at most 30 seconds obsolete.

An origin server can also probe proxies that access it to see if they accept HTTP DELETE, PUT, or POST requests, and if so, use them to implement a variety of the cache invalidation techniques discussed in Chapter 10. Recall that the origin server can distinguish proxies from browsers through the `via` request header.

13.2.2 Utilizing Cached Stale Content

Caches are overly conservative in deciding when cached information is usable. When an object changes at the origin, the entire object is downloaded anew, no matter how small the modification. A closer look at Web data reveals that, at least for textual objects, modifications usually involve a small portion of a object [Banga et al. 1997; Mogul et al. 1997]. It therefore seems wasteful to delete the entire cached object. A better solution is for the cache to obtain just the modification, or *delta*, and apply it to the object to arrive at the correct content. Using deltas involves an extension to HTTP called *delta encoding* [Mogul et al. 1997]. The extension incorporates the following main ideas.

When validating an object, the client uses entity tags (`ETags`), to avoid possible ambiguities of the `last-modified` date (see Section 5.1). As an indication that the client understands delta encoding, these requests also specify delta formats the client can decode using optional HTTP 1.1 headers such as the `accept-encoding` header.

Upon receiving such a request, a server checks whether the object identified by the request `ETag` is still valid, just as it normally would. If the object has changed, the server that understands delta encoding checks whether it still has the client's older version, identified by the entity tag from the request, and if it can produce the delta in any of the formats specified in the request. If so, the server may decide to use delta encoding for the response, in which case the server chooses a format, computes the delta in this format, and sends it to the client. The response uses a new response code indicating that the response contains a delta (as opposed to the entire object). The response also specifies the format of the delta (for example, in the HTTP 1.1 `content-encoding` header) and the entity tag of the new object version. The latter will allow the client to use delta encoding for future requests.

Delta encoding can be used in communication between the browser and proxy, the proxy and origin server, the browser and origin server, or two proxies in a cooperative proxy system. In addition, the presence of the proxy provides some extra opportunities for performance gains.

Consider a situation where the client requests an object from the proxy, and the proxy has the object in its cache but the page has expired. Normally, the proxy would send the `if-modified-since` request to the origin server, obtain the current version of the object (perhaps using delta encoding to reduce bandwidth consumption), and send the new version to the client. Notice that the proxy sends nothing to the client until it has at least an initial portion of the current object ready; the link between the proxy and the client stays idle. Instead, the proxy could start sending the *stale* object to the client right away while obtaining the current version of the object [Banga et al. 1997]. When the current version is available, the proxy computes the delta between the current proxy and the version it had sent and sends the delta to the client, allowing the client to reconstruct the current version of the object. The delta is sent over the same TCP connection used for sending the stale data.

The proxy sends the stale object in the hope that the object has not changed at all or the delta will be small and that by the time the current object is available at the proxy, much of the obsolete object will have been transferred to the client. If the delta turns out to be large, the proxy may have to abort the transfer of the stale object and send the current version. In this case, the work and bandwidth for sending the stale data, as well as the work for computing the delta would be wasted. Moreover, existing delta-computing algorithms require the proxy to accumulate the entire current object before it can produce the delta. This may increase the latency seen by the client, since normally proxies pipeline objects from the origin server to the client. Thus, this approach is appropriately called *optimistic deltas* [Banga et al. 1997].

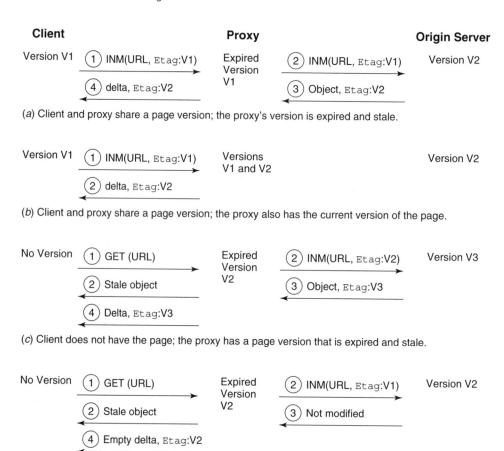

Figure 13.3 Optimistic deltas protocol (INM denotes a conditional `if-none-match` request.)

Figure 13.3 shows various cases of interactions between a client, proxy, and origin server in this approach. Columns indicate the version of the object kept on a corresponding party at the beginning of the interaction. The arrows indicate information flow and the labels on the arrows correspond to time when the flow starts. When the client and the proxy share a version of the object, the proxy simply uses delta encoding to reduce bandwidth consumption on the link to the client (Figures 13.3a and 13.3b). Figure 13.3b in particular illustrates that the proxy may retain an older version of an object to be able to compute and send just the delta to the client. When the proxy and the client do not have a common version, there are again two possibilities. If the proxy deems its version current, it simply sends it to the client. If, however, the proxy's version is expired, optimistic transfer of stale data takes place (Figures 13.3c and 13.3d). Stale data transfer pays off especially well when the expired version turns out to be still valid. In this case, no delta need be sent to the client (Figure 13.3d). A frequent occurrence of HTTP responses with a "304 Not Modified" response code[2] indicates that this pure-win situation would occur rather often. We should note that some of the proposals for better cache consistency management discussed in Chapter 10 may make this pure-win situation less frequent.

13.3 Cookied Content

Cookies are typically used to personalize pages for a given user (see Section 5.6). In this section, we refer to responses containing a `set-cookie` header, as well as responses to requests with a `cookie` header, as *cookied content*. A cookie may encode user preferences for page appearance and other information that the server uses to personalize the page for this user. When a request for an object contains a cookie, it is typically passed through to the origin server without utilizing the cache. (While HTTP 1.1 decouples the treatment of cookies from the cacheability issue, most proxies do not rely on HTTP 1.1 compliance and do not cache cookied content.)

Interestingly, Wills and Mikhailov [1999] showed that requests with cookies in most cases return identical responses, no matter what the cookie contains. It is especially true for images: 87 percent of cookied images were found to be identical regardless of the cookie content. This indicates that cookies are often used indiscriminately, whether or not content personalization is performed.

13.3.1 Cache-Friendly Usage of Cookies

All too often Web developers use cookies for their entire Web site when only a small fraction of pages actually requires them. Unfortunately, it takes very little effort to do so: for a Web site www.firm-x.com, any response with the `set-cookie:domain= www.firm-x.com` response header with an empty path atribute will make all subsequent requests from this client to this Web site carry a cookie. The consequence of such a design is that many proxies will not cache any of the objects from this site. One could argue formally that, since HTTP 1.1 does not disallow caching of any response unless it contains headers expressly prohibiting caching, the indiscriminate use of cookies does not constitute cache busting. However, it is cache busting for all practical purposes because, as we have frequently mentioned, proxies do not usually cache cookied content.

A much better approach would be to concentrate all content that needs cookies into a separate directory and specify this directory in the path attribute of the `set-cookie` header. Then only requests for the objects in this directory will carry

---

[2] For example, Nahum reported that 30 percent of all responses from IBM's Web site, www.ibm.com, had 304 response codes [Nahum 1998]. The trace of accesses from modem users studied in Feldmann et al. [1999] contained a similar number of 304 responses (26 percent). Arlitt et al. [1999] reported a lower but still significant number of these requests (15 percent) in their trace of accesses by cable modem users.

cookies, and the rest of the site can be freely cached. For example, the developer of the firm-x.com Web site could put all cookied content into the directory "user-specific," so a personalized page would have a URL such as http://www.firm-x.com/user-specific/welcome.html. Then responses from this site would have a `set-cookie` header that includes the `path=user-specific` attribute.

13.3.2 Caching Cookied Content

Better design of Web sites, where cookies would be used only when needed, would certainly be the best way to help proxy caching. In the interim, proxies can partially compensate for poor design in various ways.

Some commercial proxies offer an option of simply caching cookied images. However, the data by Wills and Mikhailov [1999] suggest that this option may introduce wrong behavior in 13 percent of cases where images differed for different cookies. The latest version of Squid also caches cookied content but issues `if-modified-since` (IMS) requests to the origin server for requests with different cookies. The IMS request carries the cookie from the current request, and if the cached content (corresponding to a different cookie) is different, the origin server will return the new version of the object. Otherwise, the origin server will return a short "304 Not Modified" response and the content itself will be served from the cache.

This method properly distinguishes cases in which the content is specific to a single request from cases in which the content is independent of the cookies and hence can be cached. However, some uses of cookies may still create a problem. Assume that the content exists in English and French and the cookies are used to determine the language of the response. Assume that both versions were created at the same time T and have never been modified. Now consider a situation where a proxy caches the French version of the object and a request arrives with the cookie specifying the English version (denote this cookie E). The proxy will send the IMS request to the origin server with cookie E and the last modified time of T. Since the content has not changed, the origin server will return a "Not Modified" response. Then the proxy will serve the cached French copy to the client, which is not the language it requested. We grant that two versions of the page might not have the same last-modified time. Still, with the last-modified time granularity of a second and the proliferation of authoring tools that may automatically create multiple variations of the same content (image-rich, text-only, frames-based, and so on), it is possible. When servers provide `ETag` headers with responses, the proxy can use them to identify precisely the cached copy of the object and achieve fully transparent caching of cookied data.

Regardless of server support for `ETags`, an ISP can autonomously employ delta-encoding between its own proxy and clients as another fully transparent way to cache cookied data.[3] When a request for a cached cookied object arrives, the proxy would

---

[3] By full transparency we mean that users never see the difference between environments with and without caching.

obtain the proper version of the object from the origin server. If the proxy and the client share an earlier version, the proxy would compute and send the delta to the client. When the proxy and client do not share a common version, the proxy can use optimistic deltas and send its stale cached copy to the client while obtaining the current version and computing the delta. Given the statistics in the Wills and Mikhailov [1999] study, in most cases this delta will be empty. However, when the delta is not empty (that is, when the content does depend on the cookie), it is likely that the two versions will be drastically different (as in the example of different languages or images). This increases the likelihood of the proxy aborting the stale transfer and sending the entire current version.

Delta encoding and optimistic deltas used between the proxy and its clients achieve full transparency at the expense of reduced caching benefits. These methods do not save any bandwidth on the link between the proxy and the Internet when processing cookied content; only bandwidth on the proxy-client link as well as some latency may be saved.

13.3.3 The Semantic Transparency Issue

The previous subsection brings up a general question: How far should the infrastructure go to accommodate unintended uses of the technology? As an extreme, consider an example showing that caching can never be done with absolute safety.

Consider objects generated dynamically by CGI scripts. Most proxies do not cache dynamic objects. To identify these objects they use the heuristics described in Section 5.10, such as the presence of "cgi-bin" or a question mark in the URL. However, Web servers allow any URL prefix to be specified as a CGI script, with the remaining part of the URL specifying parameters to the script. For instance, the developer of the firm-x.com Web site may configure its server to invoke an executable when a URL starts with http://firm-x.com/stock-market. Assume that this executable returns one of the current stock indices, and the remaining portion of the URL specifies exactly what index is needed. Thus, users may request http://firm-x.com/stock-market/dow.html or http://firm-x.com/stock-market/nasdaq.html to get the current values of the corresponding stock indices.

These URLs do not have any features that would reveal the dynamic nature of the corresponding objects. So, unless firm-x.com explicitly prohibits caching of these objects via HTTP headers, proxies will cache these objects and may deliver stale indices to users. In other words, the firm-x.com site works properly without caching and breaks when caching is introduced.

This example shows that content providers must be aware of caching when developing Web sites. If caching were to be made fully transparent to Web developers, then no content could ever be cached. Given that developers must be aware that certain designs will not work with caching, the question arises: How forgiving should the proxies be to the developer? For cookies specifically, we have considered the following alternatives for proxy behavior, in increasing order of forgivingness and decreasing order of efficiency:

1. Simply follow HTTP 1.1 and cache cookied content unless expressly prohibited. This is the least forgiving alternative, because any use of cookies for content personalization will not work unless accompanied by an appropriate `cache-control` header. However, this alternative caches the most content and penalizes sloppy design.

2. Limit caching of cookied content to images.

3. Issue conditional requests for cookied content, like Squid Version 2. For content with `ETag` headers, this is a fully transparent method.

4. Use optimistic deltas to transfer cookied content from proxy to clients. This is semantically a fully transparent method, but the least efficient one. Cookied responses can be drastically different (such as a page in a different language), causing frequent aborts of stale content transfers and, therefore, extra processing delay and bandwidth consumption.

5. Do not cache cookied objects at all.

The first alternative is preferable, because it encourages good practices. Ideally, content providers would soon learn that indiscriminate use of cookies breaks their sites and would start being more selective. However, following this route would require some vision from an ISP with a large number of customers like AOL. A small ISP cannot afford to alienate its customers by introducing cache solutions that abruptly break access to significant portions of existing content. In practice, proxies choose among alternatives 2, 3, or 5.

13.4 Expressly Uncacheable Content and Hit Metering

Similar to the problems of caching cookied content is the situation in which the Web site explicitly prohibits caching some content. We refer to such content as *expressly uncacheable content*. Often the only reason content providers disallow caching is to get accurate usage statistics for their content. However, disallowing content caching for this purpose is a huge overkill on the part of Web site developers.

13.4.1 Cache-Friendly Approaches to Hit Metering

A special *hit-metering protocol* [Mogul and Leach 1997] has been designed to allow accurate usage tracking without completely defeating content caching. While the hit-metering protocol has not gained much acceptance in practice, there are numerous other ways to collect accurate statistics short of cache busting.

For an HTML page, embedding a 1-byte uncacheable dummy object (using a "hidden embedded object" feature) is all that is needed to track accesses to the page. Another method, suitable for non-HTML objects also, is for an origin server to supply with the object a `must-revalidate` header. A proxy then validates the object on every request, allowing the server to collect the usage statistics. For embedded images, a popular method is to make the origin server always return a "307 Temporary Redirect" or other redirection response that points to the actual image, instead of immediately returning the image. The server designates the redirection response uncacheable while allowing the actual image to be cached freely. The client always obtains the redirection response from the server any time it accesses the image, so that the server can collect the usage data. Since the redirection response is usually much shorter than the image, much of the bandwidth savings from caching are retained. Yet another alternative for embedded images is to make the client validate the encompassing HTML page on every access, as described earlier. Every time the server receives a validation request, it knows that all embedded objects in the page will be accessed as well. This method amortizes the overhead of statistics collection over all images embedded in the page.

13.4.2 Caching Expressly Uncacheable Content

Proxies can partially compensate for poor design of Web sites by applying optimistic deltas or straight delta encoding to expressly uncacheable content. The use of these techniques in the context of uncacheable content is similar to their use in the case of content with cookies. On the other hand, since these expressly uncacheable objects account for fewer Web accesses than cookied content (see Section 6.3), their effect on caching is less significant.

13.5 Dynamic Content

Dynamic objects are generated by programs that run on servers every time the corresponding objects are accessed, in order to produce a different object for every access. Responses from search engines or stock-quote sites provide typical examples of dynamic objects.

Understandably, proxies try to identify and not cache dynamic objects, although the example from Section 13.3.3 shows that dynamic objects cannot always be identified reliably. On the other hand, caching dynamic pages promises a disproportionately high performance payoff. Indeed, since each access returns different information, these pages are more likely to be revisited multiple times than static pages. One study of Web accesses shows an 85 to 87 percent rate of repeated access to dynamic objects (see Sections 5.1 and 5.2 in the paper by Mogul et al. [1997]). Thus it is important to design dynamic content in a cache-friendly way and to extend cache benefits to dynamic content as much as possible.

13.5.1 Cache-Friendly Design of Dynamic Content

It turns out that not all information in a dynamic page is different for each access. Frequently, a large portion of the page is devoted to formatting specifications, headers and footers, and other information that does not change across accesses. An extreme but typical example of such mostly static pages is when an otherwise static page contains a dynamic variable, for example, an access counter or the time of day. A naive implementation would insert the dynamic variable into the page at the server, thus making the entire page uncacheable. A cache-friendly implementation would create an embedded object containing the variable; then the page itself would remain cacheable and only the embedded object would have to be downloaded on every access.

Although encapsulating dynamic portions of a page into embedded objects is a useful technique in many situations, it falls short in two kinds of pages. The first includes pages with multiple bits and pieces of dynamic data scattered around the page. For example, the page in Figure 13.4 contains three dynamic items. Including all dynamic items in a single embedded object would make this object encompass most of the page, defeating the purpose of the technique. On the other hand, encapsulating each dynamic item into a separate object would entail multiple downloads of small objects from the server, which would increase the server load and may therefore be unacceptable.

The second kind of page unsuitable for encapsulating dynamic content is represented by responses from search engines. Such responses usually contain a variable number of answers to a search query. Figure 13.5 shows the structure of a typical search-engine response, with dynamic information highlighted in bold. In this figure, the dynamic page starts with a header that might identify the search engine, then lists a number of answers (only the first two are shown), and concludes with a footer, which might contain the copyright clause, the Web designer's email address, and so on. Each answer on the page has the same structure: besides general formatting instructions, each answer includes the URL of a page that the search engine believes is relevant to the query and a measure of the page relevance.

Answers typically take up most of the content on these dynamic pages. Since the encapsulation technique would require inclusion of the entire list of answers in a dynamic object, this dynamic object would cover most of the information in the page. As mentioned earlier, this defeats the purpose of encapsulation. Yet a close

```
<HEAD>
<TITLE>Joe Smith</TITLE>
<BODY>
...
This page has been active for 10 days.
It has been accessed 23 times.
Avg. times accessed per day: 2.3
</BODY>
```

Figure 13.4 A simple dynamic page

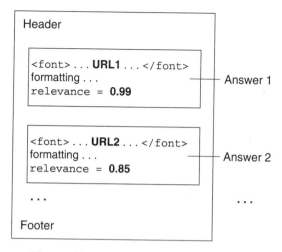

Figure 13.5 A dynamic page with a loop

examination reveals that page fragments corresponding to individual answers contain, to a large extent, static information. For example, responses to the query "caching dynamic objects" put to Lycos and AltaVista search engines contained only 27 and 18 percent of truly query-specific information, respectively [Douglis et al. 1997c]. The rest is a static page skeleton consisting of a variable number of answer skeletons.

Several proposals allow caching of static page portions when the encapsulation technique falls short. We consider them in the following subsections.

13.5.2 Base-Instance Caching

Consider an origin server sending a dynamic page to a client. If both share the same instance of the page, the server could use delta encoding to reduce the amount of data it needs to send. For example, assume that the client previously performed the query "tall green trees" on a search engine. If it now wants to perform the query "caching dynamic objects," it can send the engine an indication that it already has the result of the "tall green trees" query. This could be done, for example, by including with the second query an MD5 fingerprint of the first query. The search engine could now send just the delta between the second and first query results to the client.

Unfortunately, to use this approach the server would have to store instances of the pages it previously sent to each client. Given the number of clients accessing popular servers and the load on these servers, this approach is clearly impractical. Instead, the server can designate a certain *base instance* of the dynamic page and arrange that every client has the same base page instance. Then the server needs to store only one base instance to be able to delta-encode future responses. The Web Express product from IBM [Housel and Lindquist 1996] implements this idea.

Let the server designate some instance of the dynamic page to be base instance B (in our example, this may be the result of the query "tall green trees"). Conceptually, when a client sends its very first request Q_1 to the server (the "caching dynamic objects" query in our example), the server sends it three pieces of information:

- The instance B of the dynamic page, together with its `ETag`

- The indication that B is the base instance

- The delta of the page instance generated for request Q_1 over the base instance (the difference of the "caching dynamic objects" query response over the "tall green trees" query response)

When the client receives this response, it reconstructs the page instance Q_1 by applying the delta to base instance B and caches the base instance. For subsequent accesses (for example, a "hot red cars" query), the client includes the identity of its cached base instance (that is, its `ETag` supplied with B by the server). If the server still has B as the base instance, it will send only the deltas back (the delta of the "red hot cars" query response over the "tall green trees" query response). If the base instance at the server has changed, the server will have to send both the new base version and the delta again.

Consider our examples in Figures 13.4 and 13.5. In the first example, if the client already caches the base version, it obtains only a small delta of the current over the base version on each access, and it does so in a single access to the server. In the second example, if the current version of the page has a greater number of answers, the delta will contain the extra answers in their entirety. So, conceptually, base instance caching is not very suitable in the example of Figure 13.5. In practice, however, some delta-encoding algorithms produce deltas that are inherently compressed [Hunt et al. 1998]. These deltas would compress away repeating answer segments and therefore would still be useful in this case.[4]

The client can directly implement base-instance caching using a colocated custom proxy (see Section 13.1). When receiving a request, the custom proxy must first identify what base instance corresponds to the request. If the request uses a GET method, the stem of the requested URL (that is, the URL prefix up to the question mark, which signifies the start of the argument list) can be used to identify the base instance. POST requests pass arguments as data streams and not as part of the URL. Their URLs can therefore be used directly as the base-instance identity. This approach involves new functionality at the request sending phase, which adds to the request an indication of whether the client has the base instance of the requested object. Therefore, as we explained in Section 13.1, the approach as described cannot be implemented using plug-ins or applet wrapping.

Since applet wrapping allows legacy browsers to use new technology immediately, it will be instructive to consider a variant of base-instance caching that is amenable to

---

[4] By the same token, simply compressing search engine responses would go a long way toward decreasing their effective size. Mogul et al. [1997] provide a detailed discussion of compression and delta encoding in HTTP.

```
<html>
<body>
<applet codebase="http://www.bestsearch.com/custom-applet/"
  code="BaseInstanceCaching.class">
<param name="BaseInstanceURL"
  value="http://www.bestsearch.com/query">
<param name= "ETag"
  value="ETag of the current base instance">
<param name="delta"
  value="delta between the actual query response and base instance">
</applet>
</body>
</html>
```

Figure 13.6 Base-instance caching using applet wrapping

applet-wrapping implementation. In this variant, the server makes the base instance a separate object with its own URL; the actual responses are wrapped in an applet that first downloads the base instance—ideally from a cache—and then applies the delta to it.

For instance, let the browser request the query, "http://www.bestsearch.com/query?phrase=*query keywords*". The search engine might return the page shown in Figure 13.6. The browser invokes the `BaseInstanceCaching` method and passes it the parameters received: the URL and `ETag` of the base instance and the deltas. To implement base-instance caching, the `BaseInstanceCaching` method would fetch the base instance using the specified URL and utilizing a cached copy if available, verify its validity using the provided `ETag`, and reconstruct the actual response using the delta.

13.5.3 Template Caching

Template caching [Douglis et al. 1997c] separates dynamic and static portions of the page explicitly. The static portion is augmented with *macro-instructions* for inserting dynamic information. The static portion together with these instructions is called the page *template*. Macro-instructions use *macro-variables* to refer to dynamic information. The dynamic portion contains the *bindings* of macro-variables to strings specific to the given access. Prior to rendering the page, the client expands the template according to the macro-instructions and using the bindings that are downloaded from the server for each access. The rationale behind template caching is that the client caches the template and downloads only the bindings for every access instead of the entire page.

To see why template caching is free of the limitations of the encapsulation technique described in the beginning of Section 13.5, consider again the pages in Figures 13.4 and 13.5. Figure 13.7 gives the template and bindings encodings for the first page.[5]

---

[5] The syntax we use in our template caching examples, taken from Douglis et al. [1997c], is for illustrative purposes only. One can implement template caching using any language for template-based specification of pages, such as JavaServer Pages.

```
<HEAD>
<TITLE>Joe Smith</TITLE>
<BODY>
...                                      <HTML>
This page has been active               <TEMPLATE HREF="query.hpp">
for <VAR daysactive> days.              <BODY>
    It has been accessed <VAR count>    daysactive = 10;
    times.
Avg. times accessed per day:            count = 23;
    <VAR count/daysactive>              </BODY>
</BODY>                                  </HTML>
```

(*a*) The template   (*b*) The bindings

Figure 13.7 Template/bindings encoding for the page from Figure 13.4

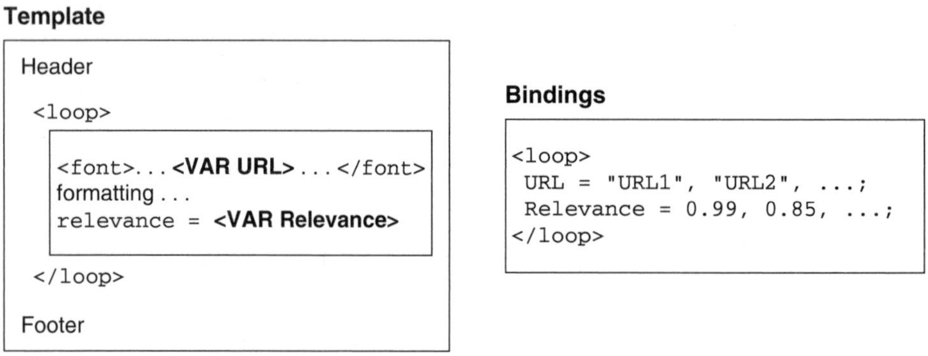

Template

```
 ┌─────────────────────────────────────────┐
 │ Header                                    │
 │   <loop>                                  │
 │     ┌───────────────────────────────────┐│
 │     │ <font>...<VAR URL>...</font>      ││
 │     │ formatting ...                     ││
 │     │ relevance = <VAR Relevance>       ││
 │     └───────────────────────────────────┘│
 │   </loop>                                 │
 │ Footer                                    │
 └─────────────────────────────────────────┘
```

Bindings

```
<loop>
 URL = "URL1", "URL2", ...;
 Relevance = 0.99, 0.85, ...;
</loop>
```

Figure 13.8 Template and bindings encodings for a search-engine response

The bindings encoding groups together all dynamic items in a single object. Unlike encapsulation, the bindings object allows the client to obtain all dynamic items in a single download. The dynamic items are then scattered throughout the page according to template macro-instructions (such as VAR tags in Figure 13.7a).

The template and bindings encodings of the page shown in Figure 13.5 is illustrated in Figure 13.8. The template describes all answers in the response using a single loop macro-instruction. The corresponding loop construct in the bindings contains a list of values for every macro-variable in the loop, one value per answer. To arrive at the actual page, the macro preprocessor expands the template loop body as many times as the number of values assigned to macro-variables, consuming the next value of each variable with every expansion. Again, the syntax is not important here; what is important is that variable-length pages such as search-query responses can be represented by a single template describing only one repeating page fragment. In particular, unlike encapsulation, template caching avoids considering the entire answer list in the query response as dynamic content.

Template caching is similar to various mechanisms for template-driven page generation at the origin server. These mechanisms range from rather simple server-side includes, which allow pieces of dynamic information to be inserted into the specified places in an otherwise static HTML page, to such tools as Sun's JavaServer Pages (JSP) or Microsoft's Active Server Pages (ASP), which provide complex languages for expanding the page template prior to sending it to the client. The only differences are that template caching expands templates at the client rather than the server, and that care must be taken to obtain all dynamic information in one download to keep the number of interactions with the origin server to a minimum.

Server-side template techniques exploit the explicit separation of dynamic and static portions of a page to simplify authoring and administering Web sites. In addition, template caching utilizes this separation to enable partial caching of dynamic objects and thus improve performance.

Extending client functionality for template caching is exactly analogous to base-instance caching, both for custom proxy and applet-wrapping approaches, with templates replacing base instances and bindings replacing deltas.

Several companies now implement template caching at surrogate servers, so that surrogates reconstruct the actual pages. Akamai refers to template caching by surrogates as *edge-side includes* and leads a group of companies in defining a new template language for this purpose [edge 2001].

13.5.4   Base-Instance Caching versus Template Caching

As we mentioned, base-instance caching and template caching are very similar. The main assumption behind both is that the size of the inherently dynamic data is much smaller than the total size of the original page.

Figure 13.9, adapted from Douglis et al. [1997c], gives an indication that this assumption holds for two popular search engines, AltaVista and Lycos.[6] The figure gives the size of the original response to the query "caching dynamic objects," the size of the template and bindings for this response, and the size of the compressed deltas between the original response and the template (assuming that the template is used for the base instance). It shows that the deltas and bindings are drastically smaller than the original page. This suggests that both base-instance caching and template caching would lead to significant performance gains at least for the pages shown. Further, the compressed deltas and compressed bindings have almost the same sizes, indicating that base-instance and template caching promise similar bandwidth savings.

Curiously, in both search engines the total size of the uncompressed template and bindings together is smaller than the uncompressed original page. The reason is that template loops encode repeated information in loop fragments only once. For example, the font and formatting information appears in every answer in the page of Figure 13.5 but only once in the template of Figure 13.8. This is a nice property, since it avoids

[6] All numbers in this subsection were obtained during the summer of 1997 and apply to the versions of the pages that were valid at that time.

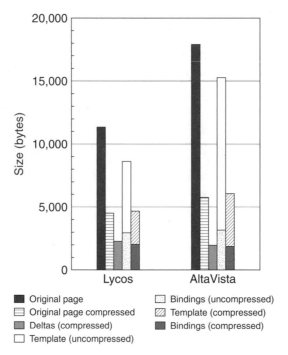

Figure 13.9 Sizes of the original pages and their templates and bindings

a bandwidth penalty on a miss in the template cache, as compared to not caching dynamic objects at all.

The big advantage of base-instance caching is that it is transparent to Web developers who create content. In particular, it can be applied to legacy content. Only the underlying server and client platforms must be extended.

The benefit of template caching is that the template need not be generated at the time of access. Instead, it can be precomputed and possibly precompressed once. Further, in some implementations, when the client does not already have the template in its cache, the server can start transmitting it to the client in parallel with computing the bindings.

Also, as with all techniques based on delta encoding, base-instance caching adds the overhead of computing the delta to the critical path of the request processing. Furthermore, current algorithms for delta computation require both versions of the content to be available in their entirety. Thus the server must first compute the page instance, then compute the delta. This prevents the server from pipelining the page to the client as it is being produced, which may increase latency.

Finally, if a complete version of a page and not the template is used for the base instance, the total size of the base instance and deltas is likely to exceed the total size of the original page. Thus, the very first client access, as well as the first client access after a base-instance change, downloads *more* information. With a high base-instance hit rate and small delta size, this overhead will be amortized over subsequent accesses. In other cases, it may have a detrimental effect on performance.

It is important to note that it is the Web site developer who decides to use base-instance or template caching. The decision is especially simple with applet wrapping, where only those pages that are supposed to use these techniques will be wrapped.

13.6 Active Proxies

We mentioned a general mechanism to inject new functionality into a browser by using Java applets. A similar mechanism has been proposed for extending proxy caches [Cao et al. 1998]. It is based on injecting executable modules called *cache applets* into a proxy cache; the proxies that implement this mechanism are called *active*. In this mechanism, a Web object carries in its entity headers a reference to a cache applet that a proxy must invoke any time it serves the object. In particular, this mechanism could be used to implement at the proxy level many of the ideas for caching uncacheable content described in this chapter. An object carries a new entity header, CacheApplet, that identifies a Java applet to be invoked before the object can be sent to the client. The proxy caches the object and its associated cache applet independently. When processing a request, the proxy first identifies the URL of the object by truncating the arguments from the request's URL (in the same way as one of the base-instance caching implementations uses stem URLs to identify base instances) and checks whether the object is in its cache.

If it is, the proxy parses its entity headers to identify the associated cache applet. This applet may be found in the proxy cache or downloaded; either way, the proxy invokes the applet and gives it the full request string (including the argument list and all headers) and the handle (that is, the file descriptor) of the object. The applet processes the object, perhaps customizing it for the given arguments and request headers (for example, the cookie header), or implementing any additional functionality desired by the content provider. The proxy then sends the resulting page to the client.

If the object is not in the cache, the proxy forwards the full request to the origin server. The server now has the choice of returning the object with or without a CacheApplet entity header, depending on whether or not the content requires the cache applets mechanism.

When the object arrives, the proxy checks for a CacheApplet entity header. If it is not present, the object does not use the cache applet mechanism and the proxy handles the object in the same way it handles objects without this mechanism. If the CacheApplet header is present, the proxy invokes the specified applet, giving the newly obtained object and the full request as arguments, and returns the result to the client. The preapplet object may be cached for future use.

Now let us look at how cache applets can be used to implement some of the ideas we described earlier in this chapter.

Delta encoding: To implement delta encoding, objects are given fictitious expiration dates far into the future. The actual expiration dates are listed in an optional entity header, perhaps `ActualExpiry`. Given the fictitious expiration time, the proxy always assumes that the cached object is valid and invokes its cache applet. The applet then interprets the `ActualExpiry` header and, if the object has actually expired, sends the request and the last-modified date of the object to the origin server. The server responds with the delta between the current and cached versions, which the applet uses to reconstruct the current version. The server and the applet are free to implement any protocol details involved in the above communication.

Base-instance caching: Implementing base-instance caching is straightforward. Pre-applet objects contain base instances of actual objects. Given the argument list of the request, the applet then obtains the delta between the base instance and the proper instance and applies this delta to arrive at the latter.

Template caching: One can obtain template-caching functionality by storing templates in the preapplet objects and associating them with a cache applet that downloads the bindings for the request and expands the template into the actual page. Notice that standard cache consistency mechanisms govern when to validate cached templates or base instances.

Optimistic deltas are an example of a feature that cannot be implemented using active proxies. This is because optimistic deltas involve modifying proxy behavior prior to the time a cache applet can be invoked.

An interesting issue related to active proxies is raised by cooperative caching. Consider a request that is forwarded along a chain of cooperating proxies, $P_1, \ldots, P_n$. As the response travels back, only one proxy in the chain, say P_i, can apply the applet. The rest of the proxies, $P_{i-1}, \ldots, P_1$, will see only the postapplet page. Thus they will not be able to use their active proxy capability unless they also download the preapplet object. But downloading both pre- and postapplet versions of the object would be bandwidth-expensive.

This means that cooperating proxies must decide when to apply the cache applet and send the postapplet object to the client and when to simply send the applet and preapplet object, letting the requesting proxy reconstruct the page. It appears that this should occur as close to end users as possible, since postapplet objects are often uncacheable. At the extreme, this would mean applying applets at the browser itself. On the other hand, certain applets assume the existence of multiple clients. For instance, to make sense, an applet that strips a page of embedded images for poorly connected clients must be applied before the response is sent over the low-bandwidth links. Furthermore, preapplet objects may carry more information (for example, a set of rotating advertisements from which only one is chosen by the applet) than their postapplet counterparts. So filtering extra information early may save bandwidth. Cases like this make less obvious the choice of where in the proxy chain to apply applets.

13.7 Summary

This chapter considers the problem of uncacheable content from two sides. On one side, we argue that while there are many legitimate needs causing the content provider to disallow or limit caching, the content provider can often satisfy these needs by designing the Web site in a cache-friendly way. Through cache-friendly design, content providers can leverage someone else's infrastructure—proxies' for example—to improve access to their content. Blind cache busting is not in the interests of content providers and, conversely, being cache friendly is not just a question of good network manners.

Table 13.1 summarizes reasons why a content provider may need to disallow caching, methods of designing a site to satisfy content provider needs while minimizing the effect on caching, and technological proposals that promise further help in these matters.

The other issue this chapter considers is how to extend the scope of caching to uncacheable content, whether it occurs because of sloppy content design or because of legitimate needs. We consider several proposals. Delta encoding and optimistic deltas allow proxies to utilize partially stale cached content. A hit-metering protocol allows Web sites to periodically obtain hit statistics from proxies and thus derive accurate usage data without making every request synchronously travel to the Web site. Base-instance caching allows dynamic content to benefit from caching when instances of the content do not differ drastically from one another. Template caching also addresses the cacheability of dynamic content and allows a content provider to explicitly separate truly dynamic data from static page templates. Finally, active proxies provide a general framework that can implement many of the above techniques.

Table 13.1 Reasons for Uncacheable Content, Cache-Friendly Content Design, and Technological Proposals to Extend Caching Benefits to this Content

Reason	Cache-Friendly Approaches	Technology Proposals
Stale delivery avoidance	Forced validation Short TTLs HTTP invalidation	Delta encoding Optimistic deltas Consistency schemes of Chapter 10
Personalized pages (cookied content)	Use cookies sparingly Supply ETags with HTTP responses	
Usage data collection	Forced validation Dummy embedded object Uncacheable HTTP redirect	Hit metering
Dynamic pages	Concentrate dynamic content in embedded objects	Base-instance caching Template caching

Part III
Web Replication

With Part III, we turn our attention to content replication on the Web. Replication refers to creating extra content copies on a system that is controlled by the provider of Web content. A replication platform seeks to improve Web access to a particular Web site or a selected group of Web sites no matter which clients access these sites. In this book, we only consider *transparent replication*, which refers to those replication techniques that require no user involvement or even awareness of whether or not a Web site utilizes replication.

There are several fundamental issues any replicated system faces.

Request distribution: How to transparently distribute requests for content among servers that hold replicas of that content.

Server selection: How to select a server replica for satisfying a given request. While the previous item concerns the *mechanisms* for request distribution, server selection refers to the *policies* that these mechanisms use to decide which server replicas to assign to which requests.

Content placement: How to decide how many replicas of given content to have and on which servers to place these replicas. This problem is related to but different from the *server location* problem that addresses the issue of finding the optimal network locations for content servers. The content placement problem concerns placing copies of various content on already deployed servers. We do not focus on server location in this book because this problem has already been well documented in the theoretical computer science community, under the name of the *facility location problem*. On the other hand, the topic of content placement has not matured enough to be included in this part; we give an overview of this problem in the context of replicated applications in Section 17.7 of Part IV.

Replica consistency: How to ensure that all replicates serve the same content at a particular point in time.

Chapters 14 and 15 are devoted to the request distribution problem. Chapter 14 describes the basic mechanisms for request distribution on the Web, while Chapter 15 shows how these mechanisms are applied in a content delivery network (CDN) environment. Chapter 15 also considers the issues of replica consistency, performance implications of providing secure Web access via a CDN, and delivery of streaming content. The server selection problem is discussed in Chapter 16, which concludes Part III.

This part discusses two kinds of servers, DNS servers and origin server replicas. Following a common shortcut, we often refer to the latter as simply *servers* but always qualify the former as *DNS servers*, thereby avoiding any confusion.

Chapter 14

Basic Mechanisms
for Request Distribution

As we mentioned in the introduction to Part III, this book focuses on *transparent replication:* replication techniques that require no user involvement or even awareness of whether or not a Web site utilizes replication. Transparent replication requires that clients use a single logical name when requesting a resource, regardless of the physical server that ends up processing the request. So a fundamental requirement of transparency is a mechanism for the redirection of logically identical requests to distinct servers.

There are a variety of points on the request processing path where such redirection may occur: at the client, at the intermediate proxies, at various points in the DNS system, at the primary origin server, or somewhere in the network. This chapter presents the basic alternatives for request redirection, while the next chapter describes how CDNs use these building blocks to implement their architectures. Sections 14.1 and 14.2 of this chapter discuss request redirection mechanisms that are oblivious to requested objects; the mechanisms that take into account which objects are requested are considered in Section 14.3.

14.1 Content-Blind Request Distribution with Full Replication

This section considers request distribution mechanisms that are oblivious to the requested objects; we refer to those mechanisms as *content-blind* mechanisms. The granularity of request distribution in these schemes is a Web site; all requests to a given site are distributed in the same way regardless of which objects are requested. These mechanisms include client redirection, redirection by a balancing switch, redirection by the Web site's DNS servers, and anycast.

14.1.1 Client Redirection

One way to implement request redirection is to use a Web client's DNS [Fei et al. 1998]. Client DNS servers either are colocated with the Web clients on the same machines or run on separate machines. In any case, a client is configured to use its DNS server.

This mechanism is illustrated on Figure 14.1. When the client wants to access a URL, for example, http://www.company.com/home.html, it issues a query to its client DNS server to find the IP address of the site. The client DNS ultimately obtains the response to this query from the Web site's DNS (see Section 4.3 for details). In this approach, the response from the Web site's DNS server contains a list of IP addresses of physical servers rather than a single IP address. The client DNS server then chooses a server from the list and returns its IP address to the client. Finally, the client requests the required object, home.html, from the chosen server.

Another approach is to perform request redirection directly at the client. This mechanism also requires the Web site's DNS to return a list of server replicas. But the client DNS server will convey the whole list to the client instead of making a choice itself. The client then will decide which server to use. The main advantage of this scheme over doing redirection by the client DNS server is that the client can monitor the performance of accesses to different servers and use these observations to make a more intelligent choice (see Section 15.5). Active clients such as forward proxies are especially well suited for redirecting requests, since they generate more traffic than individual clients and therefore have a better chance to collect enough performance measurements of prior accesses to different server replicas.

An advantage of client-based schemes is that the client is in a good position to make the server selection. It can compare routing paths from itself to various servers, or it can measure response times, packet loss rates, or other metrics. Another advantage is that these schemes do not interfere with DNS caching (we will see that some schemes do).

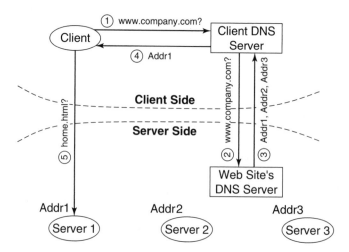

Figure 14.1 Request redirection by client DNS

Since the response from the Web site's DNS server contains the entire replica list, it can be freely cached within the DNS infrastructure as long as the replica list remains valid. For instance, in the case of redirection by the client DNS server, the client DNS server can cache the received server list and use it for many client queries, each time performing a different server selection.

The main disadvantage is that the Web site cedes control over server selection to the client. The client may choose suboptimal servers or perform no intelligent selection at all; its capabilities are not known to the Web site. Overall, client-based approaches are not widely used at the present. If a response from a Web site's DNS contains multiple IP addresses, most clients simply use the first address on the list.

Another disadvantage, at least from the practical perspective, is that these approaches require a modification to either the client DNS server or the client itself. So while transparent to the end user, these approaches are not transparent to the current software used at the client side. A more transparent approach, which requires only client configuration but no software modification, uses Java applets and is described in the context of content-aware request distribution (see Section 14.3.1).

14.1.2 Redirection by a Balancing Switch

A widely used approach incorporates a hardware-based solution to redirect requests. In this approach, a special load-balancing switch, a *balancer* for short, is placed in front of a group of servers that host a Web site. A server group that uses a balancer is often called a *server farm*. Figure 14.2 illustrates this scheme. The domain name of the Web site is mapped to the IP address of the balancer, so all clients send their packets to it. When the first packet from a client arrives, the balancer selects a server and forwards the packet (and all subsequent packets in the same session) to this server.

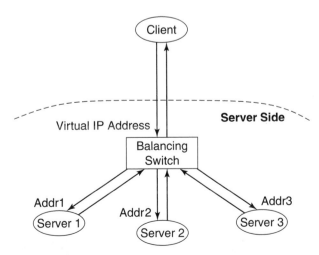

Figure 14.2 Request redirection by a balancing switch

The balancer also modifies the response packets as they pass from the server to the client, so that the packets' headers contain the balancer's IP address rather than that of the server. Thus, all clients have the illusion that they communicate with a single host with the IP address of the balancer while actually connecting to one of the servers in the server group. For this reason, the IP address of the balancer is sometimes called a *virtual IP address* of the site. The balancer can be either content blind or content aware. We consider content-aware balancers in Section 14.3 and concentrate on content-blind balancers here.

The balancer maintains a *sessions database*, which records a server chosen for each active communication session. The sessions database is needed to ensure that, once a server is chosen for servicing a request, all packets from this client in this session go to the same server. In the simplest case, the content-blind balancer considers a session to be over when no more packets arrive from the client for a certain time, say 60 seconds. In this case, the balancer examines only Layer 3 information in packet headers: source IP addresses in packets from clients to associate these packets with sessions, and source IP addresses in packets from servers to replace these addresses with the virtual IP address.

Alternatively, the balancer can equate sessions with TCP connections and consider sessions to be over when TCP connections are closed. In this case, the balancer must examine TCP headers to determine the TCP port numbers and detect FIN or RST packets that close connections. This is Layer 4 information, and the balancer then becomes an L4 switch. Note, however, that the functionality of this L4 switch is very different from the intercepting L4 switches we considered in the context of forward proxies (see Chapter 8). The main function of an intercepting switch is to intercept packets and direct them to proxies. In contrast, clients explicitly address their packets to the balancing switch, so no interception is needed. While intercepting L4 switches usually select a proxy to send a packet to based on the packet destination IP address, balancing switches choose between servers based on the packet source IP addresses. In practice, many L4 switches, such as those offered by Foundry and Nortel's Alteon division, are capable of functioning as both intercepting and balancing switches, depending on how they are configured.

Whether the balancing switch considers only Layer 3 information or also Layer 4 headers, this approach to request redirection is often called *IP balancing*. IP balancing uses standard clients and DNS and Web servers. However, by having a focal communication point at the balancing switch, it does not scale geographically. Thus, it is mostly used for load sharing in a server farm on a local area network.

Some products, such as IBM Network Dispatcher and Radware, add an interesting twist to IP balancing. Their balancers select servers and forward client packets to them as before. But servers respond to clients directly, bypassing the balancer and using the balancer's IP address as the sender address. This results in triangular communication: from the client to the balancer to the server and back to the client (Figure 14.3). Technically, this mechanism can be implemented using either network address translation (NAT) or IP-in-IP encapsulation (see Section 8.3.2).

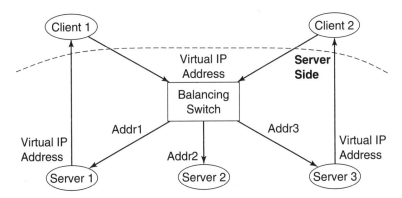

Figure 14.3 IP balancing with triangular communication

With network address translation, the balancer modifies the destination IP address of every packet to that of the chosen server. The server then responds to the client using the IP address of the switch as the source IP address of its packets. IP-in-IP encapsulation is more general because it does not require the servers to know the virtual IP address in advance. In this scheme, the switch encapsulates an entire packet from the client into a new IP packet with new headers. The new headers indicate the switch IP address (the site's virtual IP address) as the source IP address and the chosen server IP address as the destination. The server unwraps the client packet and replies to the client using, again, the IP address of the switch. In contrast with network address translation, the server learns the switch IP address from the wrapper headers of the packet. Being able to learn which IP address to use as its source IP address becomes especially handy when a server is forwarded packets by more than one balancing switch (which is sometimes the case in content delivery networks, see Section 15.6).

With both NAT and IP-in-IP encapsulation, a client cannot tell that the host it sends its request to is different from the host that replies, because both hosts use the same IP address to communicate with the client. Because content flowing from servers to clients takes a direct route, and because it constitutes most of the data exchanged between clients and servers, this approach improves geographical scalability, especially from the bandwidth-consumption perspective. The latency gain is limited by the need for client acknowledgments to travel via the balancer. Still, it can reduce response time considerably, because the aggregate bandwidth available to the Web site increases.

14.1.3 Redirection by a Web Site's DNS

Many DNS implementations—including Cisco Distributed Director, Alteon's GSLB, Arrowpoint's Content Smart Site Selector, F5 Networks 3DNS, and others—allow the Web site's DNS server to map a host domain name to a set of IP addresses and choose one of them for every client DNS query. DNS redirection by a Web site's DNS is far more widely used than DNS redirection by client DNS servers; therefore we often

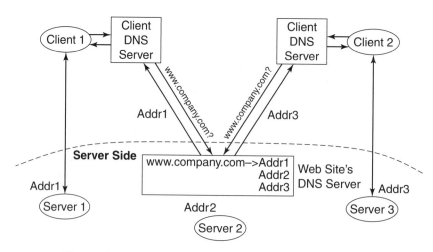

Figure 14.4 Request redirection by a Web site's DNS server

use shorter terms such as "DNS-based redirection," or "DNS server selection" in the remainder of the book, meaning by default that the redirection is performed by a Web site's DNS.

The scheme is illustrated in Figure 14.4. In this example, the site's domain name (www.company.com) is mapped to three IP addresses. When a query arrives, the site's DNS server selects a server replica and includes its IP address in the response. Then the client sends its request directly to this Web server. Notice the difference with DNS-based client redirection considered in Section 14.1.1. In the client-based approach, the site's DNS returned the entire set of IP addresses corresponding to the domain name, leaving server selection to the client DNS. Here, the site's DNS server itself makes the selection and returns only the IP address of the selected server. Server selection is based on such factors as the query origin and the load on server replicas. We discuss selection algorithms in detail later in Chapter 16.

Several advantages have made this approach widely used. It scales well geographically since clients can communicate directly with nearby servers, balancing load among them and balancing traffic among distinct routing paths. Like IP balancing, it is implemented entirely by the content site; no modification of the client or its DNS is needed.

On the other hand, DNS response caching by clients complicates changing replica sets and controlling request distribution among replicas. In Figure 14.4, for example, once client 1 obtains the DNS response that maps www.company.com to server 1, this client will continue using this server while the mapping is cached, regardless of the server load and availability. In fact, since clients usually acquire DNS mappings through client DNS servers, the cached mapping will be used by all Web clients connected to client 1's DNS server.

To counter the caching effect, Web sites often reduce the lifetime of cached DNS responses, by assigning them low time to live (TTL) values (see Section 4.2). However, this forces clients to perform DNS queries (and incur the latency of these queries) more often. Also, some client DNS servers and most Web browsers set a minimum lifetime for DNS responses and refuse to reduce it any further.

All this leads to the general observation that DNS redirection is good for request distribution based on stable metrics. For example, the network proximity of clients to servers does not change often, and DNS redirection would be appropriate for proximity-based request distribution. On the other hand, conditions related to server load and network congestion may change quickly and may call for more responsive mechanisms.

There are several other issues with redirection by a Web site's DNS. Because this method lies at the foundation of CDNs, we discuss the subject further in Chapter 15, which is devoted to CDN architectures.

14.1.4 Anycast

The principal idea behind *anycast* is that multiple physical servers use a single IP address called an *anycast IP address*. Each server advertises both the anycast IP address and its regular IP address to its routers, which advertise them to their neighbor routers in a normal manner. As a result, each router builds a path corresponding to the anycast address that leads to the server closest to this router. In other words, different routers will have paths to different servers for the same anycast IP address. In this setup, the routers perform request distribution based on router metrics without being aware of it. Anycast was first proposed to replicate the root DNS servers; a good discussion of anycast is provided by Partridge et al. [1993].

To illustrate anycast, consider the example in Figure 14.5. Routers r1, r5, and r6 contain the anycast route that leads to server 1, while routers r2 and r4 point toward server 2 for the same anycast IP address. Thus packets addressed to the same anycast address arrive at different servers depending on the first router that handles them. So packets from client 1 will arrive at server 1, while packets from client 2 will end up at server 2.

There is virtually no overhead for request redirection with anycast, since packets travel along router paths anyway. Further, packets automatically choose the closest servers according to the metric used by the routers. Unfortunately, anycast requires a change in TCP implementation in order to operate correctly. Otherwise, a problem similar to the multipath problem of interception proxies may break TCP connections. To see the problem, consider client 3 in Figure 14.5, which is connected to two routers, r4 and r6 (in the real world, this often happens when a client buys Internet connectivity from more than one ISP). Nothing prevents this client from alternating packets between the two routers. For instance, it can send the TCP SYN packet to router r6, but then send the next packet with an HTTP request to router r4. The first packet will arrive at server 1 while the second packet will be received by server 2, which will drop this packet since it does not belong to an established TCP connection as far as server 2 is concerned.

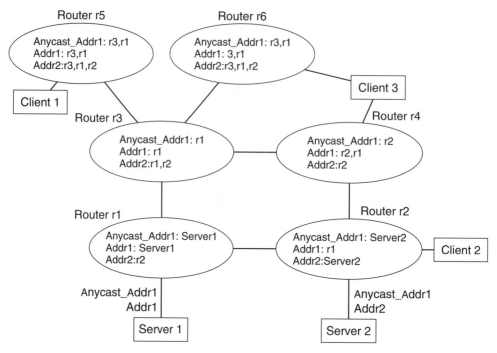

Figure 14.5 Request redirection by anycast (Each router is shown with a part of its routing table. The routing table contains the destination address followed by the path taken to reach this address.)

To fix this problem, a server could enclose its regular IP address with its TCP SYN/ACK packet, using a TCP header. The client must then send all future packets for this connection to the regular IP address. This will ensure that all these packets will arrive at the server that received the initial SYN packet. Obviously, changing TCP is a major impediment to adoption of anycast for HTTP request redirection. Anycast is much better suited to redirect DNS queries, as we show in Section 15.4.3.

Another issue with anycast is that it postulates rather static replica sets: any change in the replica set would need to be reflected in router tables throughout the Internet, which could take minutes. Finally, anycast can only perform request distribution based on a single criterion, router metrics. This may be overly rigid; for instance, it cannot take server load into account.

14.2 Content-Blind Request Distribution with Partial Replication

When a request redirection mechanism is oblivious to the objects being requested, a request for any object may be sent to any available server that replicates the Web site. This implies that any server must be able to fulfill any request. To have this ability, it may seem that every server must have a full replica of the entire Web site. While full replication is indeed often used, it is rather wasteful, considering that typically only a small fraction of content is responsible for most of the requests; it may become prohibitively wasteful for hosting service providers, due to their scale. This section describes two techniques that allow partial replication while still performing content-blind request distribution: surrogates and distributed file systems.

Since the requirement that any server in the replica set of a Web site be able to fulfill any request is fundamental for content-blind request redirection, both techniques provide a way for a server to satisfy the request even if it does not have a copy of the requested object.

14.2.1 Using Surrogates as Server Replicas

The surrogate approach, illustrated in Figure 14.6, distributes requests among surrogates that are distinct from the ultimate origin servers. A surrogate can satisfy any request. If the requested object is in its cache, the surrogate processes the request locally. Otherwise, the surrogate obtains the object from the origin server, sends it to the requester, and also caches it for future use if appropriate. Thus, every surrogate contains only a partial replica of the Web site, comprising the objects that reside in its cache. Furthermore, the more popular portions of the Web site tend to be more widely replicated across the surrogates. All redirection mechanisms in this chapter can be used to distribute requests among surrogates. However, the DNS redirection described in Section 14.1.3 has become the method of choice. We discuss this approach in more detail in the context of CDNs in Chapter 15.

The main disadvantage of surrogates is that they, like forward proxies, usually can only distribute cacheable content. Thus uncachable content may require other replication means. Also, unless the surrogates cooperate with each other to share their caches, it is difficult to control the degree of replication of various objects; each surrogate normally caches any cacheable object it has downloaded regardless of its popularity. However, with storage costs dramatically decreasing, this limitation is losing its importance.

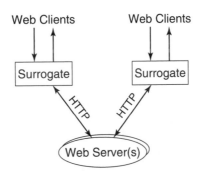

Figure 14.6 Using surrogates for partial replication of a Web site

14.2.2 Back-End Distributed File Systems

A simple way to allow every Web server replica to fulfill every request without storing the entire site is to run all Web servers on top of a distributed file system that provides a shared files environment and allows every server to access every file [Katz et al. 1994; Spasojevic et al. 1994]. This approach is illustrated in Figure 14.7. Web server replicas in this approach obtain all their files from the underlying distributed file system (DFS), instead of their own local file systems. Given that DFSs typically provide a programming interface similar to the standard UNIX file system, virtually no modification of the Web server code is required.

Conceptually, this architecture is somewhat similar to surrogates, with the main difference being that the surrogates use HTTP to obtain data from back-end servers and the DFS-based architecture relies on a DFS-specific protocol to do so. One implication of using a DFS is that Web server replicas perform all computing locally, only pulling in any files required for the computation. Since a DFS client can cache any downloaded file, all content (represented in this case as sets of files needed to produce HTTP responses) becomes cacheable. This includes dynamic content, for which a DFS client retrieves the software and data needed to produce the dynamic content locally. On the other hand, all Web server replicas in the DFS approach must provide identical computing environments and be able to perform the same computations.

Several sites reportedly use a DFS-based implementation, including the National Center for Supercomputing Applications, Carnegie Mellon University, and Transarc Corporation (now part of IBM).

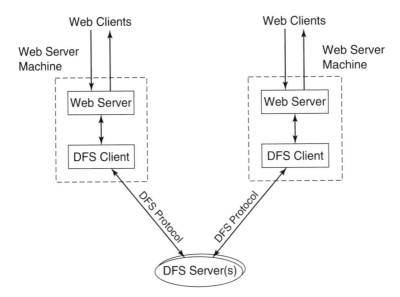

Figure 14.7 Web servers on top of a distributed file system

14.3 Content-Aware Request Distribution

All request redirection mechanisms discussed so far share one property: they are oblivious to what objects are requested. Consequently, a request for any object on a given Web site may be sent to any server, and every server must be able to fulfill any request. However, there can be multiple reasons to perform request redirection differently for different objects. One reason we discussed in Section 14.2: to support partially replicated Web sites. While the tricks described in that section accommodate partial replication, content-specific request redirection supports it directly: a request is directed only to a server that has a copy of the requested object. Other reasons for content-aware request distribution are similar to those discussed in Section 8.3.5: redirecting requests among specialized servers tuned for particular content types and implementing fine-grained quality of service policies.

This section considers content-aware methods of request distribution: redirection by a Java applet, HTTP redirection, L7 switch indirection, and the use of fine granularity domain names.

14.3.1 Client Redirection by a Java Applet

A Web site can instruct the client to perform content-aware redirection by wrapping a requested object into a Java applet [Yoshikawa et al. 1997; Vingralek et al. 1999]. In this approach, which is similar to the applet wrapping described in Section 13.1, the URL of an object points not to the object itself but to a small wrapper HTML page containing the applet invocation and the list of replica URLs as the parameter to the applet.

For example, the URL http://www.firm-x.com/home.html might point to the page shown in Figure 14.8. When clicking on the URL http://www.firm-x.com/home.html, the client downloads and runs the redirector applet. The applet chooses the URL of an object replica, perhaps http://www1.firm-x.com/home.html, obtains the object and renders it in the browser window. The initial server, www.firm-x.com, acts just as the redirector of requests and stores only the wrapper pages that correspond to actual objects. The redirector applet is the same for different objects and is likely to be cached at the browser from previous accesses.

```
<HTML>
<BODY>
<APPLET codebase="http://www.firm-x.com/redirector/"
      code="Redirect.class">
  <PARAM name="physicalURLs"
  value="http://www1.firm-x.com/home.html;
         http://www2.firm-x.com/home.html;
         http://www3.firm-x.com/home.html">
</APPLET>
</BODY>
```

Figure 14.8 A wrapper page for client redirection by a Java applet

This approach chooses a replica based on the performance of previous downloads from different servers to this client. Its main advantage is that it allows this client-centric replica selection without any modifications to any systems on the client side in contrast to the client-based redirection approaches of Section 14.1.1. Moreover, the redirector applet can communicate with the redirector server from which it was initially downloaded to obtain server-side statistics such as load on individual hosts and combine them with client-centric measurements. Further, the content provider retains control over server selection.

However, the practicality of this approach is rather limited. First, many browsers do not allow Java applets for security reasons. Second, running Java takes up a large amount of resources on the browser and might slow it down considerably. Finally, this approach is limited to browsers because proxies currently do not execute applets. This last limitation, however, may be removed in the future if active proxies (see Section 13.6) become widely adopted.

14.3.2   HTTP Redirection

HTTP allows a Web server to respond to a client request with a response that tells the client to resubmit its request to another server (see Section 5.3). This mechanism can be used by a special Web server, which accepts client requests, chooses replicas for them, and redirects clients to these replicas. The mechanism is content-aware because requests for different objects can be redirected to different servers.

HTTP redirection is quite costly. It requires the client to establish two sequential TCP connections: one to receive the HTTP redirection response and a second to download the object. For small objects, once the connection is established, it can be almost as fast to send the requested object as the redirection HTTP response. An additional drawback of HTTP redirection is that most Web browsers indicate in their status bars that they have been redirected, therefore revealing the names of the replicas to end users. Moreover, browsers might display the final URL of the object in the URL window, in which case the user can even bookmark it for future use. This compromises the user transparency of this approach. Some time ago, several companies based their load balancing on HTTP redirection or offered it as an option. Today this mechanism is usually deemphasized because of its performance problems.

Still, HTTP redirection cannot be dismissed altogether. It is true that it is costlier than, for example, the triangular communication illustrated by Figure 14.3 when we consider the delivery of a single object in isolation. However, HTTP redirection has a nice property: if embedded objects in a composite Web document use relative URLs, then redirecting the request for the container page to another server makes the client fetch *all* embedded objects from the new server as well. Furthermore, the client obtains those objects from the new server directly, with the old server being completely out of the way. Thus, the high overhead of HTTP redirection is amortized over many object downloads. In contrast, with triangular communication all client packets including those for embedded objects come to the balancing switch, and the switch must stay in the loop forwarding packets to the server for the entire interaction.

14.3.3 Redirection by an L7 Switch

Consider a Web server that stores a part of a Web site and processes its requests locally. This server can, therefore, process requests only for the content that resides on it. Thus, request distribution must take into account requested objects when assigning requests to servers. One can do this by using an L7 switch (see Section 8.3.5) in place of the L4 switch indicated in Figure 14.2.

L7 switches allow a system administrator to specify rules that determine which servers can be used for which objects. When an L7 switch redirects a request, it chooses a server in accordance with the rules. In particular, rules may specify servers that are to receive requests for certain objects or object types.

As in the case of forward proxies discussed in Section 8.3.5, the L7 switch can direct requests for different content types to different servers tuned specifically for those content types. Another advantage, more specific to replication, is that the switch can be configured to implement fine-grained quality of service policies. Consider a Web hosting service provider that hosts many Web sites using virtual hosting to share the same servers among these sites (see Section 5.7). In the environment of Figure 14.2, assume a modern implementation of virtual hosting, where the provider's DNS server resolves the domain names of all hosted Web sites into the single virtual IP address of the balancing switch, and the Web servers behind the switch use the host request header to identify the Web site for the request. Using the L7 switch, requests for certain Web sites or even for selected objects on those Web sites can be given preferential treatment by, for example, being sent to a more powerful or less-loaded server. The L7 switch could even set aside some fixed bandwidth to serve requests for particular Web sites. An L4 switch, on the other hand, cannot differentiate between different Web sites in this environment, because request packets to any of these sites have the same destination IP address.

A third often-cited advantage of the L7 switch's ability to distribute requests for different objects among different groups of servers is its direct support for partial replication. Indeed, popular content can be replicated on all available servers and the switch can be told to distribute requests for this content among these servers. Less-popular content can be replicated only on a subset of the servers, and the switch can use only these servers for the corresponding requests. Selective replication according to popularity of content reduces storage demands for servers. Although the cost of disk storage has been decreasing rapidly, such selective replication allows more popular content to reside in the main memory of the servers, and that allows the servers to process requests for this content more efficiently.

On the other hand, as with L7 intercepters of Section 8.3.5, content awareness in request redirection does not come free. The switch must establish an initial TCP connection with the clients, manage TCP state information, interpret HTTP requests, and perform a lookup to determine which Web servers have the requested objects. All this extra work can significantly reduce the capacity of the switch. As more functionality is placed on the L7 switch to implement differentiated quality of service and partial replication, the performance gap between it and Web servers decreases, which means that the switch can distribute load among fewer servers before becoming the bottleneck. A modern Web server may process over a thousand simple requests per second. Assuming a 10K average response size, it can saturate a 100Mbps network link easily. Thus, a gigabit throughput is necessary for a switch to be able to load-balance among several such servers. This kind of performance is difficult to achieve at the application layer. In Section 15.6.1, we discuss a somewhat similar redirection method aimed at a CDN, which offloads configuration rules processing from request-distributing L7 switches to separate application-level servers.

14.3.4 Fine-Granularity Domain Names

A third approach for content-aware request distribution keeps network elements (like switches) fast and simple and implements content awareness separately. There are a variety of ways to achieve that, depending on how much control the Web site has over the network. Fundamentally, two things are needed: a name service, which maps logical object names to physical names of the replicas of these objects, and a way to include the name service in the processing path of requests.

Since the Internet already has a name service, DNS, it can be used for content-aware replication. We have seen how DNS can be used for site-level replication. To use it at finer granularity, the Web site developer can add an object ID into the host portion of the object URL. For example, consider a site firm-x.com that has three objects, sales.html. marketing.html, and tech_support.html. Instead of assigning these objects URLs http://firm-x.com/sales.html and so on, the developer would assign them URLs http://1.firm-x.com/sales.html, http://2.firm-x.com/marketing.html, and http://3.firm-x.com/tech_support.html, where 1, 2, and 3 are compact identifiers of the respective objects on the site. Now when a client accesses an object, it sends a DNS query to the site's DNS server, for example, 2.my.company.com. The DNS server can resolve the name to the IP address of a Web server that has object 2 (that is, marketing.html). Notice that the sets of Web servers hosting different objects can be different.

Of course, running the DNS service at the granularity of individual objects increases the load on the DNS servers significantly. Instead of having to deal with just one domain name of the entire site, they now must handle perhaps thousands of different domain names of individual objects. Instead of sending just one DNS query to access all objects on the site, each client now must issue a separate query for each object (since each has a different domain name). Thus, reducing a replication unit from the entire Web site to an individual object might be excessive. One can use a middle ground instead: group several objects into a set and assign a domain name to the set. For instance, the Web site developer could group marketing.html and tech_support.html into a set and give this set the domain name 2.firm-x.com. Then the URLs of these objects will be http://2.firm-x.com/marketing.html and http://2.firm-x.com/tech_support.html, and the number of different domain names will be reduced. Note that now marketing.html and tech_support.html must always reside on the same set of servers. According to the patent application by its founders, Akamai uses this type of fine-granularity domain name that incorporates identities of "content chunks" [Leighton and Lewin 2000].

Even when using coarser replica granules, the scale of the site may still call for a distributed implementation of the site's DNS service. We consider some methods for such implementations in the next chapter.

14.4 Summary

This chapter has discussed a variety of mechanisms for request distribution. These mechanisms can be broadly divided into those that are oblivious to requested objects (content-blind request distribution) and those that take this information into account (content-aware request distribution).

Content-blind request distribution can in principle be performed by the client DNS server, the client itself, network routers using anycast, a balancing switch in front of a server farm, or the Web site's DNS server. All content-blind approaches require that every server replica be able to process every request for the Web site. This requirement normally means that each server must contain a replica of the entire Web site. However, using surrogates in place of Web server replicas or running Web server replicas on top of a distributed file system allows a Web site to bypass this restriction. Client-based approaches require software modifications at the client side, which impede their use in practice; although transparent to the end user, they are not transparent to client-side software and therefore cannot be considered fully transparent. Anycast in the context of HTTP requires a modification to the protocol stack implementation. Thus Web sites mostly use balancing switches or Web site's DNS servers for content-blind request distribution.

Content-aware request distribution can occur at the client, Web server, L7 balancing switch, or the Web site's DNS server if the site uses fine-granularity domain names. The client-based solution uses Java applet implementation, which limits the applicability of this solution to browsers that enable the execution of such applets. Request distribution at the Web server uses HTTP redirection to instruct the client to resubmit its request to a server replica. This approach often requires the client to establish two sequential TCP connections, one to the initial Web server and another to the server replica. L7 balancing switches allow very flexible request distribution and enable fine-grained differentiated quality of service as well as selective replication of content. This flexibility, however, comes at the expense of lower performance compared to L4 switches. Fine-granularity domain names provide a way to introduce limited content awareness to DNS-based request distribution. On the other hand, this approach increases the number of DNS resolutions a client has to perform. In practice, fine-granularity domain names and especially L7 switches are prevalent methods for content-aware request distribution.

With so many alternatives for request distribution, a careful performance study that would compare the benefits of different schemes is clearly needed. Cardellini et al. [1999] performed a simulation study comparing some of the approaches discussed in this chapter. However, this study does not consider many factors and therefore is not sufficient to resolve the performance question conclusively.

Chapter 15
Content Delivery Networks

Having considered basic mechanisms for request redirection, we are now ready to discuss architectures for scalable content delivery from content providers to consumers. These platforms are also known as content delivery networks (CDNs). Although forward proxies, especially the cooperative proxy platforms considered in Chapter 9, have the same goal, the term *CDN* is historically applied only to platforms that act as agents of content providers.

A CDN signs up individual content providers for scalable content delivery and delivers their content to any client that accesses the Web sites of these content providers. Contrast this with the forward proxy platforms of Chapter 9, which attempt to improve content delivery to their own clients only, but do so regardless of the Web site these clients access. We refer to content providers who sign up with a CDN for content delivery as *CDN customers*, and users who request content as *CDN users*. CDN users have no business relationship with the CDN. Web clients that download content through a CDN we call *CDN clients*. One should not confuse CDN clients with CDN customers: the former download content from a CDN while the latter provide content and, depending on the CDN, run origin servers.

A CDN promises two main benefits to content providers.

Global reach: A CDN serves content from multiple *CDN servers* deployed around the globe. By signing up with a CDN, a content provider gains instant presence around the globe at virtually no upfront cost. A CDN usually has servers in multiple locations and ISPs, and therefore can potentially deliver content to clients in many parts of the world from nearby servers.

Flash event protection: Sometimes a Web site experiences a sudden increase in demand called a *flash event*. In some cases flash events are predictable, as when a site posts new content that generates great interest. For example, news sites that posted the Starr report on the investigation of President Clinton could easily have predicted an increased demand. In other cases an unforeseen incident, such as a popular TV program's profiling a site, can trigger a flash event. A CDN offers an easy way to prepare for a predictable flash event or to protect from an unforeseen one, by shouldering part of the load that the origin server would otherwise have to carry.

Forward proxies appear to address the same two issues by allowing clients to download content from nearby locations. If ISPs deployed forward proxies ubiquitously, would CDNs still be needed? Gadde et al. [2001] analyzed the additional utility of CDNs under this assumption and found that CDNs would bring little additional benefits for cacheable content. Still, this does not mean that forward proxies obviate the need for CDNs, for the following reasons:

- Assuming ubiquitous deployment of forward proxies is unrealistic with the current protocols, because explicit deployment is awkward and transparent deployment is not always possible (see Chapter 8).

- Unlike forward proxies, CDNs leave full content control to content providers. This allows effective consistency control over content replicas (see Section 15.7) and accurate collection of usage statistics. In combination, these features eliminate any reason for cache busting.

- CDNs can improve access to types of content that are normally uncacheable by forward proxies, such as dynamic content, streaming content, and secured content.

- CDNs can prepopulate their servers with content from their customers. While forward proxies also can prefetch content, they are decoupled from content providers, and therefore the accuracy of their prefetching is limited. In addition, CDN server prepopulation is governed by business relationships between the CDN and content providers, where content providers pay for the privilege. This eliminates guesswork from the CDN.

Fundamentally, a CDN is an intermediate layer of infrastructure between origin servers and clients (a buzzword for this is *middleware*). A CDN can achieve scalable content delivery by distributing load among its servers, by serving client requests from servers that are close to requesters, and by bypassing congested network paths. CDN servers are similar to the surrogates considered in Section 14.2.1. The distinguishing features of a CDN are that its infrastructure is shared among multiple content provider sites and that it has a close relationship with the underlying networks. A technical consequence of shared infrastructure is that CDNs must implement a mechanism for finding the origin server for a given piece of content (see Section 15.3). By "a close relationship with the underlying networks," we mean that CDNs place their servers within points of presence or backbone nodes of ISPs (see Section 8.1). The remainder of this chapter considers various architectures and mechanisms used to implement CDNs.

15.1   Types of CDNs

CDNs can be classified according to two properties, their relationships with ISPs whose networks they use, and their relationships with their customers and the mechanism for delivering client requests to CDN servers.

The relationship between a CDN and ISPs may take several forms. A CDN may be a stand-alone company not affiliated with any particular ISP. Instead, it partners with multiple ISPs and deploys its servers in as many ISPs as possible. We refer to such a CDN as a *multi-ISP CDN*. CDN servers of a multi-ISP CDN are colocated with ISP points of presence or with entry points into ISP backbones, typically on the LAN with their access routers. For this reason, multi-ISP CDNs are said to follow a *colocation* model. An advantage of multi-ISP CDNs is that they can often deliver content from the same ISP that the requesting client uses. In this way they minimize the number of peering links or NAPs used in the delivery. Since most packet loss and network congestion occurs at certain peering points and NAPs, minimizing their number is desirable for better performance. On the other hand, to realize this advantage, a colocation CDN must deploy and maintain servers in numerous ISPs, which increases their capital costs. Examples of multi-ISP CDNs include Akamai and Digital Island.

Alternatively, an ISP itself may decide to provide CDN services. To this end, the ISP deploys CDN servers around the edge of its network, resulting in a *single-ISP CDN*. AT&T, for example, offers single-ISP CDN service. An ISP with a global network can achieve good geographical coverage this way without relying on any other ISPs. It also has a cost advantage over a multi-ISP CDN because it owns its network and does not have to purchase bandwidth from a partner. In addition, belonging to the same company makes it easier for the CDN to take advantage of low-level nonstandard network features such as multicast. On the other hand, a single-ISP CDN cannot bring its servers as close to clients as a multi-ISP CDN. An emerging technology of content delivery internetworking (see Chapter 18), if it takes hold, might address this limitation.

Turning now to CDNs' customer relationships and request delivery mechanisms, Figure 15.1 shows different types of CDNs according to these characteristics. A *CDN with hosting service*, or *hosting CDN* for short, has both the CDN servers for relaying content from origin servers to clients and also the origin servers. If a content provider wants full control over its content, the customer can use a staging server that maintains a connection to a CDN's origin server. The customer has complete freedom to create, update, and debug content on its staging server. Once ready, the new version of the content is uploaded from the staging server to the CDN origin server. The staging server is thus never used for servicing client requests. Digital Island is an example of a CDN that also offers service in the role of a hosting CDN.

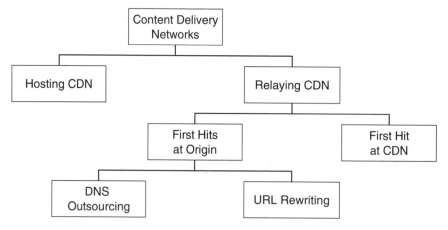

Figure 15.1 CDN types

Besides the benefits that hosting service providers offer their customers (such as relieving them from the headache of Web server management and proper resource provisioning for their Web site), a hosting CDN has the advantage of having both origin servers and CDN servers under the control of the same entity. The platform is therefore free to implement efficient proprietary techniques involving coordination between origin servers and CDN servers. These techniques can be useful in implementing flexible mechanisms for the distribution of content from origin servers to CDN servers, in keeping content at CDN servers consistent with the content at origin servers, and so on. In contrast, CDNs where origin servers are operated by customers must cooperate with the customers in implementing any such mechanisms.

In some cases, a Web site requires such complicated back-end processing that it is difficult to recreate within a hosting platform, even with custom deployment. For example, it would be difficult for a hosting CDN to take over the operation of a large search engine. In these cases, a *relaying CDN* would be more appropriate. In a relaying CDN, origin servers remain external to the CDN and are under full control of the content provider. The CDN directs all requests it cannot satisfy to origin servers at the customer sites. The content delivery solution offered by Akamai Technologies is a prime example of a relaying CDN.

Relaying CDNs can be further divided into two types, based on where client requests for container pages (as opposed to embedded objects) go.[1] CDNs with *first hit at the origin*, or *origin-first CDNs* for short, do not attempt to service container page requests. Instead, they focus on delivering embedded and, more recently, hyperlinked content. For example, Figure 15.2 shows a request flow in a relaying origin-first CDN when a client accesses the container page, home.html. This page embeds two images,

---

[1] Recall from Section 4.5 that container pages are HTML pages that include embedded objects.

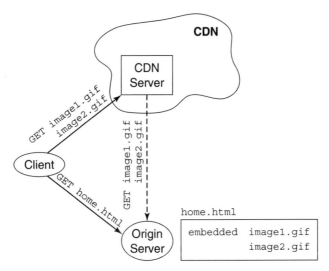

Figure 15.2 A request flow in a relaying CDN with first hit at origin

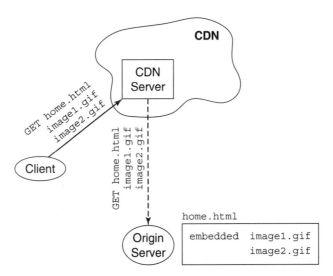

Figure 15.3 A request flow in a relaying CDN with first hit at CDN

image1.gif and image2.gif. The request for home.html goes to the origin server, and the requests for embedded images go to a CDN server. The CDN server in its turn may have to request the images from the origin server unless the CDN server already has them due to previous requests from other clients. In contrast, CDNs with *first hit at CDN*, or *CDN-first*, service all requests, including those for container pages (Figure 15.3).

15.2   Delivering Requests to a CDN

Before deciding how to deliver content to clients, a CDN must first decide how to make clients send their requests to its network rather than the customer's origin server. We refer to mechanisms that achieve this as *request-delivery* mechanisms.

Hosting CDNs do not face the request-delivery issue because they have control over their customers' origin servers and usually also control the DNS servers for their customers' domain names. Relaying CDNs commonly use various DNS tricks for request delivery, but details vary in different CDN types.

Relaying CDNs with first hit at CDN use a *DNS outsourcing* technique illustrated in Figure 15.4. Consider a company called firm-x that signs up with such a CDN for delivery of its Web site, www.firm-x.com. With DNS outsourcing, firm-x delegates its DNS service for domain www.firm-x.com to the CDN. Typically, the delegation is implemented by firm-x's DNS server, which responds to DNS queries with a pointer to the CDN's DNS server. This can either be achieved by using a CNAME DNS record that points the client DNS server to another domain name within the control of the CDN, such as firm-x.cdn-foo.com or by delegating the authority for the DNS name www.firm-x.com to CDN's DNS servers using an NS DNS record (see Section 4.2). In the second case the customer DNS will list the CDN's DNS servers as the authoritative DNS servers for the outsourced domain.

To download a CDN-delivered object such as www.firm-x.com/home.html from this site, a client sends the DNS query for www.firm-x.com to its *client DNS server*, or *client DNS* for short (step 1 in Figure 15.4). The client DNS works through the DNS hierarchy and ultimately sends this query to the DNS server that is responsible for domain names under firm-x.com. This DNS server is operated by firm-x and referred to as the *customer DNS server*, or *customer DNS* (step 2). The customer DNS redirects

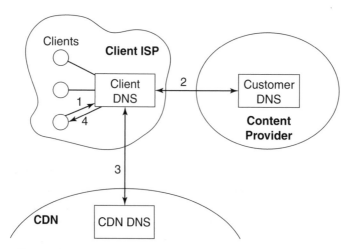

Figure 15.4 Request delivery to CDN with DNS outsourcing

the client DNS to a CDN's DNS server using either a CNAME or NS DNS record (step 3). The CDN's DNS resolves this query to the IP address of one of the CDN servers, and thus makes the client send its request to the chosen CDN server and not the customer's origin server. Thus at least three DNS entities are involved in this mechanism: client DNS, customer DNS, and CDN's DNS.

For communication unrelated to Web content delivery, firm-x will use a different domain name over which it will retain authority. For instance, the company can use firm-x.com for its email so that its workers have email addresses of the form name@firm-x.com. Firm-x's DNS server will be the authoritative DNS server for firm-x.com and will resolve this name to a host within the company that implements the mailbox.

Relaying CDNs with the first hit at origin can use one of two methods for request delivery. One method is almost identical to request delivery in the case of first hit at CDN and is also called DNS outsourcing. In this method, embedded URLs that the CDN is supposed to deliver use host names from subdomains of the customer domain name, and the CDN's DNS servers are ultimately responsible for resolving these subdomains. For instance, firm-x may have www.firm-x.com as its main domain name and images.www.firm-x.com as a subdomain for embedded objects. In this scheme, firm-x's DNS server retains authority over domain www.firm-x.com (and resolves queries for this name to the company's Web server) and points requests for the subdomain images.www.firm-x.com to the CDNs DNS server. The only difference between this method and the case of first hit at CDN is that the latter outsources the DNS name used in the URL of the container page as well as embedded objects, while the former outsources DNS names of embedded URLs only.

In the other method of request delivery, embedded content uses DNS names belonging to the CDN domain directly. For example, if page www.firm-x.com contains an image with host name images.firm-x.cdn-foo.net, then no delegation of a subdomain is required from a customer; on the other hand, the customer will likely have to convert embedded-content URLs to use the CDN domain names. Akamai calls this process "akamaizing the content." We refer to it as *URL rewriting*. CDNs using this method provide a special script to automate URL conversion. These conversion scripts parse container Web pages and convert embedded URLs to use the CDN host names as well as comply with any other format requirements that the CDN imposes. Even with scripts, explicit URL conversion is cumbersome, since it must be executed any time the customer adds new content or modifies existing content. Moreover, conversion scripts are useless for dynamically generated container pages. For dynamically generated pages, URL rewriting can be achieved only by dynamically modifying the generated page with a specialized component that will rewrite embedded URLs in the page on the fly. While this functionality is available in Volera's ICS server, it imposes performance overhead. Alteon, now part of Nortel, offers a dedicated appliance that performs URL rewriting.

All these mechanisms can be used to deliver requests for hyperlinked content, besides embedded content. For example, firm-x may outsource delivery of video clips by using a subdomain video.firm-x.com and delegating this subdomain to a CDN. Then a Web document may have a hyperlink to a clip, http://video.firm-x.com/clip1.mpeg. When the user clicks on this link, its request will be delivered to the CDN.

Comparing origin-first CNDs with CDN-first CDNs from the request-delivery perspective, the former require that embedded URLs use distinct domains from container pages. In particular, these CDNs preclude using relative URLs for embedded objects (as a reminder, relative URLs do not contain host names; instead, they assume implicitly the same host name as the container page). In contrast, CDN-first CDNs allow embedded objects to share the same domain name as the container page and to have relative URLs. Sharing the domain name is important because it enables the same CDN server to deliver both the container page and embedded objects. Therefore, all content can be served over the same persistent connection with the client.

In the case of origin-first CDNs, by contrast, the client must establish two separate TCP connections and perform two separate DNS name resolutions (unless they have been cached from previous accesses) to download a document: one to obtain the container page from the origin server and the other to fetch embedded content from a CDN server. Worse, in the case of secure HTTP interactions, separate secure session setups are required for container pages and embedded content. Given the high cost of establishing a secure session (see Section 15.9), origin-first CDNs impose a significant performance penalty in such cases.

15.3 Finding Origin Servers

In a relaying CDN, a CDN server must be able to determine which origin server to contact on a miss. To illustrate the problem, consider a URL http://images.firm-x.com/blah.jpg. When a CDN server receives a request for this object, the request identifies the object only by the path portion of the URL, /blah.jpg, and not the host portion. Fortunately, the CDN server can still tell that this page belongs to the origin server images.firm-x.com from the request's host header. (To recall, the host header contains the host-name portion of the requested URL, images.firm-x.com in our example.) But if the CDN server does not have the requested image, how would it find out the IP address of the origin server for images.firm-x.com? Doing a DNS lookup will not help, because presumably the CDN manages the domain name images.firm-x.com and maps it into its own CDN server IP addresses, not those of the external servers.

There are a few basic ways to let CDN servers find external sites.

- As part of service provisioning, the customer provides the IP address of its origin server. The CDN DNS server stores this address along with the IP addresses of the CDN servers. Depending on the originator of a DNS query, the CDN DNS differentiates between client queries and CDN server lookups. The CDN DNS responds to client queries with IP addresses of CDN servers and to CDN server queries with the IP address of the external origin server.

- Somewhat as in the previous mechanism, as part of service provisioning the customer provides the IP address of its origin server or a non-outsourced DNS name for the origin server. For example, the outsourced name images.firm-x.com could either be associated with the IP address of the origin server or with the non-outsourced DNS name, such as origin.firm-x.com, of the origin server. Each CDN server then stores the association between the outsourced name and the non-outsourced name or IP address in a table and uses this association to find the origin server on a miss. Volera proxies use this method if configured as CDN servers.

- Instead of storing the association between an outsourced DNS name and the origin server in a table, the CDN establishes a transformation rule that maps outsourced host names that the CDN manages to corresponding non-outsourced names that the customer manages. For instance, the rule could say that the non-outsourced name is obtained by adding a "-real" postfix to the lowest-level portion of the outsourced name. Then, the rule would transform the outsourced name images.firm-x.com to the non-outsourced name images-real.firm-x.com. When a CDN server receives a missed request, it applies the transformation rule and then performs a DNS query on the resulting non-outsourced host name. The customer DNS server resolves this query to the external origin server.

- With URL rewriting, the rewritten URL can embed both the host name of a CDN server complex and the host name of the actual origin server, for instance http://images.firm-x.cdn-foo.net/images-real.firm-x.com/blah.jpg. On a miss, the CDN server can then extract the host name of the external origin server and obtain the object. A similar method is used by Akamai [Leighton and Lewin 2000].

15.4   Request Distribution in CDNs

CDNs employ many CDN servers for content delivery. Large multi-ISP CDNs can have several thousand CDN servers. Once a request is delivered to its network as discussed in Section 15.2, the CDN must distribute this request to one of its servers. We considered a number of basic request-redirection mechanisms in Chapter 14. CDNs typically combine them in an attempt to gain the benefits of each. The goals of the resulting mechanism include allowing both wide-area and local-area request distribution and providing service to very high-volume Web sites. This section describes some combinations of the basic request-redirection mechanisms that can be used by a CDN.

15.4.1   DNS/Balancing Switch Redirection

Redirection by a balancing switch is best suited for request redirection among servers on a LAN. DNS-server-based balancing is best for request distribution across WANs,

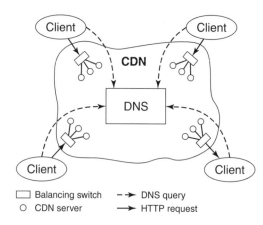

Figure 15.5 DNS/balancing switch request redirection

because client-server proximity metrics change infrequently. This suggests a two-level request redirection schema: DNS-based redirection to distribute requests among geographically distributed server farms, and redirection by a balancing switch within each farm. The first level is often called *global request distribution*. Such a two-level scheme is shown in Figure 15.5. In this scheme, the CDN DNS returns the IP address of the balancing switch that front-ends the chosen server farm. The client packets then arrive at the switch, which forwards them to one of the servers in its farm. AT&T's CDN service is an example of a CDN using this two-level scheme.

In principle, the two redirection levels can be kept completely decoupled, and any CDN DNS server product can be combined with any balancing switch. However, extra benefits can be gained from an integrated solution where the two levels cooperate. In an integrated solution, each balancing switch monitors the server load in its cluster, it alerts the CDN DNS server if the overall load in the cluster reaches a dangerous level. The CDN DNS server takes this into account in distributing future requests among balancing switches. The CDN DNS server and balancing switch can also exchange *healthcheck* messages containing information about failures in the server clusters. If healthcheck messages from a balancing switch stop arriving or indicate a dangerous number of failures within a cluster, the CDN DNS server stops sending requests to this balancing switch. The balancing switch can be either L4 or L7. Several companies—including Nortel's Alteon division, F5, iPivot, Foundry Networks, Radware, and Cisco—offer integrated DNS/balancing switch solutions.

15.4.2 Two-Level DNS Redirection

One problem with DNS-based request redirection as described in Section 14.1.3 is that effective control over server selection compels the DNS server to assign a short time to live to DNS responses. This in turn increases the number of Web requests that would require a DNS query, which in our case must be answered by the CDN DNS. The

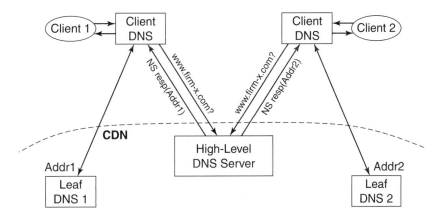

Figure 15.6 A two-level DNS system in a CDN

number of such Web requests increases even further if the CDN uses fine-granularity domain names for content-aware request distribution (see Section 14.3.4). A higher rate of DNS queries may cause an increased user latency (because more requests must wait for the DNS query result) and higher load on the DNS server.

To alleviate these problems, the CDN DNS is sometimes split into two levels as shown in Figure 15.6 [Leighton and Lewin 2000]. The DNS mapping database for all objects is replicated or partitioned among a number of leaf DNS servers. These leaf servers are front-ended by another server, which is denoted a high-level DNS server. The high-level DNS server registers as the authoritative server with higher-level DNS servers, such as those responsible for the .com or .net domains. Thus, this DNS server receives initial DNS queries from clients. When a query arrives, the high-level DNS server sends a response indicating that the authoritative DNS server for this domain is actually one of the leaf DNS servers. The leaf DNS server chosen is one close to the client DNS server that originated the query. Moreover, the high-level DNS assigns a very long TTL to the response, so that it would be cached by the client DNS server for a long time. The actual name resolution occurs at the leaf DNS servers.

This two-level DNS architecture distributes the DNS load among leaf DNS servers and allows client DNS servers to use nearby DNS servers for queries while they cache high-level DNS responses. Lower latency and distributed load allow leaf DNS servers to set a very low (or zero) TTL to their responses, improving their control over load balancing.

15.4.3 Anycast/DNS Redirection

A more radical solution to DNS scalability is to exploit anycast. In this case, the CDN's DNS database is fully replicated on several DNS servers placed at different corners of the network. Anycast is used to deliver a DNS request to the DNS server that is closest in the network to the query originator. What makes anycast work here is that, unlike HTTP, the DNS protocol is connectionless: DNS interactions involve a simple exchange of UDP messages. Thus the main anycast problem discussed in Section 14.1.4—which is that unstable routing may disrupt connections—does not arise, and this approach can be used in the Internet as it exists today, without modification of any of its protocols.

15.5   Pitfalls of DNS-Based Request Distribution

Because DNS request distribution plays such an important role in CDNs, let us consider the issues around this mechanism in more detail. We have already mentioned how client caching of DNS responses may hurt DNS-based request distribution. There are several other problems as well. How severe these problems are is currently an open question. However, it is useful to understand the architectural limitations of this scheme.

A major goal of a CDN is to deliver content from a CDN server that is at the edge of the network and close to the requesting client. Unfortunately, when trying to direct the client to a nearby content server, the only information the DNS server has is the IP address of the originator of the DNS query. As Figure 15.4 illustrates, it is the client DNS server, not the Web client, that sends this query on the client's behalf. Large networks often have few centralized DNS servers that all clients use. For example, most AT&T Worldnet clients use only two DNS servers, no matter where the client is located. Therefore, the browser may be far removed from its DNS server, causing the CDN DNS server to choose a distant CDN server for the request. We call this problem the *originator problem*.

Another problem is that the number of Web clients behind different client DNS servers can be drastically different. In a large ISP, millions of users can share a DNS server, while a small organization may have only a few users behind its DNS server. As a result, a single DNS resolution by the CDN DNS may generate drastically different load on the selected CDN server: a DNS request from a large ISP's DNS server may result in millions of HTTP requests, while a DNS request from a small organization may generate a negligible HTTP load. The load on a Web or CDN server that results from a single DNS resolution is called the *hidden load factor* [Colajanni et al. 1998a]. Hidden load factors make it very difficult for the DNS-based server selection algorithm to predict the effect of its Web server choice.

Finally, a relaying CDN with DNS outsourcing faces another problem, which we refer to as a *client DNS masking problem*. Client DNS servers are typically configured to always request recursive DNS resolution. Virtually all DNS servers, except for root DNS servers (see Section 4.2) honor requests for recursion. To see the consequence of this obedience, consider Figure 15.7 and contrast it with Figure 15.4. After a client sends its DNS query to its client DNS (step 1), the client DNS forwards this query to the customer DNS (step 2). When the customer DNS receives a DNS query from a client DNS, the customer DNS honoring requests for recursion resolves the

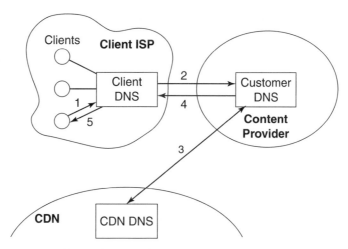

Figure 15.7 A client DNS masking problem

query itself and sends the final result to the client DNS. That means that it is the customer DNS that sends the DNS query to the CDN DNS (step 3). So not only does the CDN DNS not know who the actual Web client is, it does not know who the client DNS server is either. All DNS requests for customer content will arrive from the customer DNS server, making the CDN deliver customer content from a CDN server that is closest to the customer, regardless of where requests originated. The whole purpose of delivering content from points close to clients will be defeated.

A simple way to avoid this problem is to configure the customer DNS servers not to honor requests for recursive DNS resolution. Most DNS server implementations can be configured this way. However, this would cause the customer DNS servers not to use recursion for all DNS requests, even those that have nothing to do with CDNs. While the consequence of denying recursion is unclear, it is certainly a deviation from the current practice to honor recursion requests. Note that hosting CDNs or CDNs that use URL rewriting for request delivery do not have this problem, because the customer DNS in these CDNs is not on the processing path of requests for CDN-delivered content.

15.6 Fine-Tuning DNS Request Distribution

We have seen that proper DNS-based request distribution can be impaired because of the originator problem, unknown hidden load factors, and client DNS masking. The originator problem may cause DNS to select CDN servers that are not close to HTTP clients, hidden load factors may lead to wrong load-balancing decisions by DNS, and the client DNS masking problem defeats DNS request distribution completely. Fortunately the DNS masking problem can be resolved by properly configuring the customer DNS servers, and therefore we assume this problem has been addressed. To alleviate the other two problems it may be beneficial to fine-tune DNS request distribution at the CDN server chosen by DNS and send the HTTP request to another CDN server. We refer to this fine-tuning as *post-DNS request distribution*.

There are three ways to perform post-DNS request distribution: triangular communication (see Section 14.1.2), HTTP redirection, and URL rewriting. Several L4 and L7 switches support triangular communication, including Arrowpoint (now part of Cisco) and IBM's eNetwork Dispatcher. HTTP redirection is supported by most Web servers, and an increasing number of products support URL rewriting, for example Volera's ICS proxy server and Alteon's Akamaizer.

15.6.1 Post-DNS Request Distribution by Triangular Communication

Let CDN server A be the one chosen by the DNS and CDN server B be a better server for the request. If server A knows that B is a better server, it can use triangular communication, where it forwards all packets from the client to B. Server B responds to the client using A's IP address, so that the client is not aware that response packets arrive from a different server. Note that A would need to continue forwarding client packets, including TCP acknowledgments, to B for the whole duration of the interaction. IP-in-IP encapsulation is more convenient than network address translation for the implementation of triangular communication because each CDN server can potentially receive forwarded packets from any other CDN server, and because, with IP-in-IP encapsulation, a recipient of a forwarded packet can learn the forwarding server IP address (which the recipient must use in its response packets) directly from the packet itself (see Section 14.1.2).

One pitfall of this approach arises from the fact that server B has to impersonate server A using A's IP address. Since IP impersonation (also known as *IP spoofing*) is used by many attacks against servers on the Internet, an increasing number of routers filter IP packets based on the knowledge of where a particular server is located. For example, if a router receives a packet with A's IP address as source address, and if the router knows that A is not located behind the link on which this packet arrived, the router might drop the packet. Therefore, to make triangular communication work, a CDN must take great care to ensure that no such filtering routers are on the route between the client and server B, or that packets from both A and B arrive at such routers by the same link.

Although conceptually triangular communication can be implemented by CDN servers as described above, in practice it is usually implemented by balancing switches that front-end CDN servers, as in Figure 15.5. However, making request distribution decisions places extra burden on balancing swtiches: they must now keep track of each other's loads, maintain information on Internet topology and possibly other metrics used in request distribution, and identify the best server or server farm for a given request from a given client.

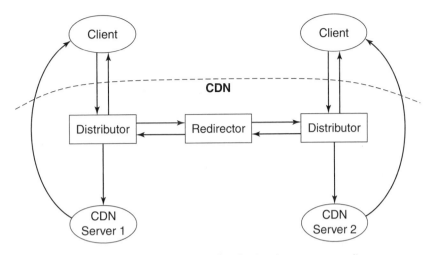

Figure 15.8 Post-DNS request distribution by separate redirectors

Another approach to request distribution, derived from the RaDaR architecture [Rabinovich and Aggarwal 1999], relieves switches of this burden by concentrating request distribution in separate units. This architecture is shown in Figure 15.8. It contains request *distributors* and request *redirectors*. Distributors fulfill the role of L7 balancing switches in Figure 15.5. DNS redirection is used to send client requests to the distributors that are closest to the clients as far as CDN's DNS knows. Redirectors make all post-DNS request distribution decisions. Although Figure 15.8 shows only one redirector, many redirectors can be deployed throughout the CDN.

A distributor accepts an HTTP request, parses it, and forwards it to a redirector responsible for the requested URL. The redirector chooses a CDN server for this request and sends the server identity back to the distributor. This message exchange occurs over UDP, so it involves no connection establishment overhead. The distributor then forwards all request packets to the chosen CDN server; the remainder of the interaction uses triangular communication between the client, the distributor, and the CDN server.

The distributors in this approach are quite similar to L7 switches. However, the functionality of an L7 switch is split here between distributors and redirectors, allowing independent decisions on how much resource to deploy for each component. Redirectors can be easily scaled up by partioning the URL namespace among a larger number of redirectors. The number and location of distributors, redirectors, and CDN servers can be decided independently.

15.6.2 Post-DNS Request Distribution with HTTP Redirection and URL Rewriting

HTTP redirection (see Section 14.3.2) and URL rewriting (see Section 15.2) can be used even if all that the CDN server knows is that it is not an appropriate server for this request and it does not know which server is better. Both methods rely on agreement between CDN servers and its DNS on a special domain name format that embeds a client IP address.

Consider HTTP redirection. If a CDN server does not know to which server to forward the request, it will redirect the client to a URL with a special host name that embeds the client's IP address. For example, if the original URL was http://www.firm-x.com/page.html and the client has IP address 192.105.10.25, then the new URL could have the form http://192-105-10-25.www.firm-x.com/page.html. To follow the redirection, the client sends a DNS query for domain name 192-105-10-25.www.firm-x.com to the CDN DNS server. This time, the DNS server knows the client IP address from the domain name and performs server selection relative to this client. Thus the originator problem will not arise.

With URL rewriting, a CDN server serves the requested page to the client, but rewrites all embedded URLs (and possibly hyperlinks) on this page according to the above format. Then the embedded URLs include the client IP address in their host-name portion, and the CDN DNS server receives DNS queries for domain names that encode the HTTP client origin IP address. As in the case of HTTP redirection, the DNS server is then able to select a server relative to the client.

If the CDN server knows the proper CDN server for the received request, the server receiving the request can use the IP address of the proper CDN server in place of the special domain names in both methods, saving an extra DNS query resolution. Assume that the proper CDN server's IP address is 127.150.30.155 and the original URL was http://www.firm-x.com/page.html. Then, in the case of HTTP redirection, the CDN server receiving the request can redirect the client to URL http://127.150.30.155/page.html, and the client will send the request for page.html to the proper CDN server directly, without a DNS query. Similarly, in the case of URL rewriting, the receiving CDN server can replace the domain name www.firm-x.com with 127.150.30.155, and the client will go directly to the proper CDN server for the embedded content.

Note that URL rewriting requires access to container pages and therefore applies mostly to hosting CDNs or CDNs with first hit at CDN. In fact, the same is often true of HTTP redirection, because using it does not usually pay unless its overhead can be amortized over the container page and its embedded objects (see Section 14.3.2).

15.7 Data Consistency in CDNs

An important selling point of CDNs over forward proxies is that they allow closer coupling of CDN servers with content providers. This coupling allows a CDN to enforce strong replica consistency and supply accurate usage statistics to content providers. In fact, strong consistency is almost imperative for CDNs, because clients in this case assume they obtain content directly from origin servers. Thus clients can rightfully expect to always receive current content from a Web site.

The CDN may use its ability to provide strong consistency in a variety of ways: to help in marketing its services by claiming strong consistency of all delivered content, or to sell different levels of content delivery service, charging more for stronger consistency. In any case, it is essential that a CDN have the ability to maintain strong consistency of any content it replicates on its servers.

Strong data consistency in CDNs can be achieved by invalidation of content cached at CDN servers when it becomes stale. Cache invalidation is much more practical for CDN servers and surrogates in general than for forward proxies. A CDN may have tens, hundreds, or perhaps thousands of CDN servers but still nothing close to the millions of potential clients in the Internet at large. A small number of caches to invalidate removes many challenges related to client list maintenance and the number of invalidations, the two main limiting factors of invalidation as discussed in Chapter 10. Furthermore, CDN servers and origin servers either are under the same administrative domain (in the case of a hosting CDN) or are parties to an explicit business agreement, thus making the use of proprietary or nonstandard protocols feasible. As a result, surrogates and CDNs are the only environments where invalidations are currently used. Several companies offer add-ons to proxies and servers that implement proprietary protocols for invalidation. Among commercial offerings, Webspective Corporation, now part of Inktomi, implements invalidation with delayed updates.

To minimize impact on the origin server and its load, server-side functionality is sometimes implemented on a separate invalidation server. Interestingly, a general purpose off-the-shelf event notification server can be used as the invalidation server. For example, any event server that complies with the Event Notification specification of the Object Management Group will do [OMG 1999]. These event servers allow applications to define event types with arbitrary attributes, and they allow event *producers* to deposit these events on the event server and event *consumers* to *subscribe* to events of certain types with certain attribute values. The event server delivers events that match subscriptions to appropriate consumers.

To implement cache invalidation using a general event server, a CDN might define an event type `ObjectChange` with an attribute containing an object identifier, such as the object URL. When a CDN server acquires object X, it subscribes to `ObjectChange` events that have the attribute containing X's identifier. When the CDN server removes or invalidates object X, it unsubscribes to these events. If any object changes at the origin server, the origin server deposits event `ObjectChange` with the attribute containing this object's identifier on the event server; this event is then delivered to all CDN servers that currently store this object. The CDN servers then invalidate this object and unsubscribe to these events or obtain the new version of the object.

Subscription lists at the event server are equivalent to client lists in the basic invalidation mechanism of Section 10.2. By separating event notification functionality from the content servers one can divide the load and leverage highly optimized third-party event services.

A completely different mechanism for CDN data consistency is described by Akamai cofounders Leighton and Lewin [2000]. Their mechanism includes a fingerprint (see Section 5.1) of an object served through the CDN into its URL. For example, assume that MD5 hash functions are used to produce fingerprints, and let object http://domain-name.com/image1.gif have fingerprint 28765. Then the URL is transformed into http://domain-name.com/28765/image1.gif. Should image1.gif change, its fingerprint and hence the derived URL will also change. As long as clients use the new URL, they are guaranteed to see the new content. Consistency is enforced even if stale objects are stored in forward caches, since current object versions have different URLs. This approach is applicable only to embedded objects, because container pages are usually required to have stable URLs, such as http://www.att.com/. Therefore, this approach is geared toward origin-first content distribution networks.

This approach also implies that any change of an object entails the transformation of its URL. That in turn requires that the object URL be changed in all pages on the site that refer to the object. In other words, a *local* change to an object now leads to a *global* parsing of all container pages on the Web site, to find and update those that contain references to the changed object. Products such as Volera's ICS proxy and Alteon's Akamaizer allow on-the-fly URL rewriting and alleviate this problem. With these devices, an object change requires a change in only the device configuration, letting it know of the new URL transformation rule. As HTML pages flow through such a device, it rewrites any references to this object to include the new URL.

Another limitation of this approach is that forward caching of container pages may lead to stale content delivery. Consider a container page X that embeds object Y. After Y changes to Y', the container page is modified to point to Y' instead of Y. However, if a forward proxy caches the stale version of X, it will continue serving the old version of Y to its clients. Thus, in general, the level of consistency of this method is limited by the level of consistency provided by forward caches. The only way it can enforce strong consistency is by disallowing caching of container pages. In some cases when the content provider makes container pages uncacheable for unrelated reasons, this requirement is not a limitation. In other situations it can lead to a significant reduction in cacheable content and increase in bandwidth consumption and CPU loads experienced by the Web site.

15.8 Streaming Content Delivery

Just like forward proxies, CDN servers can also be used to scale up streaming content delivery. The initial idea is simple: clients are redirected to CDN servers that are used as broadcasting relays between the origin server[2] and the clients. Similar to forward proxies, a CDN server concentrates many client requests into a single stream from the origin server and hence reduces traffic and server load.

---

[2] Origin servers are often called source servers or stream sources in the context of streaming data. We continue to use the term *origin server* for uniformity.

Streaming content delivery poses especially interesting challenges in cases of delivering live streams, often referred to as *Webcasts*. The challenges stem from the fact that live streams cannot be stored in advance on CDN servers. Thus the delivery of the stream to the CDN servers must occur in real time during the Webcast. Since a large CDN deploys numerous CDN servers globally, a popular Webcast may strain the network and the origin server just from the need to deliver the content to all the CDN servers around the globe. Much of the effort in the area of streaming CDNs has been devoted to addressing this challenge.

15.8.1 Using Multicast for Streaming Content Delivery

A single-ISP CDN can use IP multicast for streaming content delivery. The transmission from the origin server to the CDN servers in this case can be done using multicast, while the transmission from a CDN server to its clients would be via unicast. Before the origin server begins transmitting the live stream, it creates a multicast group for this stream and then transmits the stream to the multicast address. When a CDN server receives a client request for this stream, the CDN server first learns the multicast address of the stream from the origin server and then joins the multicast group.

Concentrating streams in CDN servers provides a feasible way to address some of the multicast problems discussed in Section 7.4. As a reminder, these issues included a large multicast state at the routers, a high rate of multicast group membership changes, a high drop rate of multicast packets, and the lack of universal deployment.

No matter how many CDN servers a CDN has, this number still pales in comparison with the potential number of clients of the Webcast. Thus CDN servers limit the size of the multicast group and the multicast state maintained by the routers in the ISP network. Moreover, a CDN server generates a change in the multicast group only when the first client arrives or the last one departs. With many clients per CDN server, the rate of changes to the multicast group are greatly reduced.

Further, caching at the CDN servers can address the issue of dropped packets. Maxemchuk et al. [1997] defined a protocol in which a CDN server caches a sliding fragment a few seconds long of live video before transmitting it to the client. To accumulate the initial fragment, transmission to clients is delayed by the duration of the fragment. Then, while the fragment is being transmitted, a new segment is being received from the content server. As the new segment accumulates at the CDN server, the CDN server recovers any lost packets by requesting them from the origin server or from another CDN server (which may have been luckier and received the packet); so by the time the transmission of the new segment begins, the CDN server has received or recovered nearly all packets.

In this approach, the content provider (the Webcaster) can specify if a slight delay can be tolerated when provisioning the live video event. When a CDN server receives the first request for the stream, as part of the transmission setup between the origin server and the CDN server, the origin server informs the CDN server of a stream delay. The CDN server then either uses the packet recovery mechanism (if a stream delay is specified) or transmits immediately.

Finally, the usage of multicast in this case is contained entirely within the ISP owning the network. Thus it is not predicated on the adoption of multicast by other networks.

15.8.2 Using Application-Level Multicast for Streaming Content Delivery

A multi-ISP CDN, or a single-ISP CDN that is not willing to use IP multicast, must find other means for scalable Webcasting. One possibility is to use satellite broadcasts, similar to the forward proxy approach described in Section 9.5.3. Other approaches revolve around the idea of *application-level multicast*. Application-level multicast relies on a distribution tree of relay servers that use IP unicast to forward content from the root toward the leaves of the tree. In other words, the distribution tree is *overlaid* on the IP network, which itself remains purely point-to-point and does not use multicast. Consider Figure 15.9. With a hierarchy of relay servers, each relay server concentrates all streams of its descendants into a single stream in the next level up the tree. The traffic flow from the origin server to CDN servers via relay servers resembles multicast packet delivery (see Section 2.4), with the difference that it is implemented by application-level relay servers rather than routers.

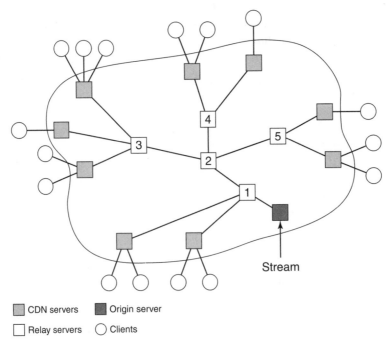

Figure 15.9 An overlay distribution tree for streaming data delivery

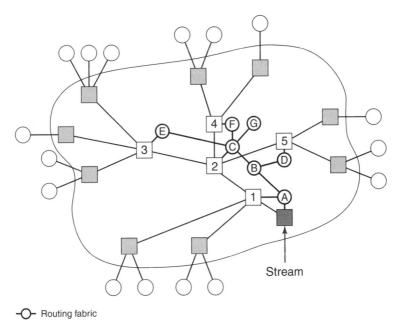

-O- Routing fabric

Figure 15.10 Suboptimal overlaying of a distribution tree

To maximize bandwidth savings and balance traffic in the network, the overlay tree must follow physical network topology. An example of suboptimal overlaying is shown in Figure 15.10, which depicts the overlay tree of Figure 15.9 along with the underlying physical topology. In this figure, relay server 5 obtains the stream from relay server 2 via routers C, B, and D. At the same time, relay server 2 obtains its stream from relay server 1 via routers A, B, and C. The result is that the physical link between routers B and C carries the stream twice, once from relay server 1 to relay server 2 and the second time from relay server 2 to relay server 5. The same overlay topology could be implemented more efficiently if relay server 5 were located at router G instead. Then the physical network would carry no duplicates.

The simplest overlay approach assumes a manual configuration of the overlay distribution tree. In this approach, called *splitter networks* by RealNetworks, configuring the distribution tree becomes part of the provisioning of the Webcasting event.

A more automated approach is offered by FastForward Networks, now part of Inktomi. In this approach, relay servers (which FastForward calls *media bridges*) are statically configured to form an overlay mesh network. The mesh is defined by configuring each media bridge to communicate with some other media bridges as neighbors in the mesh. All Webcast events use this common mesh, from which each event dynamically carves out its own distribution tree. As an example, Figure 15.11 shows a mesh that carries two Webcasts, streams 1 and 2, each using its own distribution tree.

15.8.3 Constructing a Distribution Tree

How does a Webcast construct its distribution tree? FastForward's approach is essentially as follows. Media bridges build routing paths to all potential Webcast origin servers in the overlay mesh, just as routers do in the physical network. The first client to join the Webcast sends its request to its CDN server, which forwards the request to the Webcast origin server along a media bridge path. This path becomes the initial branchless tree. In the example of Figure 15.11, if a client using CDN server E1 is the first to request stream 1, then the initial tree will consist of the path comprising the origin server of stream 1, media bridges B2 and B1, and CDN server E1.

Subsequent client requests also travel along paths toward the origin server. However, these paths terminate at the first media bridge that is already part of the distribution tree of the stream and become new branches of the tree. For instance, when a client using CDN server E2 in Figure 15.11 requests stream 1, its request terminates at media bridge B2, and the new branch comprising media bridges B2 and B6 and CDN server E2 is attached to the tree, resulting in the final tree shown in bold dashed lines in Figure 15.11.

A disadvantage of this tree construction method is that it tends to create rather skinny trees with long parallel paths and few branches. For example, the tree of stream 2 in Figure 15.11 consists of two long branches with no common edges. A path from E3 to the origin server of stream 2 via media bridges B2, B6, and B7 would have terminated at media bridge B6 and resulted in fewer media bridges and edges in the distribution tree and hence lower load on the infrastructure. However, assuming that

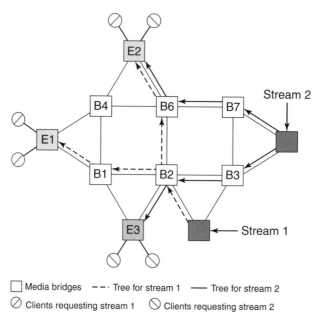

Figure 15.11 Multiple distribution trees on top of a common overlay mesh

all edges in the mesh are assigned equal cost, the system will not consider this path because it is longer than the path via B2 and B3.

Automatic configuration of distribution trees means less work to provision a Webcast: once the mesh is configured, new Webcasts require no topology configuration. Another advantage is that, when a media bridge fails, the distribution tree can quickly rebuild itself to bypass the failed node, assuming the mesh has redundant paths that allow that rebuilding. To enable this feature, each neighbor pair monitors the health and cost (such as message delay and drop rate) of its connection; a surviving neighbor of a failed media bridge will trigger tree reconfiguration.

Neither of the above approaches excludes using IP multicast in the portions of the network where it is available. The inclusion of multicast into streaming content delivery is most explicitly articulated by Chawathe et al. [2000], although in a somewhat different context. FastForward Networks also has announced support for multicast and satellite clouds.

Consider a multi-ISP CDN where multicast is available within individual ISPs but not globally. We can view such an environment as a collection of IP multicast clouds stitched together by unicast links between gateway nodes (see Figure 15.12). This environment is equivalent to the overlay mesh where nodes correspond to the multicast clouds and neighbor links to the intergateway connections. Gateway nodes are a special kind of relay servers. At the entrance of a stream to a cloud, the ingress gateway receives a unicast stream and forwards it to the stream's multicast address within the cloud. As the stream leaves the cloud, the egress gateway forwards the stream to the peer gateway using the peer's unicast IP address.

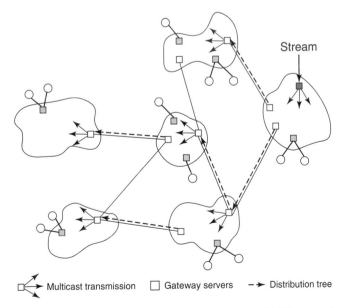

Figure 15.12 An overlay distribution tree in a multi-ISP streaming
CDN with multicast clouds

Of interest is the question of allocating multicast addresses to a Webcast, since each cloud has to assign its own local multicast address to the Webcast and make this address known to all CDN and relay servers in the cloud who might be interested in receiving the Webcast. When the overlay distribution tree is configured manually for each Webcast, multicast address assignment can be part of the Webcast provisioning process. In other words, for each cloud that the administrator includes in the distribution tree, he or she also assigns a multicast IP address that the Webcast will use within that cloud.

For automatic configuration of the distribution tree, FastForward uses the following trick. Within each multicast cloud, all CDN and relay servers as well as gateways use the same hash function to map an arbitrary stream name to a multicast address within a block of addresses assigned by an administrator. As a client request travels toward the Webcast origin server, each relay and gateway path on the path joins the multicast group with the address to which the requested stream maps. Since they all use the same hash function, they all join the same address. The last gateway in the cloud takes on the responsibility of sending the stream packets to this multicast address when the packets start arriving.

There are numerous other problems related to streaming content distribution besides delivering content from the origin server to CDN servers. These problems include protocol design (which is far from being standardized, with at least three competing protocols—Apple QuickTime, RealVideo, and Windows Media—in existence), the architecture of a streaming and relaying server, efficient support of VCR-like functions (for example, stop, resume, rewind) which can be implemented to some extent even for a live Webcast, and so on. Streaming content constitutes a field in itself, and in this book we are unable to cover it in detail.

15.9 Supporting Secure Content Access

The Secure Socket Layer (SSL) protocol [Freier et al. 1996] has become the standard for authenticating Web servers and protecting the privacy of information transmitted over the Internet. It is therefore important that CDNs be capable of supporting SSL-protected traffic. This section highlights the most important issues SSL-protected traffic faces in a CDN environment. A content distribution network using other secure protocols, such as IP Security Protocol (IPSec), would face many of the same problems.

15.9.1 SSL Overview

On a very high level the properties of the SSL protocol can be summarized as follows.

- The server is authenticated so that a client can be sure that data comes from the site to which the client intended to connect.

- Traffic is encrypted to prevent an attacker from reading any data in transit between the client and the server.

- Integrity checks are performed on the data to ensure that the data was not modified while in transit.

- Optionally, the client can also be authenticated. This allows the server to ensure that it is communicating with a particular client. In most cases this option is not used and clients are authenticated using other means like cookies or user IDs and passwords.

These high-level properties are achieved by establishing a *secure session* between the client and server. Each session has a session state associated with it which contains the identities of the server and, if available, the client; the cryptographic algorithms used; and a shared secret key which is used to encrypt and authenticate the data exchanged between the client and the server. The shared secret key is generated during session establishment and at a minimum the server is authenticated during this phase. A so-called public key cryptographic algorithm is used to establish the session.

This algorithm requires, at a minimum, performance of two computationally expensive operations, also known as public key operations, one operation on the client and one on the server. To amortize the overhead of session establishment over longer periods, SSL allows a session to persist across multiple TCP connections.[3] Each session is identified by a session ID which is passed by the client in the clear (that is, without encryption) at the beginning of every TCP connection, allowing the server to decide if an already existing SSL session should be reused or if a new session should be established.

To authenticate itself, each SSL-protected server uses two keys. One of the keys is publicly available (the *public key*) and the other is private to the server (the *private key*). The authentication algorithm allows everybody who has access to the public key to verify whether or not someone else has the private key. This property of the algorithm is used to authenticate a server by verifying that the server has possession of the private key. The private key is therefore extremely sensitive information. If it is revealed, the site can be impersonated by other sites, and subsequently all security properties of the SSL-protected traffic would be lost. On the other hand, the public key has to be certified by a trusted certification authority such as VeriSign to ensure that the key is the correct public key that should be used to authenticate a site. Otherwise, an imposter could pass a phony public key that would match the imposter's private key and claim that this public key belongs to another site. The imposter would then be able to pose as this other site without stealing the site's private key. To protect against this possibility, a legitimate site obtains a *certificate* from a certification authority that binds the DNS name of the site to its public key.

---

[3] In theory there might also be multiple SSL sessions within a single TCP connection. However, we believe that this functionality is rarely used in today's Internet.

SSL inherently impacts the performance of an origin or CDN server in two ways: first, all data has to be encrypted; second, a secure session has to be established for each client. To quantify this impact, consider that one typical public key operation takes on the order of 10ms on a dedicated 600MHz Pentium. The same hardware can encrypt data with a rate of 38Mbps after the shared secret has been established using IDEA, a common encryption algorithm [Lia and Massey 1991]. The combination of both impacts requires the deployment of substantially more hardware to support the same amount of Web traffic.

15.9.2 Performance Impact of Supporting SSL in a CDN

In the CDN environment, SSL poses additional performance challenges beyond the already high overhead required to establish and maintain an SSL session between a client and an SSL-protected server. The additional performance requirements stem from the fact that in a CDN a client might be redirected to multiple CDN servers. Each of these servers requires a new SSL session establishment, since the CDN servers will not have valid SSL session states for a particular client. For example, if the client is redirected to 10 different CDN servers for 10 embedded objects, the client would have to establish a total of 10 SSL sessions. Especially on slow clients, this would lead to unacceptable performance. It would also require that the aggregate performance of the CDN servers serving the content would have to be 10 times higher compared to the case in which only one session is established.

This impact depends on whether the CDN is of CDN-first type or origin-first type.

CDN-first: In a CDN-first CDN, the client goes to a CDN server first. Then, to eliminate multiple SSL session establishments, the CDN must redirect the same client to the same CDN server farm and to the same CDN server within that farm. These two problems must be addressed differently, because different mechanisms redirect the client to a server farm and to an individual server within the farm. Request distribution between farms is usually performed by the CDN's DNS. Thus, to address the first problem, the CDN's DNS must remember how it responded to past DNS queries and attempt to resolve future queries from the same client DNS servers to the same CDN server farms.

Request distribution within a CDN server farm is commonly performed by a balancing switch such as an L7 switch. L7 switches can keep track of SSL sessions and which CDN server in the farm established which session. Using this information, the L7 switch can redirect a new TCP connection that uses a previously known SSL session to the CDN server which established this session. L4 switches can also address this problem, by considering client IP addresses in arriving packets and redirecting packets with the same client IP address to the same CDN server. However, the L4 solution limits the fliexibility of load-balancing in the CDN server farm, since all traffic from a particular client is always redirected to the same CDN server even if this traffic does not belong to the same SSL session.

Origin-first: In an origin-first CDN, it is unavoidable to perform at least two SSL session establishments: one with the origin server and one with a CDN server. Once both SSL sessions are established, the CDN faces the same issues as a CDN-first CDN, to ensure that future requests from this client do not cause even more SSL connection establishments.

15.9.3 Key Management

To distribute the content of a Web site, the CDN has to possess a private/public key pair and a certificate that binds the public key to the DNS name used to retrieve the document from the CDN. For example, if a CDN were to distribute objects with images.cnn.com as host name in their URLs, the CDN would need a private/public key pair for images.cnn.com and a certificate issued by CNN or by a certification authority like VeriSign binding the public key to images.cnn.com.

If this private key is stolen by an attacker, the attacker might intercept traffic to the CDN. The attacker could then pose as the Web server for images.cnn.com. In this scenario, the client is under the impression that the server is authenticated and, therefore, might provide the attacker with sensitive information like passwords, credit card numbers, or other personal data. The security of the site images.cnn.com can only be reestablished if the certificate *expires:* clients then stop using the old public key, and the CDN obtains a new private/public key pair and a new certificate. The attacker would need to steal the new private key to continue its attack. Therefore, it is advisable to give the certificates stored on CDN servers a short expiration time to minimize the impact of such an attack.

On the other hand, short expiration times raise the problem that whenever a certificate expires, the CDN must obtain a new private/public key pair and the certificate from the customer.[4] In addition, the CDN must distribute this information to all CDN servers serving the secure content.

An alternative approach is to serve secure content from the CDN's own domain, for example, images.cnn.cdn-foo.com. Then the CDN needs no separate private key for CNN's content since the private key for cdn-foo.com can be used. The advantage of this approach is that fewer keys have to be managed and that the keys are managed solely within cdn-foo.com's administrative control. In particular, keys do not have to be passed between the CDN and its customers. The drawback of this approach is that it is limited to embedded objects. If the container HTML page is served using this approach, the URL shown in the Web browser would contain cdn-foo.com and, therefore, the user would recognize that the document was not provided by CNN. This is usually not the intent of the content provider.

---

[4] The CDN cannot generate this information itself since the certification authority would issue the certificate only if the request comes directly from the customer.

15.9.4 Content Retrieval from the Origin Server

To protect secured content, CDN servers obviously must use secure connections to communicate with clients. Perhaps less obvious but also essential is that CDN servers must use a protected and authenticated channel to retrieve content from the origin server. This is because security is only as strong as the weakest link in the information path. If content is substituted by an imposter on the path from the origin server to a CDN server, sending this fake content to clients in the most secured way is not going to provide any protection.

For example, assume that DNS outsourcing is used to deliver client requests to the CDN, and that the CDN is responsible for the images.cnn.com domain in URLs, while the DNS name of the origin server for these images is original.cnn.com. The CDN must then ensure that CDN servers use SSL to connect to original.cnn.com and that original.cnn.com provides a valid certificate to prove to the CDN servers that it is indeed original.cnn.com.

It is also important, for the same reason, that traffic within the CDN and between the CDN servers and the origin server uses the same level of protection as traffic between the CDN servers and clients. Different types of keys provide different levels of protection: larger keys are harder to guess and thus provide better protection. On the other hand, larger keys involve higher computational overhead for SSL session establishment and content encryption. Using different key lengths to communicate between CDN servers and the origin server and between CDN servers and clients means, therefore, either that content does not receive the intended level of protection or that some communication incurs unnecessary overhead.

For example, if objects from images.cnn.com require a 128-bit key, the CDN must ensure that CDN servers do not retrieve these objects from original.cnn.com using a much weaker 40-bit key. On the other hand, if the origin server does use 40-bit keys, the CDN can safely reduce its overhead by using 40-bit keys for images.cnn.com as well.

15.10 Summary

Potential benefits that a CDN offers to content providers include improved performance of their Web sites and protection from sudden demand surges called flash events. CDNs can be stand-alone companies that seek presence in networks of multiple ISPs (multi-ISP or colocation CDNs) or they can be services provided by a large ISP itself (single-ISP CDNs). CDNs can also be broadly classified into hosting CDNs, which maintain both surrogates (called CDN servers in the context of CDNs) and origin servers, and relaying CDNs that have only surrogates. Among relaying CDNs, one can distinguish between origin-first and CDN-first types of CDNs, depending on whether container HTML pages are served by the origin or CDN server.

Compared to CDN-first, the origin-first CDN involves an extra TCP connection and DNS query for a document download, except when the container page is already cached by the client. In addition, container pages in an origin-first CDN are excluded from CDN delivery. Secure content delivery incurs further performance costs in an origin-first CDN because of the need to establish an extra SSL session. An advantage often cited by origin-first CDNs is that their customers see every request to their sites; however, this argument is not well grounded, because a CDN-first CDN can always provide usage statistics to its customers in a pre-agreed format. In fact, a CDN has to provide similar information to its customers already as part of billing, since billing is based on usage. Finally, a CDN customer can always track the usage of container pages by a number of methods described in Chapter 13. While origin-first CDNs have been historically the first CDN types on the market, CDNs are increasingly switching to the CDN-first approach.

The core components of a relaying CDN include mechanisms to deliver client requests to the CDN network instead of the customer's origin server and to distribute these requests among CDN servers. (Hosting CDNs do not face the first problem since they already include origin servers.) CDN-first CDNs use DNS outsourcing for request delivery, while origin-first CDNs can use either DNS outsourcing or URL rewriting for this purpose. Most CDNs use DNS redirection to distribute requests among CDN servers, but they rarely use it in the basic way described in Chapter 14. Instead, they combine it with other mechanisms, such as IP redirection, fine-grained domain names, two-level DNS redirection, and anycast.

Still, DNS-based request distribution has inherent limitations, including the originator problem and hidden HTTP loads. A CDN has a number of mechanisms at its disposal to correct DNS-based request distribution at a post-DNS stage of request processing. These mechanisms include triangular communication, HTTP redirection, and URL rewriting.

CDNs compete with forward proxies as an overall approach to scalable content delivery. This makes it especially important for CDNs to distribute a variety of content types. We have considered some issues that CDNs face in delivering streaming data and SSL-secured content in this chapter. Part IV includes a discussion on providing scalable access to applications, which is deferred because it is a less mature direction at the time of writing.

Chapter 16

Server Selection

We considered an architectural aspect of request distribution in Chapters 14 and 15 and identified various components on the request processing path that can perform request distribution. This chapter examines an algorithmic aspect of request distribution, which addresses the issue of how these components actually select from among multiple servers that can process the request. The discussion in this chapter applies to server selection among CDN servers, surrogates in general, and replicated origin servers. Thus we use the generic term *server* to refer to all these kinds of servers.

The problem of server selection is similar to the problem of load-balancing in distributed systems that has been extensively studied over the past twenty years.[1] However, the latter concentrates on load distribution over a local area network. Including wide area networks brings a significant new aspect to Web server selection. Also, the Web presents a very different workload from that used in traditional load-balancing studies. Among the differences are heavy demand on the server communication system (giving rise to new load metrics such as the number of open TCP connections at a server) and practically unbounded potential load from Web users (bringing into doubt results obtained under the assumptions that all users are known). Still, many ideas in traditional load-balancing are relevant for Web server selection, especially as discussed in Section 16.2.2.

16.1 Metrics

Our first concern is performance metrics that drive server selection algorithms.[2] Three main groups of metrics are used: the *proximity metrics* that measure proximity of servers to a client, the *server load metrics* that measure the load of servers or network

---

[1] We refer an interested reader to Shirazi et al. [1995] for a good introduction to the load-balancing area.
[2] Following a general practice in experimental computer science, we use the term *metric* to mean a measure of performance. This usage is different from mathematics, where metrics are assumed to satisfy specific mathematical properties.

paths to the servers, and the *aggregate metrics* that implicitly measure the effects of both load and proximity.

Metrics are also distinguished based on the measurement method. *Passive measurements* obtain metrics by simply observing the normal operation of the system. For example, a Web client takes passive measurements if it records the time of its Web accesses that would have been performed anyway. In contrast, *active measurements* involve actions that the system performs only for the purpose of obtaining the metric. A typical example is a probe that the client may send to a server to measure its response time. This distinction is rather ambiguous, as even passive measurements involve some action performed just for the sake of the measurement (such as recording the measurement result). In the context of the Web, measurements are sometimes considered passive or active based on whether or not they inject any extra packets into the network. Finally, measurements can be synchronous or asynchronous. *Synchronous measurements* occur at the time of a client request, while the request is waiting (put differently, they occur on the *critical path* of the request). *Asynchronous measurements* do not delay the request. For example, they may occur after processing the request, or on a schedule that is independent of request processing.

No matter how the measurement is performed, the correctness of a particular measurement usually diminishes over time. This is because the characteristics of the Web are highly variable. Accounting for the diminished value of old measurements in a metric is called *aging* the metric.

All things being equal, asynchronous passive measurements are obviously the least intrusive. One must always justify using active and, especially, synchronous measurements by showing that the benefits outweigh the extra overhead caused by the measurements themselves.

16.1.1 Proximity Metrics

A perennial motivation for Web caching and replication is to serve clients from a nearby server. But what is the goal of doing so? Two potential benefits come from the proximity of servers to clients. One is latency. Just the electromagnetic propagation delay places a significant lower bound on latency when clients and servers are far away. For example, a coast-to-coast round-trip in the U.S. will take about 30ms. Globally, the delay can be 100ms or more. In fact, the propagation delay can be much higher than the geographical distance would suggest, since packets do not follow a straight line but rather traverse a series of zigzag network links. The effect of the propagation delay is further magnified by the fact that a single Web interaction often involves a number of consecutive round-trips. For example, to access a Web site requires a round-trip to obtain the DNS resolution of the site's host name, a round-trip for the initial exchange of control messages for the new TCP connection, a round-trip to download the container page, and a round-trip to download images embedded in the container page. The number of round-trips increases even more if the client does not use persistent connections and pipelining. A far-away client may therefore easily experience a half-second delay just because of the speed of light limit.

The other benefit is lower bandwidth consumption. When clients interact with nearby servers, the traffic they generate is localized to small sections of the Internet and does not load the rest of the network. The network as a whole is then capable of carrying more interactions, and overall the experience of users improves.

Three metrics are typically considered to capture the degree of proximity between two hosts: *geographical distance*, the number of network routers between the two as revealed by the `traceroute` utility described in Section 2.2 (otherwise called *network hops*), and the number of autonomous systems traversed by packets on their way from one host to the other (usually referred to as *autonomous system hops* or AS path length).

A crucial issue is how a particular metric correlates with end performance. As is often the case on the global Internet, the difficulty of staging a convincing experiment leads to contradictory observations. Carter and Crovella [1997] found that neither geographical distance nor network hops have any bearing on the file download time from a server. In fact, they found that a random server selection results in better download time than a server selection based on either of these proximity metrics. A possible explanation for this surprising result is an extremely small sample size: only 10 servers were examined. Gwertzman [1995] observed moderate positive correlations between these two proximity metrics and download time. He also found a stronger correlation of download time with network hops than with geographical distance, which would suggest that the former may be a better measure of proximity. McManus considered the AS hops measure [McManus 1999]. By sending ICMP pings [Postel 1981b] to a sample of almost 20,000 servers, he found that the higher the number of AS hops to a server, the higher were its mean ping response latency, the variance of the latency, and the packet loss. This suggests that the number of AS hops is potentially a reasonable proximity measure.

Geographical distance may not be indicative of either the propagation delay or bandwidth consumption, because messages may take drastically different routes from those suggested by the geography. Because different ISPs exchange messages at a relatively small number of exchange points in the network (see Section 2.3), messages between hosts belonging to different ISPs must travel to one of the exchange points, regardless how close they are geographically. Gwertzman gives an example of two hosts in the Boston area that communicate through Washington, D.C. Still, geographical distance is a useful measure of coarse granularity. One expects that communication between two European hosts would be more efficient than between a European and an American host. On the other hand, it would be much riskier to assert that communication between New York and Princeton is more efficient than between New York and Boston, just because Princeton is 40 miles away and Boston is 200.

Network and AS-hops metrics reflect the actual message path between hosts. However, they have their own weaknesses. The network-hops measure equates local area hops, wide area hops, and hops across ISP exchange points. On the other hand, certain exchange points are often the bottlenecks responsible for the most packet loss and queuing delays at routers. As an extreme example, two hosts with one LAN router between are probably incomparably closer to each other than two hosts divided by a congested network access point; however, the network-hop count is the same in both cases. Another disadvantage of the network-hops measure is that obtaining it requires an active measurement using a `traceroute`-like procedure. This is much more intrusive than obtaining geography or AS-hops metrics, which can be done from the data that already exist.[3]

The AS-hops measure counts only autonomous systems, which roughly correspond to ISPs and corporate networks. This measure thus discriminates between servers based on the number of exchange points on the message paths to these servers. And yet the measure does not discriminate between a cross-Atlantic AS hop and a hop connecting two regional ISPs. Furthermore, a large number of host pairs have the same AS-hops count. The AS hops measure therefore fails to discriminate between servers in many cases. For example, McManus found that over 90 percent of all routes announced by the BGP routers in his network had just three distinct AS path lengths.

Overall, finding a good proximity metric remains an open problem. In the absence of a better solution, various combinations of the three proximity metrics are often used as a proximity discriminator. Consider, for example, the following combination. Let us divide the globe into large regions, such as Europe, North America, South America, the Far East, Australia, and so on. We could apply the following rules to compare the proximity of host A to hosts B and C:

1. A is closer to a host in its same region than to a host in a different region (geography measure).

2. If step 1 fails to discriminate between B and C, then A is closer to a host that is fewer AS hops away (AS hops measure).

3. If steps 1 and 2 fail to discriminate and all three hosts belong to the same AS, use network hops (or OSPF path costs, see Section 2.3.1) to discriminate between B and C.

4. In all other cases, declare B and C equidistant.

With all their limitations, a big advantage of proximity metrics is their stability over time. Once collected, the proximity database can be used for a long time without constant updating.

16.1.2 Server Load Metrics

Beside distributing requests to nearby servers, server selection must also spread the load among servers to avoid overloading some servers while others have spare

---

[3] The NetGeo service [NetGeo 2001] maps an IP address to a postal address; AS hops can be obtained from the information maintained by and exchanged among BGP routers.

capacity. A number of load metrics have been proposed. The most popular are the number of connections, number of requests, ready queue length, and response time.

The number of connections measures the number of open TCP connections (see Chapter 3) at the server. The higher the number, the higher the server load. The rationale is that an overloaded server will be slow in fulfilling requests and thus will accumulate a larger number of open TCP connections. Another reason behind this measure is that the number of open connections seems to be a frequent bottleneck at the servers. This measure does not count multiple requests over the same persistent connection.

The number of requests corresponds to the request-arrival or request-fulfillment rate or to the average number of outstanding requests at a server awaiting execution (otherwise known as a request queue length). This measure fails to reflect the fact that different requests may impose drastically different load on the server. The belief behind this measure is that with a large request rate, these differences will average out and the number of requests will still provide a reasonable yardstick to compare server loads.

The ready queue length is basically the output of UNIX's `uptime` command, which gives the number of tasks at the server that are ready to run, averaged over some period of time. It is often used as a measure of server utilization.

Finally, the response time measures the time it takes a server to execute a request. The response time may be drastically skewed by different service demands of different requests: a request for a small icon image may take much less time to execute than a request for a computationally intensive dynamically generated object, regardless of server load. Therefore, discriminating among server loads based on response time may be deceptive, just as with the number of requests measure.

16.1.3 Aggregate Metrics

Important factors affecting perceived performance are bandwidth and load on network paths to a given server. A lightly loaded nearby server may produce worse download time than a distant, more heavily loaded server if the network path from the client to the former has lower bandwidth or is more congested. Thus when discriminating among servers on a WAN, it is desirable to account for not only server load, but also network load and capacity of the communication paths to the servers. We call metrics that reflect both these components *aggregate metrics*. These metrics include ICMP ping latency, TCP ping latency, TCP request latency, HTTP request latency, download time, datagram round-trip time, download latency, effective transfer bandwidth, and packet loss rate.

ICMP ping latency [Chankhunthod et al. 1996; Carter and Crovella 1997] measures the delay between sending an ICMP echo message to a host and receiving the response. This metric reflects propagation delay and router queuing delay, and also, indirectly, server load, because a very busy server will presumably take longer to process the ping. A limitation of this metric is that it measures the delay of an ICMP packet, which may be treated differently than TCP packets by the routers and especially the

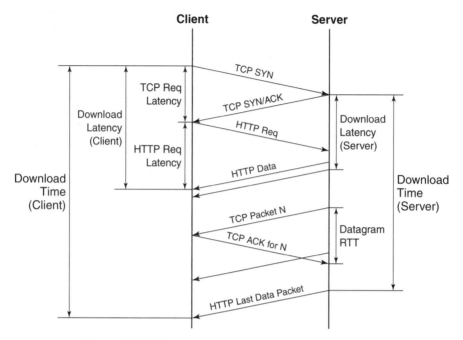

Figure 16.1   Some aggregate metrics for server selection

end host. Thus its delay may not accurately predict the delay of TCP packets. Another downside is that it involves an active measurement.

TCP ping latency [Dykes et al. 2000] measures the time between sending a TCP SYN request to a nonexistent port and receiving an error response (TCP RST message) back. Unlike ICMP pings, TCP ping packets are treated as normal data packets by routers and end hosts.

The remaining metrics can be obtained either passively, assuming there is frequent communication between the client and the server involved, or actively. These metrics are illustrated in Figure 16.1. TCP request latency is the delay between the time the client requesting an object sends a TCP SYN packet to the server and the time it receives the TCP SYN/ACK back; this measure reflects the network delays as well as the time the server takes to initialize the TCP connection. HTTP request latency is the delay between the time the client sends out an HTTP request packet and the time it receives the first response packet. These metrics can only be obtained at or near a client. In contrast, the datagram round-trip time can be obtained at the server, by measuring the delay between sending the TCP SYN/ACK packet and receiving the HTTP request packet, or the delay between sending a portion of the response and receiving the TCP ACK for this portion. The datagram round-trip reflects only the network condition and not the server load.

Download latency [Vingralek et al. 1999] and download time [Karaul et al. 1998] are higher-level metrics. They reflect the time between the start of a client request and either the start or finish, respectively, of receiving the response, including opening the TCP connection if necessary. While most naturally measured at the client, these metrics can also be estimated at the server. As Figure 16.1 shows, the server side always underestimates these metrics since it does not account for the network delay of the initial packet from the client to the server, as well for the final response packet from the server to the client.

The effective transfer bandwidth [Dykes et al. 2000] is the document size divided by the download time and can be measured by both the client and server (the latter will overestimate the effective bandwidth since it underestimates the download time). Finally, both the client and the server can also measure the packet loss rate by analyzing the stream of TCP packets. Packet loss may occur in the congested network as well as at a busy server and so can be considered an aggregate measure. A path with a high loss rate indicates a suboptimal server.

We are not aware of a comprehensive study that compares all these metrics. Dykes et al. [2000] compared client-side server selection using download latency, effective bandwidth, and TCP pings, and found that TCP pings provided the best overall response time. However, this study used latency and bandwidth measurements from a four-month calibration period and did not refresh their values during the experiment itself, which ran for the subsequent three months. The experiment therefore used bandwidth and latency measurements that were between three and seven months old, which may have influenced the conclusions. Sayal et al. [1998] compared download latency with ICMP pings and also with network hops, a proximity metric. This study found that download latency is superior to ICMP pings and to network hops, while the comparison of ICMP pings with network hops was inconclusive. Carter and Crovella [1997] observed ICMP pings (and especially a series of pings) to be superior to the proximity metrics of network hops and geographical distance, both of which performed even worse than random server selection. As we have already mentioned, the last conclusion contradicts several other studies [Gwertzman 1995; Sayal et al. 1998; McManus 1999] and may be an aberration caused by a small sample size.

Many metrics discussed in this section require that a host record the time when certain packets are sent or received. To enable such packet-level measurements, one may modify the host where the measurement occurs: the clients, the servers, or the load-balancing element that front-ends the servers. An alternative is to install a facility that logs all packets the host sends and receives, including their time stamps.[4] A log analyzer then obtains various metrics by examining the log. A challenge is to make this packet logger and analyzer fast enough to keep up with the packet rates. With modern Web servers and proxies capable of delivering hundreds of megabits of content per second, this is not an easy task. Feldmann [2000] describes an approach for architecting such a facility.

---

[4] A UNIX utility, `tcpdump`, provides this functionality.

16.1.4 Internet Mapping Services

Obtaining metrics can be intrusive (when it involves active measurements such as `traceroute` or probe packets) or require infrastructure that a host may lack (such as a packet logger and analyzer). In addition, it may also rely on cooperation from the ISPs providing the connectivity to the measuring host (such as supplying the routing data to compile the AS hops metric), which usually is hard to obtain. In all these cases, a possible solution is to have a special service on the Internet that can provide some metrics of path quality between any two hosts on the Internet. Anyone could then simply use such a service for server selection instead of performing measurement independently.

The NetGeo system [NetGeo 2001] provides such a service for the geographical distance metric. It maps an arbitrary IP address to a postal address as well as to the longitude and latitude that correspond to the network administrator location for the subnet to which the IP address belongs. The geographical coordinates of a pair of hosts can be easily translated into the geographical distance. NetGeo does not have entries for all Internet destinations, and the geographical mapping can be imprecise because of the coarse granularity of the mapping, since an entire network may map to a single geographical point regardless of how large an area the network spans. Still, it can be used successfully to identify large distances between hosts, for example, those on different continents.

The IDMaps system [Francis et al. 1999] has a more ambitious goal of providing latency and bandwidth estimates for paths between any pair of hosts. Although it performs active measurements to obtain these metrics, the results of these measurements are intended to be reused by a large number of Web sites and clients, which would justify the extra load these measurements impose on the Internet.

However, a mapping service like IDMaps faces scalability challenges of its own. When an individual host (a Web client or a server) estimates path metrics to other destinations, it faces a task of linear complexity: the amount of work is proportional to the number of destinations being measured. In contrast, an Internet mapping service has a task of quadratic complexity, since it must measure paths between every pair of destinations.

The IDMaps project proposed several ways to reduce the scale of the problem [Francis et al. 1999]. Still, mapping the entire Internet will always be more difficult and less accurate than doing so from the perspective of a single host. The stated goal of IDMaps service is to provide metric estimates within a factor of two of a true value. However, Internet maps provide a very useful service in cases where a host lacks infrastructure to obtain measurements itself, has an occasional need for a metric estimate that would not justify measurement implementation, or needs a metric estimate between two third-party hosts rather than between itself and another host.

16.1.5 Aging of Metrics

Consider a proxy server that uses passive measurements of download latency from replicated servers in its server selection. Should the proxy use the latest measurement for every server? Clearly, the volatility of server and network conditions can make a single measurement a very unreliable metric of expected performance. Another option is to average several past measurement results. For example, a proxy can use the average of the last five download latencies from a given server, or average download latencies over the last five minutes in its server selection. But this represents another extreme, where all these measurement results are given the same weight even though the more recent ones may better reflect current conditions.

The middle ground is provided by schemes that take past measurement results into account but *age* them by assigning them lower weight. One such scheme, called *exponential aging* and well known from its use in TCP implementations, has also been proposed for use in the Web context [Vingralek et al. 1999]. This scheme computes the metric value recursively as follows. Let ave_{cur} be the current value of the metric. After the first measurement, ave_{cur} is set to the obtained measurement result. After a subsequent measurement result *sample* is obtained, the new value ave_{new} of the metric is calculated as

$$ave_{new} = (1 - r) \times ave_{cur} + r \times sample$$

where r is an aging factor between 0 and 1 that reflects the speed of aging. The closer r is to 1, the faster the influence of old measurements diminishes. If $r = 1$ then only the last measurement is taken into account. If r is set dynamically to equal $1/k$ where k is the number of the current measurement, then ave_{cur} represents the mean value of the k measurement results, each with equal weight.

A crucial issue in deciding how quickly to age a metric is understanding how quickly the measured condition on the Web changes and, therefore, how fast individual measurments become obsolete in practice.

Two independent studies considered this issue for download latency and download time and provided an indication that these metrics are relatively stable server differentiators. Vingralek et al. [1999] measured download latency from 50 of the most popular servers in their trace. They performed these measurements for each server every minute for three days. They then considered the difference between a given sample and subsequent samples for an individual server. They found that 90 percent of subsequent samples were within 10 percent of the value of the base sample for an average of 41 minutes after the time of the base sample. If one allowed 30 percent deviation, then 90 percent of subsequent samples stayed within the allowed deviation for eight hours after the base sample. Unfortunately, this study does not report the variance of the value of this time interval, which limits the usefulness of this result.

Myers et al. [1999] considered download times from three popular Web sites each having between 11 and 20 mirrors. Rather than focusing on changes in absolute metric values, this study concentrated on how server ranking would change under newer or older metric values. A server rank is its position in the sequence of servers ordered according to the metric, in this case download time; it is ranking that ultimately counts in server selection. One experiment measured the probability that the rank change of a server during a given time interval will not exceed a given limit. This experiment produced inconclusive results. Two of the sites showed rather stable ranking: for instance, on the site with 20 mirrors, in 85 percent of the cases server rank changed by at most four positions in up to two hours. However, the third site showed much greater variability, with rank changes similar to random permutations for all time scales considered (one hour and above).

In another experiment, Myers et al. [1999] studied whether a change in download time from a server indicates a change in its ranking. They found that, while a larger change in the metric value does increase the likelihood of a significant change in ranking, the dependency is not very strong. Considering a site with 11 mirrors, a 1-second change in download time led to a rank change of at most three positions in 90 percent of cases, while a 128-second change in download time reduced this probability only to 80 percent. Thus small changes in download time do not indicate a need to take new measurements from all servers and reassess server selection, especially because the goal of server selection in practice is to avoid poor servers rather than find the optimal one [Johnson et al. 2001].

While more research is clearly needed, these studies provide an indication that prior download time probably remains useful for a period of tens of minutes, and that small metric changes observed on high-ranking servers need not trigger active measurements of the rest of the servers.

16.2 Algorithms

In Chapter 14 we considered a variety of points in the network where a request may be diverted to one of several server replicas. Any of these points has an opportunity to select the most appropriate server for the request. However, different metrics would be most appropriate or even obtainable at different points.

DNS-based request distribution (see Section 14.1.3) often uses a proximity metric as the primary server selection criterion. Using load metrics for fine-grained server selection is difficult at the DNS level because of the hidden load problem (see Section 15.5). Section 16.4 discusses DNS server selection in more detail.

On the other hand, server-load metrics are the primary metrics used by a load-balancing switch that distributes requests among a server farm on a single LAN (Section 14.1.2). This is because all servers on the same LAN are so close to each other that there is no benefit to considering proximity. At the same time, it is easy for the switch to obtain fine-grained server-load measurements. The switch sees every request going to any of the servers in the farm and thus can perform very fine-grained load-balancing. Some metrics even require no feedback from the servers. For example, the switch itself can keep track of the number of requests in progress, the number of active connections, and server response time. In principle the switch can estimate the last metric even if responses from the servers bypass the switch (as in Figure 14.3), by measuring the spacing in time of TCP acknowledgments from the clients. Generally, the larger the spacing, the higher the response time, although in this case the metric values can be skewed by Internet delays. It is server selection by a balancing switch that is most closely related to traditional load-balancing work [Shirazi 1995].

Clients often drive their selection by aggregate metrics such as download time, because many of these metrics are readily available for clients and seem to be the best predictors of access performance. High-volume clients such as Web proxies are in an especially good position to use these metrics, since these clients are more likely to perform downloads frequently enough to obtain the metrics by passive measurements.

Given a metric, the simplest server selection algorithm is to always choose the best server for the current request according to the current metric values. In fact, this simple algorithm is often used. Examples of this class of algorithms include choosing a server that has the fewest active connections, the one with the fewest outstanding requests, the one that has been selected least often so far (this is also known as a *round-robin* approach, implemented by simple rotation among servers), or the one with the shortest ready queue length or the shortest response time. However, selection algorithms often deliberately choose a suboptimal server. Why would one ever want to select a suboptimal server? There are four main reasons: to obtain passive measurements from suboptimal servers; to avoid oscillations in request distribution; to send requests from the same client to the same server, often referred to as *client stickiness;* and to respect the *affinity* of requests to server caches. The following sections describe these reasons.

16.2.1 Obtaining Passive Measurements

Consider a Web proxy that selects servers based on previously observed download latency. Assume that a site is replicated on two servers. At some point let server A have a temporary slowdown so the metric favors server B. If the proxy always chooses the optimal server, it will choose server B. Then the proxy will keep obtaining fresh values of server B's metric while having an increasingly obsolete value of server A's metric. So even after A recovers from its slowdown, the proxy may not ever select it again.

A *randomization* approach addresses this problem. With randomization, the server selection algorithm *favors* the best server but can with some probability still select suboptimal ones. Consider, for example, a proxy server that uses download latency for server selection. The best server would be the one with the lowest latency, but a randomized algorithm may select servers with probability inversely proportional to their latency [Sayal et al. 1998]:

$$P_i = \frac{1/L_i}{\sum_{j=1}^{n}(1/L_j)}$$

where L_i is the latency of a download from server i, n is the number of replicated servers and P_i is the probability of choosing server i. A similar method using total download time as a metric was proposed by Karaul et al. [1998].

If some servers are still not accessed frequently enough to accumulate enough passive measurements, the proxy may supplement this strategy with some active measurements by issuing HEAD requests to these servers.

16.2.2 Avoiding Oscillations

When server selection is based on the load metric, the freshness of metric values becomes important. If the balancing element always has instantaneous server-load information, selecting the best server is often the best strategy. It has been shown, for example, that if each server processes requests sequentially in first-come-first-served order and if request service demands do not differ drastically, then always selecting a server with the shortest request queue is optimal in terms of the average response time [Winston 1977; Weber 1978].[5] A Web site implemented as a server farm with a balancing switch in front fits into this model. The switch can keep track of the current values of most load metrics directly because it sees every request. It can therefore maintain accurate values of such metrics as the number of open connections, the number of outstanding requests, and the response time.

However, in many situations a balancing element must rely on periodic load reports from the servers. One example is request distribution by Web site's DNS based on load. The balancing element (the DNS server in this case) cannot accurately track instantaneous load on the servers. Instead, it relies on load reports from the servers and therefore its load information becomes stale between the reports.

Another example is a CDN with a number of server farms, each with its own balancing switch (see Figure 15.5), where switches can forward requests to each other to fine-tune DNS server selection (see Section 15.6). Assume that a switch selects remote switches for request forwarding depending on the load of the server farms these switches are directly connected to. This requires all switches to exchange periodic reports about the load of their server farms. As a result, switches may have stale load information.

The best server according to stale information may no longer be the best at the time it is selected. In particular, using stale information may lead to load oscillations, or as Dahlin [2000] calls it, the *herd effect*. This effect occurs when the best server according to a stale metric is selected for all future requests and quickly stops being the best while other servers become idle. After the next round of load measurements, the situation reverses.

Consider a system where a balancing element distributes load among four servers based on periodic load reports, for example, the average server utilization in the prior period. Assume that the balancing element always selects the best server according to this metric. The scenario is illustrated on Figure 16.2a. At time t1, server 1

---

[5] For requests with highly variable service demands this policy has been shown not to be optimal [Whitt 1986; Harchol-Balter 1999].

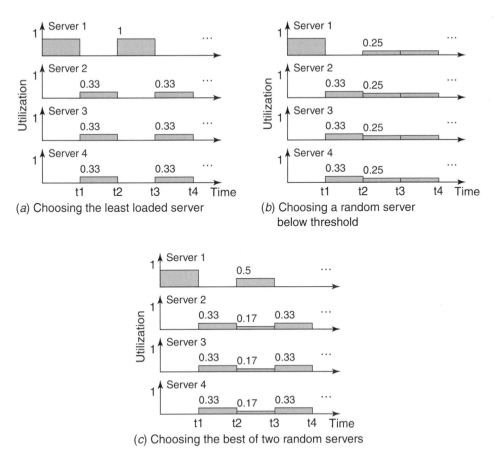

(a) Choosing the least loaded server

(b) Choosing a random server below threshold

(c) Choosing the best of two random servers

Figure 16.2 Oscillations in load balancing

reported 100 percent utilization while other servers were idle. The algorithm that always chooses the best server will then use servers 2, 3, and 4 for requests in the next time interval. Assuming server 1 has no backlog of requests, this request distribution leads to role reversal at time t2, when server 1 reports being idle and the rest of the servers are sharing the load. The algorithm will now select server 1, and so on, resulting in load oscillations. Although this example is intentionally exaggerated, oscillations may occur in many situations where an optimal server is always selected based on possibly stale information.

Similar to passive measurements, randomized server selection can be used to avoid oscillations. One such technique, exemplified by the algorithm proposed by Mirchandaney et al. [1989], uses load thresholds and randomly distributes requests evenly among all servers whose load (according to stale load information available to the balancing element) is below the threshold. In the example from the previous paragraph, assume that the threshold is 80 percent utilization. Figure 16.2b gives the time diagram for this algorithm. At time t1, server 1 reports a load above the threshold and thus is excluded from any requests. From time t3 on, all servers are below the threshold and share the load evenly without oscillations.

Another technique randomly chooses k servers among the total servers available and then selects the best server among them [Mitzenmacher 1997]. By analyzing a queuing model of replicated servers, Mitzenmacher found that selecting the best among just two randomly chosen servers seems to be a good strategy in most situations, especially if the number of servers is large. This algorithm guarantees that the worst $k-1$ servers according to the most recent metric measurements will receive no requests until the next round of measurements. This is because any subset of k servers will have another server with a better metric value, which will be chosen. If the number of servers is small, a complete exclusion of these servers can negatively affect load distribution when they have no request backlog to keep them busy until the next round of measurements. Figure 16.2c shows the time diagram for this algorithm in our four-server example using a load metric. It still exhibits load oscillations, but they are smaller than those in the algorithm that always chooses the best server.

Dahlin [2000] proposed two more randomized algorithms, which use as a load metric the request-queue length at a server and try to explicitly equalize its value across all servers. Assume that servers report their request-queue length to the balancing elements every T seconds, and the latter then use these reports until the new reports arrive. We refer to the time intervals between the load reports as phases. Let L_i be the request queue length at server i and λ be the total arrival rate for all servers. Then, the total number of new requests that arrive in the system between reports is $new\_requests = \lambda T$. So if we want each server to have an equal number of requests by the time of the next load report, each would have the following number of requests:

$$srv\_requests = \frac{\sum_{i=1}^{n} L_i + new\_requests}{n}$$

where n is the number of servers. Since each server i starts with L_i requests at the beginning of the phase, it must be sent $srv\_requests - L_i$ extra requests, if $L_i < srv\_requests$.[6] With randomization, each server is selected with probability proportional to the extra requests it must receive:

$$P_i = \frac{srv\_requests - L_i}{new\_requests}$$

The preceding algorithm attempts to equalize server loads toward the end of the current phase. Dahlin's second algorithm tries to achieve equal loads as quickly as possible. The basic idea is that the algorithm starts the phase by always selecting the least-loaded server until the number of requests at this server (its reported queue

---

[6] If L_i already exceeds $srv\_requests$, then server i has so many requests that even if it receives no more new ones it will still have more requests than the average server. So the algorithm does not select such servers during the current phase. We omit the details of dealing with this more complicated case.

length plus new requests) catches up with that of the second-least-loaded server. At this point the algorithm starts selecting these two servers with equal probability, until each has the same number of requests as the third-least-loaded server. Then the algorithm starts load-balancing among these three servers and so on until all servers have an equal load. Then all servers will be selected with equal probability until the end of the current phase.

Instead of counting the number of requests sent to each server (which would be difficult in the case of multiple balancing elements, since each element would be unaware of the number of requests sent to servers by others), the algorithm precomputes the time points in the current phase when it should switch from using j least-loaded servers to $j + 1$ least loaded servers. Assume for convenience that all servers are sorted by their load, and so L_j is the load of the jth-least-loaded server. Let t_j be the time when the algorithm starts using j servers. (Initially, t_1 is the beginning of the phase.) If by time t_j the algorithm has successfully equalized the load of $j - 1$ least-loaded servers to the next load level L_j, each of these $j - 1$ servers now has received L_j requests. Thus there are now j servers with load L_j. To bring their load the next level, L_{j+1}, each of these servers must receive $L_{j+1} - L_j$ more requests, and the total number of these extra requests to j servers is $extra\_requests = j \times (L_{j+1} - L_j)$. Given the total request arrival rate λ, it will take time $extra\_requests/\lambda$ to receive these requests. Then

$$t_{j+1} = t_j + \frac{extra\_requests}{\lambda}$$

Using a queuing model similar to the one used by Mitzenmacher, Dahlin showed that his algorithms outperform Mitzenmacher's algorithm in most situations. At the same time, Dahlin's algorithms require estimates of the total request arrival rate. When server selection is done on the server side (such as CDN's or Web site's DNS), one can assume the availability of this metric. For client-side server selection, the other two randomized techniques are more appropriate.

16.2.3 Supporting Client Stickiness

Client stickiness refers to a server selection strategy that sends requests from the same client to the same server. There are several reasons why it is desirable. Performance is enhanced when a client using the same server sends its requests over persistent connections and uses pipelining. The performance penalty for switching servers may become even higher if the client accesses the server via a secure protocol like SSL (see Section 15.9). From the perspective of functionality, a server may maintain locally client-specific information such as user profiles between requests; if some requests from this client end up at a different server, it would lack information necessary to function properly.

Ensuring stickiness depends on the request redirection mechanism used. In a client-side DNS-based redirection (see Section 14.1.1), giving a long TTL to DNS responses provided by the client DNS server to clients can do the trick. The client caches the

DNS resolution and uses the prescribed server for the TTL duration; however, the TTL that the client DNS server can give is limited to the TTL it received from the Web site's DNS server, and eventually the TTL will time out and the client might be redirected to a different server. On the other hand, this method must be applied with care for DNS-based redirection done by the Web site's DNS server (see Section 14.1.3), because a DNS response from a Web site goes to the client DNS server and will be reused by all clients using that client DNS. Giving a large TTL to such a response may thus exclude a potentially large group of clients from load-balancing for a long time. Recall from Chapters 14 and 15 that Web site's DNS redirection often uses short TTL for this precise reason.

Other redirection mechanisms, such as HTTP or L4 or L7 switch redirection, may use *client hashing* or provide explicit support for stickiness. With client hashing, the redirecting element chooses a Web server for a request by applying a hash function to the client IP address. By applying the same hash function to all requests, the redirector guarantees that all requests from the same client hash to the same server. This scheme is very similar to hash-based load-balancing among proxies (see Section 8.3.3) and the URL hashing method for cooperative proxy caching (see Section 9.3.3); the only difference is that the client IP address rather than the server IP address or URL is used as the hash argument. The consistent hashing idea described in Section 9.3.3 also applies here to improve load-balancing at a minimum hash disruption. A disadvantage of client hashing is that it is difficult to combine with other selection factors. For example, it would be difficult to devise a hash function that would account for proximity.

With explicit support for stickiness, offered for example by IBM's eNetwork Dispatcher, the redirecting element maintains state that records previous server selections for individual clients. Once a server is selected for a client, the client's subsequent requests are directed to the same server. The concern with this scheme is the overhead associated with state maintenance and lookup.

16.2.4 Respecting the Affinity of Server Caches

Respecting cache affinity refers to a server-selection strategy that tries to optimize the use of server caches. The idea is that once a server has processed a request for an object, the object is likely to be in the server's main memory cache, so this server can process another request for this object much more quickly than for a new object that would require disk access. Conversely, a selection strategy oblivious to existing server cache contents could degrade server performance because of *cache thrashing*, where objects are constantly replacing each other in the cache. A server selection algorithm may therefore improve server performance by accounting for cache affinity. Once such an algorithm selects a server for processing a request for an object, it selects the same server for all subsequent requests for this object.

Note that DNS redirection or an L4 switch in front of a Web server farm cannot respect cache affinity because they have no information on which objects are being requested. Nor is it a useful strategy for client-based redirection, since repeated requests for the same object are likely to be satisfied from the client cache anyway. This strategy is therefore most appropriate for an L7 balancing switch in front of a Web server farm.

Just as with client stickiness, the two approaches for respecting server cache affinity are based on hashing and explicit affinity support. Hash-based affinity support assumes that the L7 switch selects a server by applying a hash function to a requested URL. Since the same URL always hashes to the same server, affinity is assured. Explicit support, described by Pai et al. [1998], requires the switch to maintain state about prior server selections for object requests, which allows the switch to direct subsequent requests for an object to the server that was selected for the initial request for the same object. Just as with client stickiness, the main trade-off between the two schemes is that a hash-based solution is difficult to combine with other factors, such as client-server proximity or fine-grained load-balancing, while explicit support adds overhead to the redirecting element (the L7 switch in this case). Trace-driven simulations [Pai et al. 1998] have shown that the total throughput of a server farm respecting cache affinity can achieve several times the throughput of an affinity-oblivious server farm, unless each server cache is large enough to hold almost all the content referenced in the trace.

16.3 Server Selection with Multiple Metrics

Many server-selection algorithms rely on a combination of several metrics. One should not confuse these algorithms with those using aggregate metrics: the latter algorithms use a single metric, albeit one that reflects several aspects of system performance. A typical example using multiple metrics is the approach to server selection in which the algorithm selects the nearest server to the client (a proximity metric) provided overloaded servers are not selected (a load metric). We refer to algorithms that follow this general approach as *proximity-load-threshold* algorithms.

The most natural proximity-load-threshold algorithm is one that considers the servers in order of increasing distance from the client and selects the first server whose load is below a threshold. This algorithm, however, serves as a good illustration of problems described in Section 16.2.2, since it is prone to load oscillation when using stale load information.

Consider, for instance, the situation where all requests arrive from clients to which server A is closest and server B is next closest. The redirecting element selects server A for all requests, which results in overloading that server; once the redirecting element realizes the problem, it starts selecting server B for all requests. As a result, server B becomes overloaded while server A is idle. The redirecting element then starts using server A for all requests again, and so on. This oscillation only occurs if most clients are closer to A than to B, which is not always the case; however, this scenario occurs frequently enough—for example, during a local event—to make it a concern in the design of a server-selection algorithm.

loop through the servers in order of increasing distance from the client
for each server i
  if $load(i) < LW$
    forward request to server i
  if $(load(i) > LW)$ and $(load(i) < HW)$
    forward request to server i with probability $\frac{HW - load(i)}{HW - LW}$
    and do not forward to server i with probability $1 - \frac{HW - load(i)}{HW - LW}$
endfor
in case request has not been forwarded, send it to the least loaded replica.

Figure 16.3 Feedback-based algorithm for selecting a replica

We already know (Section 16.2.2) a general solution to the oscillation problem: randomization. One such algorithm has been described by Aggarwal and Rabinovich [1998]. This algorithm is shown in Figure 16.3. It assigns two load thresholds to a server, a high watermark *HW* and a low watermark *LW*. The algorithm always selects the closest server if its load is below the low watermark, and it never selects a server with load exceeding the high watermark. When server load is between these watermarks, it is selected with a probability that depends on the server load; this probability decreases to zero as the load increases to the high watermark. Trace simulations by Aggarwal and Rabinovich indicated that this algorithm successfully prevents load oscillations.

16.4 DNS-Based Server Selection

DNS is currently the main mechanism for request distribution over wide area (and sometimes even local area) networks. Both stand-alone Web sites and CDNs use DNS request distribution. The former often follow the basic architecture of Section 14.1.3, while the latter are likely to combine DNS request distribution with other mechanisms described in Section 15.4. The discussion in this section applies to both architectures; however, for simplicity, we only discuss server selection in the context of the basic architecture. In a CDN with server forms (see Figure 15.5), a server would correspond to a server farm, and communication between the DNS and a server would correspond to communication between the DNS and the switch in front of a server farm. Likewise, we have seen that CDN DNS service is often a distributed system in its own right; we, however, refer to it simply as the DNS server in this section.

16.4.1 A Typical DNS Server-Selection Scheme

A DNS server can use various combinations of the metrics discussed earlier, with server load and aggregate metrics reported to it by servers. For example, the following is a typical scheme.

  1. The DNS server chooses a nonoverloaded server that is closest to the originator of the DNS query, according to some proximity metric. For many

proximity metrics, such as autonomous systems hops, many servers may be equidistant from the query originator.

2. To break ties and avoid oscillations, the DNS server uses load-metric values collected from the servers and favors less loaded servers.

3. The DNS collects healthcheck reports from servers (these can be the same messages that carry load reports) and excludes failed servers.

In this scheme, the DNS server must be able to predict the effect of its server selection on the load of the chosen servers. For example, if the same server is closest for two consecutive DNS queries, should this server be chosen for both queries or should the second query be resolved to another, even if more distant, server? The answer depends on whether or not the load that results from the first query will overload the closest server. Similarly, predicting the load effect of server selection can be useful in balancing load among equidistant servers in step 2 of the above procedure.

Predicting the load of a Web request is difficult in general, because requests for different content may generate very different loads. In practice, algorithms often assume that all requests generate some average load and rely on load feedback from servers to correct any significant imbalances that result from this assumption. However, DNS exacerbates this problem by introducing hidden load factors (see Section 15.5). As a reminder, *hidden load factors* refers to potentially drastically different loads on HTTP servers that result from different DNS queries.

If hidden load factors were known, they could be easily accounted for in a server-selection algorithm. Several such algorithms have been proposed [Colajanni et al. 1998a; Colajanni et al. 1998b]. The goal of one of these algorithms, the *two-tier round-robin* [Colajanni et al. 1998b], is pure load-balancing, without accounting for the proximity aspect. This algorithm simply classifies all client DNSs as *hot* or *normal*, depending on whether their estimated hidden load factors are above or below a threshold. The algorithm then performs round-robin server rotation among DNS queries originated from normal client DNSs and a separate round-robin server rotation among DNS queries coming from hot client DNSs. Another algorithm, *adaptive TTL* [Colajanni et al. 1998a], performs server selection using any existing policy but then assigns a TTL to each DNS response that is inversely proportional to the hidden load factor of the query originator. The idea is to compensate higher hidden loads by lower TTLs and therefore equalize the load each DNS resolution imposes on the CDN server.

16.4.2 Estimating Hidden Load Factors

Any algorithm that accounts for hidden load factors can only be as good as the estimates of the hidden load factors. Finding these estimates requires the system to know which HTTP requests come as a result of which DNS queries, or which HTTP client IP addresses are behind which client DNS IP addresses. Building these associations is a difficult problem.

There are various means by which one can try to match DNS and HTTP clients [Shaikh and Tewari 2000].

1. Associating HTTP requests with the DNS request that occurred a short time earlier

2. Associating an HTTP client with the DNS server that has a common high-level DNS name or which belongs to the same autonomous system

3. Associating an HTTP client with the DNS server that shares the longest common IP address prefix

The reasoning behind the first method is that a Web interaction involves a DNS query followed by an HTTP request. Unfortunately, DNS caching muddies this scenario. Many HTTP requests reuse the same DNS query and occur long after the DNS query was answered. Conversely, a DNS query can easily occur just prior to an unrelated HTTP request and be mistakenly associated with the latter. Shaikh and Tewari [2000] were able to associate only 6 percent of HTTP clients with client DNSs based on this method, and then it remained unclear how accurate the resulting associations were.

The second method assumes that HTTP clients and their DNSs belong to the same domain or autonomous system. However, this assumption may not hold in some cases, and in other cases the domain or AS may have more than one DNS server, raising a problem of how to apportion clients among these DNS servers. The combination of the two methods seems like a more reliable way to build the association, but Shaikh and Tewari were able to find matches this way for just 1.4 percent of all clients.

The third method is similar to the "common AS" method above and assumes that HTTP clients and their DNSs are located on the same network and therefore share common prefixes in their IP addresses (see Chapter 2). Again, a large network may partition its HTTP clients among multiple client DNSs and a small network may use a DNS server from another network, in which case HTTP clients in the first network may not share an IP prefix with their DNS server. Overall, Shaikh and Tewari found that among the client-DNS associations they were able to build, only 37 percent of the clients shared IP prefixes with their DNS servers.

More reliable ways of building the association between HTTP clients and client DNSs require a dedicated *calibrating server* or a *calibrating DNS name*. The calibrating server method involves dedicating a special surrogate, called a calibrating server, for the purpose of associating Web clients with their DNS servers. [Rabinovich 2001; Bestavros and Mehrotra 2001]. To find which clients use a given DNS server in the context of a CDN, the CDN's DNS occasionally resolves a DNS query from this server to the calibrating server. The CDN's DNS assigns zero TTL to this *calibrating response* and waits between consecutive calibrating responses long enough to ensure that no client DNS or HTTP client caches previous calibrating responses. The system can then confidently associate Web clients that send HTTP requests to the calibrating server with the client's DNS server to which the preceding calibrating response was sent. The calibrating server method also lets the system measure the hidden load factor for a given client's DNS by observing the load imposed on the calibrating CDN server as a result of sending the calibrating DNS response to this DNS server.

Alternatively, a *calibrating DNS name* method can be used to associate clients with their client DNS servers. Let the DNS name of the Web site be firm-x.com and let a Web client request a page http://firm-x.com/page.html. If the system wants to associate this client with its client DNS server, the Web server can dynamically insert a dummy embedded object into page.html whose URL has a special domain name, which encodes the client IP address. For example, if client IP address is 127.30.155.11 then this domain name can have a form 127-30-155-11.calibrating.firm-x.com. The client will need to resolve this name. So, the next DNS query for this name must come from its client DNS server. The system can now associate the client whose IP address is embedded in the queried domain name with the client DNS server that issued the query.

Using a combination of these methods, the system can gradually build a database of the associations of Web clients with their DNS resolvers. A significant limitation of these methods is that they would not work well with Web clients that frequently change their IP addresses, such as dial-in clients that get different IP addresses at the start of every dial-in session. Using the calibrating server method to measure hidden load factors would still be possible, but building associations between clients and client DNS servers is useless if clients change their IP addresses all the time. It appears that IP prefix matching is the only feasible way to assign such clients to their DNS resolvers.

16.5 Why Choose a Server When You Can Have Them All?

Consider a client that has a choice of N servers from which it can download a page. Several studies indicate that active probing of servers just prior to download provides the best prediction of server performance [Dykes et al. 2000; Sayal et al. 1998; Carter and Crovella 1997]. Unfortunately, active measurements create extra network traffic and server load and add latency to the download itself. However, HTTP range requests (see Section 5.4) allow probes to perform useful work. Indeed, assuming that a client knows the size of the requested object, the client can send separate range requests for portions of the object to multiple servers as once. The only thing a client needs to know in advance to determine the range boundaries is the object size. Fortunately, the client can easily determine the object size by issuing an initial HEAD request to one of the servers. Once the size S of the object is known, the client splits it into k blocks, where k exceeds the number of servers, and requests the first N consecutive blocks from the servers in parallel using appropriate range requests. The server that finishes first with its block is sent a request for the next outstanding block until all blocks are received. All requests to a given server, including the initial HEAD request, reuse a single persistent TCP connection. This idea has been proposed by Rodriguez et al. [2000].

A performance analysis of this scheme showed that, with the appropriate choice of k, if the bottleneck is at the servers, the overall download time is even lower than if the best server was used, because of the parallelism. If the bottleneck is in the client link to the Internet (as is the case with a dial-in client), the scheme downloads most bytes from the best server and results in just slightly worse performance than if only the best server were used. Individual range requests act as server performance probes, yet all of them, even those to suboptimal servers, contribute to the completion of the overall task.

The two important aspects of this scheme are the proper choice of the number of blocks and the need for the extra initial HEAD request. A block size should be small enough to ensure that suboptimal servers have to transfer only small amounts of data. Yet small blocks increase the idle times the best server incurs between the time it services one block request and the time it receives the next block request. A possible variation of the scheme is to start with small blocks to probe the servers and then complete the download in one large block request to the best server.

The initial HEAD request would not add any significant overhead to accessing large objects for which the scheme is intended. However, if the object turns out to be too small for the scheme to be worthwhile, the extra delay due to a HEAD request may become a noticeable portion of the download time. Given that most objects are small, it may be beneficial to use an initial range request instead of a HEAD. For instance, assuming that the scheme is worthwhile for objects over 10KBytes, the client may start by issuing a request to one of the servers for the initial 10KBytes of the object. If the object is smaller than that, the server simply returns the object. Otherwise, the server returns the initial 10KBytes of the object including the object-size information that the scheme needs. The scheme will be worthwhile if the remaining portion of the object is over 10KBytes, meaning that the object size is at least 20KBytes. Thus, for objects between 10KBytes and 20KBytes the initial request would still be unnecessary; however, there are many fewer objects in this size range than in the range from 0KByte to 10KBytes.

16.6 Summary

Whichever point on the request processing path implements request redirection must select the server for a given request. Server selection is based on performance metrics of individual servers. The main types of metrics are proximity metrics measuring the geographical or network distance between the client and a server, load metrics that measure the load of individual servers, and aggregate metrics that reflect the overall performance of client fetches from various servers.

Aggregate metrics are the best predictors of the relative performance of replica servers because these metrics directly reflect the download performance. Clients are well equipped to use aggregate metrics; however, performing server selection at a client requires modifying the client and relies on Web site cooperation in providing the client with the list of servers.

On the server side, DNS-based server selection is necessarily coarse-grain, because of the implications of client DNS caching, the originator problem, and hidden load factors. On the other hand, it is very simple and lightweight. It remains the main means of request distribution over a wide area. An L4 or L7 switch in front of a server farm offers fine-grain server selection, but is most appropriate on a LAN.

Overall, we describe a variety of metrics and algorithmic approaches for Web server selection. Few comprehensive performance studies exist in this area. Our discussion, for the most part, is a design-space description and is deliberately short on any specific recommendations. The topic of server selection allows for many choices in terms of metrics and algorithms used, with often contradictory requirements (such as high TTL of DNS responses for client stickiness versus low TTL of these responses for finer-grain control). Given the difficulty of the problem, the appropriate goal of server selection ought to be to avoid bad servers, not to choose the optimal one [Johnson et al. 2000].

Part IV
Further Directions

We conclude the book with a discussion of less established trends in the use of proxies and CDNs. While many details of the mechanisms described earlier will undoubtedly change over time, we believe that the underlying concepts introduced so far will be valid for an extended period of time. On the other hand, the concepts introduced in this part are less proven and may still change.

We begin by discussing the use of forward proxies and surrogates for purposes other than improving performance. Having a highly flexible and powerful proxy in the network provides the opportunity to implement a variety of services. Chapter 17 describes several of these services.

Another recent trend is so-called content distribution internetworking (CDI). CDI allows a content provider to use forward proxies or CDN servers from multiple ISPs and CDNs. This approach is appealing to CDNs because it promises them higher capacity, better proximity to the client, and increased fault tolerance while reducing their capital costs. The main disadvantage is the added complexity of allowing proxies and CDN servers to interact. CDI is discussed in Chapter 18.

Chapter 17
Adding Value at the Edge

Our discussion so far has focused on the performance benefits of caching and replication. However, the role of forward proxies and surrogates can extend beyond performance. As focal points of Web traffic at the edge of the network, they provide an opportunity to implement a variety of services that would not otherwise be feasible. In other words, proxies and surrogates stop being viewed as just performance boosters but rather as a platform for implementing various value-added functions. The idea of using a proxy for value-added services was actually put forward quite early by Brooks et al. [1995]. This chapter examines some important but often overlooked benefits of proxies and surrogates, which are often called *edge servers*.

17.1 Content Filtering

Like it or not, content filtering (or, as some put it, censoring) is going to be a part of Internet practices. Examples of benign uses of this technology include companies that are increasingly limiting the kind of information their workers can access and parents who are concerned with the content accessible to their children.

Many approaches to content filtering have been proposed. Some use automatic content classification, for example, a CYBERsitter filtering product or Virtual Control Agent component of SuperScout Web filter. Some use extensive lists of potentially questionable URLs classified into subject categories; these lists are offered by a number of companies such as N2H2, SonicWALL, SuperScout, and Net Nanny. Most use proprietary technologies while others such as SafeSurf follow a Platform for Internet Content Selection (PICS) protocol [Resnick and Miller 1996], an open protocol for supplying Web content ratings.

Various approaches to content filtering differ in several areas, including where the filtering occurs. One common place is the browser. Its advantage is that the deployment and operation of filtering is under the full control of the end user. In particular, it can be deployed autonomously, regardless of what the rest of the network does. This advantage, however, is at the same time the main weakness of this filtering location: with children often more computer-literate than their parents, they can uninstall local filtering as easily as their parents can install it.

Now consider a user who connects to an ISP at a point of presence (POP) with an interception forward proxy (see Chapter 8). If this proxy performs filtering, there is no way for the user to bypass it, short of changing the ISP. So a proxy in the network enables a new service to users, which allows the user, for example, to specify content filtering rules using a Web-based interface. These rules can never be bypassed and are protected by a password. The user can block access to certain sites or particular pages, or prohibit pages containing certain keywords. These filtering rules become part of the user profile and are consulted by the proxy on every Web access. Processing an HTTP request by the filtering proxy thus includes the steps of accessing the user profile, checking the filtering rules, and obtaining the object itself only if the applicable rules allow. This approach is especially attractive to ISPs because it delegates the task of choosing filtering rules to users themselves. The ISP remains content-neutral, and therefore immune to both accusations of censorship and liability for delivering content deemed inappropriate or harmful.

17.2 Content Transcoding

The Internet explosion has led to a variety of consumer devices, from desktop computers to handheld devices such as the PalmPilot. These devices have different screen sizes, color capabilities, processing power, and supported graphics formats. Some devices may be unable to make use of content as it is provided by origin servers. These devices first download the content and then transform it locally to a lower-quality form. Since the lower-quality encoding is usually smaller, the time and bandwidth used for downloading high-quality content are wasted.

Using a forward proxy for such devices allows the ISP to offer the service of dynamically transforming the content into a more efficient form. Such transformation is often referred to as *content transcoding* or *distillation* [Fox and Brewer 1996]. Examples of possible content transformations include:

- Turning a high-resolution image into a lower-resolution image with smaller image size

- Turning a color image into a grayscale image, again, reducing the image size

- Turning a PostScript file into an HTML document, which is not only smaller but also displayable on devices that do not support PostScript, such as PalmPilots

There are two basic types of content transcoding. *Transparent transcoding* does not affect the content quality as seen by the end user. For example, converting a color image into a grayscale image for a device not capable of displaying color is completely transparent to the end user because the user cannot see color images anyway. *Nontransparent transcoding,* on the other hand, results in some degradation of content, trading content quality for response time. Examples of nontransparent transcoding include stripping a page of some of its embedded images or lowering image resolution to reduce the image size. Such transcoding may be especially valuable for users connected to ISPs by a low-bandwidth line such as a dial-up modem.

If a proxy can determine the client capabilities (for example, when clients supply a `user-agent` HTTP header with their requests), the proxy may do transparent transcoding unilaterally. For nontransparent transcoding, or when it is not possible to determine the capabilities of the client, the distillation service must provide an interface for the user to specify preferences. The preferences may include stripping documents of their embedded images or lowering image resolutions. The user may specify these rules unconditionally or make them applicable only when using a low-bandwidth connection. In the latter case, the proxy must determine the bandwidth of the connection before applying the transcoding. It can do so dynamically by measuring the spacing between the TCP acknowledgments it receives from the client [Carter and Crovella 1997]. Alternatively, the ISP may implement a closer integration of the proxy with its connectivity platform, so that the proxy is directly informed by the platform of the connection bandwidth to the client.

Two basic transcoding techniques can be used by a proxy.

Real-time distillation: In this technique a proxy stores only original documents in its cache and performs the transformation in the course of request processing. The main advantage of this approach is its simplicity. The proxy cache does not have to deal with multiple encodings of the same document, and the caching algorithm requires no changes. A disadvantage of real-time distillation is the increased latency imposed by the proxy performing image transformation for each request.

Cached distillation (sometimes called soft caching): In this technique a proxy keeps the result of the distillation in the cache [Kangasharju et al. 1998]. This may cause the proxy to store several encodings of the same document in the cache. It reduces the cache latency (since in some cases it may find the desired encoding in the cache without having to compute it on the fly), but involves a more complex caching algorithm in order to preserve the freshness of all encodings of the same object.

Fox and Brewer [1996] were among the first to provide a system for content distillation. This system has been commercialized by ProxiNet (now owned by Puma Technologies). Among other systems implementing content distillation, we can mention the Mirror Image Internet proxy and the now-defunct QuickWeb proxy from Intel.

17.3 Watermarking

The Internet as a communications medium raises a variety of security concerns. One especially worrisome concern for many content providers is that Internet access simplifies unauthorized copying and distribution of content. Indeed, once the content moves to a user's computer, the content provider loses control over its future fate.

There is not much a content provider can do to prevent an unscrupulous user from redistributing an object once that user is in possession of it. But what can be done is at least to make sure that when an unauthorized copy is discovered, the perpetrator can be traced and face the consequences [Brassil et al. 1994]. The possibility of getting caught could serve to deter many people from unauthorized content distribution.

The technology that allows tracing content copies is called *watermarking*. With watermarking, an object can be indiscernibly modified upon each access so that each copy can be uniquely associated with the access and the client that retrieved it. When an unauthorized copy turns up, the initial access at the root of the distribution of this copy can be traced. Nontextual objects such as images, video, and audio are amenable to watermarking. Textual objects such as HTML and plain text cannot be watermarked effectively.

An ISP may partner with a content provider so that the content provider would make its content cacheable by the ISP's forward proxy (thus allowing the ISP to improve performance to its clients) in return for the forward proxy's using watermarking to control content distribution. But watermarking service could be even more compelling when offered by a CDN that operates surrogates. Watermarking involves managing the archive of tracking records of object copies (or the secret keys required to recompute watermarked copies from the original reference version) and users to whom those copies were served. Some content providers may lack resources to do all this. To these content providers, a CDN can offer a watermarking service implemented by its surrogates. The surrogates would watermark content as it flows through on its way from the content server to the client, and send tracking records to the archive. The CDN can exploit its own size to manage the archive efficiently.

17.4 Custom Usage Reporting

Another service a CDN can offer to a content provider is custom usage reporting. This service allows the content provider to receive a variety of usage reports at various levels of detail. The service also allows the content provider to generate useful statistics based on its usage database. The SiteWise Service from Akamai Technologies is one commercially available example of custom usage reporting.

Similar to watermarking, custom usage reporting is most compelling when offered by a CDN. To receive this service, the content provider becomes the CDN's customer, and the surrogates of the CDN log user accesses. The log is then used for generating custom usage reports or for data mining. The CDN provides the customers of this service with a Web-based interface for specifying and downloading reports.

In principle, the origin server itself could perform the same task. But as in the case of watermarking, it would involve maintaining an extensive archive of usage records and implementing numerous data-mining queries and reporting procedures. A CDN, on the other hand, gains efficiency of scale by having a large archive database server and common data-mining and reporting modules used by many customers. We should note that CDNs bill content providers based on usage and thus already supply content providers with some usage statistics. However, billing reports do not subsume the usage reporting service. While billing is based on aggregate statistics such as the number of bytes served by surrogates, the usage reporting service would be specific to individual documents and provide much richer data-mining queries and analysis.

17.5 Implementing New Services with an Edge Server API

We have seen that an edge server can provide a platform for implementing a variety of applications. In addition to the user-visible services described in this chapter, we have described numerous techniques throughout the book that involve modifications to proxy functionality. One way to implement these functionalities is to modify the source code of a publicly available edge server implementation. The problem is that this approach creates a modified version of the code, which must be maintained. Given the rate of changes in Web technologies, keeping that modified version current would require constant porting of the modifications to new releases of the base product.

Alternatively a large potential customer may be able to talk a vendor into implementing desired extensions into the vendor's code. But the customer would be at the mercy of the vendor.

A third possibility, and the one we argue for, is for the edge server to export an application programming interface (API) that would allow the operator of the edge server to flexibly extend or modify the edge server's functionality. In this way, extensions do not create a new branch in edge server evolution. When a new release appears, the extensions can be installed easily on the new release, assuming that the new release's API is upward-compatible. Also, the edge server operator does not need to rely on the goodwill of the vendor every time a new extension is needed. Moreover, we even imagine the standardization of an edge server API so that the same extensions could run on top of different edge server products.

It is important to distinguish between an API to an edge server and a programming toolkit that can be used to implement an edge server, like libwww [Nielsen et al. 2001]. While both aim at achieving edge server extensibility, there is an important difference between the two. An edge server with a well-defined API is an operational product with default functionality, while an edge server toolkit is a collection of building blocks that implement some actions typically performed by edge servers. These building blocks by themselves are meaningless; they must be glued together in a master program in order to obtain an operational product. This is typically a much more time-consuming task than writing to the API of an edge server. On the other hand, a toolkit gives the programmer the ultimate flexibility in implementing his or her own edge server.

Edge server products come in two flavors. An *appliance edge server* is basically a black box that includes both hardware and software. The box often uses a specialized operating system tightly integrated with the edge server code itself. A *software-based edge server* is an application implemented on top of a standard operating system (typically a flavor of UNIX); this application can run on any computer capable of running the underlying operating system. An example of the appliance approach is NetCache from Network Appliance. Inktomi's Traffic Server and Squid are examples of the software approach. The appliance approach promises a performance advantage from a stripped-down operating system specifically optimized for the single application. However, it makes exposing a meaningful API difficult.

The problem with providing an API on an appliance edge server is that a developer writing to this API would not be able to use system calls to the operating system (since system calls are not exposed). Implementing system calls in an appliance that are general enough to support software development may turn the specialized operating system into a general one, and move the appliance edge server toward a software-based solution. To date, we are not aware of an appliance edge server that would provide an API suitable for new service implementation by third parties, while some software-based products, for example, Traffic Server, do provide it. We thus view the main tradeoff between the appliance and software approaches to be performance versus flexibility.

17.6   The ICAP Protocol

The Internet Content Adaptation Protocol (ICAP) is a proposed protocol that allows a more distributed solution to the problem of extending the functionality of edge servers.[1] The basic concept is to offload custom processing from the edge server to a special ICAP server. Then the edge server has to be only slightly modified to remotely call the ICAP server in cases that require custom processing. This approach allows highly optimized appliances to be used for routine operation while maintaining a high level of flexibility in an ICAP server that is implemented in software on top of a standard operating system. The edge server itself would still have to export an API, but this API would be quite simple, just a set of rules to specify requests and responses that must be shipped off to the ICAP server for extra processing.

ICAP describes three different modes of custom processing. The *request modification* mode, depicted in Figure 17.1a, allows the modification of requests as they are transmitted from the client via an edge server to the origin server. In this mode,

---

[1] It should be remarked that despite the fact that many companies active in the caching and content distribution field favor ICAP and support the Open Pluggable Edge Services (OPES) effort with the goal of standardizing an ICAP-like protocol, ICAP is neither widely used nor an Internet standard at this point. Information about the status of ICAP can be found at http://www.i-cap.org/.

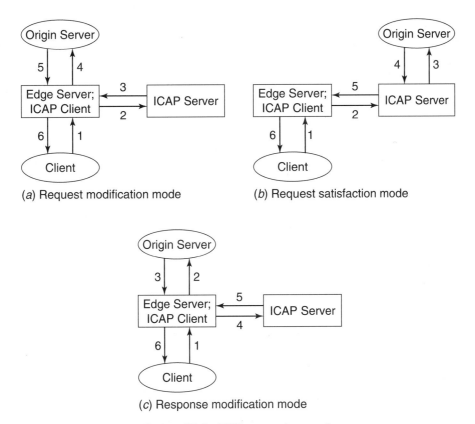

(a) Request modification mode

(b) Request satisfaction mode

(c) Response modification mode

Figure 17.1   ICAP processing modes

after the client request arrives at the edge server (step 1), the edge server issues an ICAP request, which contains the original client HTTP request, to the ICAP server (step 2). The ICAP server has the option to modify the HTTP request according to a custom policy that this server implements before returning this request to the edge server (step 3). In particular, the ICAP server may modify the URL or the Web server specified in the client request. The edge server sends the modified request to the Web server specified in it, which may be different from the Web server specified in the original client request (step 4). That server sends its response to the edge server (step 5), which then forwards this response to the client (step 6).

One scenario where the request modification mode might be useful is content filtering. If, for example, a company policy limits employees' Web access to nonoffensive sites, a regular ICAP-enabled interception proxy can be used at the company boundary. The ICAP server would replace requests to offensive sites with the URL of a page describing the company policy. The benefit of ICAP in this example is that a fast and inexpensive proxy appliance can be used for caching and that the more complicated policy decision is made on the ICAP server. The ICAP server in this scenario might even be operated by a company specialized in filtering, like Net Nanny or N2H2, which removes the burden from the company to keep their filter rules up to date.

The second ICAP mode is called *request satisfaction* mode and is shown in Figure 17.1b. The edge server sends the client's HTTP request to the ICAP server as in the request modification mode. However, the ICAP server itself satisfies the request as it sees fit, consulting the origin server if necessary. The ICAP server then sends the response to the edge server, which forwards it to the client. It is unclear how this approach differs from a cache hierarchy (see Section 9.3.2) in which the ICAP server represents the parent of the ICAP client, and in fact the edge server could just as well use HTTP to communicate with the ICAP server.

Finally, the *response modification* mode shown in Figure 17.1c allows the modification of the object returned from the origin server. In this mode, after the edge server has received the content from the origin server (step 3), the edge server forwards the content to the ICAP server, which then can adapt the content as required. Example applications for this ICAP mode include transcoding Web objects for special devices, human language translation, virus checking, and so forth.

The three ICAP modes are implemented as a simple request-response protocol similar to HTTP 1.1 on top of TCP. Neither the details nor the policy and security considerations of the ICAP protocol have been finalized yet and hence cannot be discussed further in this book. However, we should mention that all three ICAP modes offer an additional chance for an attacker to hijack Web traffic and that especially the request satisfaction and response modification modes will generate a substantial amount of additional traffic. The request satisfaction mode requires that objects be transferred from the ICAP server to the edge server. The response modification mode transfers objects twice, from the edge server to the ICAP server and back.

17.7 Distributing Web Applications

So far we have discussed in this chapter how to extend edge server functionality using an edge server API and how to offload custom processing from the edge server using ICAP. Both of these approaches preserve the notion of an edge server as a file-caching device, be it a forward proxy or surrogate. A more radical approach of moving additional functionality into the network is to replicate an entire application including the data the application accesses. For example, instead of computing the results of a search in an online encyclopedia at a central location, the search application and the encyclopedia files could be replicated in multiple places in the network, and individual results could be computed at each replica. The challenges of this approach are to decide how to replicate the application and where to replicate it.

17.7.1 How to Replicate Applications

Obviously, an application requires a server architecture with specific capabilities. For example, a UNIX application cannot run on an NT server, some applications may require a certain amount of disk or main memory, and some may rely on a certain nonstandard computing environment. At this point there is no standard environment for replicated applications; however, we assume for the remainder of this section that an application is replicated among servers that are capable of running it.

Replicating an application involves two main tasks. First, all related files must be copied and the new server must be initialized to run the application; second, the new application replica must remain consistent with the primary copy, with all updates propagated from the latter to the former. Consistency maintenance of application replicas is complicated because the mirror must acquire all updated files together in order to ensure the integrity of the application. Otherwise, the set of items required for page generation may be inconsistent, with some items new and some still old. In general an application might contain a set of executable modules, underlying data that these modules use to compute responses, and some resident processes that these modules may call. Any inconsistency among these components may cause unpredictable consequences including server failure.

To fulfill these tasks, the replicated applications can use an approach similar to the approaches used for software distribution, such as the technology developed by the Marimba Corporation [Hoff et al. 1999]. The following discussion reflects in part Marimba's approach, which is based on the notion of an application *index page*. Conceptually, the index page consists of two parts: the list of all files comprising the application along with their last-modified dates; and the *initialization script* that the recipient server must run before accepting any requests. In addition to describing the application, the index page provides an effective solution to the consistency maintenance problem.

The index page reduces the problem of maintaining consistency of applications to maintaining consistency of an individual static page. Every server that has a copy of an application assumes that it caches the application's index. The system only needs to ensure that all cached copies of the index are consistent. When some object in the application changes, the application's primary server updates the index accordingly. When replica servers detect that their cached copies of the index are not valid, they download the new index and then copy the modified objects as prescribed in the index.

The mechanism for maintaining consistency of cached copies of the index page itself is orthogonal to our discussion here. Any mechanism discussed elsewhere in the book can be used. It can be a direct invalidation by the primary server; it can be the adaptive validation by replica servers; it can also be an "always-validate" scheme where the index page is validated by the replica server on every user access to the application.

17.7.2 Where to Replicate Applications

In principle, an application could be replicated on a server when the first request for the application arrives to this server, similar to static Web content on a proxy cache miss. However, due to the size of a typical Web application (including its data), this would likely add an unacceptable delay for the user. In addition, such on-demand application replication might result in transferring a large application and its data to fullfill a single user request, increasing instead of decreasing the required bandwidth. Therefore, it becomes important to replicate applications judiciously. This can be done with one of the following methods.

Static replication: In this method, the system administrator determines servers to distribute the application to. The administrator then prepopulates the chosen servers with the application. In other words, this method involves human replica placement decisions. Such decisions are often driven not by technical virtues but by business agreements between content providers and the service providers, such as a CDN that distributes the application.

Dynamic asynchronous replication: The system periodically analyzes usage patterns for various applications and makes dynamic decisions on the number and location of replicas of these applications.

Static replication is appropriate when it is prescribed by business agreements. In other cases, it imposes a daunting task on system administrators, which becomes ever more difficult as the scale of the system increases. It is also error-prone and not responsive enough to changes in access patterns for various content. Therefore, we concentrate on dynamic asynchronous replication of Web applications in the remainder of this section. We should also mention that very little work has been done on this topic.

With dynamic asynchronous replication, the system must periodically examine past usage patterns and decide how many replicas of a given application to place where. We refer to the algorithm used in this decision as a *content placement algorithm.* This algorithm has to address several issues.

Accounting for proximity and load: The main challenge in designing such an algorithm is that it must achieve both network proximity (that is, it must locate replicas close to the clients accessing them) and load-balancing between replica servers.

Convergence: The algorithm should *converge:* under steady usage patterns, the algorithm should eventually arrive at a steady content placement configuration and, ideally, stop moving replicas around. To illustrate convergence, consider a content placement algorithm which adds a replica if the load of a replica reaches 500 requests per second and removes a replica if its usage drops below 250 requests per second. If this algorithm is used and replica A reaches exactly 500 requests per second, the algorithm would configure a second replica, B. However, if the load is not spread exactly equally between A and B, the algorithm would remove one of the replicas, since it serves less than 250 requests per second, only to create it again shortly after that. Therefore, this algorithm would not converge.

Responsiveness and stability: The algorithm must respond quickly to a meaningful change in demand patterns (responsiveness); at the same time, it should not move replicas around in response to minute demand changes (stability). For example, the content placement algorithm introduced previously to illustrate convergence is responsive but not stable. The algorithm would instantly introduce a new replica if the request rate reaches 500 requests per second, which makes it responsive. On the other hand it would remove the replica again if the request rate drops below 250 requests per second for only a short period of time, which makes the algorithm unstable. In general, responsiveness and stability are contradictory and vaguely defined requirements (what is meaningful change?) and are usually satisfied by hand-tuning algorithm parameters.

Distributed operation: Another desirable requirement for such an algorithm is that it be distributed, since the scale of a large set of replicated applications might make a centralized replica placement algorithm problematic.

One such algorithm has been proposed in which each application server makes its own autonomous content placement decisions for the applications that are present on the application server [Rabinovich et al. 1999; Rabinovich and Aggarwal 1999]. An application server may create an additional replica of an application on another application server, or it may migrate the application from itself to another application server, or it may drop (uninstall) the application, provided other replicas of this application exist elsewhere in the CDN.

17.8 Summary

In addition to improving performance of Web accesses, forward proxies and surrogates (collectively called edge servers in this chapter) can implement a rich set of value-added services. Edge servers are a convenient place to do so because they are a focal point for Web traffic in an ISP, a corporation, or a CDN. Functional services are more tangible than performance improvement and, therefore, are easier to market. They can also be a more compelling differentiator between competing ISPs or CDNs.
Examples of services that might be implemented on edge servers are

- Content filtering to prevent users from viewing certain content on the Internet

- Content transcoding to make content more suitable for a wide variety of devices

- Watermarking to track the illegal distribution of content

- Custom usage reporting to supply the content provider with detailed information about the clients viewing the content

To implement extra services, it is important to be able to extend the functionality of an edge server. In general, software edge servers built on top of a general-purpose operating system are more amenable to such extensions than appliance edge servers.

On the other hand, appliance edge servers typically have higher performance. ICAP aims to break this tradeoff by offloading custom processing to a separate ICAP server. Standard processing can then be done on a high-performance appliance edge server and custom processing on an ICAP server that is implemented on top of a general operating system and is flexible enough to be extended.

Whether the extra services are implemented on an ICAP server or on an edge server directly, the implementation requires a suitable set of APIs to interact with either unit. Some edge server products, such as Inktomi's Traffic Server, already provide such APIs. The next step, clearly, is to allow an implemented service to run on a variety of different edge server products with no or little change. Otherwise, adding extra services would increasingly tie the edge server operator to its edge server vendor. This portability goal calls for a standardized set of edge server APIs. While the need for a standardized framework to implement value-added services has been recognized, actual work in this area is still in its infancy.

A more radical approach to distribute processing within the network is to replicate an entire application including the data the application needs to function properly. Since replicating entire applications is an expensive operation, great care has to be taken to decide when and where an application and its data should be replicated.

Chapter 18
Content Distribution Internetworking

Another extension of the use of forward proxies as well as CDNs is *content distribution internetworking (CDI)* [Biliris et al. 2001]. The goal of CDI is to allow collaboration between forward proxies and CDNs, as well as between individual CDNs, in improving access to certain Web content. By involving forward proxies and CDNs, the CDI model exhibits features of both caching and replication. Like replication, the CDI model leaves the content under complete control of the content provider. Participating CDNs also follow the usual replication model: they sell their services to content providers and try to improve delivery of this content to any client that requests it. On the other hand, participating forward proxies follow the caching model in that they cater to their clients and not content providers. In addition, the different components involved in delivering the service can be under different administrative control, similar to cooperative proxy caching as described in Chapter 9.

The CDI effort is being defined within the Internet Engineering Task Force (IETF) and no citable documents have been produced yet. Therefore we only outline the main issues and approaches here, including the advantages and disadvantages of CDI, the problem of request distribution, and content distribution and accounting issues.

18.1 Pros and Cons of CDI

Following is a list of the main advantages of CDI.

Greater reach: A CDN can expand its reach to a larger client population by utilizing partner CDN servers and forward proxies deployed close to these clients. This is especially valuable in situations where the CDN is not allowed to deploy its own surrogate servers close to clients. For example, in many cases, an ISP providing Internet access over cable modems allows CDNs to deploy surrogates only in data centers, but not directly in the cable infrastructure. However, the ISP itself may have forward proxies within the cable infrastructure, and the ISP could make these forward proxies accessible to partner CDNs via CDI.

Higher capacity: CDI provides a benefit even when multiple forward proxies and CDN servers cover the same set of clients. In this scenario, CDI allows a CDN to outsource requests to other CDNs and forward proxies in case of unexpected high demand.

Increased fault tolerance: CDI can increase the reliability of a CDN since the CDN can continue serving content through its partners even in the event of a total failure of all of its own CDN servers.

Larger scale: Separating the server selection process into inter-CDN and intra-CDN stages increases the scalability, similar to separating IP routing into inter- and intra-AS routing.

All these advantages lower the cost of content distribution. With CDI, multiple CDNs are able to share the same CDN server. This reduces the total number of such servers that have to be deployed by all CDNs. For example, a CDN that wants to have a CDN server close to every client in the Internet would have to deploy servers in remote locations for small sets of clients. In the case of CDI this investment can be shared among multiple CDNs. Including forward proxies operated by ISPs would reduce the cost even further.

On the other hand, CDI has to overcome some difficult challenges to be viable. The following are the most challenging issues.

Complexity of Layer 7 interaction: Internet designers deliberately chose Layer 3 as the layer at which all networks interconnect. This was deemed to be the layer that had the least complexity while providing all functionality necessary to interconnect multiple networks. CDI revises this decision by interconnecting networks at Layer 7. Therefore, a large amount of Layer 7 information has to be exchanged to make CDI work, which greatly increases the complexity of CDI.

Quality of service: One reason for introducing CDNs was to provide some sort of quality of service on top of the Internet, despite its unreliable, best-effort nature (see Chapter 2). A challenge of CDI is to preserve this gain in the quality of service while working with partners under separate administrative control.

18.2 Request Distribution

The goal of request distribution[1] is to find the appropriate forward proxy or CDN server for a given client and request. In the forward proxy case, the forward proxy receives all requests from the clients it serves; thus, the proxy can redirect these requests to CDI partners as specified by the CDI redirection policy. The most common

---

[1] Request distribution is also referred to as *request routing*. However, the term *routing* implies Layer 3; therefore, we prefer the term *request distribution*.

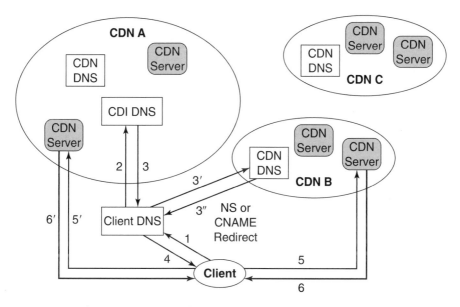

Figure 18.1 Example CDI request distribution using DNS

mechanisms of distributing requests within a CDN are described in Part III. The same mechanisms can be extended to distribute requests across multiple CDNs. In particular, DNS-based redirection can be used between CDNs in several ways.[2]

- A CDN DNS server can return an A record (with a suitable TTL) that contains the IP address of a server within its own CDN or a partner CDN. This is the most efficient option, but it requires the closest cooperation between the CDNs and is therefore mainly used when choosing among servers that are in the same administrative domain as the DNS server returning the record. This method can also be used to redirect a request to a partner forward proxy.

- A CDN DNS server can return a CNAME record (with a suitable TTL) that contains a new domain name whose authoritative DNS server resides in a partnering CDN. The DNS resolution scheme of the partnering DNS then takes over and ultimately returns an A record (IP address) of a server in its CDN to the client DNS.

- A CDN DNS server can return an NS record (with a suitable TTL), redirecting the query to the DNS server of a partnering CDN. The DNS server of the partnering CDN then takes over, and ultimately returns an A record (IP address) of a server in its CDN to the client DNS.

Figure 18.1 illustrates the use of these three redirection methods. The example consists of CDN A, CDN B, CDN C, and a client. Similar to DNS request distribution in

---

[2] Please see Section 4.2 for details on DNS.

the single CDN case, the client contacts its local DNS server (client DNS) to resolve a domain name of a Web site (step 1). The client DNS server then contacts the authoritative DNS server for the domain, which in the case of CDI would be a CDI DNS server (step 2). The CDI DNS server uses one of the three options outlined above to redirect the client to one of the three CDNs. In the simplest case the CDI DNS server chooses a CDN server which is within its own administrative boundary. In this case the CDI DNS would return an A record to the client DNS (step 3), which returns it to the client (step 4) pointing the client directly to the CDN server. The client can then retrieve the content from the CDN server specified in the A record returned by the client DNS server (steps 5' and 6').

If the CDI DNS server decides to use another CDN, it returns a CNAME or NS record to the client DNS server. The client DNS server then contacts the CDN DNS server indicated by the CNAME or NS record (step 3'), which resolves the DNS query further to return an A record to the client DNS server (step 3''). This A record will be returned to the client (step 4), which retrieves the content from the identified CDN server (steps 5 and 6).

An alternative to the DNS-based approach is URL rewriting. With URL rewriting, a CDN would serve HTML content while replacing embedded URLs and hyperlinks to point to other CDNs.

So far we have discussed mechanisms of request distribution between CDI partners; however, we have not yet discussed the policy behind the request distribution decision. In general, the policy should reflect the performance different partners can deliver for particular clients and requested content. In addition, the decision is probably also based on the cost of delivering content via a particular partner. It is unreasonable to expect that all CDI partners will utilize a single metric or algorithm. However, the algorithms used are likely to follow the following outline.

1. From all partner CDNs and forward proxies, select the ones that could deliver the content to the particular client in question.

2. From the partners chosen in the previous step, select the ones that will fulfill all performance agreements made with the provider of the requested content.

3. From the partners chosen in the previous step, select the least expensive one.

If at any time during steps 1 to 3 no CDN or forward proxy is left, the request distribution mechanism will use the best partner from the set in the previous step.

18.3   Content Distribution

In addition to distributing requests between CDI partners, it is also necessary to distribute the content to CDN servers and forward proxies which will eventually serve it. At a minimum, this requires the transfer of information about the content that allows partners to find the origin servers for the given content. This problem has already been discussed in Section 15.3 in the context of CDNs. However, in the context of CDI, it becomes necessary to distribute this information in a globally understood format. Invalidation of objects stored at partner proxies and CDN servers is another example of information that must be exchanged between CDI participants. Many of the mechanisms introduced in Sections 10.2 and 15.7 apply here. However, it is again necessary to standardize these information exchanges to solve the same problems in the context of CDI.

18.4 Accounting

Another important problem CDI has to address is accounting. Most content providers demand detailed statistics on how much content was served to which client and when. This information in its unaggregated form is extensive. For example, the Web site of a popular TV game show logs about 1Byte of data for every 10Bytes of data served. Sending these logs to the content provider will saturate its links to the Internet and partly defeat the purpose of CDNs. Therefore, the data clearly has to be aggregated before it can be transferred to the content provider. In the context of CDI these aggregation methods and the resulting log formats have to be standardized.

In addition to the log aggregation issue, the accounting system also has to provide the request distribution system with real-time feedback to support performance sensitive request distribution algorithms. For example, the algorithm described in Section 18.2 eliminates in step 2 all CDNs that cannot fulfill a given performance agreement. To make this decision, the request distribution system has to know how each partner is performing at each point in time. Therefore, each partner must periodically advertise its performance to all partners. It is interesting to note here that the better performance a CDI partner advertises to other partners, the more content it will serve. Since in general payments are made based on the amount of content served by a partner, this creates an incentive for individual partners to overstate their performance. Therefore, it is important to have a verification mechanism, so that this performance feedback can be trusted despite the fact that it comes from another CDI participant. To solve this problem, one could envision adding an accounting-only CDN into the CDI architecture. This CDN has the sole purpose of providing information about the performance of various forward proxies and CDN servers to the request distribution systems of all partners. Since this CDN does not possess caches by itself and derives its revenue from providing performance reports, it can be trusted as a neutral source of this information.

A closely related issue is accounting for pay-per-view content. A CDN or forward proxy serving this content might be responsible for verifying that a client has paid the content provider before processing the request from this client. Again, this verification in the context of CDI has to be standardized to ensure that all participating proxies and CDN servers perform this verification.

18.5 Summary

Content distribution internetworking allows a combination of multiple CDNs and ISPs to deliver content better and cheaper by sharing the cost of deploying their CDN servers and forward proxies. The main problem to be addressed is how to combine the request distribution, content distribution, and accounting mechanisms used by different CDNs while maintaining a certain level of quality of service. In the case of the request distribution system, for example, this requires finding the best proxy or CDN server in the network by using multiple request distribution mechanisms, such as DNS, Layer 7, or URL rewriting, and multiple levels of request distribution algorithms, such as inter- and intra-CDN request distribution algorithms. The general challenge in content distribution and accounting is to standardize the complex interactions between multiple CDNs and ISPs without restricting innovation.

Glossary

A record: A record type in the DNS protocol used by a DNS server to provide the IP address of the host with a particular domain name.

anycast: A request distribution mechanism where request redirection to a server replica is performed by routers. The principal idea behind anycast is that multiple hosts use a single IP address called an anycast IP address in addition to their individual IP address. Hosts advertise both the anycast IP addresses and their individual IP addresses to their routers, which advertise them to their neighbor routers in a normal manner. As a result, each router builds a path corresponding to the anycast address that leads to the host closest to this router. Therefore, a client request is routed to the host closest to the client, according to the routing metric, among the hosts with the given anycast IP address.

AS (Autonomous System): A part of the Internet for which BGP routing is under single administrative control. An AS has a unique identifier and usually contains a large number of hosts. For example, AT&T's main AS has the identifier 7018 and contains the AT&T backbone and some of AT&T's customers.

authoritlative DNS server: The authoritative DNS server for a particular domain name such as www.att.com is the DNS server that can answer DNS queries regarding this domain name authoritatively. The authoritative DNS server for a domain name can be found by traversing the authoritative DNS server hierarchy starting with the root DNS servers. Examples of authoritative DNS servers in this book include a Web site's DNS server and the DNS servers of a CDN.

backbone: Any large ISP has a network that connects all its routers located around the world. This network is called a backbone network.

BGP: The Border Gateway Protocol is the routing protocol used between ASs. BGP determines which ASs a datagram has to traverse to reach its final destination. It is the foundation that lets independent networks join the Internet.

browser: A Web client that obtains Web content for consumption by a human user or an application on the same computer. Browsers therefore represent final destinations of Web objects. The most common examples of browsers are Microsoft Internet Explorer and Netscape Navigator.

byte hit rate: The ratio of the number of bytes that a Web component, such as a Web proxy, serves from its cache to the total number of bytes served by this Web component.

cacheable: A response is cacheable if a cache is allowed to store a copy of the response and return this copy on subsequent requests. Also, in this book, we call a request cacheable if it can be satisfied by a cached response. A request for an uncacheable object is obviously uncacheable; a request for a cacheable object may or may not be cacheable depending on the HTTP request headers.

caching: Storing a copy of data close to the consumer of the data to allow faster data access. In the context of this book, the term *caching* mainly refers to storing Web responses closer to the Web client requesting the content. An additional benefit of caching is that communication with the place where the data was originally stored is reduced. Examples of caches in this book are browser caches and proxy caches.

cache hit: A request that can be satisfied using a cached response.

cache miss: A request that cannot be satisfied using a cached response.

caching proxy: A Web proxy that performs caching.

client: An application that requests service from another application (server), which typically executes on a different host. For example, a Web browser such as Microsoft's Internet Explorer or a proxy are both Web clients.

client DNS server: The DNS server that hosts such as HTTP clients are configured to use when they need to resolve domain names of other hosts, such as Web servers, into the corresponding IP addresses. Client DNS servers are distinguished from authoritative DNS servers.

CDN: A Content Delivery Network is middleware between content providers and consumers. A CDN serves content from multiple surrogates deployed around the globe. The distinguishing features of a CDN are that its infrastructure is shared among multiple content provider sites and that it has a close relationship with the underlying networks.

CDN client: A Web client that downloads content through a CDN.

CDN customer: A content provider who signed up with a CDN for content delivery.

CDN user: A Web user who requests content delivered through a CDN.

CGI script: A program that is invoked at the server when a client accesses a URL which specifies this program in its path field. CGI scripts are used to generate Web objects dynamically at the time of the client access. CGI stands for Common Gateway Interface.

CNAME record: A record type in the DNS protocol used by a DNS server to indicate that a particular domain name is a synonym of a another canonical domain name, and to provide the canonical name. A host that receives a CNAME record in response to its DNS query will repeat the query using the canonical name.

container object or page: In this book, a container object or page is defined as an HTML object that embeds other Web objects.

content provider: Web objects are created and owned by people and companies who are collectively called content providers.

content replica: A duplicate of a content object stored on a server replica.

cookie mechanism: An HTTP extension that allows an HTTP server to store information (a cookie) on browsers and tell the browsers to include this information with future requests. Cookies are commonly used by servers to keep track of user sessions that involve multiple interactions between the user and the Web site. Examples include storing the contents of a shopping cart or a user profile.

DHCP: The Dynamic Host Configuration Protocol is used to dynamically assign and distribute configuration information to a host. The configuration information can include the host's IP address, DNS server, or default router.

DNS: The Domain Name System is an online database mainly used to convert human-readable domain names like www.att.com into IP addresses.

DNS server: DNS servers implement the Domain Name System. DNS servers receive a request to resolve a domain name from a client or another DNS server and return one or more response records. These records may have a wide variety of record types and either provide the answer or redirect the requester to another DNS server.

document: In this book a document is defined as a collection of objects which are displayed as a single entity in a browser. For example, an HTML object and all its embedded images constitute a single document.

domain: A part of the DNS namespace. For example, att.com is a domain in the domain name space.

dynamic object: A Web object that the server generates each time it processes a request for this object, as opposed to serving the object from a file.

dynamic replication: A replication technique that dynamically determines the portions of Web sites that must be replicated, based on user demand and other factors.

explicit mirroring: A mirroring technique that involves maintaining mirror Web sites; that is, the technique whereby each mirror has its own URLs that are distinct from other mirrors. With explicit mirroring, users must consciously choose a mirror to access the Web site.

explicit (Web) proxy: A proxy that receives client requests because clients explicitly address their requests to the proxy using the proxy IP address. Compare with *interception proxy*.

forward (Web) proxy: A computer application that provides a shared cache to a set of clients. With a forward proxy, client requests arrive at the proxy regardless of which origin servers these requests are pointed at; the forward proxy either responds to these requests using previously cached responses or obtains the responses from the origin servers on behalf of the clients, forwards the responses to the clients, and optionally stores the responses in its cache for future use. The proxy acts as a Web server to its clients and as a client to origin servers.

FTP: The File Transfer Protocol allows the sending of files to, retrieval of files from, and deletion of files on a remote FTP server. It was one of the predecessors of HTTP.

handshake: An initial message exchange to establish a TCP connection between two hosts. It involves three sequential messages: a SYN segment from the host that is initiating the connection, a SYN/ACK segment from the recipient host, and a SYN/ACK segment from the initiating host.

hashing: Mapping every item from one set to an item from another set. Examples in this book include mapping an arbitrary URL to a proxy identifier in hash-based proxy cooperation, mapping packet destination IP addresses to proxy identifiers in transparent proxy deployment with load-balancing across multiple interception proxies, and mapping an arbitrary URL to a 16-byte value using the MD5 hash function. A mapping algorithm used in hashing is called a hash function.

hit rate: A ratio of requests that a component such as a Web proxy satisfies using cached objects to the total number of requests that arrive at this component.

host: Any type of device connected to the Internet that has its own IP address.

hosting service provider: A company that implements and maintains Web sites for other businesses and individuals. A hosting service provider relieves content providers of the necessity to maintain their own Web servers and other facilities.

HTML: Hypertext Markup Language is a language used to encode documents on the Web.

HTTP: The Hypertext Transfer Protocol is used in the Web to transfer objects between servers and clients.

hyperlink: A reference in an HTML object that points to another object on the Internet. In most browsers, a hyperlink is highlighted and if the user clicks on the hyperlink, the browser loads and displays the object the hyperlink points to.

ICAP: The Internet Content Adaptation Protocol allows a distributed solution to the problem of extending the functionality of proxies and surrogates. The basic concept is that the proxy or surrogate remotely calls an ICAP server for the adaptation of the content. This approach separates the caching and the adaptation of content and allows for highly optimized proxy and surrogate appliances for routine processing while maintaining a high level of flexibility at the ICAP server.

ICMP: The Internet Control Message Protocol is used to exchange control messages about host reachability, status, congestion, datagram flow, local route change requests, and other network-layer problems within the Internet.

IETF: The Internet Engineering Task Force is the standards body of the Internet (see *http://www.ietf.org/*).

interception proxy: (also known as: transparent proxy, transparent cache). A Web proxy that receives requests from clients by intercepting the flow of traffic between the client and the server. Since no configuration of the clients is required to enable interception proxies, this proxy deployment is considered transparent from the client's perspective. Compare with *explicit proxy*.

Internet: A collection of connected data networks using the TCP/IP protocol suite.

ISO/OSI model: The ISO/OSI model defines a stack of seven network protocol layers as a set of standards for the interfaces a layer should provide to the next layer up the stack and the services a layer should offer. Despite the fact that the ISO/OSI model has been overshadowed by the Internet protocols, its terminology is widely used.

IP: The Internet Protocol is the protocol used to connect multiple data networks to the Internet.

IP address: Each host on the Internet has at least one 32-bit-long unique Internet address identifying the host. Typically, IP addresses are written in decimal dotted notation where each decimal number represents 8 bits in the address. For example, the IP address of www.att.com, which is 11000000 00010100 00000011 00110110, is written as 192.20.3.54.

IP-in-IP encapsulation: (also known as: IP tunneling) A technique in which an IP datagram is encapsulated in another IP datagram. The purpose of this technique is to redirect the original IP datagram to another destination without losing any of the original information.

ISP: An Internet Service Provider is a company that provides Internet access to the public. In most cases, the access allows the customer to send and receive IP traffic and, therefore, participate in the Internet. Examples of ISPs include America Online, AT&T Worldnet, and EarthLink.

L2 switch: A switch that only considers Layer 2 information such as a MAC address when it decides where to forward traffic. See also *switch*.

L4 switch: A switch which takes into account Layer 4 information when it decides where to forward traffic. L4 switches commonly base their forwarding decision on the source or destination IP address, the transport protocol of the datagram, such as TCP, and the source or destination port number of the transport protocol, such as TCP port numbers. See also *switch*.

L7 switch: A switch that considers application-layer information (Layer 7) when it decides where to forward traffic. L7 switches are mainly found in the Web environment, where they establish a TCP connection with a Web client, parse the HTTP request in the first few packets of the TCP connection, and base their forwarding decision on the application-layer information contained in the request, such as the requested URL. See also *switch*.

latency: The elapsed time between the moment a client issues a request and the moment it receives the response. Sometimes a distinction is drawn between download latency and download time, in which case the latter includes the time for the client to receive the entire response, whereas the former includes only the time to receive the first byte of the response.

layering: See *ISO/OSI model*.

MAC address: The Medium Access Control address is the address used on Layer 2 to identify communication endpoints on a single physical network.

MD5: A hash function that maps an arbitrary string of characters to a 16Byte value with extremely low probability of mapping distinct character strings to the same value. The 16Byte values produced from character strings are often used as compact identifiers of the corresponding character strings, which can potentially be much longer.

mirror: A full or partial replica of an origin server. The terms *mirror* and *mirroring* are often used as synonyms to the terms *server replica* and *replication,* with the vague difference being that mirrors are usually meant to be static—that is, manually configured.

mirror Web site: A Web site that has the same content as another Web site but has a distinct URLs (especially the URLs' hostnames differ).

mirroring: Creating and maintaining a mirror.

multicast: IP multicast is a mechanism that allows efficient delivery of a datagram to multiple hosts on the Internet. Multicast is useful in situations when many hosts, called a multicast group, are interested in the same content. The idea behind IP multicast is to optimize the transmission of IP datagrams in such a way that an identical datagram traverses the link between two routers only once.

NAP: A network access point is a local area network which allows different Internet service providers to exchange Internet traffic. NAPs are exchange points where arbitrary ASs can connect to each other.

NAT: Network address translation is a mechanism which allows the rewriting of IP addresses and TCP port numbers to redirect IP datagrams to another destination. The mechanism requires that the device, which performs the NAT, maintain enough state to rewrite subsequent datagrams and reply datagrams of the same TCP connection in a similar manner.

NS record: A record type in the DNS protocol used by a DNS server to indicate that another DNS server is responsible for a particular domain name. For example, when a host sends a DNS query for host www.firm-x.com to a root DNS server, the root server will respond with an NS record indicating a DNS server responsible for the .com domain.

object: (also known as: resource). A single piece of data identifiable by a URL. An object in the Web context is generally retrieved with a single HTTP request-response pair. Examples of objects are a single HTML object or a single image.

origin server: The Web server where a Web object ultimately resides is called the origin server for that object. Web objects are placed on their origin servers by content providers; thus, origin servers act as authoritative sources of Web content.

persistent HTTP connection: A feature in HTTP that allows a client to download multiple objects from a server using a single TCP connection.

pipelining: A feature in HTTP 1.1 that allows an HTTP client to send requests over an existing TCP connection to an HTTP server without waiting for responses to earlier requests sent over the same TCP connection.

POP: A point of presence of an ISP is a place where the ISP has equipment that allows the public to connect to its network.

port number: The port number addresses an individual application on a host rather than the host itself. For example, TCP port number 80 is the port on which Web server applications expect to receive HTTP requests.

prefetching: Performing work in anticipation of future needs. For example, a browser might download a Web object before the user demands it.

proxy: In this book the term *proxy* is used interchangeably with the term *forward proxy* (see *forward proxy*).

proxy appliance: (also known as: cache appliance) A particular implementation of a proxy as a preconfigured, easy-to-install, single-purpose computer system.

replication: Creating and maintaining a duplicate of a resource under the control of the content provider.

reverse proxy: See *surrogate*.

router: A host that participates in a routing protocol like BGP and forwards IP datagrams toward the destination using the information gathered by the routing protocol.

RTT: Round trip time is the time it takes to send an IP datagram from a source to its destination and back.

server: An application that receives requests for service from other applications (clients), which typically run on other hosts. Examples include a Web server, a DNS server, and an ICAP server.

server replica: A mirror, a partial mirror, or a surrogate.

SSL: The Secure Socket Layer protocol is used to secure traffic between a client and a server that communicate using TCP. The level of security provided by SSL is configurable and allows protection of the privacy, integrity, and authenticity of both parties involved.

static object: A Web object that is stored in a file and used without change for multiple requests.

streaming content: Content that is transmitted while being displayed. Examples include live and nonlive video or audio content.

surrogate: (also known as: reverse proxy). An intermediary application that operates on behalf of an origin server. Similar to a forward proxy, a surrogate either responds to a client request using the locally stored object replica or obtains the object from the origin server, sends the response to the client, and optionally stores the object for future use. In contrast to a forward proxy, a surrogate is under the control of the provider of the content, not the consumer.

switch: A device that forwards data received on an incoming network link to an outgoing network link. Switches come in multiple flavors, from simple L2 switches to highly complex L7 switches. The difference between these switches is in the amount of information they consider in deciding where to forward data. For example, L2 switches consider Layer 2 information such as a MAC address. In contrast, L7 switches consider application-layer (Layer 7) information, such as the URL of an object.

TCP: The Transmission Control Protocol is a transport-layer protocol used by the Web to deliver requests from clients to servers and Web objects from servers to clients. TCP is built on top of IP to provide extra functionality that applications commonly need so that each application does not have to implement them anew. In particular, TCP tries to provide the application with connection-oriented, reliable, only-once, in-order, full duplex data delivery between two hosts in the Internet.

TCP slow start: The phase in which TCP doubles its transmission rate after transmitting and acknowledging an entire congestion window. TCP slow start always occurs at the beginning of a TCP connection and sometimes after a packet loss during a TCP connection. Because of the low initial transmission rate, slow start is one of the reasons why the effective throughput of TCP is lower than the capacity of the underlying network.

traffic interception: The process of using a network element to examine network traffic for the purpose of determining if the traffic should be diverted from its intended destination to another host. For example, traffic interception is the basis of transparent proxy deployment.

transparent mirroring: A mirroring technique that allows all mirrors to have common object URLs. With transparent mirroring, the existence of multiple mirrors is hidden from users.

transparent replication: A replication technique that allows all replicas of a Web object to share the same URL.

TTL: Time to live fields are found in different contexts. In general, a TTL indicates how long a particular object or datagram should exist. In particular, the IP TTL indicates how many routers an IP datagram is allowed to traverse before it will be dropped; the TTL of a Web object or a DNS response indicates how long the returned object or DNS response can be cached.

UDP: The User Datagram Protocol is a transport protocol that only adds an additional address—the port number—to the functionality provided by IP. The port number addresses an individual application on a host rather than the host itself. In particular, UDP provides no notion of a connection, no reliability, and no mechanisms for avoiding traffic congestion. On the other hand, UDP has less overhead than TCP.

URL: A Uniform Resource Locator is a compact string of characters for identifying the network location of an object. An example of an URL is http://www.att.com/.

Web browser: See *browser.*

Web caching proxy: See *caching proxy.*

Web client: See *client.*

Web object: See *object.*

Web server: See *server.*

Web site: A collection of Web objects that belong to the same content provider. Objects from the same Web site usually share a common prefix in the host name of their URLs—for example, www.research.att.com, library.research.att.com, and help.research.att.com. There is no inherent relationship between Web servers and Web sites, although in practice a Web site often resides on a single server, and the two terms are often used interchangeably.

Bibliography

[Abdulla 1998] Abdulla, G. (1998). *Analysis and Modeling of World Wide Web Traffic*. PhD thesis, Virginia Polytechnic Institute and State University.

[Abrams et al. 1995] Abrams, M., Standridge, C., Abdulla, G., Williams S., and Fox, E. (1995). Caching proxies: Limitations and potentials. In *Proceedings of 1995 World Wide Web Conference*.

[Aggarwal and Rabinovich 1998] Aggarwal, A., and Rabinovich, M. (1998). Performance of replication schemes on the Internet. Technical Report HA6177000-981030-01-TM, AT&T Labs.

[Aggarwal et al. 1999] Aggarwal, M., Wolf, J., and Yu, P. (1999). Caching on the World Wide Web. *IEEE Transactions on Knowledge and Data Engineering*, 11:95–107.

[Albrecht et al. 1999] Albrecht, D. W., Zukerman, I., and Nicholson, A. E. (1999). Pre-sending documents on the WWW: A comparative study. In *Proceedings of the 16th International Joint Conference on Artificial Intelligence*, pp. 1274–1279.

[Almeida and Cao 1998] Almeida, J., and Cao, P. (1998). Measuring proxy performance with the Wisconsin Proxy Benchmark. *Computer Networks and ISDN Systems*, 30:2179–2192.

[Almeida et al. 1996] Almeida, V., Bestavros, A., Crovella, M., and de Oliveira, A. (1996). Characterizing reference locality in the WWW. In *Proceedings of the IEEE International Conference on Parallel and Distributed Information Systems*, pp. 92–103.

[Arlitt et al. 1999] Arlitt, M., Friedrich, R., and Jin, T. (1999). Workload characterization of a Web proxy in a cable modem environment. Technical Report HPL-1999-48, Hewlett Packard Labs.

[Arlitt and Jin 1999] Arlitt, M., and Jin, T. (1999). Workload characterization of the 1998 World Cup Web site. Technical Report HPL-1999-35R1, Hewlett Packard Labs.

[Arlitt and Williamson 1996] Arlitt, M., and Williamson, C. (1996). Web server workload characterization: The search for invariants. In *Proceedings of the ACM SIGMETRICS Conference*, pp. 126–137.

[Bakre and Badrinath 1995] Bakre, A., and Badrinath, B. R. (1995). I-TCP: Indirect TCP for mobile hosts. In *Proceedings of the 15th International Conference on Distributed Computing Systems*, pp. 136–143.

[Balakrishnan et al. 1996] Balakrishnan, H., Padmanabhan, V. N., Seshan, S., and Katz, R. H. (1996). A comparison of mechanisms for improving TCP performance over wireless links. In *Proceedings of the ACM SIGCOMM Conference*, pp. 256–269.

[Banga et al. 1997] Banga, G., Douglis, F., and Rabinovich, M. (1997). Optimistic deltas for WWW latency reduction. In *Proceedings of the 1997 USENIX Technical Conference*, pp. 289–303.

[Barford and Crovella 1998] Barford, P., and Crovella, M. (1998). Generating representative Web workloads for network and server performance evaluation. In *Proceedings of the ACM SIGMETRICS Conference*, pp. 151–160.

[Barford et al. 1998] Barford, P., Bestavros, A., Bradley, A., and Crovella, M. (1998). Changes in Web client access patterns: Characteristics and caching implications. Technical Report BUCS-TR-1998-023, Computer Science Department, Boston University.

[Barford et al. 1999] Barford, P., Bestavros, A., Bradley, A., and Crovella, M. (1999). Changes in Web client access patterns: Characteristics and caching implications. *World Wide Web*, 2:15–28.

[Bell et al. 1990] Bell, T. C., Cleary, J. G., and Witten, I. H. (1990). *Text Compression*. Prentice Hall, Englewood Cliffs, NJ.

[Berners-Lee and Connolly 1995] Berners-Lee, T., and Connolly, D. (1995). RFC 1866: Hypertext Markup Language 2.0—*http://www.ietf.org/rfc/rfc1866.txt*.

[Berners-Lee et al. 1994] Berners-Lee, T., Masinter, L., and McCahill, M. (1994). RFC 1738: Uniform Resource Locators (URL)—*http://www.ietf.org/rfc/rfc1738.txt*.

[Berners-Lee et al. 1996] Berners-Lee, T., Fielding, R., and Nielsen, H. (1996). RFC 1945: Hypertext transfer protocol, HTTP/1.0—*http://www.ietf.org/rfc/rfc1945.txt*.

[Bestavros 1995] Bestavros, A. (1995). Using speculation to reduce server load and service time on the WWW. In *Proceedings of the 4th ACM International Conference on Information and Knowledge Management*, pp. 403–410.

[Bestavros 1996] Bestavros, A. (1996). Speculative data dissemination and service to reduce server load, network traffic and service time in distributed information systems. In *Proceedings of the 12th International Conference on Data Engineering*, pp. 180–189.

[Bestavros and Mehrotra 2001] Bestavros, A., and Mehrotra, S. (2001). DNS-based internet client clustering and characterization. Technical Report BUCS-TR-2001-012, Boston University.

[Biliris et al. 2001] Biliris, A., Cranor, C., Douglis, F., Rabinovich, M., Sibal, S., Spatscheck, O., and Sturm, W. (2001). CDN brokering. In *Proceedings of the 6th International Workshop on Web Caching and Content Distribution*.

[Bloom 1970] Bloom, B. (1970). Space/time trade-offs in hash coding with allowable errors. *Communications of the ACM*, 13:422–426.

[Brassil et al. 1994] Brassil, J., Low, S., Maxemchuk, N., and O'Garman, L. (1994). Electronic marking and identification techniques to discourage document copying. In *Proceedings of INFOCOM*, pp. 1278–1287.

[Bray 1996] Bray, T. (1996). Measuring the Web. In *Proceedings of the 5th World Wide Web Conference*, pp. 993–1005.

[Breslau et al. 1999] Breslau, L., Cao, P., Fan, L., Phillips, G., and Shenker, S. (1999). Web caching and Zipf-like distributions: Evidence and implications. In *Proceedings of INFOCOM*.

[Brooks et al. 1995] Brooks, C., Mazer, M., Meeks, S., and Miller, J. (1995). Application-specific proxy servers as http stream transducers. In *Proceedings of the 4th World Wide Web Conference*, pp. 539–548.

[Cáceres and Iftode 1995] Cáceres, R., and Iftode, L. (1995). Improving the performance of reliable transport protocols in mobile computing environments. *IEEE Journal on Selected Areas in Communications*, 13:850–857.

[Cao and Irani 1997] Cao, P., and Irani, S. (1997). Cost-aware WWW proxy caching algorithms. In *Proceedings of the Usenix Symposium on Internet Technologies and Systems*, pp. 193–206.

[Cao et al. 1998] Cao, P., Zhang, J., and Beach, K. (1998). Active cache: Caching dynamic contents on the Web. In *Proceedings of the 1998 Middleware Conference*, pp. 373–388.

[Cardellini et al. 1999] Cardellini, V., Colajanni, M., and Yu, P. S. (1999). Dynamic load balancing on Web-server systems. *IEEE Internet Computing*, 3:28–39.

[CARP n.d.] Cache Array Routing Protocol (CARP), and MS Proxy Server v2.0 (White Paper)— *http://www.microsoft.com/technet/proxy/technote/prxcarp.usp*.

[Carter and Crovella 1997] Carter, R. L., and Crovella, M. E. (1997). Server selection using bandwidth probing in wide-area networks. In *Proceedings of INFOCOM*, pp. 1014–1021.

[Cate 1992] Cate, V. (1992). Alex—a global filesystem. In *Proceedings of the USENIX File Systems Workshop*, pp. 1–12.

[Chankhunthod et al. 1996] Chankhunthod, A., Danzig, P., Neerdaels, C., Schwartz, M., and Worrell, K. (1996). A hierarchical internet object cache. In *Proceedings of the 1996 USENIX Technical Conference*.

[Chawathe et al. 2000] Chawathe, Y., McCanne, S., and Brewer, E. (2000). RMX: Reliable multicast in heterogeneous networks. In *Proceedings of INFOCOM*, pp. 795–804.

[Claffy et al. 1998] Claffy, K., Miller, G., and Thompson, K. (1998). The nature of the beast: Recent traffic measurements from an Internet backbone. In *Proceedings of the INET Conference*.

[Cohen and Kaplan 2000] Cohen, E., and Kaplan, H. (2000). Prefetching the means for document transfer: A new approach for reducing Web latency. In *Proceedings of INFOCOM*, pp. 854–863.

[Cohen and Ramanathan 1997] Cohen, R., and Ramanathan, S. (1997). Using proxies to enhance TCP performance over hybrid fiber coaxial networks. Technical Report HPL-97-81, Hewlett-Packard Labs.

[Colajanni et al. 1998a] Colajanni, M., Yu, P. S., and Cardellini, V. (1998a). Dynamic load balancing in geographically distributed heterogeneous Web servers. In *Proceedings of the 18th IEEE International Conference on Distributed Computing Systems*.

[Colajanni et al. 1998b] Colajanni, M., Yu, P. S., and Dias, D. M. (1998b). Analysis of task assignment policies in scalable distributed Web-server systems. In *Proceedings of the IEEE International Conference on Parallel and Distributed Information Systems*, 9:585–600.

[Comer 1991] Comer, D. E. (1991). *Internetworking with TCP/IP Vol I: Principles Protocols, and Architecture, Second edition*. Prentice Hall, Englewood Cliffs, NJ.

[Conover 1999] Conover, J. (1999). Layer 4 switching: Unraveling the "vendorspeak"— *http://www.networkcomputing.com/1009/1009ws1.html*.

[Crovella and Barford 1998] Crovella, M., and Barford, P. (1998). The network effects of prefetching. In *Proceedings of INFOCOM*, pp. 1232–1239.

[Crovella and Bestavros 1995] Crovella, M., and Bestavros, A. (1995). Explaining World Wide Web traffic self-similarity. Technical Report 1995-015, Computer Science Department, Boston University.

[Crovella and Bestavros 1996] Crovella, M. E., and Bestavros, A. (1996). Self-similarity in World Wide Web traffic: Evidence and possible causes. In *Proceedings of the ACM SIGMETRICS Conference*, pp. 160–169.

[Cunha 1997] Cunha, C. R. (1997). *Trace Analysis and Its Applications to Performance Enhancements of Distributed Information Systems*. PhD thesis, Boston University.

[Cunha et al. 1996] Cunha, C. R., Bestavros, A., and Crovella, M. E. (1996). Characteristics of WWW client-based traces. Technical Report BU-CS-95-010, Computer Science Department, Boston University.

[Cunha and Jaccoud 1997] Cunha, C. R., and Jaccoud, C. F. B. (1997). Determining WWW user's next access and its application to pre-fetching. In *Proceedings of the Second IEEE Symposium on Computers and Communications*, pp. 6–11.

[Curewitz et al. 1993] Curewitz, K. M., Krishnan, P., and Vitter, J. S. (1993). Practical prefetching via data compression. In *Proceedings of the ACM SIGMOD International Conference on Management of Data*, pp. 257–266.

[Dahlin 2000] Dahlin, M. (2000). Interpreting stale load information. *IEEE Transactions on Parallel and Distributed Systems*, 11:1033–1047.

[Danzig 1998a] Danzig, P. (1998a). Netcache architecture and deployment. *Computer Networks and ISDN Systems*, 30:2081–2091.

[Danzig 1998b] Danzig, P. (1998b). Personal communication.

[Day and Zimmermann 1983] Day, J. D., and Zimmermann, H. (1983). The OSI references model. *Proceedings of the IEEE*, 71:1334–1340.

[Deering and Hinden 1998] Deering, S., and Hinden, R. (1998). RFC 2460: Internet Protocol, Version 6 (IPv6) specification—*http://www.ietf.org/rfc/rfc1883.txt*.

[Dilley 1999] Dilley, J. (1999). The effect of consistency on cache response time. Technical Report HPL-1999-107, Hewlett-Packard Labs.

[Dilley et al. 1999] Dilley, J., Arlitt, M., Perret, S., and Jin, T. (1999). The Distributed Object Consistency Protocol. Technical Report HPL-1999-109, Hewlett-Packard Labs.

[Dingle 1996] Dingle, A. (1996). Cache consistency in the HTTP 1.1 proposed standard. In *Proceedings of the 1st Workshop on Web Caching—http://w3cache.icm.edu.pl/workshop/ program.html*.

[Douglis 2000] Douglis, F. (2000). Personal communication.

[Douglis et al. 1997a] Douglis, F., Feldmann, A., Krishnamurthy, B., and Mogul, J. (1997a). Rate of change and other metrics: A live study of the World Wide Web. In *Proceedings of the USENIX Symposium on Internet Technologies and Systems*, pp. 147–158.

[Douglis et al. 1997b] Douglis, F., Feldmann, A., Krishnamurthy, B., and Mogul, J. (1997b). Rate of change and other metrics: A live study of the World Wide Web. Technical Report #97.24.2, AT&T Labs–Research.

[Douglis et al. 1997c] Douglis, F., Haro, A., and Rabinovich, M. (1997c). HPP: HTML macro-preprocessing to support dynamic document caching. In *Proceedings of the USENIX Symposium on Internet Technologies and Systems*, pp. 83–94.

[Droms 1993] Droms, R. (1993). RFC 1531: Dynamic Host Configuration Protocol—*http://www.ietf.org/rfc/rfc1531.txt*.

[Duchamp 1999] Duchamp, D. (1999). Prefetching hyperlinks. In *Proceedings of the USENIX Symposium on Internet Technologies and Systems*, pp. 127–138.

[Duska et al. 1997] Duska, B. M., Marwood, D., and Feeley, M. J. (1997). The measured access characteristics of World-Wide-Web client proxy caches. In *Proceedings of the USENIX Symposium on Internet Technologies and Systems*, pp. 23–35.

[Duvvuri et al. 2000] Duvvuri, V., Shenoy, P., and Tewari, R. (2000). Adaptive leases: A strong consistency mechanism for the World Wide Web. In *Proceedings of INFOCOM*, pp. 834–843.

[Dykes et al. 2000] Dykes, S. G., Robbins, K. A., and Jeffery, C. L. (2000). An empirical evaluation of client-side server selection algorithms. In *Proceedings of INFOCOM*, pp. 1361–1370.

[edge 2001] edge (2001). Edge Side Includes—*http://www.esi.org/*.

[Egevang and Francis 1994] Egevang, K., and Francis, P. (1994). RFC 1631: The IP network address translator (NAT)—*http://www.ietf.org/rfc/rfc1631.txt*.

[Eriksson 1994] Eriksson, H. (1994). MBONE: The Multicast Backbone. *Communications of the ACM*, 37:54–60.

[Fan et al. 1998] Fan, L., Cao, P., Almeida, J., and Broder, A. (1998). Summary cache: A scalable wide-area Web cache sharing protocol. In *Proceedings of the ACM SIGCOMM Conference*, pp. 254–265.

[Fan et al. 1999] Fan, L., Cao, P., Lin, W., and Jacobson, Q. (1999). Web prefetching between low-bandwidth clients and proxies: Potential and performance. In *Proceedings of the ACM SIGMETRICS Conference*, pp. 178–187.

[Fei et al. 1998] Fei, Z., Bhattacharjee, S., Zegura, E. W., and Ammar, M. H. (1998). A novel server selection technique for improving the response time of a replicated service. In *Proceedings of INFOCOM*, pp. 783–791.

[Feldmann 1999] Feldmann, A. (1999). Personal communication.

[Feldmann 2000] Feldmann, A. (2000). BLT: Bi-layer tracing of HTTP and TCP/IP. In *Proceedings of the 9th World Wide Web Conference*.

[Feldmann et al. 1999] Feldmann, A., Cáceres, R., Douglis, F., Glass, G., and Rabinovich, M. (1999). Performance of Web proxy caching in heterogeneous bandwidth environments. In *Proceedings of INFOCOM*, pp. 107–116.

[Fielding 1995] Fielding, R. (1995). RFC 1808: Relative Uniform Resource Locators—*http://www.ietf.org/rfc/rfc1808.txt*.

[Fielding et al. 1999] Fielding, R., Gettys, J., Mogul, J., Frystyk, H., Masinter, L., Leach, P., and Berners-Lee, T. (1999). RFC 2616: HyperText Transfer Protocol, HTTP/1.1—*http://www.ietf.org/rfc/rfc2616.txt*.

[Fox and Brewer 1996] Fox, A., and Brewer, E. A. (1996). Reducing WWW latency and bandwidth requirements by real-time distillation. *Computer Networks and ISDN Systems*, 28:1445–1456.

[Francis et al. 1999] Francis, P., Jamin, S., Paxson, V., Zhang, L., Gryniewicz, D., and Jin, Y. (1999). An architecture for a global Internet host distance estimation service. In *Proceedings of INFOCOM*, pp. 210–217.

[Freier et al. 1996] Freier, A. O., Karlton, P., and Kocher, P. C. (1996). The SSL Protocol, version 3.0—*http://www.netscape.com/eng/ssl3/draft302.txt*.

[Fuller et al. 1993] Fuller, V., Li, T., Yu, J., and Varadhan, K. (1993). RFC 1519, Classless Inter-Domain Routing (CIDR): An address assignment and aggregation strategy—*http://www.ietf.org/rfc/rfc1519.txt*.

[Gadde et al. 1997a] Gadde, S., Chase, J., and Rabinovich, M. (1997a). Directory structures for scalable Internet caches. Technical Report CS-1997-18, Department of Computer Science, Duke University.

[Gadde et al. 1997b] Gadde, S., Rabinovich, M., and Chase, J. (1997b). Reduce, reuse, recycle: An approach to building large Internet caches. In *Proceedings of the Workshop on Hot Topics in Operating Systems*, pp. 93–98.

[Gadde et al. 1998] Gadde, S., Chase, J., and Rabinovich, M. (1998). A taste of Crispy Squid. In *Proceedings of the Workshop on Internet Server Performance*.

[Gadde et al. 1999] Gadde, S., Chase, J., and Rabinovich, M. (1999). CRISP Distributed Web Proxy—*http://www.cs.duke.edu/ari/cisi/crisp/*.

[Gadde et al. 2001] Gadde, S., Chase, J., and Rabinovich, M. (2001). Web caching and content distribution: A view from the interior. *Computer Communications*, 24:222–231.

[Glassman 1994] Glassman, S. (1994). A caching relay for the World Wide Web. In *Proceedings of the 1st World Wide Web Conference*, pp. 69–76.

[Gonnet and Baeza-Yates 1991] Gonnet, G., and Baeza-Yates, R. (1991). *Handbook of Algorithms and Data Structures*. Addison-Wesley, Reading, MA.

[Gray and Cheriton 1989] Gray, C. G., and Cheriton, D. R. (1989). Leases: An efficient fault-tolerant mechanism for distributed file cache consistency. In *Proceedings of the 12th ACM Symposium on Operating System Principles*, pp. 202–210.

[Gribble and Brewer 1997] Gribble, S. D., and Brewer, E. A. (1997). System design issues for Internet middleware services: Deductions from a large client trace. In *Proceedings of the USENIX Symposium on Internet Technologies and Systems*, pp. 207–218.

[Grimm et al. 1998] Grimm, C., Neitzner, M., Pralle, H., and Vöckler, J.-S. (1998). Request routing in cache meshes. *Computer Networks and ISDN Systems*, 30:2269–2278.

[Gundavaram 1996] Gundavaram, S. (1996). *CGI Programming on the World Wide Web*. O'Reilly, Sebastapol, CA.

[Gwertzman 1995] Gwertzman, J. (1995). Autonomous replication in wide-area internetworks. B.S. thesis (Technical Report TR-17-95), Department of Electrical Engineering and Computer Science, Harvard University.

[Gwertzman and Seltzer 1996] Gwertzman, J., and Seltzer, M. (1996). World-Wide Web cache consistency. In *Proceedings of the 1996 USENIX Technical Conference*, pp. 141–151.

[Hanks et al. 1994] Hanks, S., Li, T., Farinacci, D., and Traina, P. (1994). RFC 1702: Generic routing encapsulation over IPv4 networks—*http://www.ietf.org/rfc/rfc1702.txt*.

[Harchol-Balter et al. 1999] Harchol-Balter, M., Crovella, M. E., and Murta, C. D. (1999). On choosing a task assignment policy for a distributed server system. *Journal of Parallel and Distributed Computing*, 59:204–228.

[Hoff et al. 1999] Hoff, A. V., Payne, J., and Shaio, S. (1999). Method for the Distribution of Code and Data Updates (U.S. Patent Number 5,919,247).

[Hoffman et al. 1998] Hoffman, P., Masinter, L., and Zawinski, J. (1998). RFC 2368: The mailto URL scheme—*http://www.ietf.org/rfc/rfc2368.txt*.

[Housel and Lindquist 1996] Housel, B. C., and Lindquist, D. B. (1996). WebExpress: A system for optimizing Web browsing in a wireless environment. In *Proceedings of the Second Annual International Conference on Mobile Computing and Networking*, pp. 108–116.

[Hunt et al. 1998] Hunt, J. J., Vo, K.-P., and Tichy, W. F. (1998). Delta algorithms: An empirical analysis. *ACM Transactions on Software Engineering and Methodology*, 7:192–214.

[Huston 1999] Huston, G. (1999). Interconnection, peering, and settlements. In *Proceedings of the INET Conference*, p. 2.

[InfoLibria 1999] InfoLibria, Inc. (1999). Dynacache—*http://www.infolibria.com/products/f-dyna.htm*.

[InfoLibria 2001] InfoLibria, Inc. (2001). Dynacache—*http://www.infolibria.com/products/dynacache_overview.htm*.

[Inktomi 1998] Inktomi (1998). New network caching standard proposed—*http://www.inktomi.com/new/press/1998/wpad.html*.

[Jacobson 1995] Jacobson, V. (1995). How to kill the Internet. A presentation at SIGCOMM '95, Middleware Workshop. Available at *http://www.root/obs.com/ip-development/talks/vj-webflame.pdf.gz*.

[Jacobson et al. 1992] Jacobson, V., Braden, R., and Borman, D. (1992). RFC 1323: TCP extensions for high performance—*http://www.ietf.org/rfc/rfc1323.txt*.

[Jiang and Kleinrock 1998] Jiang, Z., and Kleinrock, L. (1998). An adaptive network prefetch scheme. *IEEE Journal on Selected Areas in Communications*, 17:358–368.

[Jin and Bestavros 2000] Jin, S., and Bestavros, A. (2000). Sources and characteristics of Web temporal locality. In *Proceedings of the 8th International Symposium on Modeling, Analysis and Simulation of Computer and Telecommunication Systems*, pp. 28–36.

[Jin and Bestavros 2001] Jin, S., and Bestavros, A. (2001). GreedyDual* Web caching algorithms: Exploiting the two sources of temporal locality in Web request streams. *Computer Communications*, 24:174–183.

[Johnson 1999] Johnson, E. (1999). Increasing the performance of transparent caching with content-aware cache bypass. In *Proceedings of the 4th International Web Caching Workshop*.

[Johnson et al. 2001] Johnson, K. L., Carr, J. F., Day, M. S., and Kaashoek, M. F. (2001). The measured performance of content distribution networks. *Computer Communications*, 24:202–206.

[Kangasharju et al. 1998] Kangasharju, J., Kwon, Y. G., and Ortega, A. (1998). Design and implementation of a soft caching proxy. *Computer Networks and ISDN Systems*, 30:2113–2121.

[Karaul et al. 1998] Karaul, M., Korilis, Y. A., and Orda, A. (1998). A market-based architecture for management of geographically dispersed, replicated Web servers. In *Proceedings of the First International Conference on Information and Computation Economies*, pp. 158–165.

[Karger et al. 1997] Karger, D., Lehman, E., Leighton, T., Levine, M., Lewin, D., and Panigrahy, R. (1997). Consistent hashing and random trees: Distributed caching protocols for relieving hot spots on the World Wide Web. In *Proceedings of the Twenty-Ninth Annual ACM Symposium on Theory of Computing*, pp. 654–663.

[Katz et al. 1994] Katz, E., Butler, M., and McGrath, R. (1994). A scalable Web server: The NCSA prototype. *Computer Networks and ISDN Systems*, 27:155–164.

[Krishnamurthy and Rexford 2001] Krishnamurthy, B., and Rexford, J. (2001). *Web Protocols and Practice: HTTP/1.1, Networking Protocols, Caching, and Traffic Measurement*. Addison-Wesley, Boston.

[Krishnamurthy and Wills 1997] Krishnamurthy, B., and Wills, C. E. (1997). Study of piggyback cache validation for proxy caches in the World Wide Web. In *Proceedings of the USENIX Symposium on Internet Technologies and Systems*, pp. 1–12.

[Krishnamurthy and Wills 1998] Krishnamurthy, B., and Wills, C. E. (1998). Piggyback server invalidation for proxy cache coherency. *Computer Networks and ISDN Systems*, 30:185–193.

[Krishnan and Sugla 1998] Krishnan, P., and Sugla, B. (1998). Utility of co-operating Web proxy caches. *Computer Networks and ISDN Systems*, 30:195–203.

[Kristol and Montulli 1997] Kristol, D., and Montulli, L. (1997). RFC 2109: HTTP state management mechanism—*http://www.ietf.org/rfc/rfc2109.txt*.

[Kroeger et al. 1997] Kroeger, T. M., Long, D. D. E., and Mogul, J. C. (1997). Exploring the bounds of Web latency reduction from caching and prefetching. In *Proceedings of the USENIX Symposium on Internet Technologies and Systems*, pp. 13–22.

[Lawrence and Giles 1999] Lawrence, S., and Giles, C. L. (1999). Accessibility of information on the Web. *Nature*, 400:107–109.

[Leighton and Lewin 2000] Leighton, T., and Lewin, D. (2000). Global document hosting system utilizing embedded content distributed ghost servers. World Intellectual Property Organization, International Publication Number WO 00/04458.

[Li and Cheriton 1999] Li, D., and Cheriton, D. R. (1999). Scalable Web caching of frequently updated objects using reliable multicast. In *Proceedings of the USENIX Symposium on Internet Technologies and Systems*, pp. 92–103.

[Lia and Massey 1990] Lia, X., and Massey, J. L. (1990). A proposal for a new block encryption standard. In *EUROCRYPT '90: Workshop on the Theory and Application of Cryptographic Techniques*. (Reprinted as Vol. 43, *Lecture Notes in Computer Science*, pp. 55–70. Springer-Verlag, Berlin.)

[Loon and Bharghavan 1997] Loon, T. S., and Bharghavan, V. (1997). Alleviating the latency and bandwidth problems in WWW browsing. In *Proceedings of the USENIX Symposium on Internet Technologies and Systems*, pp. 219–230.

[Makpangou et al. 1999] Makpangou, M., Pierre, G., Khoury, C., and Dorta, N. (1999). Replicated directory service for weakly consistent replicated caches. In *Proceedings of the 19th IEEE International Conference on Distributed Computing Systems*, pp. 92–100.

[Manley and Seltzer 1997] Manley, S., and Seltzer, M. (1997). Web facts and fantasy. In *Proceedings of the USENIX Symposium on Internet Technologies and Systems*, pp. 125–133.

[Markatos and Chronaki 1998] Markatos, E. P., and Chronaki, C. E. (1998). A top 10 approach for prefetching the Web. In *Proceedings of the INET Conference*.

[Mattson et al. 1970] Mattson, R. L., Gecsei, J., Slutz, D. R., and Traiger, I. L. (1970). Evaluation techniques for storage hierarchies. *IBM Systems Journal*, 9:78–117.

[Maxemchuk et al. 1997] Maxemchuk, N. F., Padmanabhan, K., and Lo, S. (1997). A cooperative packet recovery protocol for multicast video. In *Proceedings of the International Conference on Network Protocols*, pp. 259–266.

[McManus 1999] McManus, P. R. (1999). A passive system for server selection within mirrored resource environments using AS path-length heuristics—*http://www.gweep.net/~mcmanus/proximate.pdf*.

[Michel et al. 1998] Michel, S., Nguyen, K., Rosenstein, A., Zhang, L., Floyd, S., and Jacobson, V. (1998). Adaptive Web caching: Towards a new global caching architecture. *Computer Networks and ISDN Systems*, 30:2169–2177.

[Mirchandaney et al. 1989] Mirchandaney, R., Towsley, D., and Stankovic, J. (1989). Analysis of the effect of delays on load sharing. *IEEE Transactions on Computers*, 11:1513–1525.

[Mitzenmacher 1997] Mitzenmacher, M. (1997). How useful is old information. In *Proceedings of the 16th ACM Symposium on Principles of Distributed Computing*, pp. 83–91.

[Mogul et al. 1997] Mogul, J., Douglis, F., Feldmann, A., and Krishnamurthy, B. (1997). Potential benefits of delta-encoding and data compression for HTTP. In *Proceedings of the ACM SIGCOMM Conference*, pp. 181–194.

[Mogul and Leach 1997] Mogul, J., and Leach, P. (1997). Simple hit-metering and usage-limiting for HTTP, RFC 2227—*http://www.ietf.org/rfc/rfc2227.txt*.

[Moy 1998] Moy, J. T. (1998). *OSPF: Anatomy of an Internet Routing Protocol*. Addison-Wesley, Reading, MA.

[Myers et al. 1999] Myers, A., Dinda, P., and Zhang, H. (1999). Performance characteristics of mirror servers on the Internet. In *Proceedings of INFOCOM*, pp. 304–312.

[Nahum 1998] Nahum, E. M. (1998). WWW workload characterization work at IBM Research. In *Position Paper at Web Characterization Workshop, World Wide Web Consortium*.

[NECP 2001] The Network Element Control Protocol (NECP)—*http://www.netapp.com/necp/*.

[NetGeo 2001] NetGeo (2001). NetGeo: The Internet geographic database—*http://www.caida.org/tools/utilities/netgeo/*.

[Netscape 1996] Netscape (1996). Navigator proxy auto-config file format—*http://www.netscape.com/eng/mozilla/2.0/relnotes/demo/proxy-live.html*.

[Nicholson et al. 1998] Nicholson, A. E., Zukerman, I., and Albrecht, D. W. (1998). A decision-theoretic approach for pre-sending information on the WWW. In *Proceedings of the 5th Pacific Rim International Conference on Topics in Artificial Intelligence*, pp. 575–586.

[Nielsen et al. 2001] Nielsen, H. F., Berners-Lee, T., and Groff, J. F. (2001). Libwww—The W3C Protocol library. World Wide Web Consortium (W3C)—*http://www.w3.org/Library/*.

[NLANR 2001] National Laboratory for Applied Network Research (NLANR) hierarchical caching system usage statistics—*http://www.ircache.net/Cache/Statistics/*.

[Nottingham 1999] Nottingham, M. (1999). Optimizing object freshness controls in Web caches. In *Proceedings of the 4th Web Caching and Content Delivery Workshop—http://workshop99.ircache.net/Papers/nottingham-final.ps.gz*.

[OMG 1999] Object Management Group, Inc. (1999). Notification Service specification—*http://ftp.omg.org/pub/docs/telecom/99-07-01.pdf.*

[Padhye et al. 1998] Padhye, J., Firoiu, V., Towsley, D., and Kurose, J. (1998). Modeling TCP throughput. In *Proceedings of the ACM SIGCOMM Conference*, pp. 303–314.

[Padmanabhan and Mogul 1996] Padmanabhan, V. N., and Mogul, J. C. (1996). Using predictive prefetching to improve World-Wide Web latency. In *Proceedings of the ACM SIGCOMM Conference*, pp. 26–36.

[Pai et al. 1998] Pai, V. S., Aron, M., Banga, G., Svendsen, M., Druschel, P., Zwaenepoel, W., and Nahum, E. (1998). Locality-aware request distribution in cluster-based network servers. In *Proceedings of the 8th International Conference on Architectural Support for Programming Languages and Operating Systems*, pp. 205–216.

[Partridge et al. 1993] Partridge, C., Mendez, T., and Milliken, W. (1993). RFC 1546: Host anycasting service—*http://www.ietf.org/rfc/rfc1546.txt.*

[Paxson and Floyd 1997] Paxson, V., and Floyd, S. (1997). Why we don't know how to simulate the Internet. In *Proceedings of the 1997 Winter Simulation Conference*, pp. 1037–1044.

[Peterson and Davie 1996] Peterson, L., and Davie, B. (1996). *Computer Networks: A Systems Approach*. Morgan Kaufmann Publishers, New York.

[Pitkow 1999] Pitkow, J. E. (1999). Summary of WWW characterizations. *World Wide Web*, 2:3–13.

[PolyMix 3 n.d.] PolyMix 3—*http://www.web-polygraph.org/docs/workloads/polymix-3/.*

[Postel 1980] Postel, J. (1980). RFC 768: User Datagram Protocol—*http://www.ietf.org/rfc/rfc768.txt.*

[Postel 1981a] Postel, J. (1981a). RFC 791: Internet Protocol—*http://www.ietf.org/ rfc/rfc791.txt.*

[Postel 1981b] Postel, J. (1981b). RFC 792: Internet Control Message Protocol—*http://www.ietf.org/rfc/rfc792.txt.*

[Postel 1981c] Postel, J. (1981c). RFC 793: Transmission Control Protocol—*http://www.ietf.org/rfc/rfc793.txt.*

[Postel 1983] Postel, J. (1983). RFC 879: TCP maximum segment size and related topics—*http://www.ietf.org/rfc/rfc879.txt.*

[Rabinovich 2001] Rabinovich, M. (2001). Resource management issues in content delivery networks (CDNs). Presentation at DIMACS Workshops on Resource Management and Scheduling in Next Generation Networks.

[Rabinovich and Aggarwal 1999] Rabinovich, M., and Aggarwal, A. (1999). RaDaR: A scalable architecture for a global Web hosting service. In *Proceedings of the 8th World Wide Web Conference*, pp. 467–483.

[Rabinovich et al. 1998] Rabinovich, M., Chase, J., and Gadde, S. (1998). Not all hits are created equal: Cooperative proxy caching over a wide-area network. *Computer Networks and ISDN Systems*, 30:2253–2259.

[Rabinovich et al. 1999] Rabinovich, M., Rabinovich, I., Rajaraman, R., and Aggarwal, A. (1999). A dynamic object replication and migration protocol for an Internet hosting service. In *Proceedings of the 19th IEEE International Conference on Distributed Computing Systems*, pp. 101–113.

[Resnick and Miller 1996] Resnick, P., and Miller, J. (1996). PICS: Internet access controls without censorship. *Communications of the ACM*, 39:87–93.

[Rexford et al. 1999] Rexford, J., Sen, S., and Basso, A. (1999). A smoothing proxy service for variable-bit-rate streaming video. In *Proceedings of the Global Internet Symposium*.

[Rexford and Towsley 1999] Rexford, J., and Towsley, D. (1999). Smoothing variable-bit-rate video in an Internetwork. *IEEE/ACM Transactions on Networking*, 7:202–215.

[Rodriguez et al. 2000] Rodriguez, P., Kirpal, A., and Biersack, E. W. (2000). Parallel-access for mirror sites in the Internet. In *Proceedings of INFOCOM*, pp. 864–873.

[Rodriguez et al. 2001] Rodriguez, P., Sibal, S., and Spatscheck, O. (2001). TPOT: Translucent proxying of TCP. Technical Report TR 00.4.1, AT&T Labs–Research.

[Rousskov and Wessels 1998] Rousskov, A., and Wessels, D. (1998). Cache digests. *Computer Networks and ISDN Systems*, 30:2155–2168.

[Rousskov et al. 2000] Rousskov, A., Wessels, D., and Chisholm, G. (2000). The second IRCache Web cache cache-off—The official report. Technical report, Web Polygraph.

[Saltzer et al. 1984] Saltzer, J. H., Reed, D. P., and Clark, D. D. (1984). End-to-end arguments in system design. *ACM Transactions on Computer Systems*, 2:277–288.

[Sayal et al. 1998] Sayal, M., Breitbart, Y., Scheuermann, P., and Vingralek, R. (1998). Selection algorithms for replicated Web servers. In *Proceedings of the Workshop on Internet Server Performance*.

[Schechter et al. 1998] Schechter, S., Krishnan, M., and Smith, M. (1998). Using path profiles to predict HTTP request. In *Proceedings of the 7th World Wide Web Conference*, pp. 457–467.

[Shaikh and Tewari 2000] Shaikh, A., and Tewari, R. (2000). On the effectiveness of DNS-based server selection. IBM Research Report RC 21785.

[Shirazi et al. 1995] Shirazi, B. A., Hurson, A. R., and Kavi, K. M. (1995). *Scheduling and Load Balancing in Parallel and Distributed Systems*. IEEE Computer Society Press, New York.

[Simmons n.d.] Simmons, C. Configuring automatic discovery for ISA server clients—*http://www.isaserver.org/pages/tutorials/autodiscovery.htm*.

[Spasojevic et al. 1994] Spasojevic, M., Bowman, C. M., and Spector, A. (1994). Using wide-area file systems within the World-Wide Web. In *Proceedings of the 3rd World Wide Web Conference*.

[SpecWeb 1999] SpecWeb99 (1999)—*http://www.specbench.org/osg/web99/*.

[Stewart 1999] Stewart, III, J. W. (1999). *BGP4: Inter-Domain Routing in the Internet*. Addison-Wesley, Reading, MA.

[Tewari et al. 1999] Tewari, R., Dahlin, M., Vin, H., and Kay, J. (1999). Beyond hierarchies: Design considerations for distributed caching on the Internet. In *Proceedings of the 19th IEEE International Conference on Distributed Computing Systems*.

[Thaler and Ravishankar 1998] Thaler, D. G., and Ravishankar, C. V. (1998). A name-based mapping scheme for rendezvous. *IEEE/ACM Transactions on Networking*, 6:1–14.

[Totty 1999] Totty, B. (1999). Personal communication.

[Turau 1998] Turau, V. (1998). What practices are being adopted on the Web? *IEEE Computer*, 31:106–108.

[Vingralek et al. 1999] Vingralek, R., Breitbart, Y., Sayal, M., and Scheuermann, P. (1999). Web++: A system for fast and reliable Web service. In *Proceedings of the 1999 USENIX Technical Conference*, pp. 171–184.

[Wang 1997] Wang, Z. (1997). CacheMesh: A distributed cache system for World Wide Web. In *Proceedings of the 2nd Workshop on Web Caching—http://workshop97.ircache.net/ minutes/html*.

[Wang and Crowcroft 1996] Wang, Z., and Crowcroft, J. (1996). Prefetching in World Wide Web. In *Proceedings of the Global Internet Symposium*.

[WCCP n.d.] Cisco Systems. WCCP: Web Cache Communication Protocol—*http://www.cisco. com/warp/public/732/wccp/protocol.html*.

[Web Polygraph 2001] Web Polygraph—*http://www.ircache.net/polygraph/*.

[Weber 1978] Weber, R. (1978). On the optimal assignment of customers to parallel servers. *Journal of Applied Probability*, 15:406–413.

[Webstone 2001] Mindcraft. Webstone benchmark—*http://www.mindcraft.com/ webstone/*.

[Wessels and Claffy 1997] Wessels, D., and Claffy, K. (1997). RFC 2186: Internet Cache Protocol (ICP), version 2—*http://www.ietf.org/rfc/rfc2186.txt*.

[Whitt 1986] Whitt, W. (1986). Deciding which queue to join: Some counterexamples. *Operations Research*, 34:55–62.

[Williams et al. 1996] Williams, S., Abrams, M., Standridge, C. R., Abdulla, G., and Fox, E. A. (1996). Removal policies in network caches for World-Wide Web documents. In *Proceedings of the ACM SIGCOMM Conference*, pp. 293–305.

[Wills and Mikhailov 1999] Wills, C. E., and Mikhailov, M. (1999). Examining the cacheability of user-requested Web resources. In *Proceedings of the 4th Web Caching and Content Dlivery Workshop—http://workshop99.ircache.net/Papers/wills-final.ps.gz*.

[Winston 1977] Winston, W. (1977). Optimality of the shortest line discipline. *Journal of Applied Probability*, 14:181–189.

[Wolman et al. 1999a] Wolman, A., Voelker, G., Sharma, N., Cardwell, N., Brown, M., Landray, T., Pinnel, D., Karlin, A., and Levy, H. (1999a). Organization-based analysis of Web-object sharing and caching. In *Proceedings of the USENIX Symposium on Internet Technologies and Systems*, pp. 25–36.

[Wolman et al. 1999b] Wolman, A., Voelker, G., Sharma, N., Cardwell, N., Karlin, A., and Levy, H. (1999b). On the scale and performance of cooperative Web proxy caching. In *Proceedings of the 17th ACM Symposium on Operating System Principles*, pp. 16–31.

[Woodruff et al. 1996] Woodruff, A., Aoki, P. M., Brewer, E., Gauthier, P., and Rowe, L. A. (1996). An investigation of documents from the WWW. In *Proceedings of the 5th World Wide Web Conference*, pp. 963–979.

[Wooster and Abrams 1997] Wooster, R. P., and Abrams, M. (1997). Proxy caching that estimate page load delays. In *Proceedings of the 6th World Wide Web Conference*.

[Yin et al. 1998] Yin, J., Alvisi, L., Dahlin, M., and Lin, C. (1998). Using leases to support server-driven consistency in large-scale systems. In *Proceedings of the 18th IEEE International Conference on Distributed Computing Systems*, pp. 285–294.

[Yin et al. 1999] Yin, J., Alvisi, L., Dahlin, M., and Lin, C. (1999). Volume leases for consistency in large-scale systems. *IEEE Transactions on Knowledge and Data Engineering,* 11: 563–576.

[Yoshikawa et al. 1997] Yoshikawa, C., Chun, B., Eastham, P., Vahdat, A., Anderson, T., and Culler, D. (1997). Using smart clients to build scalable services. In *Proceedings of the 1997 USENIX Technical Conference,* pp. 105–117.

[Yu et al. 1999] Yu, H., Breslau, L., and Shenker, S. (1999). A scalable Web cache consistency architecture. In *Proceedings of the ACM SIGCOMM Conference,* pp. 163–174.

[Zipf 1949] Zipf, G. K. (1949). *Human Behavior and the Principle of Least-Effort.* Addison-Wesley, Cambridge, MA.

[Zukerman et al. 1999] Zukerman, I., Albrecht, D., and Nicholson, A. (1999). Predicting users' requests on the WWW. In *Seventh International Conference on User Modeling,* pp. 275–284.

Index

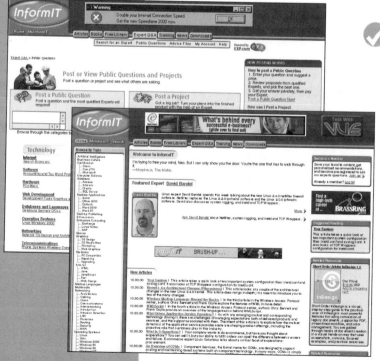